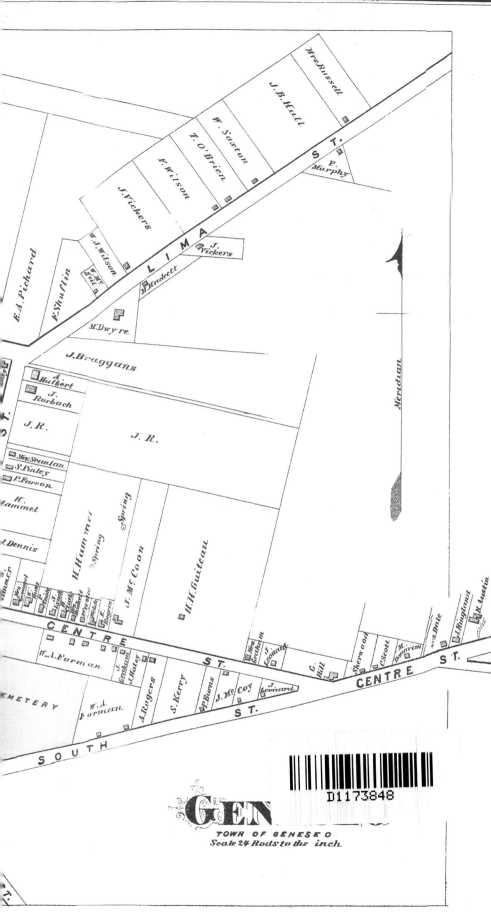

Geneseo
Business Notices

Abbott A. J...Attorney and Counselor
Ayrault Mrs B...Resident
Allen H...Agent W. W. Wadsworth Est
Austin J. R...Auctioneer and Propr of Livery, Sale and Exchange Stables
Armstrong C. P...Farmer and Stock Grower
Arnold H. L...Sheriff Livingston Co
Angel B. F...Farmer
Armstrong C. O...Farmer, Dist No. 7
Adams & Strang...Attorneys
Brodie Wm. A...Book-keeper for J. S. Wadsworth, Est
Binge S. P...Dealer in Dry Goods, Groceries, Crockery Ware, &c
Beach C. O. & Co...C. O. Beach, L. DeWitt Smith, Dealers in Dry Goods, Groceries, Crockery, Carpets, Paper Hangings, &c
Beckwith Thos. D...(Beckwith & Shepard), Dealers in Boots and Shoes, and Agents for Singer's Improved Sewing Machines
Burley W...Farmer and Stock Grower, Dist No. 1
Bateman A...Farmer, Dist No. 8
Butler F. W...   "   "   6
Butler E. E...   "   "   7
Cone James J...Banker
Clement James W...Pub. Livingston Republican
Chase Enos G., M. D...Physician and Surgeon, No. 40 Second St
Craig John, M. D...Physician and Surgeon, Centre St
Clark L. & Son...L. Clark & A. Clark, Custom and Merchant Millers, Farmers and Lumber Merchants, Millville Mills
Curtiss E. F...Agent for James W. Wadsworth Est
Clark I. A...Farmer and Surveyor
Doty C. F. & Co...Dealers in Hardware, Stoves, Tin and Copper Ware, Agricultural Implements, &c
Davison J...Jeweler, Dealer in Clocks, Gold and Silver Watches, Silver Ware, Fine Jewelry, Tea Sets, Cake Baskets, Table and Pocket Cutlery, &c., Agent for Morton's Gold Pens, Depot for Genuine Pebble and Crystal Spectacles
Davis Chas...Farmer
Denison B. F...Farmer, Dist No. 7
Fish J. C...Croquet Manufr
Forsyth M. L...Agent for Elias Howe Sewing Machines
Ferguson Saml...Manufr of Carriages
Finley Saml...Farmer, Dist No. 6
Goheen Charles...Dealer in Flour, Feed, Salt, Water Lime, Cement Pipe, &c
Griswold Aaron D...Farmer and Stock Grower, Dist No. 4
Getsinger Christian...Farmer, Dist No. 7
Gearhart N. A...Deputy Co. Clerk
Gray Thomas...Farmer, Dist No. 3
Hubbard S...Attorney and Counselor
Howe H...Steward at the State Normal School
Harrison H...Carriage Maker
Hamilton J. A...Propr "Tremont House"
Hustin Alexander...Farmer and Stock Grower
Hawley H...   "   "   "   Dist No. 1
Hudnutt E. W...Machinist and Pattern Maker
Haynes J. H...Farmer, Dist No. 7
Hawley James...Stock Grower and Farmer
Hall J. T...Farmer and Surveyor
Jackson A...Dealer in Tobacco and Manufr Cigars
Johnson H. L...Dealer in Pine and Hemlock Lumber, Flooring, Siding, Mouldings, Shingles, Lath, Sash, Doors and Blinds, Rochester Lime, Water Lime, &c
Janes Nelson...Agent James S. Wadsworth Est
Jones Chas...Farmer and Coal Dealer
Jones Rev. J., A. M...Principal of Geneseo Academy
Jones John H...Farmer and Stock Grower, Dist No. 4

Kneeland R. A...Farmer, Dist No. 4
Lauderdale W. E...Physician, Centre St
Lord Scott...Attorney and Counselor
Lewis J. D...Auctioneer, Drover, Wool Merchant and Farmer
Larwill J. C...Carpenter, Joiner and Builder
Lowery Thomas...Farmer and Stock Grower, Dist No. 1
Lamason J. T...Farmer, Dist No. 6
Mercer & Goode...Merchant Tailors, Ready-made Clothing and Gents' Furnishing Goods
McClintock A...Dealer in Boots and Shoes
Milne Wm. J...Principal of Geneseo Normal and Training School
Munn J. E...Agent for Agricultural Implements and Grover and Baker Sewing Machines, and for Portable Steam Engines for Threshing, &c
Metcalf Geo. P...Dealer in Fancy Dry Goods, Ladies' Furs, &c
Magee John H...Farmer, Dist No. 4
Marsh A. L...   "   "   6
McClintock Chas...   "   "   7
North H. P...Farmer and Propr of Saw Mill
Neff Abram...   "   Dist No. 9
Neff C...   "   and Carpenter, Dist No. 10
Orton James S...Cashier Genesee Natl Bank
Olmsted Theodore F...Treasr Livingston Co., and Teller Genesee Valley Natl Bank
Pickard R. A...Painting, Graining and Paper Hanging
Pfaff Jacob...Farmer, Dist No. 3
Robinson W. H...Propr "American Hotel"
Rose N. W...Ins. Agent and Dealer in Clothing, Hats, Caps, Furs, and Gents' Furnishing Goods
Rollins P. & M...Stock Growers and Farmers
Richmond J...Dealer in Watches, Clocks, Jewelry and Plated Ware
Sackett E...Farmer and Lessee
Stevens D. M...Stock Grower and Farmer
Taylor L...Propr "Globe Hotel"
VanMiddlesworth H...Farmer, Dist No. 1
Vance & Weller...Livery, Sale and Exchange Stables
  C. M. Vance, ——— Weller, Genesee Valley R. R. Agents, and Agents for U. S. Express
Vance C. M...Genesee Valley R. R. Agt. and U. S. Express Agent
Wadsworth Craig W...Farmer
Wadsworth James W...   "
Wadsworth W. W...   "
West James A...Physician, Main St
Walker W. R. & Son...Dealers in Drugs, Paints, Oils, Dye Stuffs, Perfumery and Toilet Articles, Books, Stationery and Music
Willard Wm...Propr of Centl Market
Whiting Wm. H...Secretary and Treasurer Geneseo Gas Co
Wood James...Attorney and Counselor
Wingate G...Farmer and Stock Grower, Dist No 1
Weeks Harrison...Baker and Confectioner
Webb John...Farmer and Stock Grower
Warford James S...Farmer and Stock Grower, Dist No. 4
Warford Theodore P...   "   "   "   "   4
Willard A. J...Farmer
Weller J. P...   "   Dist No. 10
Warner David...   "   and Stock Grower, Dist No. 8
Walls Charles...   "   Dist No. 8
Wynn T. J...   "   and Stock Grower, Dist No. 8
Winn Benj. T...   "   "   "   8

TOWN OF GENESEO
Scale 24 Rods to the inch

SUNY GENESEO

From Normal School to Public Ivy, 1871–2007

GENESEO NORMAL AND TRAINING SCHOOL, GENESEO, LIVINGSTON CO., N. Y.

SUNY GENESEO

From Normal School to Public Ivy, 1871–2007

by Wayne Mahood
with Frederick Bright, Judith Bushnell, Paul Hepler, and James McNally

THE
DONNING COMPANY
PUBLISHERS

We dedicate this book to those who cared enough about the College to save materials
for posterity, which enabled us to do our work...
...and to our friend Fred Bright, who kept the faith.

Cover photos: Sturges Hall by Ronald Pretzer, sunset photo by Benjamin Gajewski, and Mahood and committee photos taken by Ronald Pretzer
Half-title page: Milne Archives
Title page: 1938 *Normalian*

The Donning Company Publishers
184 Business Park Drive, Suite 206
Virginia Beach, VA 23462

Steve Mull, General Manager
Barbara Buchanan, Office Manager
Wendy Nelson, Editor
Chad Casey, Graphic Designer
Derek Eley, Imaging Artist
Susan Adams, Project Research Coordinator
Scott Rule, Director of Marketing
Tonya Hannink, Marketing Coordinator

Mary Taylor, Project Director

Cataloging-in-Publication Data

        Library of Congress Cataloging-in-Publication Data

Mahood, Wayne.
SUNY Geneseo : from normal school to public ivy, 1871-2007 / by Wayne Mahood ; with Frederick Bright ... [et al.].
    p. cm.
Includes bibliographical references and index.
ISBN 978-1-57864-513-8 (alk. paper)
1. State University of New York College, Geneseo--History. I. Bright, Frederick. II. Title.
LB1921.G45M34 2008
378.747'85--dc22

                            2008026461

Printed in the United States of America at Walsworth Publishing Company

Contents

Foreword by President Christopher C. Dahl _____ 6

Acknowledgments _____ 8

Introduction _____ 12

Chapter One _____ 16
Wadsworth Normal and Training School: Establishing the Tradition (1867–1871)

Chapter Two _____ 28
Geneseo Normal and Training School: A Firm Foundation (1871–1905)

Chapter Three _____ 58
Geneseo Normal School: The "Old Main" Tradition (1905–1922)

Chapter Four _____ 84
State Normal School, Geneseo, New York: The Expanding Curriculum (1922–1934)

Chapter Five _____ 104
Geneseo State Teachers College: The Depression and War Years (1934–1946)

Chapter Six _____ 138
State University of New York Teachers College at Geneseo: The Transition Begins (1946–1963)

Chapter Seven _____ 186
State University of New York College at Geneseo: Curriculum, Construction, Conflict (1963–1971)

Chapter Eight _____ 214
State University of New York College of Arts and Science at Geneseo: The Liberal Arts Transition (1971–1979)

Chapter Nine _____ 240
State University of New York at Geneseo: A Public College with an Ivy Twist (1979–1995)

Chapter Ten _____ 274
SUNY Geneseo: "Some Achieve Greatness" (1995–2007)

Epilogue _____ 304

Appendices _____ 310

Notes _____ 319

Index _____ 332

About the Authors _____ 344

Foreword

This history is unique—an account of the State University of New York at Geneseo from its beginnings right after the Civil War to the present, written over the course of four years by five members of our college community who came together to produce the chronicle you have in your hands.

Working in the Heritage Room of our alumni center, McClellan House, the members of the "College History Project"—all of them highly respected emeritus faculty and staff members—met on more than 180 occasions to discuss the text, to examine research materials, and to consider the people and events that make up the rich tapestry of Geneseo's history. I am grateful to them for their hard work, dedication, and affection for this special place. Their herculean efforts are themselves record-breaking!

As the title page reveals, this history is very much a team effort. Although the primary author was Wayne Mahood, distinguished service professor emeritus of education, the other members of the team pored over every page of the text—in several successive drafts. More than that, the five team members also represent a substantial slice of Geneseo's history. Professor Mahood is a much-beloved professor and mentor to generations of graduates from the Shear School of Education who have gone on to distinguished careers as teachers throughout the state and nation. He is one of those special professors whom alumni ask me about whenever I am on the road for alumni events. Without him, this history would not exist, for he drafted every chapter, sometimes in the midst of other major writing projects.

Professor Paul Hepler, who came to Geneseo in 1956, is a legendary, longtime chair of the Art Department—an eloquent chronicler of College and village history and someone who has done much to preserve the visual heritage of Geneseo. He was chiefly responsible for the excellent photographs that complement and enhance the text of the history.

Dr. James McNally, former director of institutional research, was responsible for keeping the College's data for many years. As the initial chair of the committee, he provided vigorous leadership to the project.

Fred Bright, former chair of the Department of Physical Education and one of our most well-loved and successful coaches, succeeded Jim McNally as chair and brought the project to completion.

All along, Judith Bushnell, librarian emerita and former archivist for the College, provided invaluable insights, research, and attention to detail. The College community owes a debt of gratitude to all these individuals.

In the context of college history writing at Geneseo, this volume is a major event—the first full-scale history of Geneseo since Rosalind Fisher's ...*the stone strength of the past...*, published at the time of our centennial in 1971. As Professor Mahood and his colleagues point out in the introduction, for many of us the College's history begins when we first encountered it. The work is very much the product of a generation of faculty and staff who first came to Geneseo between 1956 and 1969. As such, it looks at the College from the perspective of some of the key players who built Geneseo into the SUNY campus and public liberal arts college we have become in the last half of the twentieth century. But that is not all. Its treatment of the early history of the College significantly improves upon Rosalind Fisher's previous work, and the volume adds significant new information and insights about all eras of our history, often with a lighthearted touch. It is a volume to be enjoyed, full of excellent photographs, and it is a history that will be savored by alumni, friends, and neighbors of the College from every generation. I commend it to all members of our College family for their reading pleasure.

Reading through the volume, I was personally struck by an underlying theme that has driven the development of Geneseo in good times and bad, embodied in a line from Shakespeare's *Twelfth Night* that was quoted by Dean Celia Easton as she welcomed new students to campus in 2004: "Some are born great, some achieve greatness, and some have greatness thrust upon 'em." As you will read, 2004 was a year in which the College achieved several great things—gaining a chapter of Phi Beta Kappa and winning the SUNY Athletic Conference's Commissioner's Cup among them. Early and late in this history, we read about budget cuts, political difficulties, even challenges to our existence as a college. But we have always overcome those challenges. We were not "born great" as a college, nor have we been handed greatness (or large sums of money) on a silver platter. Without a lot of state funding and often in challenging times, we have always achieved greatness at Geneseo through the efforts of our students, our faculty, our staff, our alumni, and our friends in the community. This history is the story of those achievements. At the beginning of a third century in our existence, it offers hope and confidence that we will continue to achieve great things in the years to come. That is the underlying theme in our story. As we read this volume, let us all enjoy and celebrate our history— past, present, and future.

President Christopher C. Dahl
April 2, 2008

President Christopher C. Dahl (Ron Pretzer, Spring 1996, *Geneseo Scene*)

Acknowledgments

Cynics have described a camel as a horse designed by a committee. That unflattering reference does not apply here. Rather, the committee responsible for this updated history of the State University of New York at Geneseo, creatively chaired by the inimitable Dr. James McNally, who offered coffee and chocolate chip cookies (courtesy of his good wife, Shirley), was truly a working one. Ms. Judith Bushnell, alumna (B.A. and M.L.S), former reference librarian and archivist, and rose between the thorns, located archival materials, provided a vital chronology, untiringly edited the manuscript into readable form, and prepared extensive photograph captions. Fred Bright, recognized for his thirty years of teaching and coaching, proved not only to be the college's unofficial historian (including possessing a vital collection of photos and slides), but a skillful note taker and indefatigable acting committee chairman as well. Contrary to rumors that he photographed the laying of the cornerstone in 1871, Dr. Paul Hepler offered unparalleled knowledge of ephemera illustrating the College's history (including a priceless personal collection), and critical expertise in reproducing materials. Above all, the committee provided intimate knowledge of the College from their collective experiences. Because of that quartet, we have this book.

Accepting the risk of failing to recognize important sources, we readily thank:

President Christopher Dahl, without whose interest and authorization there would have been no committee or book.

Arthur Hatton, former vice president for college advancement and president of the Geneseo Foundation, who initiated the project, offered valuable editorial suggestions, and proved an ardent supporter even when the committee doubted itself.

President Dahl, the **Geneseo Foundation,** and **Campus Auxiliary Services** for financial support.

Drs. Kenneth Levison and William Caren, vice president for administration and finance and associate vice president for enrollment services respectively, who took time from their busy schedules to offer valuable insights into the workings of the College.

Dr. Martin L. Fausold, distinguished service professor emeritus, who thoughtfully offered his unpublished *A Draft History of the State University of New York* (1988), transcripts of his numerous interviews of key SUNY and Geneseo personnel, and helpful advice.

Alumnus (B.A., M.L.S.) **Dr. Mitchell Robinson,** who, in addition to his well-researched and well-written paper, "A Freer Opportunity....," offered some very constructive advice about how this history might be written.

Dr. Bruce Leslie, professor of history, SUNY Brockport, who interrupted his writing and teaching assignments to offer insightful comments about the entire manuscript at critical moments. He can never be thanked enough.

Judson Mead, newsletter coordinator, Office of News Services, State University of New York at Buffalo, who carefully read the manuscript and offered helpful suggestions.

Joan Bush, then Geneseo Foundation secretary who—without flinching or losing her pleasant smile—helped us get started by typing meeting minutes, photocopying materials, and providing the committee with needed supplies.

Marilyn Lyon, secretary to Dr. Caren, who in a timely fashion managed to type critical transcripts from audiotaped interviews conducted on an antiquated recorder.

Sue Chichester, Laura Cook, Ryan Fraser, Nikolas Varrone, and unnamed others in Computing and Information Technology (CIT), who supplied us with a computer, printer, and accessories, and were generally as helpful as we could ask. Fraser, Varrone, and student **Mark Petrie** were particularly helpful, patient, and instructive in extricating us from software problems.

Brian A. Bennett, director of design and college publications, who interrupted his hectic schedule to locate and supply photographs that date back over forty years.

Joanna Kirk, former editor, Alumni Development Publications, for her many helpful references about faculty, staff, students, and alumni and for serving as unofficial photographer of the committee.

Anthony Hoppa, assistant vice president for communications, who took an early interest in the project and provided liaison services.

Professor emeritus **Dr. James Somerville,** whose meticulous research examining the effect of the Vietnam War on Geneseo was of particular help.

Suzanne ("Suzy") Boor, administrative associate, Alumni and Parent Relations, never lost her sense of humor regardless of how many times she was pestered with questions about alumni(ae). And, of course, we thank all others in that office for putting up with us for four years, including **Debra G. Hill,** formerly director (now assistant vice president for college advancement); **Patty Hamilton-Rodgers,** Hill's successor; **Michele Worden,** associate director; and **Allison Barley,** assistant director.

Virtually the entire Milne Library staff, particularly **Liz Argentieri, Tim Finnigan, Sheila Freas, Harriet Sleggs,** and **Donna Howe.**

David W. Parish, alumnus, former College government documents librarian and village and town historian, who never failed to meet requests however obscure the reference, even when longtime village residents drew blanks.

Amie Alden, Livingston County historian, for sharing many photos which enhance this production.

Nancy Johncox, principal offset print shop operator, who unfailingly reproduced voluminous copies of strategic materials to meet the committee's needs.

Dr. Thomas Matthews, director of leadership education development and training, SUNY Geneseo, for anecdotes about entertainers the College has booked during his almost forty years at Geneseo.

Donald P. Lackey, former director of personnel, SUNY Geneseo, for laboriously updating a list of Geneseo faculty and staff after half a century's lapse, which proved helpful to our writing and which will find a home in the College Archives.

Joseph M. Dolce, multimedia coordinator, Computing and Information Technology, who provided audio taping equipment and duplicated audio tapes.

Elizabeth Horek Anderson, Geneseo '48, advisor to Valley Hall 3, who shared her memories of the students living there in 1948, and **Barbara Myers Scoville** ('52) who even prepared a drawing and contacted other roommates of Valley Hall 3 to help us get some feeling for what student housing was like during that post-World War II era.

Elizabeth "Wid" Adams and **Judy Mendoza** for lending photographs of ancestor Colonel John Rorbach and early Geneseo scenes.

Harrison "Flops" Phillips ('42), who readily answered questions about Geneseo in the late 1930s and early 1940s by mail and phone, while **Gordon Schiller** ('63), helped us with the 1959–1963 period.

Paul Kreher, a '93 biology major with a master's degree in physical therapy, who provided some wonderful recall of the college from 1989 to 1993.

Alumna **Jean Trescott,** whose graduate paper "A History of Education in the Town of Geneseo" twice has come in quite handy.

Alumni **Bill Brewer** ('69), **Barbara Finkle** ('68), and **Doug Brode** ('65), for reminiscences about the "Greek Tree," and **Dr. Paul Scipione** ('68), and **Robert Avalone** ('76), for reminiscing about Prometheus fraternity. **Dr. Bruce Godsave** ('65), **Charles "Dutch" VanRy** ('64), **Dr. George Wilkerson** ('64), and **James Brunner** ('62) enlivened the committee's treatment of the 1960s with their wonderful anecdotes.

Craig Shaw, Stratus Imaging, who graciously donated copies of photographs of the Integrated Science Center taken with airborne equipment to celebrate the center's dedication.

Former College photographers **Roger Smith** and **Ronald Pretzer,** who documented so many Geneseo events from the 1960s into the new millenium—often without attribution—and many other photographers whose names are sadly forgotten.

Benjamin Gajewski ('08), former photo editor for *The Lamron*, for permission to use his wonderful photo of a Geneseo sunset and for making a CD copy for the committee.

Mary McCrank, Geneseo's former media relations officer, whose news releases, instant responses to inquiries, and photographic memory were so helpful.

Jeff Kaplan and **Robert Lyon,** Facilities Planning and Construction, who provided a listing of buildings, architectural plans, and expertise unavailable elsewhere.

Mrs. Robert W. MacVittie, who gave Martin Fausold a collection of invaluable items her husband had collected over the years, which Fausold shared with us and which helped us to get to know President MacVittie better.

President Christopher C. Dahl, Ms. Theodora Greenman, Dr. William Caren, Dr. Martin L. Fausold, Dr. Kenneth Levison, Mrs. Ruth Linfoot, Dr. Myrtle Merritt,

Dr. Robert Redden, Ms. Gloria Tarantella, Dr. Wilbur Wright, and **Brenda Webb Conlon** and **Thomas Conlon** ('52), who graciously allowed us to interview them.

Matt and **Joseph Griffo, Robert McDonald, Daniel Scoville, Theodore** and **Peter Bondi, Mary Ann Fink, Andrew Chanler, Patricia Fennell, Dr. James Walker, Dr. Robert Isgro, Adrian "Bud" Prince, Hans Tanner, John Linfoot,** and **Dominic Mazza** for supplying photographs, identifying individuals in photographs, or offering useful anecdotes.

Cathy Reinholtz, longtime secretary to the art department, for visual support correspondence.

Noeme Panke Dueker and **Rochester Photographics** for expertly duplicating nearly four hundred photographs.

Mary Taylor, project director, and **Richard Horwege,** senior editor, the Donning Company Publishers, who patiently and reassuringly answered the committee's many questions and allowed an unprecedented delay in delivery of the manuscript.

Wendy Nelson, editor, and **Chad Casey,** graphic designer, also of the Donning Company Publishers, for their working with us to complete our book.

Rosalind R. Fisher, Clayton C. Mau, Colonel John Rorbach, and **Frank Welles,** from whose earlier histories of SUNY Geneseo we benefited, as well as the student editors and writers whose prose in *The Lamron,* including the priceless fiftieth anniversary booklet, and the various yearbooks dates back more than one hundred years.

And spouses **Shirley, Joan, Shirlee,** and **Bobbi,** who put up with our absences and occasional inattentiveness.

W. M.

Introduction

The beginning of the college at Geneseo dates from: (a) 1871, (b) 1904, (c) 1948, (d) 1964, (e) 1985, (f) when you, the reader, first encountered it, or (g) it depends.

Of course, the answer is (f), "when you, the reader, first encountered it." But a case can be made for (g), "it depends." That is, the Geneseo Normal and Training School opened in 1871, but 1904 identifies a major curriculum change for educational institutions in New York State. The State University of New York was created in 1948, while 1964 marks the year the first four-year liberal arts freshmen matriculated. In 1985, Associated Press reporter Peter Coy proclaimed Geneseo a "success story." Still, for many of us, nothing really happened until **we** became associated with the College—and maybe nothing has since.

Enough of the multiple-choice questions; school's out, though you may still have occasional nightmares about being unprepared for a test, about being in the wrong room, or about showing up at the wrong time. Yet, SUNY Geneseo remains a special place to alumni, current or retired faculty and staff members, contributors to the College, village residents, and others who benefit from the College's local presence.

It is remembering that "special place" that motivated us, a committee of five who met frequently and laughed even more frequently, to agree to undertake a new history. We were determined to preserve "institutional memory," a notion emphasized by then-vice president for college advancement Arthur Hatton, who convened this committee in February 2004. Too often, after participants fade from the scene, a sense of what happened before is lost. Unless records are maintained and resurrected, a society's, or in this case, a college's "roots" are forgotten. So, what follows is an attempt to preserve the history of a college that has transformed itself from a normal school to a public ivy, without knowing how the story will end. Further, we recognize that, unfortunately, there will be gaps in the ongoing story.

Shortly after we began, it struck us forcibly what we had gotten ourselves into. Events of the College's earlier days resemble faded pho-

Opposite Page: Sturges Hall, with its memorable chiming clock tower, has been a campus landmark for more than seventy-five years. (Roemer House collection)

tographs. They are just events. Only what we, ourselves, know personally seems meaningful. The problem for us, then, has been to make that far-off past equally meaningful, because it is the foundation for the current College.

Committee member and former art department chairman, Dr. Paul Hepler, still vividly recalls some of those earlier days: "...of a small college on the Genesee when students wore clothes that had labels on the inside...a time when female students had to wear skirts, coffee hour meant you saw many staff *not* in your discipline, and everyone went to Mrs. Schutz for their paychecks. The basketball team practiced in the tiny Holcomb [now Welles] gym and played games at the high school [Doty building]. Class attendance was actually checked at sessions starting after Labor Day, and Thanksgiving once was just a one-day vacation. Students...

Phi Sigma Epsilon's 1963 homecoming float depicting the 1939 World's Fair trylon and perisphere was hinged so the trylon could be lowered to pass below power lines along the parade route. The hard work paid off with first-prize honors. (Milne Archives)

labored for weeks on amazing homecoming floats so huge they could barely get through Main Street. *In loco parentis* was not considered an administrative pox, and there was a chance you could see all of the 750 students at least once during the school year."

Though memoirist Hepler was remembering the College barely fifty years ago, to most readers it might be "ancient" history. Just compare the change in the number of buildings that make up the campus in that same time—from five to forty-three. Or contrast the enrollment: from 750 to 5,419, including 5,104 full-time undergraduates. From dress codes and dorm hours to designer jeans, sneakers, and caps on backward—or whatever represents the latest fashion statement. From basketball practices in a bandbox to games in a fieldhouse. From the Blake dorms to Saratoga Terrace and Putnam Hall. From big, old Underwood manual typewriters for faculty to desktop and laptop computers.

What we hope has not changed is the affection for Geneseo that was brought home so poignantly by a recent panel of alumni in the renovated Mary Jemison Dining Hall. Articulate, humorous, bright, and genuine, the panelists have pursued a wide variety of careers, but they have one thing in common—a Geneseo education, for which they are grateful. One recalled having found himself at the College after entering as a twenty-six-year-old social outcast. Another, a seventeen-year-old, was in shock her first semester but left with needed self-reliance. Still another learned to analyze, to "read the fine print," while the final panelist took seriously SUNY's motto when he graduated, "Let each become all he is capable of being."

What stood out was not only an affection for Geneseo, but a genuine appreciation for having been part of a community where they were encouraged to grow, to test their values, and to better themselves.

Those who have invested in, presided over, or taught at Geneseo should be gratified if that is the way Geneseo is remembered. Maybe what follows will invoke similar pleasant memories for you, the reader, and encourage you to share those memories with others and with the College.

Wadsworth

NORMAL and TRAINING SCHOOL

Establishing the Tradition (1867–1871)

According to lore, in 1575, as a reward for their heroic defense of the city against a siege by the Spaniards in 1573–1574, William of Orange offered a choice to the citizens of Leiden in the Netherlands: they could be free from taxes forever or have a university. The citizens chose a university, which became one of the most famous in Europe.

There is a rough parallel to this story in Geneseo. The citizens here, too, had a choice in the late 1860s, even more difficult than that which the citizens of Leiden faced. They could use their hard-earned money to rebuild the downtown after two major fires, finance two new iron bridges to cross the Genesee River, construct a new water line to Conesus Lake to protect against future fires, or underwrite a college. The Geneseoans chose to do it all—to obligate themselves to the hilt. However, ahead lay numerous, often acrimonious, public meetings, long trips to Albany by advocates, discouraging setbacks, and renewed efforts by those with a faith in the cause. For a full treatment, one has to read Rosalind (affectionately known as Rhody) Fisher's impressive history of the College written to commemorate its centennial, ...*the stone strength of the past*....[1]

Opposite Page: Geneseo's Main Street was still a dirt road in the late nineteenth century, and the view from the northwest was dominated until 1884 by the Presbyterian church ("White Church") steeple with the official village clock. (Fred Bright collection)

To set the stage for Fisher's and this history, we must go back to 1784, when the state created the University of the State of New York (not to be confused with the State University of New York, established in 1948). This earlier university was a department of state government headed by a Board of Regents formed "to charter and regulate secondary and higher educational institutions." Shortly, the Regents recognized the need for common, or public, schools to instruct children "in the English language or be taught grammar, arithmetic, mathematics, and such branches of knowledge as are most useful and necessary to complete a good English education." The plan took root, as the number of New York schools and pupils being served rapidly expanded.[2]

The 1823 Livingston County Court House was the site of some of the earliest community meetings about a possible Normal School. (Bright Collection)

The Need for Teachers and Teacher Education

The resulting growth in common schools required a proportionate increase in teachers, but, as Geneseo history professor emeritus Dr. Martin Fausold points out, "teacher training was practically non-existent." At best, most of the teachers were barely older than their students, like Jesse Stuart, a school dropout at age nine, who became a one-room school teacher before attaining a high school education. Speaking at Geneseo years later, he asserted that a common school teacher's best tools, especially in more rural areas, were two fists with which to handle the toughest—and quite possibly older—boys. He had learned that from his older sister, who had suffered black eyes, courtesy of a male student in her class. However, Stuart acknowledged that a college education, which he subsequently achieved, was an even better tool.[3]

The idea of teacher "training" at Normal Schools was imported from France, which founded the first, *Ecole Normale*, in Paris in 1794. Such schools offered models or patterns for teaching, which were to be disseminated in public schools. Horace Mann, state superintendent of schools in Massachusetts in 1837, also saw teacher education as an opportunity to instill societal values in elementary-level school children. Additionally, Normal Schools could benefit from selecting teachers more carefully than had been the case. Too often in those formative days American schools were staffed by young men teaching only during college breaks while preparing for the ministry or law. (President John Adams comes readily to mind as an example of a budding lawyer who taught very briefly.) Further, the liberal arts education of most of those temporary male teachers was considered superfluous for those teaching young children. Finally, women, typically viewed as nurturers, seemed the right fit, and by 1850 they represented well over half of all elementary teachers.[4]

Despite the clear need for teacher education and institutions to fulfill the mission, disagreement arose over the instruction—a debate that continues today. Four approaches were suggested, all distinguished by the emphasis to be placed on academic instruction. One approach called for a secondary, or better yet, collegiate preparation. A second called for "helpful hints regarding teaching" in addition to a secondary education. The third position emphasized "the art of teaching" and methodology, while the fourth was split into two camps: one stressing the theoretical aspects of specific academic disciplines, the other imitating Oswego's emphasis on methodology put to the test in a training or practice school.[5]

Geneseo's interest in teacher education went back at least to James Wadsworth, who came to the Genesee Valley in 1790 with his brother William. In 1843, approaching seventy-five and increasingly aware of his mortality, he reminded his older son, James Samuel, that "uneducated man always has been and always will be a puppet in the hands of designing demagogues." To prepare "educated" men, James had spearheaded the creation of Temple Hill Academy, or Livingston County High School (later Geneseo Academy) in 1827, which attracted Cornelius Felton, a future Harvard president, as one of the first tutors.[6]

Until mid-century, the education of teachers in the U.S. largely had been entrusted to such academies funded in part by the state, though as early as 1834 "special seminaries" were proposed. The first such seminary in the United States was the Lexington (Massachusetts) State Normal School, founded in 1839. Following Massachusetts' lead, the New York State legislature took a gingerly first step in 1844 when it revoked subsidies to the academies and created a Normal School in Albany. The next Normal School, at Oswego, did not come for another seventeen years. Then, in 1866, Governor Reuben E. Fenton prodded the legislature further—to offer the enabling legislation and to solicit proposals for four more Normal Schools. Geneseoans (and representatives from thirteen other villages) were quick to pick up on the invitation.[7]

Fredonia, Cortland, Potsdam, and nearby Brockport beat out Geneseo. Legislators serving those villages wanted a piece of the action for their constituents. A college meant jobs, student purchases locally, and board and room fees to house students and faculty. (This practice of protecting one's turf continues to the present, of course.) Undaunted, representatives from the village, encouraged by Geneseoan Lockwood L. Doty, who headed the state Bureau of Military Statistics and enjoyed influence in Albany, appealed not only to the legislature again, but to the governor and superintendent of public instruction. To sweeten the pot, Geneseo voters pledged an additional ten thousand dollars from a trust fund set up by James Wadsworth in 1833 as an inducement. However, as Colonel John Rorbach recalled in his address on the first twenty-five years of the College, the creation of a school that would compete with Temple Hill Academy was a "delicate subject for any of us to attempt to handle." But, as he lamented, "this once prosperous school [the Academy] had been for years upon a slow but steady decline," which opponents of the Normal School refused to admit.[8]

In fact, looking back over the first twenty-five years, Rorbach was still awed that so much opposition to a Normal School in Geneseo was overcome. He vividly recalled that "the suspicions and oppositions of our friends of the rural parts of our town had been excited against a few of us by those malcontents of our village—what ridiculous misrepresentations and calumnies...." It seemed to him at the time that it was obvious that the future of Geneseo Academy was in jeopardy. The Presbyterian Synod, its sponsor, had split into the "New School" and the "Old," depriving it of much help. He also remembered that the city of Syracuse had "greedily" stolen nearby Lima's Methodist "College" (Genesee College) to resurrect it as Syracuse University.[9]

Geneseo Academy.   GENESEO, N. Y.

The Temple Hill and SUNY Geneseo Connection

The link between Temple Hill Academy and the College continues today, though the Academy was dissolved by the state legislature in December 1891. In 1896 the remaining assets ($8,190.39, with accrued interest of approximately $2,400) were turned over to county treasurer William A. Brodie, who also was then the Geneseo Normal School's local board secretary. Thereafter interest was to be paid to the treasurer of the Geneseo Normal and Training School to aid "worthy and needy [Presbyterian] students" by Chapter 372, Laws of New York of 1890. In fact, some Presbyterian students' tuition was paid out of these funds earlier, beginning in 1887 when "Miss Kadashaw" from Alaska was awarded twenty-five dollars. Another was Flora B. Tallchief, a sixteen-year-old Iroquois, who was given money from the fund at least three times to help her graduate in January 1918 in the English course, five years after she entered the school.[10]

The postscript is a story in itself. From 1890 to the present, the interest from this money, known as the Temple Hill Fund, has served two purposes: (1) as short-term loans for needy students and (2) as an endowment for scholarships. In 1948, the earlier act governing the fund was amended to require the county treasurer to pay the income to the president of the College. In turn, the president was to recommend to the College Council worthy and

This view shows the Presbyterian-sponsored Temple Hill Academy from Academy Street (now Prospect Street). One building still stands and is a private residence. (Balding Postcards, Bright collection)

needy students at the College. Preference was to be given to "the children of clergymen of the Presbyterian church," a reminder that the funds had originally been raised "by subscription from members of said church."[11]

In 1988, the College obtained legislation to transfer the assets from the county treasurer to the Geneseo Foundation, Inc. This belatedly recognized that starting in 1971, the College could maintain a non-profit, tax-exempt corporation to administer its own private funds. Then, following more recent non-discriminatory laws, the clause giving preference to Presbyterian students was deleted by agreement of all parties concerned. The interest from the principal, totaling approximately sixty-two thousand dollars in 2004, still provides short-term loans and scholarships for all, not just deserving Presbyterian, students. So the dreams and aspirations of the founders and alumni of Temple Hill Academy still live through "The Temple Hill Scholarship Endowment Fund."[12]

Raising Money to Fund the Normal School

An equally delicate matter was the need to raise forty-five thousand dollars for a Normal School. While Geneseo was considered wealthy because of the presence of the two branches of the Wadsworth family, that was not the case. In fact, the village had suffered two disastrous fires (1864 and 1866), wiping out much of the downtown and incurring an estimated uninsured loss of $83,750. Then there was the bill for thirty-six thousand dollars to cover the town's share of the cost of erecting two new iron bridges, and a six-thousand-dollar obligation for an abutment to the Cuylerville bridge. Finally, the town still owed its share of bounties paid to the county's Civil

Among the costly projects facing Geneseo residents shortly after the Civil War was the need to replace this bridge over the Genesee River near the current intersection of Court Street and Route 63. (John Balding and Son, Geneseo, N.Y., Bright Collection)

War enlistees. (Colonels John Rorbach and John R. Strang, two prominent Geneseoans who later served as local board members of the College, soldiered with the 104th New York Volunteer Infantry which trained at Geneseo's Camp Union.) Rhody Fisher estimated the total indebtedness of the Village and Town of Geneseo at $129,000. (Add a zero and you have the approximate amount in today's dollars, $1,290,000!!) Nonetheless, on September 24, 1867, by a 321 to 176 vote at a special meeting called by the village trustees, the villagers agreed to raise the forty-five thousand dollars for a school.[13]

A January 1864 fire (seen here) destroyed twenty-two businesses on the west side of Main Street, and an April 1866 fire claimed an additional seventeen businesses. (Livingston County Historian and Andrew Chanler)

Less than a year later, by a seventy-two to five vote, the village upped the ante, pledging a maximum of one hundred thousand dollars to be paid in fifteen installments, by levying real and personal property taxes in the village, and to obtain the necessary site. (The village would only have to raise forty-five thousand dollars through taxes, using ten thousand dollars from the Wadsworth Trust and twenty thousand dollars from the county board of supervisors, assuming seventy-five thousand would be enough to provide the building and equipment.) Lockwood L. Doty and Colonels Craig W. Wadsworth and John Rorbach were appointed to obtain the land. But opposition was led by those whom Rorbach anonymously labeled "malcontents." The principal opponent was B. F. (Benjamin Franklin) Angel, an early graduate and trustee of Temple Hill Academy, village mayor in 1850 and minister to Norway and Sweden. (Ironically, he once owned what is now the McClellan House at 26 Main Street, presently occupied by the College's Alumni and Parent Relations and the Lockhart Gallery.) The accepted version to explain his opposition is that Angel feared the threat to Temple Hill Academy and the unwelcome prospect of higher taxes. However, the triumvirate of John Rorbach, William A. Brodie (replacing Doty), and Craig W. Wadsworth overcame Angel's objections.[14]

Normal School Founding Fathers

Several local residents were instrumental in getting state approval for a Normal School.

Civil War veteran, lawyer, and entrepreneur Colonel John Rorbach (1826–1899) served on the Board of Visitors for many years. (Elizabeth "Wid" Adams and Judy Mendoza)

William A. Brodie (1841–1917) was a thirty-third degree Mason who laid the Statue of Liberty cornerstone. (Geneseo Masonic Lodge, reproduced by Daniel Fink)

Civil War veteran and lawyer Colonel John S. Strang (1840–1909) served on the Board of Visitors from 1892 to 1909. (Geneseo Village/Town Historian)

Lockwood Lyon Doty (1827–1873) held several political appointments and wrote the first history of Livingston County. (Livingston County Historian)

Civil War veteran Brev. Col. Craig Wharton Wadsworth, Sr. (1841–1872) helped obtain a building site for the Normal School and served as one of its commissioners. (Livingston County Historical Society, reproduced by Ronald Pretzer)

Genesee Valley Bank president James S. Orton (1816–1892) was appointed a Normal School commissioner. (Livingston County Historian)

Making the Normal School a Reality

Geneseoans finally had authorization for a college in late April 1868, when the legislature granted Geneseo the right to establish the Wadsworth Normal and Training School. (It was rumored that the legislature was thereby honoring Geneseo's General James Samuel Wadsworth, the 1862 GOP gubernatorial candidate who lost his life rallying Union infantry at the Civil War's Battle of the Wilderness in 1864.) The next step was to secure the land and obtain another eighteen-thousand-dollar appropriation from the state. Obtaining the land proved an unexpected obstacle. B. F. Angel, a thorn in the side of Normal School proponents, once again raised objections. Angel successfully argued that using the village "Park," albeit undeveloped, for a Normal School was a base injustice to the villagers. Craig Wadsworth, the General's middle son, then offered to sell land just west of the park (where the Doty building, once Geneseo Central High School, is today). Thus, rather than a gift of the first parcel, the Wadsworth property had to be purchased by the village. On February 2, 1870, the late James S. Wadsworth's heirs sold almost seven acres of his "Home Farm" for $2,019.60 to the three newly appointed school commissioners, Craig Wadsworth, John Rorbach, and James S. Orton. In turn, they deeded the land to the State for the nominal sum of one dollar in 1871, to be used "to procure a site and to erect buildings thereon."[15]

Benjamin Franklin Angel (1811–1894), U.S. ambassador to Norway and Sweden, was one of the chief opponents of establishing the Normal School. (Geneseo Village/Town Historian)

The school now would become a reality, though not without further carping. According to Rorbach, the school's building committee was "liberally censured and our motives again maligned for locating the buildings in such an outlandish and out-of-the-way place." (The Normal School was to be located "downhill" both literally and figuratively. By contrast, the Temple Hill Academy overlooked the village in an Olympian manner.) The commissioners had the last laugh, for the Academy had only two acres, clearly insufficient to meet the College's need in less than twenty-five years. And the chosen location, just uphill from the Erie Railroad Station east of the flats, would assure students well into the future the benefit of an unobstructed view of the beautiful sunsets across the valley.[16]

Students and faculty turned out in force to pose for what may be the earliest extant Old Main photo, taken before the chapel was added to the north end of the building in 1875. (Livingston County Historian)

Meanwhile, on June 15, 1869, given the offer of land, though it was not yet deeded, ground was broken for the College's first building. Adapting Fredonia's building plans, the Normal School erected an 11,418-square-foot, three-story, steam-heated, gas-lighted building, with hot and cold water. It was actually five connected buildings: a forty-eight by seventy six-foot center building, thirty-three by forty-foot wings on either side, and thirteen by twenty-foot extensions to each wing. The school cafeteria and the "Primary Department" were located in the ten-foot-high-ceilinged basement. Classrooms and offices for the "Intermediate, Academic and Normal Departments" were located on the fourteen-foot-high first and second floors, while the upper story, "the boarding hall," was to accommodate the young ladies who paid $3.50 per

week for room and laundry facilities. The architect's description for that floor reads like a commercial advertisement: "Parlors for students, assembly room, which might be used for calisthenics for lady students, lavatories, and sleeping apartments for those boarding in the building."[17]

The building, soon affectionately known as "Old Main," would stand for eighty years, though many changes would be necessary. Changes included converting the entire third story into a dormitory months after the first students arrived. Within five years, an auditorium ("suitable assembly room") was erected, and, still later, a library and gymnasium.[18]

Geneseo was about to embark on a venture that would lead to a college with an enviable reputation for excellence.

Geneseo

NORMAL *and* TRAINING SCHOOL

·

A Firm Foundation (1871–1905)

On the night of July 1, 1872, graduate Frank A. Winnie, president of the Delphic Society and future faculty member, entertained an appreciative audience gathered in the Geneseo Normal and Training School concert hall with a brief address. It was the beginning of a two-part celebration that would conclude the next morning with the school's first graduation.

That graduation—after barely a year's operation—was a momentous event for the fledgling school. Although it would not rank with the transcontinental railroad, the Atlantic telegraph cable, telephones and electric lights, or other major advances in technology, farming, and industry, it marked a milestone for the village. What makes that commencement so memorable is not only the breakneck speed with which Geneseo graduated its first students, but that it had overcome so many obstacles.

Even the name of the school seems to have been problematic over the years. For example, on September 13, 1871, when the school opened with 354 students—71 enrolled in the "Normal Department," 203 younger students in the "Training Department" (later practice

Opposite Page: Geneseo's Main Street was decorated with arches made of foliage, flags, and banners to celebrate the 1879 centennial of the Revolutionary War Sullivan Campaign to destroy Native American villages. (Dan Fink from Merrell glass plate negative)

school) and 80 in the "Academic Department" (secondary school)—it had already been retitled. The name change, dropping Wadsworth from the title, was the beginning of a pattern of name, but not necessarily role, changes. According to William Lane, the College's first archivist, "Board Minutes and Board secretaries seemed to use whatever appealed to them from [1871] on, dropping the term 'and training' finally in 1899." Advocate for the school and later local Board of Visitors (now College Council) chairman, William Brodie, recalled a town meeting, a vote, and an unsuccessful appeal to the legislature to restore the original name. A quarter-century later John Rorbach recalled that "…the name of the school was changed…at the procurement of its old enemies…," though what he meant by that is unclear. An alternative explanation is that the College was renamed in keeping with the general nomenclature of the other schools in the state.[1]

Today's Big Tree Inn was built in 1833 as Allen and Bethiah Ayrault's residence. Over the years, the building's width was doubled, a third floor was added, the back was extended, and the home became a popular restaurant and inn, which was purchased by Campus Auxiliary Services and reopened in 1999. (Bright collection)

It can be argued that the College's name changes also reflect a persisting identity crisis. For example, in February 1965, Arthur Brooks, Geneseo's public information officer, wrote the following to the Rochester area media:

"WE HATE TO BRING THIS UP, BUT....................

Some of our friends in the newspaper, radio and television fields sometimes refer to us as Geneseo Teachers College, or Geneseo State College of Education, and lots of other things.

Actually we'd like to be known by our official title:

STATE UNIVERSITY COLLEGE AT GENESEO"

Brooks's boss, President Robert W. MacVittie, promptly penciled an appreciative and clever reply.[2]

Twenty-five years later, charismatic President Carol Harter also tried to clarify the College's name. In a letter to State University of New York Chancellor D. Bruce Johnstone she wrote:

"Dear Bruce:

Like others who have expressed their preference for "University Colleges" to describe our thirteen institutions, I too prefer that to the somewhat misleading "Colleges of Arts and Sciences" [sic] designation. Unfortunately I don't know how one escapes the unfortunate acronyms SUC(K) or SUC(Ks) that result from this abbreviation. And to make it worse, imagine G-SUC(Ks)....Perhaps it is even worse if one reverses the order of the acronym: SUC-P (we have several), SUC-A, SUC-F, or good lord, SUC-OW.

...In any case, if we could use University College at Geneseo without "State," I would prefer that solution but doubt that the rascals of the world will settle for UC(Ks).

Just thought I'd reinforce the obvious.

Fondly,
Carol Harter
President"[3]

Her successor, Dr. Christopher Dahl, also felt called on to set the record straight in a memo to the College's administrators on April 18, 2005:

"…When referring to Geneseo, please use, **The State University of New York at Geneseo**, **SUNY Geneseo**, or simply **Geneseo** as our official name. Please do not use State University College, or worse still, SUC in referring to Geneseo. Please also avoid the Big-Ten-style 'Geneseo State,' which is utterly incorrect."

And so it goes. By archivist Lane's count the College has had at least ten names, which offered an initial framework for this book.

The Local Board Begins

The confusion, at times conflict, over the College's name and role symbolizes its struggle just to exist, let alone succeed. After rancorous public meetings and alleged back-room deals, a slate of names for the Board of Visitors was forwarded to state superintendent of public instruction, Abram B. Weaver. (Republicans and Democrats sparred, as did Temple Hill Academy and Normal school advocates.) On August 3, 1871, Weaver officially appointed nine persons to the board: Colonel Rorbach; former County Judge Scott Lord;

General James Wood; Livingston County Judge Solomon Hubbard; Dr. Walter E. Lauderdale; manager of the Wadsworth estates Hezekiah Allen; the late General James S. Wadsworth's youngest son, James W. Wadsworth; local lawyer Adoniram J. Abbott; and Daniel Bigelow, a town official and unsuccessful candidate for county school commissioner.[4]

By the late nineteenth century, Geneseo had a new courthouse, gas streetlights, and the Wadsworth Memorial Fountain—but the streets were still unpaved. (Hans Tanner collection)

The next scuffle occurred on August 9, when the nine met at the law office of presumptive chairman Scott Lord to elect the board's officers. According to William Brodie, writing as local correspondent for the Rochester *Democrat and Chronicle*, at that meeting there was the "most bitter bandy of words between some members of the board...." After six voice votes, Mr. Hubbard's motion to resort to paper ballots was accepted, resulting in the election of General James Wood as chairman and subsequently a huffy resignation by Scott Lord. At issue was whether to have an academic department (college preparatory program) in the new Normal School, following Temple Hill's denominational (Presbyterian) tradition. Rorbach claims that Lord, one of four who unsuccessfully opposed it, resigned because of the board's decision to have an academic department. (Peter Miller, who apparently was untainted by politics and willing to serve in a lesser role, replaced Lord the following February.) The five in favor felt they had promised the voters to continue the academy instruction. Dr. Lauderdale was elected secretary, apparently without any fireworks.[5]

The board then turned to the task of soliciting applications for the school's principal, the title used for the head of the Normal School well into the twentieth century. When the board reassembled in General Wood's law office the next day, August 10, the committee headed by Mr. Hubbard announced six applicants. Six days later, after interviewing candidates, the board narrowed the choices to two: Brockport Normal School faculty member William J. Milne and a former deputy superintendent of public instruction identified only by his last name, Barr. Milne was selected principal on the second ballot at a salary of twenty-five hundred dollars, while Barr, approved as vice principal and math instructor, subsequently declined the position.[6]

The First Milne Era

The twenty-eight-year-old Milne, a Scot and professor of ancient languages at Brockport, had obtained his master's degree (and subsequently his doctorate) from the University of Rochester. Brockport would both lament the loss of his services and rec-ommend him to Geneseo: "in Prof. Milne [Geneseo] will find a ripe scholar, a courteous gentleman, and a social friend." "Prof. Milne," alternately called "Dock Milne," lost no time getting started, meeting with the board five days after being ap-pointed principal to help select the remaining faculty.[7]

Also at that first meeting, Rorbach and Lauderdale were named to the building and grounds committee, with a task possibly rivaling that of appointing the school head: negotiating for a janitor-steward who would be responsible for the buildings and grounds and for the students' rooms and meals. In fact, caring for the College's buildings and grounds would prove a major headache. (In 1875, less than four years into operation, a sixty by one-hundred-foot building, referred to as the "chapel," to be located thirty feet north of the "north tower of the present building," was authorized. And eleven years later another building, a campus school, was approved.) Complicating matters, the board's first non-academic appoint-ment—of Harmon "Ham" Howe, "popular host of the [village's] American Hotel" as a janitor-steward—did not turn out well.[8]

William J. Milne, who served as the Normal School's first principal from 1871 to 1889, was the youngest person ever appointed to head the school. (Roemer House collection)

The first major problem Howe encountered was the Gas Light Company's bills, which the board felt were excessive. But the problem was more serious than it appeared. On July 12, 1873, after a failed promise to abstain "from use of ardent spirits," Howe was released from his contract and a temporary replacement was named.[9]

Three years later L. Charles Morey, "a veteran of the late war" [Civil War], was appointed. He remained until 1913, when he was forced to retire, after a total of thirty-eight years, in part because he had come to act as if he owned the school.[10]

By the early 1880s, a northwest addition to Old Main housed the School of Practice, shown at the rear on the right. (Livingston County Historian)

L. C. Morey served from 1876 to 1913 as the Normal School's second janitor. (Ada L. Houseknecht photo, Milne Archives)

The board's first weeks were a flurry of activity and amazing progress, considering the tasks it faced. Acting much like a local public school board, the members spent an enormous amount of time hiring faculty, soliciting students, establishing student admissions and disciplinary policies, writing the curriculum, and getting the building and grounds in order. The latter included calcimining (painting) walls, building stairs, repairing blackboards, oiling the floors, buying 125 tons of coal to heat the building, and procuring twenty loads of manure and soil to landscape the front yard. The board met almost daily with "Prof. Milne" from late August into October that first year to hire faculty. Not surprisingly, given the board members' ties to the community, disagreements over awarding contracts for services and hiring faculty characterized meetings.

Yet, looking back, it appears that the board was highly successful in its hiring, especially given the shortness of time. Four of its early faculty had or would obtain doctorates while in service, including Principal Milne and his brother John M. Milne, who in 1872 was appointed to teach Greek and Latin in the Academic Department. Others were Reuben A. Waterbury (mathematics and methods), who previously had been head of an academy, and Jerome Allen (natural sciences), who left ten years later to become president of Teachers College at St. Cloud, Minnesota. (Allen, with the faraway look he is supposed to have had, accurately predicted that salt—which had not yet been discovered—would be mined from salt springs underneath nearby ground.)[11]

Less is known about the rest of the very early faculty, which included 1872 alumna Gloria F. Bennett, Sarah (or Sara) Fletcher, Delia Day Vanderbilt, J. B. Gorham, Emma S. Parsons (McMaster?), Mary E. Parks, Helen Roby ("Preceptress," or "Training Department" head), Nancy L. Van Husen, and Lizzie Killip. Most of the appointees were themselves graduates of and had taught at Normal Schools or had some elementary school teaching experience. While there were the usual appointments of locals and charges of cronyism, probably they were typical of Normal School faculty members generally. Only twenty-six percent of Normal School faculties in New York State between 1871 and 1882 held at least a baccalaureate degree. Salaries, ranging from four hundred dollars paid to "Critic" teachers in the Training Department to one thousand dollars for preceptresses in the Normal Department, were negotiated with the board. Faculty were granted annual contracts (a reminder that they served at the pleasure of the board) and were instructed to complete the school term; sickness alone excused them from their obligations. Finally, the

Old Main's hallways, featuring richly detailed walls and pressed metal ceilings, were ornately decorated with artwork. The print on the left is now in the Alice Austin Theater lobby in Brodie Hall. (Roemer House collection)

teachers were told to give "their best energies, and all their time during the sessions of the School, to its interests," an admonition repeated well into the twentieth century.[12]

William J. Milne · Reuben A. Waterbury · J. B. Gorham · Miss Lizzie Killip

Mrs. Sara F. Fletcher · Nancy L. Van Husen · Jerome Allen · Miss Mary E. Parks

Emma S. McMaster · Miss Delia Vanderbelt · John M. Milne · Miss Helen Roby

The Lamron's fiftieth anniversary booklet included these photos of 1871 faculty members and twenty-eight-year-old principal William Milne. (*The Lamron, 50th Anniversary*)

Organizing the School

The local board initially intended to admit students as young as fourteen, but to withhold diplomas until age eighteen. Subsequently they raised the admission age to sixteen to comply with regulations for the state's Normal Schools. Entrants also had to be of "good health, good moral character and average ability." Early on, possibly at the outset, the College wanted it clear that the "Normal Department [was] open only to those who intend to teach and is designed to give thorough instruction and training in all that is required in a teacher's work." To ensure attainment of that objective, beginning in 1891 the students signed a pledge binding them to teach after graduation. This contract existed well into the twentieth century, to which Geneseo President MacVittie, a 1944 Oneonta graduate, attested.[13]

To assure "the education and discipline of teachers for the common schools of the State," the new Normal School would have two major divisions, the Normal Department and the Academic Department. The Normal Department was to prepare teachers for grades one through six, and was consequently fur-

Before teaching children, Normal School students presented lessons to their peers and teachers, as in Phebe Hall's classroom. (Livingston County Historian)

ther divided into the Primary and Intermediate departments. (Geneseo, like all the other state Normal Schools except Albany, which prepared secondary teachers, was to "train" only elementary school teachers.) The students learned the subject matter from one set of faculty, after which they watched model lessons taught by other faculty to grades one through six students in the "Training Department," later called the "School of Practice," and later still the "Campus School." Then in their second year the "seniors" taught lessons to the elementary grade students. "No lesson is presented [by the senior student] to a class until the material and plan of presentation have been corrected by the critic [teacher] to whose department the subject belongs." Years later, Normal School graduates still vividly recalled teaching a "model" lesson to invited school friends and village residents.[14]

"Hide and Seek, Whoop!," a John Rogers sculpture that was the first class gift in 1879, graced the stage of the primary department assembly room. (Livingston County Historian)

Students preparing to teach "the rudiments of learning" to grades one through three enrolled in the Primary Department. Those intending to teach in the Intermediate Department (grades four through six) had to know the "four fundamental rules of arithmetic, including long division, and the multiplication table....read well in the Third Readers, and spell the words in the lesson; read, and know as much geography as is generally contained in the primary works."[15]

Conflict Over the Academic Department

The inclusion of the "Academic Department"—essentially a preparatory school—in the Normal was a source of continuing controversy. The department had been approved by the local board on August 22, 1871, to satisfy supporters of Temple Hill Academy who saw no need for a Normal School since, they argued, the Academy had prepared teachers since at least 1842. State superintendent of public instruction Abram Weaver opposed the local board's decision, arguing that the primary mission of Normal Schools was

to prepare "thoroughly trained and educated teachers," not serve also as a local secondary school. Deviating from that purpose would not only spell failure, but it would create an unnecessary burden for the taxpayers.[16]

Given that the Academic Department served a community need and that there had been parity of enrollments between the Normal and Academic departments, Superintendent Weaver reluctantly permitted Geneseo to continue the "deviation." The controversy over including academic departments in Normal Schools would decline by the late 1880s, when many (though not Geneseo's) were dropped.[17]

Superintendent Weaver's concern over the quality of a Normal School education was well founded. One early study determined that typically the Normal Schools were "glorified high schools." Twenty years later it was found that the latent function of Normal Schools, despite attempts to prevent it, was to enable local residents to educate their children, "regardless of qualifying them for teaching...." (In fact, statewide, only thirteen percent of those with a Normal School education actually were teaching in 1903. By contrast, of Geneseo's first 101 graduates, 88 had taught, 69 were still teaching in 1877, two had died, and one was an invalid.)[18]

Early art classes drew from still life objects such as the paper lanterns hanging from the chalkboard, rather than copying drawings from cards, a technique common in the early to mid-twentieth century. (Paul Hepler collection)

The Courses of Study

Three curricular options were available to students learning to teach in the Normal Department: Elementary English, Advanced English, and Classical, the latter two overlapping the curriculum in the Academic Department.

The two-year Elementary English course of study, the most popular, was not particularly rigorous. The first year's coursework included arithmetic, grammar, geography, reading (the first half of the first term only), spelling and impromptu composition, penmanship (last half of the first term), vocal music (first half), and light gymnastics (daily). The second term of the first year added botany, the first half of rhetoric and English literature, the first half of physiology and zoology, U.S. History, and drawing. The second year consisted of philosophy and history of education, school economy, civil government and education law, teaching methods, and practice teaching (second term).[19]

The Advanced English and Classical courses were available for those wanting more rigor or preparing for liberal arts degrees. The two-year Advanced English curriculum—algebra, philosophy, Latin, astronomy, geometry, and trigonometry—

followed a satisfactory examination on the content of the first year course of study. The three-year Classical Course, taught in the Academic Department, required Latin and Greek or modern languages, declamations (public speaking), methods in teaching the Advanced English course, mineralogy and geology, and practice teaching after successful completion of the first year of the Elementary English program.[20]

Fraternities and sororities were given their own Old Main meeting rooms, and members often arranged simultaneous meeting dismissal times to encourage socializing in the hallways. (Milne Archives)

Social Conduct Rules and Regulations

However striking the contrast between the school's rules at the outset and today, there are similarities. After all, the students represented the school to the village.

Pursuant to the board's instructions "to draft rules and regulations" for admission, Principal Milne laid out expectations for the incoming students. "Idleness, profanity, falsehood, obscene and indecent language, and the use of tobacco during school hours, or on school premises" were banned. Suspensions were to be meted out for unexcused absences of six consecutive school days (excluding verified sickness), malicious conduct, insolence to teachers, defacing property, and "conduct injurious to other pupils." Less than three years later, a prohibition against out-of-town Normal School students "frequenting or visiting any Saloon, Billiard Room, or other such place of amusement" without parent or guardian permission was added. (Likely, it was expected that those living at home in the village would be monitored by their parents or guardians.) Some twenty years later the board reinforced its disdain for smoking by informing the principal that it "looks with disapproval upon any student smoking on the street or in public places or coming to school with clothing saturated with tobacco." (Smoking would be an issue again in the mid-1950s and 1980s, when it was limited to designated areas before ultimately being banned from all campus buildings.)[21]

These women shared a small study table in their room, which they enlivened by attaching friends' photographs to netting hanging on the wall. (1997 *Oh Ha Daih*)

The board came to expect at least one agenda item a month devoted to enforcing the rules and regulations. The matter of the suspension of "Mr. L. M. Stratton" alone lasted through two meetings, which taxed the enforcers' tolerance for the suspended student, whose violation was not revealed, and for each other.[22]

However, some matters went unnoticed, at least publicly. For example, the administration seemed unaware of or ignored the nocturnal activities in the "glen." An 1878 graduate, back for the fiftieth anniversary celebration of the Normal School, recalled:

"…the boys' clandestine meetings with the girls who roomed in after lights were out at night…how the girls used to steal in their stocking feet and with bated breath down the long hall of the dormitory, the floor of which used to creak dismally causing the girls' hearts to thump in dire apprehension as they tiptoed cautiously past the door of Madame Kelsey [the Rhetoric teacher and the girls' supervisor] yet this did not prevent the brave girls from keeping their pre-arranged trysts."[23]

Other issues that taxed Principal Milne and the board included monitoring the arrangements for boarding female students and for helping students pay (or exempting them from paying) tuition. In-state Normal School students paid no tuition; out-of-staters and those in the Academic Department, except local students, did. While the state Normal Schools were intended only for New York State residents, the restriction was not observed until 1895. After that, as the 1898 College catalogue spelled it out: "Non-residents of the state are not solicited or encouraged to enter our Normal Schools." This may also have been to limit enrollment, which had to be capped periodically.[24]

In short, Milne and the local board wrestled with the usual problems facing a new college: constructing buildings, hiring and retaining the best faculty it could afford, offering an appropriate curriculum, teaching, disciplining, and housing its students.

The burden of providing adequate, if not comfortable, student housing fell

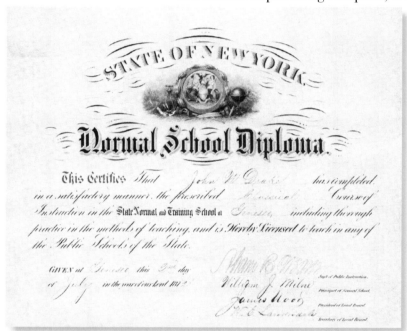

heavily on the village. An extension of Bank Street downhill from Main Street to the Erie Railroad to encourage house construction was proposed. Creating another street, running between Bank and Court streets, also was proposed. And while Miss Fisher claimed that H. P. North offered an easement on his property to create North Street for more housing, the street was laid out much earlier. It remains that the village was bent on constructing lodgings for Geneseo Normal School students.[25]

The oldest extant Normal School diploma was awarded to John Drake, member of the first graduating class in 1872. Art professor Paul Hepler bought the diploma at an antique shop, and for many years it was displayed in the Blake A College Center. (Milne Archives)

The First Graduation

That first graduation on July 1, 1872, beginning with Frank Winnie's address, was the celebratory end of a dramatic year. Against all odds, the College graduated ten students, four of whom completed the Classical Course, two the Advanced English, and four the Elementary English. All were New Yorkers who lived nearby. The exceptions were Mary P. Allen and Frank Ephraim Welles, who, as Dr. Welles, returned to teach at the College and fathered a future Geneseo principal. They were from Norwich, New York. How these students, including those who followed Principal Milne to Geneseo, graduated after only one year of coursework in a two- or three-year curriculum is a bit of a mystery. In her history of the College, Miss Fisher was under the impression that Milne wanted so much to have a graduation at the end of his first year that he arranged for some of his Brockport students to transfer to Geneseo and expedited their coursework. It may be that they took proficiency exams and met the minimum two-term requirement by counting Brockport and Geneseo. (Fifty years later, Pliny Seymour recalled "a short entrance exam" and class assignments based on the test results.) Also, likely some students benefited from having taught in rural, one-room schools.[26]

That first graduation was a splendid affair, given contemporary reports. The program was organized by the Delphic Society at the campus's Concert Hall. Frank Winnie's fellow graduates Ara Wilkinson, John N. Drake, and Frank E. Welles participated with an essay ("Fashion"), oration ("Restricted Suffrage"), and a declamation in Latin, respectively. A "rather long" debate on "Free Trade" by two society members demonstrated the "argumentative skills" of the school's students.[27] (Such "argumentative skills" may have been the undoing of 1873 Geneseo Classical Curriculum graduate James M. Milne, who was forced out after nine tumultuous years as principal of Oneonta Normal [1889–1898]. Nevertheless, he was honored posthumously when Oneonta's library was named for him, making two Milne libraries in the SUNY system. Coincidentally, at one time three Milnes were principals—William at Albany, John at Geneseo, and James at Oneonta.)[28]

Delphic fraternity members posed in front of stage scenery that may have been used for one of their dramatic presentations. (Merrell photo, Livingston County Historian)

Despite "extreme heat," at 10:00 the next day, July 2, the formal exercises were conducted at the First Presbyterian Church, "The White Church" on Main Street, before a packed house. In addition to the Delphic Society members who had performed the previous evening, the female graduates, "dressed in white," also made "themselves distinctly heard." Julia Skinner, Maggie McNaughton, Mary Allen, Sarah Watson, and Ella Chamberlain read essays on "Character," "Gold Lies Deep in the Mine," "Atmospheres," "Possibilities," and "Let There Be Light" respectively. Despite his own later experience, Frank Welles spoke about "Unsuccessful Men."[29]

Particularly gratifying, the graduates' hard work paid off. Geneseo's *Livingston Republican* reported that prior to commencement "all the male graduates and several of the lady graduates have secured situations as teachers, at salaries ranging from $900 to $1200." It might be added that those salaries matched, if not exceeded, the salaries of some of their instructors.[30]

Their efforts paid off in other ways as well. In an editorial a week after graduation the *Livingston Republican's* editor harkened back to the heated, even acrimonious, debates about the villagers' agreement to tax themselves to support a Normal School. Clearly, the village had been amply rewarded "morally, socially, pecuniarily, and educationally." For example, assuming fifty students boarded in the village, on average each spent fifty dollars there, or a total of twenty-five hundred dollars. (A study performed by Geneseo's School of Business in 2006 found that the students spent more than fifty-two million dollars per year, much of which went for housing in the village.) Additionally, a number of families had moved into the village to take advantage of the Normal's Academic Department. This may have resulted in an additional thirty-thousand-dollar income to the village. Less tangible, but no less beneficial, was the village's reputation "as the seat of a great institution of learning."[31]

More Construction

While Principal Milne and the local board were trying to make the new building and grounds presentable, the need for more buildings and land was already manifest. Less than three years after the opening, Colonel Rorbach recalled, "we had reached the stage in the rapid and uninterrupted progress of this school, when ampler facility for congregation and study room, etc., was indispensable." So the board authorized a sixty-by-one-hundred-foot building, to be known as "Normal Hall" and to be located north of the "north tower of the present building." And again the board went to the legislature for money, twice, in fact. It was successful, per Rorbach, because "Our

Old Main's chapel, also known as Normal Hall, provided ample seating for lectures, concerts, and dramatic productions that entertained community residents as well as students and faculty. (Livingston County Historian)

great commonwealth has always acted upon the theory of conviction, that intelligence is cheaper in the end than ignorance." In short, the legislature complied, but, given the nation's depression, it could not grant enough to meet the entire need. The hall was furnished, but its size was reduced from the original plans.[32]

Rorbach also remembered that in 1884 again, "we found ourselves in straitened circumstances, that is our pupils had become too numerous, and I might add, too clamorous for our accommodations." Ironically, the College's success had become a problem. It needed more room for its "School of Practice," or "Training Department," where the Normal School students taught lessons modeled by their critic teachers to younger students (initially up to sixth grade). Once more the legislature came through, but Dr. Milne was disappointed that the plans did not include some additions he felt necessary. In response, he put up eight hundred dollars of his own money— no small sum then. This led to the first College fundraising, a necessity with which we are all too familiar. Consistent with the generosity the College has come to expect, various "entertainments" by the students and faculty raised $860 to repay Milne.[33]

Ten years later, in 1894, the board addressed the need for another new building to house a gymnasium. The board also decided to move the heating plant out of the original building and the science lab to an upper floor to "get rid of the unpleasant fumes" emanating from the basement. This led to numerous meetings and extended discussions beginning March 25, at

The many poles in Old Main's gym probably made basketball games challenging. (Bright collection)

least one of which resulted in a highly contested debate. One issue was how high the new building should be. Another was whether the board dared go to the legislature again. But it had no choice, having just authorized spending thirty-five hundred dollars for "extraordinary and unforeseen repairs" to some new heaters (and another fifteen dollars for "thermometers"). The board first sought funds from what remained of the late James S. Wadsworth's estate, but the Wadsworth trust fund was earmarked for the village's Wadsworth Library. Still intent on providing the appropriate environment, on October 10, 1898, the board approved the purchase of 3.95 acres for "athletic grounds" after the Genesee Valley Park Association sold the parcel to the state for four thousand dollars, and in turn, the legislature appropriated the money. So Kelsey Field, honoring Assemblyman and new board member Otto Kelsey, came to be.[34]

The School's Lifeblood

Its students are a school's lifeblood. Consider Geneseo's class of 1893 at its tenth reunion. It boasted that it was the first to have a "young lady" president, to organize as a junior (first) class, and to have its "class song, yell, colors, flower, etc." Despite the unproven hyperbole, the reunion class's claims reflect the students' growing attachment to the budding college.[35]

This attitude also reflects the administration's encouragement of a varied and healthy academic and social life—as varied as possible in a small school in a small, still-rural village. The literary societies are ample testimony. Certainly the school's yearbook editors in 1903 bought into it: "To be elected final [second semester] president of one of the literary societies at the Normal is one of the highest honors that can be conferred upon a student, as for that office the highest literary and executive ability is required."[36]

By 1903 there were seven (or eight, depending on the source) "fraternities." (All societies were called fraternities regardless of the members' gender.) The earliest five were the Delphic (1871), Clionian (1872, for women, and the largest, with fifty-five members in 1903), Phi Alpha (1881), Philalethean (1881), and Agonian (1885, women). They were "to hold semi-monthly meetings for the purpose of debate and general literary culture." Others in those early years were Arethusa (1892, women), Gamma Sigma, and Alpha Delta (1902, women, replacing the Ladies Literary Club formed the previous year), and the Ladies Athletic Association. (Almost two decades would pass before Delta Kappa was formed to replace Delphic Fraternity, and another three decades before Phi Sigma Epsilon appeared in 1952. An anecdotal account has it that the members of Phi Sig had to hold a satisfactory tea to obtain administrative approval.) Importantly, the fraternities and sororities **were** the social life at the College until well into the 1960s.[37]

While the societies were involved in activities throughout the year, including hosting teas and other social events, typically in the early years their greatest contributions were at commencement time, which became more ambitious over the years. For example, on Tuesday evening, June 16, 1900, the six older societies performed plays. The first, *A Pair of Spectacles*, was done jointly by the two oldest societies, Clionian and Delphic. Two nights

Otto Kelsey, a Board of Visitors member and state assemblyman, was the namesake of Kelsey Field. (1934 *Normalian*)

The class of 1893, the first to elect a female class president, held many reunions, including this one in October 1955. (Livingston County Historian)

Fraternities and sororities enriched campus social life, sponsoring get-togethers such as this "Clionian spread" at the Simmons boarding house. (Livingston County Historian)

later Arethusa and Gamma Sigma teamed up to perform *The Editor*, while Saturday night, the 20th, Agonian and Philalethean brought *A Tropical Romance* to the stage. Whatever the quality of the dramatists, the relatively long essays written at the time for the school's yearbook, *Normalian*, were impressive by any standards. "The Man Without a Country" examined the notorious Dreyfus case, while "Right and Wrong in South Africa" excoriated repression and injustices. The others, "Realism in Literature," "Trusts," and "Democracy and Empire," were equally contemporary and instructive.[38]

Apparently the local board was less enthusiastic about a request earlier by a Miss W. Greenwood "to deliver a scientific lecture upon the subject of temperance" and dumped the task of corresponding with her on the first Principal Milne. Unfortunately, Milne's response is not found in the board's minutes. The board was even more evasive when the Reverend James A. Hickey, rector of St. Mary's Church, twice asked the board to prohibit "any religious exercises at the opening of school" and to omit "the reading of scripture and prayer." Both had been a part of the school's observances from the beginning. After the second attempt, board member James W. Wadsworth successfully moved adjournment of the meeting before any action could be taken.[39]

The Second Principal Milne

By 1890, similar and other matters had fallen into the lap of John M., the second "Prof. Milne" (or alternately, "Prof Jack"), who became principal shortly after the elder Milne left to lead the more prestigious Normal School

Fraternities and sororities were known for debates, rhetoric, and dramatic productions, but also provided lighter entertainment, such as the 1902 Philalethean and Agonian circus, led by ringmaster Clay Niles. (Roemer House collection)

at Albany. The younger Milne knew the duties well, having been hired on July 16, 1872, to teach in the Academic Department, thereby relieving his brother of his teaching responsibilities.

Elevating the younger Milne, who had served as acting principal during his brother's leave of absence in 1887, may have been a given. Unfortunately, the younger Milne, though as industrious as his brother, was not as hearty. Recognizing this, barely four years into his term, the local board approved a month's leave of absence for him, but he courteously rejected the offer, responding that "at present I have no need for a vacation." He would ten years later.[40]

As had his brother, "Prof Jack" struggled to ensure the College's academic quality, albeit at times through intimidation. Even the faculty were targets. In April 1891, the board forbade the faculty to hold any political office that would interfere with teaching, and it established two committees to observe classes. One was to visit during the first twenty-week term, the other during the second. This seems to have anticipated the state superintendent's 1898 call for statewide inspections of Normal Schools.[41]

Despite distractions, the younger Milne's and the board's primary focus was on the curriculum. As historian Martin Fausold has written, "more often than not...the Normal Schools in the state [including, presumably Geneseo] were niches between the grammar schools and colleges." On July 19, 1892, the board sought to remedy this in part by dropping the Elementary English course, but stopped short of doing so after consulting with the state superintendent of public instruction. Two years later the board took up the matter again,

Normal School musical ensembles, including the 1896 orchestra, enhanced Geneseo's cultural life. (Merrell photo, Roemer House collection)

when board member Adoniram Abbott moved to change the one-year "common school course." He would require those admitted by examination to undergo a "critical review" of the usual secondary school subjects along with "composition, map drawing, calisthenics, methods of teaching, essay, and vocal music." In the second term, he demanded "school law, methods of teaching, and training in the school of practice, and declamation and vocal music." The motion was twice tabled before the board agreed to drop the Elementary English course entirely. This action also may have been induced by the need to cap enrollment at six hundred students.[42]

The Demand for Professionalism

It appears that the board also was reacting to a sweeping state law enacted in 1897, upgrading requirements for teachers in larger school systems. (Only those appointed by their home school districts were exempt.) The larger schools could hire only Normal School graduates, "graduates of a training class," or those with three years of teaching experience. This meant increased enrollments at Geneseo and the other Normal Schools. Additionally, the admission age was raised to seventeen, and the school year set at two twenty-week sessions, with, minimally, four hours of instruction a day, or no less than 450 hours of class work. Graduates received certificates valid for three years. Public demand for professionalism, which waxed and waned, was in the ascendancy.[43]

Geneseo's board wanted to go further, authorizing Principal John Milne

John M. Milne succeeded his older brother as Geneseo's second principal. (*The Lamron, 50th Anniversary*)

to suspend any students who, barring the students' or a family member's sickness—or, inexplicably, "a lack of ability to do the required work"—failed all the subjects at "any periodical examination." Expulsion was to follow a second such failure. However, a year later when fourteen students failed and parents raised objections, the board suspended the policy. Apparently Milne and the board bowed to community pressure as they may have done earlier when Milne recommended that students make "public confessions" in lieu of suspensions for violating disciplinary rules.[44]

Board member Abbott's concern over the school's academic rigor possibly reflected a growing demand for professionalism generally, including in education, law, medicine, and engineering. In 1887, Columbia University, which founded Teachers College, may have been the first to focus on professionalism in education. The curriculum base would be a liberal education, with special scholarship concentrating on subject matter, followed by more technical pedagogical skills. The Normal School at Albany too would move in that direction and was imitated in time by the other Normal Schools.[45]

At issue were the role and function of state Normal Schools, including Geneseo. A Massachusetts high school principal proclaimed that "state normal schools [which promoted upward mobility] have stood for an idea...namely that special preparation of some kind is demanded and required for the business of teaching." Normal Schools should be leaders in educational thought and practice.[46]

Critics charged that preparation in the science of education was the wrong way to go. A Rhode Island Normal School head argued that "the normal school must not aspire to be a

The 1891 faculty included (first row, from left): Cora Northrup, Hubert Schmitz, Elizabeth McBride, Sara Goheen; (second row): Jennie Coe, William Milne, Maria Chichester, Emeline McMaster Curtiss; (third row): Phebe Hall, Mary Burns, Myra Burdick, Mary Parks; (fourth row): Frank Welles, John Milne, Marcia Heath Rowland, Sarah Parry; (top): Reuben Waterbury. (*The Lamron, 50th Anniversary*)

The Erie Railroad station, which originally stood near the lower end of Court Street, was preserved and moved to Geneseo's Highland Park. Geneseo was well served by railroad, as indicated by these 1899 schedules. (Hans Tanner collection, Paul Hepler collection)

college or a school of advanced pedagogical research." The focus should be on the art of teaching: "the normal school for the inspiration and instruction of the teacher; the model school where she [sic] may see good teaching; and a training school in which, for at least half a year, she may teach all the time."[47]

The training or "practice" school was "the body and soul" of teacher training. Teaching one's peers under the watchful eyes of a critic teacher (an innovation in itself) was one thing, but teaching real children (again under the critic's watchful eyes) was different altogether. Moreover, it was a double benefit. Village children not only obtained an education, they also helped older students to become better teachers.[48]

The Geneseo board, caught up in this debate virtually from the outset, could no longer ignore the demand for professional education and the need for more teachers to meet increasing enrollments in public schools. Geneseo's enrollment increased correspondingly. In the fall of 1889, the

school had a total of 464 students, the majority of whom were returnees. Modest growth followed, but by 1898 enrollment had grown to 751, which was considered "too large for the capacity of the buildings *and the best Normal School work*" [italics added]. So, the local board received permission from the superintendent of public instruction to cap enrollment in the Normal Department at 600.[49]

It may be that the school catalogue played a role in attracting students. It proclaimed that "The village of Geneseo is delightfully situated in the valley of

The Normal School's 1898 catalog boasted that students had access to the Wadsworth Library's thirteen thousand volumes. (Bright collection)

the Genesee" and it emphasized that the College was accessible by four railroads, the New York Central, the Erie, the Genesee Valley Canal Railway (or Western New York & Pennsylvania Railway), and the Delaware, Lackawanna & Western. Although only the Erie actually came to Geneseo and, at that, was a downhill trek from Old Main, the school was fortunate to have it that close. The catalogue also asserted that the students had access to "a complete TEXT BOOK LIBRARY, containing, besides the work used in the school, others for reference." If that did not suffice, the students could use the village's Wadsworth Library with "thirteen thousand volumes of carefully selected works."[50]

In 1896, with a healthy enrollment and the school's glowing description of itself, its students, faculty, and local board celebrated the first twenty-five years. It was an illustrious occasion, marked by two addresses: a short one by board member Rorbach, who recalled that difficult but exhilarating quarter century, and the principal one by Columbia University President Nicholas M. Butler. The administrators, board, and faculty took justifiable pride in the fact that ninety-five percent of the thirteen hundred graduates up to then had taught or were teaching. Two years later they claimed the honor of graduating 224, the largest class in Normal School history to that point.

Athletics

Whether Principal Milne and board member Rorbach took similar pride in the College's Fall 1896 football team is unrecorded, but they could have. After whitewashing Avon High School 24-0, the team looked forward to an even more satisfying win against the University of Rochester. But the Rochesterians were no-shows. (Geneseoans claimed that their opponents cowardly opted out

The 1901 football team included (front, from left): Claire Wilson, "Herb" Dunn, unidentified players; (middle): Purl Zielman, Gene Weller, Archibald Campbell; (back): manager Clarence Averill, "Jap" Hurlburt, "Can" Patchin, "Jo" Purdy, John Clancy. (Livingston County Historian)

of playing a stronger Normal School). Hornellsville's high school team—most of Geneseo's opponents were high schools—willingly substituted, and was routed 26-0 on an almost indescribably muddy field.[51]

However, four years later the school's yearbook editors lamented the "decided deterioration" of the football and baseball teams. (The Fall 1899 football team won only one of its nine games. The 1900 baseball team was "almost equally unfortunate.") According to the editors, a "good football team" was impossible "where students enter and leave at all times." Second, Geneseo lacked the "school spirit so necessary and desirable for school athletics...." (Allegedly, the faculty did "not enthuse" because they were concerned about the "many and serious accidents" each season.) Third, the editors sighed, baseball had entered a "new era." "In previous years semi-professional players have been secured to strengthen the team, thus placing it outside the pale of strictly inter-scholastic baseball circles." Hope lay with other sports: basketball (begun in 1901 and successful its second year with wins over Brockport and Fredonia), track, and cross country. The new gym, with locker rooms for men and women (the men took the new rooms, of course) also would help.[52]

By contrast, the editors gushed over the "Carnival of Gymnastics," held March 29, 1901. After "long and painstaking preparation" under the guidance of physical education instructor Carl Schrader, the students of all ages engaged in the "most interesting athletic event ever held in Geneseo." Events ran the gamut from calisthenics to dumb-bell and parallel bar exercises and from fencing to "military and figure marching and figure dancing," whatever they were. The editors eagerly looked forward to a repeat performance the next year. (While Schrader would make his mark at Harvard later, we remember him by the physical education building on the campus here bearing his name.)[53]

Likely, the performers' outfits would bring hoots of derision from today's students. At least the women were permitted to wear white blouses and sneakers rather than the "usual gym suits...navy blue blouses and bloomers and slippers." The men substituted "navy blue long gymnasium trousers, white sleeveless jerseys, black belts, and white gym shoes" for the regular "navy blue long sleeved jerseys and slippers."[54]

The Second Milne Era Ends

By 1900, Geneseo and the other Normal Schools faced the need to make genuine curriculum improvements. An 1895 graduate looking back over four decades recalled that "the entrance requirements were few, as anyone who wanted to teach could enter. No physical exam was necessary. Further, at the end of the semester there were no tests. Marks were received through the selection method, that is, anyone who made the average of C or higher did not have to take a final exam." Moreover, "the library at Geneseo Normal was very inadequate." To meet the challenge, Geneseo's board discussed the superintendent of public instruction's plan to expand the course of study of English to four years. Nothing came of this discussion immediately. But the issue of professionalism and the role of Normal Schools, in fact, the administration of public education in the state generally, was about to come to a head. However, John Milne, who was forced to appeal to the superintendent of public instruction to obtain a salary of thirty-three hundred dollars, which the local board had denied him by a four-to-three vote, would not live long enough to see the issue resolved.[55]

Proud members of the Philalethean fraternity's 1902–1903 championship track team demonstrated the winning athletic spirit that remains a Geneseo tradition: (from left) William Whitmore, Leland Bartoo, Charles Toole, William Flynn. (Houseknecht photo, Livingston County Historian)

Director of Physical Culture Henry Patten's 1897–1898 shinny team (a sport similar to field hockey) posed in Old Main's gymnasium surrounded by exercise equipment. Team members included Gertrude Barnum, Della Balding, Edith Warford, Alice Davey, Catherine Lotz, Anna Winans, Belle Houce, Maybell Roper, Crystine Lotz, Naomi Hooker, Mary Streamer, and Ava Hooker. (Houseknecht photo, Livingston County Historian)

On June 6, 1903, Principal Milne asked for and was granted a leave of absence for the current year and the "ensuing school year as may seem to be necessary for his restoration to health." While a leave had restored his brother's health, the younger Milne, who had also served as village mayor, was not so fortunate. He died of tuberculosis on January 7, 1905, in Denver, where he had hoped the climate would prove restorative. Three months after Milne's leave was granted, Dr. Hubert J. Schmitz, professor of science, was named "acting principal" and would serve in that capacity until April 29, 1905.

Fortunately Schmitz knew the school and was well known. A Berlin University graduate, Dr. Schmitz was hired in November 1881 to replace Dr. Allen as head of the science department. "More than one student" remembered him admonishing: "I give you ze-wo, wiz pen and ink." (Nor was Dr. Welles, one of the first graduates and at this time professor of Latin and Greek, exempt from student waggery: "Put your eyes on the book, do you see any Latin floating around the room?")[56]

Schmitz, whose status as acting principal was extended in July 1904 and whose responsibilities included serving as vice principal at a salary of twenty-one hundred dollars, was thrown into the fray almost immediately. The library and swimming pool were added to the original building, but two years later the pool ("swimming tank") was still empty due to problems obtaining water. And on August 20, 1904, as had his predecessors, Schmitz wrestled with the future of the Academic Department. A local board committee proposed continuing it another year and then establishing a high school with a regular four-year curriculum instead. But nothing was done immediately.[57]

While Schmitz apparently performed ably enough, resolving the issues facing the College (and the state's Normal Schools generally) demanded a new administrator.

****

Looking back, what can we say about the two Milnes?

It is hard to believe that William, only twenty-eight years old when appointed, accomplished so much. His appointment was, as Colonel Rorbach proclaimed, blessed by "Providence."

Milne faced a daunting challenge. He had to get a school up and running, which included attracting quality faculty while establishing a concomitant curriculum, constructing necessary buildings, and attracting students.

Above all, he valued scholarship. While he wanted to develop a community, which resulted in societies he formed or helped form, he expected those societies to be more than simply socializers. They were to be cultural experiences, which was evident in the music the members played, the debates they conducted, and the plays and pageants they performed. And Milne wanted it all, right now. Nothing made that more obvious than his graduating ten students at the end of the school's first year in operation.

In eighteen years under Milne's leadership, Geneseo Normal achieved a glowing reputation and an enviable enrollment. His leaving was a blow, but he was destined for greater things, including leading Albany, which he had renamed New York State Normal College, to greater heights.

Though brother John, seven years younger, was an able successor, his precarious health may have limited his ability to match his brother's success. Moreover, he faced the growing demand for professionalism, which put Geneseo in greater competition with other schools developing teacher education programs. And the debate over retaining the academic program, which pitted board and community members against each other, hindered the progress he sought. It remains that John Milne saw the school grow to the point that enrollment had to be capped and nearly all of its graduates actually would go into teaching, a mark few teacher education programs could match.

The leadership of the two Milnes for over thirty-four years set a high standard for those who followed, causing the *Livingston Republican* editor on September 9, 1897, to "exult" over the "tone and character" of "OUR Normal," which stood "at the head of the long column of all such institutions."

Science department head Hubert Schmitz served as acting principal while John Milne was on medical leave from 1903 to 1905. (Livingston County Historian)

Chapter Three

Geneseo
NORMAL SCHOOL
·
The "Old Main" Tradition (1905–1922)

Writing about the dawn of the twentieth century, Walter Lord claimed these were "the good years" in the United States; "good because, whatever the trouble, people were sure they could fix it." Though later tempered by a world war that erupted in Europe in 1914, the nation's belief that it would continue to solve its problems was not easily erased. The examples of the Wright brothers, Henry Ford, and President Theodore Roosevelt demonstrated that more effort and ingenuity might be required, but the problems could be fixed.[1]

New Pressures on the School

In 1906, the State Normal School at Geneseo or State Normal School, Geneseo (it used both names alternately) would need that optimism. One serious problem that needed fixing was education. But, resorting to more familiar jargon, there were systemic problems: a growing demand for pay raises, better working conditions and greater status for teachers, and more rigorous teacher training by means of an upgraded curriculum. Another pressing problem was resolving the long-standing antagonism between New York State's superintendent of public instruction and its Board of Regents.

Opposite Page: The Minckler block, located on the southeast corner of Main and Center streets, proudly displayed a World War I honor roll plaque. (Bright collection)

Necessarily, Geneseo's Normal School and a changing local board were affected by these systemic problems. Only James W. Wadsworth remained from that first board. Dr. Walter Lauderdale, who had died in 1893, had been succeeded by his son, also a Dr. Walter Lauderdale, shortly thereafter. Adoniram Abbott passed away five years later, and Colonel Rorbach, the most eloquent spokesman for the board, had died in November 1899. However, there was some overlap, including Major William Austin Wadsworth, James Wadsworth's cousin, who would serve forty years; William A. Brodie, the board's chairman, who had been very active from the school's inception; Lieutenant Colonel John R. Strang, who had honorably served with Colonel Rorbach in the 104th New York Volunteers and was appointed to the board in 1892; and Charles Fielder, who also had taken his seat that year. The newest members were Otto Kelsey, a former state assemblyman, in 1898; Lockwood R. Doty, appointed to replace Colonel Rorbach in 1899; and Floyd Crossett, whose name is familiar to those who drive the town road named for him, and who replaced the deceased Judge Hubbard in 1901.

Like the board, the College itself was manifesting changes, including adapting to new names. In part this was legislated and in part it was a concern for the image of teacher education. Increasingly, the Normal Schools were competing with universities and colleges that offered teacher education programs to accommodate an increasing number of high school graduates who might seek higher education. (In 1914, the public school year was increased from just six weeks a year to October 1 to June 1.) So, the Normal Schools not only had to appear better—thus the name changes—they had to raise standards.[2]

But this contradicted the "prevailing philosophy," that the teacher needed to know only enough "to teach the pupils." That is, teachers should not be burdened with useless knowledge (the Classical course) or be inspired to greater ambitions. Yet, the public tended to link material success with higher education, especially the liberal arts. It was a no-win situation: a liberal arts degree was perceived as unnecessary for elementary teachers, but without it the teachers lacked status.[3]

In Albany, two events would change the state's management of its Normal Schools. One was the return of Andrew Sloan Draper from the presidency of the University of Illinois to the New York State superintendency. (He beat out Geneseo's ex-principal William Milne, who had made a name for himself at Albany's Normal School.) The other was the Unification Act of 1904, which settled the long-standing differences between the office of the state superintendent of public instruction and the State's Board of Regents.

In 1906–1907, the Normal School orchestra was a small ensemble consisting mostly of string instruments. (Roemer House Collection)

An Oswego County native, Albany Law School graduate and practicing attorney, Draper was familiar not only with the legislature, having served one term in the State Assembly, but also with Normal Schools, having been on the executive board of the Albany Normal School. More importantly, as New York's school superintendent from 1881 to 1886, he had "vigorously" focused on the training and certification of teachers. One result was greater uniformity among the schools in terms of standards for admission, schedules, curricula, methods, and graduation requirements. He would make his mark once more.[4]

Draper may have been drawn back to New York by passage of the Unification Act of 1904, which he had advocated and which resolved the prolonged legislative debate over the roles of the state superintendent and the Regents. The act pared the nineteen-member Board of Regents to eleven and elevated the superintendent of public instruction to commissioner of education. More importantly, the law merged the New York State Department of Public Instruction and the Regents, thereby clarifying the roles of the Regents and the commissioner. Henceforth, the Regents would oversee colleges and universities and the commissioner would be executive officer of the Regents with control over elementary and secondary education, including teacher education. In short, Draper "successfully weaned teacher training away from the Regents" and would capitalize on his accomplishment.[5]

The 1905 faculty included (standing, from left): Emily Baker, Helen Daley, Anna Blakmer, unidentified, Barnard Bronson, Sara Goheen, unidentified, Elizabeth Rorbach, unidentified, Mary Parks, Mrs. J. Fraley, Carl Schrader, Sarah Parry; (seated): Frank Welles, Emeline Curtiss, Emma Gunther, Acting Principal Hubert Schmitz, Laura Comstock, unidentified, Edward Graber, Lydia Jones, Elizabeth McBride, Phebe Hall. (Houseknecht photo, Livingston County Historical Society)

The local board, directly affected by these changes, debated Acting Principal Schmitz's fate. It extended his contract on July 16 and appointed him vice principal as well, on November 5, 1904. But on April 8, 1905, and again a week later, the board deferred "consideration of the principalship." The suspense for Schmitz ended two weeks later, when—after reviewing the credentials of six candidates—the board recommended to Commissioner Draper that James V. Sturges be appointed principal.[6]

The May 4, 1905 *Livingston Republican* trumpeted the appointment of the tall, forty-year-old Sturges, the first principal with a liberal arts background. Sturges had earned bachelor's and master's degrees from Colgate (and a doctorate would follow in 1909), had held public school principalships in New York and New Jersey, and had headed the mathematics department at Pratt Institute in Brooklyn for six years. (Coincidentally, Geneseo graduate Leslie A. Case, class of 1896, succeeded Sturges as Tarrytown, New York principal.)[7]

Because Schmitz would continue as vice principal and science department head for another three years, an assistant was hired to help him. Guy A. Bailey ("Bugs" to the students) was appointed on August 19, 1905 at a salary of nine hundred dollars. A Cortland graduate, Bailey became an international authority on birds, devising ingenious ways to lure birds within range and to capture them on film. He served the College for thirty-four years, and had a $2.5-million building named for him on April 28, 1965.[8]

The Demise of the Academy

Upon his arrival, Principal Sturges was hit with some significant—and unpleasant—changes. On June 30, 1905, New York's assistant commissioner of education Augustus S. Downing "made a detailed and explanatory statement" about reorganizing the high school curriculum. He had dropped a bombshell. The local board had to eliminate the Academic Department, with its Classical course, so the village would have to develop its own high school. Though a board committee had recently recommended such a move, it was still a shock.[9]

James Sturges served as principal from 1905 to 1922. (Roemer House Collection)

The Unification Act forced other changes as well. The Normal Schools' curricula henceforth would be prescribed by the state education department, not developed locally and approved by the superintendent of public instruction, as had been the case. Also, entering students were required to have an approved high school diploma or its equivalent or promise to complete the high school course and the two-year regular course to obtain their teaching licenses. The regular course of study, two years in length, was beefed up, emphasizing more specialized training in subject matter. The goal of the proposed changes was single-purpose teacher training schools.[10]

Thus, Sturges was forced to drop three teachers to reorganize the Training Department (the practice school) and to reduce some faculty salaries to pay for unanticipated building maintenance. Incongruously, while releasing three teachers, he needed to make eleven appointments: a supervisor of methods, principals of the Primary and Intermediate departments, and eight new "model" teachers, including those responsible for the seventh and eighth grades. (And he had to hire a Mr. Moffat as "special policeman" in April 1912, which needs no explanation for those of us familiar with the role of the College's University Police.)[11]

Less than two years later, because of the popularity of the kindergarten program, Principal Sturges made it a separate department, resulting in even more hirings and more relocations of classes. A plus was the 1916 appointment of C. Agnes Rigney to teach fifth grade. Miss Rigney is better known for initiating the speech and drama ("dramatic arts") program and guiding it until *1955!*[12]

More Building Projects

A minor, but nettlesome problem for Sturges and the Normal School board was the matter of the empty swimming "tank." The pool had been unusable at times due to a leak and the cost of refilling it. On July 7, 1908, the frustrated board asked to meet with village authorities. The result two years later—six years after the pool's construction—was an agreement to have the village supply the water to the school, including the pool, for two hundred dollars a year.[13]

Principal Sturges also had to renovate the existing buildings to accommodate the curriculum changes and install electric lights in the gymnasium. To meet the needs of the Training Department, Sturges instructed Janitor Morey to supervise, among other projects, painting the building, grading the grounds "to make a better field for athletic work" and readying the newly constructed

C. Agnes Rigney began the speech and dramatic arts programs and served on the faculty for forty years. (1930 *Normalian*)

library for needed use. The last came about because board member and former state assemblyman Otto Kelsey had wrung twenty-five thousand dollars from the legislature for a one-story, forty-by-eighty-foot building, to the "back and side of the building next to the gymnasium" to house the school's "3000 to 5000" books. After many delays furnishing it with tables and chairs "of the latest oak design" and acquiring the needed books, the library was opened in late 1904, though it was still unfinished.[14]

This addition took on added importance in 1909 when Geneseo's Teacher-Librarian program was begun. A far cry from the School of Library and Information Science that would emerge, it was a groundbreaking program. "One of three pioneer normal schools in the U.S.," it was begun and guided by Miss Ida Mendenhall, later by Mary Richardson, both of whom gained national reputations. Under the former, the school's library was transformed from the typical Normal School library—"a small, unclassified, little-used collection behind locked doors" and protected by wire fencing—into a model one. The two-year course prepared students to teach in the upper grades while maintaining their schools' libraries. (Understandably, the closing of the Library School in 1983 was both lamented and protested by its graduates and others who had benefited from it. The graduates' achievements and record of job placements over the years were exemplary.)[15]

Janitor Morey's forced resignation in 1913 spared him from engaging in two more building projects and considerable repair work. However, removing him after almost forty years was a bit of a fiasco. On September 30, 1913, the board indicated its "desire" to have Morey resign, effective January 1, 1914. Three months later, on April 14, 1914, Mr. L. Watson Clark was hired, effective June 27, at one thousand dollars a year (changed to one hundred dol-

The library wing, with the swimming pool in the basement, was added to the south end of Old Main in 1903. (Bright collection)

lars per month six years later). Clark would live in the house on Kelsey Field after it was made habitable, rather than the rooms in Old Main where Morey and his family had been living.[16]

"Janitor" Clark and Principal Sturges were forced into undertaking long-overdue projects: adding a heating plant (which was declared inadequate only six years later), installing "toilets" (locker/shower rooms) in the gymnasium, painting Old Main inside and out while repairing its roof and chimney, and mending the Practice School's electric lights. The students themselves largely transformed the basement kindergarten room, "awkward in shape, poorly lighted and ugly...into the very attractive room" it was reported to be in 1921.[17]

More Curricular Changes

Another long-overdue project was renting, then renovating, the basement of Anthony "Tony" Aprile's Court Street house. In only eight short years the kindergarten program had outgrown its facilities. Aprile's house now bore the label "Pestalozzi-Froebel House," which stressed children's growth through action and play. Borrowing on his experience with Johann Pestalozzi, Friedrich Froebel wanted the children, employing their natural senses, to learn through practice and observation. Though the high-sounding name may have lent an aura to the house, it is unlikely it did anything to rid the former wine cellar of its fumes.[18]

The editors of *The Lamron's* 50th Anniversary booklet asserted that "the work in the Training School [in Old Main, Aprile's basement, and the Center Street School] was the most practical of any given in the Normal course."

For many years, Geneseo's School of Library and Information Science sponsored an annual lecture named for early library education chair Mary C. Richardson. (1933 *Normalian*)

Old Main kindergarten students posed to demonstrate several of their favorite activities. (Livingston County Historical Society)

Importantly, too, in 1918 the Training (or Practice) School was reorganized into the Kindergarten-Primary Department (Kindergarten and the first three grades), the Intermediate Department (grades four through six), and a new "Grammar," or Junior High School, with seventh and eighth grades. The addition of the Kindergarten-Primary and the Grammar departments needs explanation.

The Kindergarten-Primary Department, which came about rather belatedly, would prove particularly attractive to the Normal School students. Many of the older children in the Training School had to care for their younger siblings while their parents worked. The younger often accompanied their older siblings when they reached school age, so it seemed natural to teach the younger children as well. Thus, shortly the Pestalozzi-Froebel School on Court Street became better known as the "Neighborhood School," because it involved many local parents and children. By 1921 the Kindergarten-Primary program had proved so popular that Anne Blake, the head of the department and later the College's dean, had to employ assistants to teach the 116 Normal School students who had opted for that specialization.[19]

Adding the Kindergarten program in 1907 and dropping the Academic Department at the end of the 1908–1909 school year created serious problems for Principal Sturges and the village. Locating the Kindergarten program in Aprile's basement helped somewhat, but there was neither space nor an approved program for the junior and senior high school students attending the Normal School. So, beginning in September 1908, the

local board limited the eighth-grade enrollment to forty students, giving preference to students "regularly promoted and then to qualified students in the order in which they apply."[20]

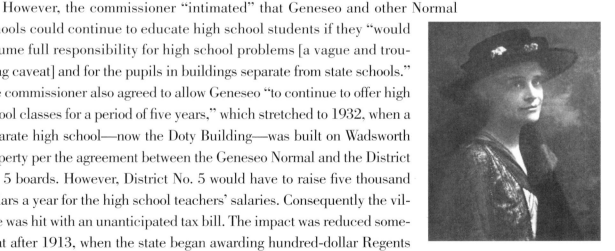

Increased kindergarten enrollment led to the February 23, 1916, opening of an additional kindergarten, the Pestalozzi-Froebel House, on Court Street. (*Snap Shots*, 1918)

This decision forced a meeting between the Normal School board and the board of education of the Union Free School District No. 5 ("the Cobblestone School") on Center Street to work out arrangements for the eighth graders in the Training School. The issue came to a head in 1914, when the commissioner of education announced, as forecast earlier, that the state would no longer offer secondary education in the state's Normal Schools.[21]

However, the commissioner "intimated" that Geneseo and other Normal Schools could continue to educate high school students if they "would assume full responsibility for high school problems [a vague and troubling caveat] and for the pupils in buildings separate from state schools." The commissioner also agreed to allow Geneseo "to continue to offer high school classes for a period of five years," which stretched to 1932, when a separate high school—now the Doty Building—was built on Wadsworth property per the agreement between the Geneseo Normal and the District No. 5 boards. However, District No. 5 would have to raise five thousand dollars a year for the high school teachers' salaries. Consequently the village was hit with an unanticipated tax bill. The impact was reduced somewhat after 1913, when the state began awarding hundred-dollar Regents Scholarships per year to three thousand qualified students. Located in Old Main, the newly designated high school had its own principal and four teachers, all supervised by Sturges, and so continued to supply athletes, actors, and singers for the Normal's activities.[22]

Thus, well into the twentieth century, most Geneseoans received their entire schooling in "Old Main" as part of the Demonstration and Practice School.

Anne Blake, namesake of the Blake buildings, headed the Kindergarten-Primary program, and in her later service as dean was often in charge of the school in the principal's absence. (1922 *Normalian*)

Geneseo's cobblestone school on Center Street now serves as the Livingston County Historical Society museum. (Roemer House Collection)

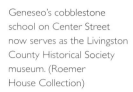

DISTRICT SCHOOL. GENESEO, N. Y.

The bulk of the village kindergarteners were consigned to the basement. First through fifth graders, taught on the first floor, entered the building on the north end. Sixth, seventh, and eighth-graders ("subfreshmen") occupied part of the second floor, while the senior high school students were spaced across the front of the building on the second floor.

In 1918, in a change that the *Livingston Republican* labeled "radical," the Training School was reorganized into "four groups of three years each." The Primary and Intermediate grades remained first through third and fourth

The 1911 football team included (front, from left): Dudley, Watson, Schaefer, K. Werner, A. Werner; (center): Davis, Friar, Campbell; (back): Stevens, Flansburg, Scott, Grey, Leonard, Barber. (Merrell photo, Livingston County Historian)

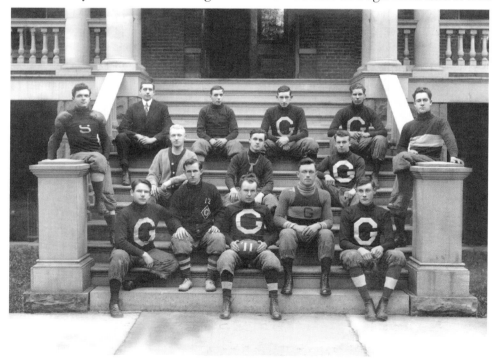

through sixth grades respectively. Ninth grade was added to the junior high's seventh and eighth grades, with the high school serving tenth through twelfth graders. This required rearranging classrooms again, enlarging the high school study hall, which was conveniently located next to Principal Lucy Buell's office, and assigning seats. Also the science department, with a new biology lab, was relocated "in the west wing of the building," and new classrooms were added to Old Main's third floor.[23]

The first summer school was introduced in 1914, fulfilling Dr. Sturges's "cherished" hope for one, and earning him "Geneseo's everlasting appreciative gratitude." The *Livingston Republican* editor crowed that only Geneseo and Oneonta were so favored by the state legislature. The summer program was designed for those with high school diplomas seeking teaching licenses, because the diploma alone no longer satisfied the requirement for a license. The six-week course, to be taught mornings by Normal School faculty, was limited to primary and kindergarten work in the "Professional" department. Since the session was equivalent to half the regular twenty-week first term, entrants were expected to attend two summer schools. The *Republican's* editor speculated that "many old teachers will come here to get up-to-date methods." In fact, many experienced teachers did, a custom that lasted for many years.[24]

Members of the 1915 women's basketball team wore the typical women's athletic costume of the era. (1915 *Pivot*)

The final important curriculum change during Principal Sturges's tenure was creation of a special education program, mandated by an act of the state legislature in 1920. Every school system with ten or more "subnormal" or "unusually retarded" children was to provide a specially prepared teacher. Though it would take many years to accept special education as appropriate for professional training, two years later, in 1922, Geneseo began implementing it.

Mrs. W. Austin Wadsworth established and funded the Elizabeth Wadsworth Nursing Home in 1915 in this house at 32 North Street, which is now a student rental property. (*The Lamron, 50th Anniversary*)

Influenza, Diversity, "Foul Antics," and Yells

Though at times building construction and renovation seemed to take precedence, the students' physical and mental health remained the College's primary concerns. For example, on January 19, 1910, all students "under suspicion of having tuberculosis [were] excluded from the school until they produce a certificate from the county bacteriologist of their exemption from the disease." More serious was the influenza that gripped the world eight years later, caus-

The Wadsworth Nursing Home's sun room also served as a sleeping porch, a feature consistent with the popular belief in the curative power of fresh air. (Merrell photo, Milne Archives)

ing an estimated 548,000 deaths in the United States. After consulting with Dr. Page, the town and village health officer, the nervous board agreed to keep the school open.[25]

Concerned about the students' conduct, the board, without publicly divulging any wrongdoing, told the Gamma Sigma Society that it was no longer welcome and ordered it to vacate its room on campus. (To encourage and to monitor the societies, the board and administration had long permitted them to have rooms in Old Main.)[26]

The 1905 baseball team members were (front): unidentified; (middle, from left): Clarence Rogers, Dallas Newton, John Fraser, John Freeman, unidentified, Tom Simms; (back): unidentified, Earl Tripp, John Stickney, coach Carl Schrader, Howard McNaughton, Charles Toole. (Livingston County Historian)

Long before today's emphasis on diversity, Geneseo benefitted from African-American students, including the village's athletic Tom Simms and the Normal's senior class treasurer, twenty-year-old Bertrand L. Twiman. The latter, a Scottsville native and Classical course graduate of June 1906, was a double minority, as one of only eighteen males in a graduating class of 116. Sister school Plattsburgh also had a black male student leader at this time, suggesting greater diversity in Normal Schools than might be suspected. Because this was long before affirmative action policies or records identifying ethnicity, there is no way to know who the first African-American to attend the College was or when he or she attended.

On the other hand, College administrators had to be embarrassed by the "foul antics" of the school's basketball players in a literally hard-fought basketball game on January 14, 1905. While the College's "lightweights" lost "a remarkably clean" first game of a double-header to the Wadsworth Shamrocks 24-14, the "heavyweight" game with undefeated Rochester Business Institute, which the Normals won 31-25, apparently turned into a brawl. One Rochester Business Institute player had nine fouls called on him, while Geneseo's Campbell was not far behind with six. Fortunately, the win over Batavia the previous Friday was without incident.[27]

Apparently other times school spirit had to be resuscitated. For example, the 1914 class secretary recorded that at the November 12, 1912, meeting a motion had carried for the class "to attend the football game in a body and

to buy tin horns." To lead the cheering "Miss Vera Norton was appointed cheer [leader] for the day," and "Several yells were practiced." No "yells" were needed when thirty-six members of the "junior" class took the 12:55 p.m. trolley car to Rochester's Schubert Theater on January 18, 1913, to see Robert Mantel in *Hamlet*.[28] (The practice of addressing each other formally, as "Miss Vera Norton" above, reflects the formality that prevailed for much

of the College's history. Teachers, of course, were routinely addressed—in public at least—as Miss, Mrs., Professor, or Dr.)

Given the protests aroused by a speaker at the College in the 1960s, it is surprising so little notice was paid a lecturer at the Normal School in March 1916. Fired from his faculty position at the University of Pennsylvania's prestigious Wharton School (and soon to be fired from the only school which then would hire him), socialist Scott Nearing was an unusual choice to be invited to staid Geneseo. In fact, the editor of the *Livingston Republican* commented that while Geneseo's students "did not subscribe to all of his theories, they agreed that he is a striking speaker whose thoughts are well worth studied consideration." Likely, the editor was less charitable later when Nearing was unfairly charged with committing espionage for opposing World War I.[29]

Boarding Houses

From the outset, providing housing for the students had been a problem. It was alleviated, but not solved, by the opening of more boarding houses as the village grew. Geneseo Town and Village historian David W. Parish reported that at one time there were "at least seventeen village residences for women students." Many were on Wadsworth Street, which extended from north of Bank Street to Park Street, just beyond which the Doty Building (formerly Geneseo Jr.-Sr. High School) is located. Among the residences were Emerson Hall, Houston, Raub, Rippey, the Wilcox House, and Bank Street's McCurdy House. Years later one local male recalled "the select bevy of pretty

Normal School students who lived at Mrs. Newton's boarding house on Wadsworth Street." By contrast, living in Old Main's dormitory with its creaking floors and walls apparently was "last resort housing."[30]

The Gooding House at 45 Wadsworth Street, erected in the 1880s, was reputedly the "Queen of Halls." Sold to Ina and Elbert Foland in 1917, the renovated, rambling three-story building, with its spacious porches, was renamed Emerson Hall after Foland's favorite author. The Folands, who housed up to forty-four women a year for thirty-five years, employed a full-time cook to make up for the lack of restaurants in the village.

These 1907 students decorated their room with school and sorority pennants as well as photographs of friends. (Milne Archives)

Possibly the most unusual house was the former croquet factory, the Bolt House at Five Main Street, in which thirty-one girls resided.[31]

Most student accounts recall only women boarding in these houses under the watchful eyes of the owners. However, 1878 graduate Pliny Seymour remembered that both males and females lived in the boarding houses, though he does not even hint at any cohabitation. The owners had to assure that their charges observed 10:00 p.m. weeknight and midnight weekend curfews and had to keep tabs on the girls and their dates. Even with curfews, boarding houses offered relative freedom. Dormitory dwellers had to obtain permission—and occasionally even a chaperone—to go uptown for soap or toothpaste or to attend Frank April's Rex Theater, the Riviera's predecessor, on Center Street.[32]

On September 11, 1911, Dr. Sturges called on his faculty advisors to visit boarding houses to determine whether the "landladies and students" were "keeping regulations." In fact, Sturges was reported to be "very strict this year." Houses that did not meet standards were stricken from the school's list of approved boarding houses. When Sturges asked his faculty whether they would report violations, only two refused, one of whom was Guy "Bugs" Bailey. (Despite some faculty resistance, the practice of assigning advisors to boarding houses was still in effect thirteen years later under Sturges's successor.)[33]

World War I and Aftereffects

The war that erupted in 1914 and shocked the world did not affect the College to the extent that another war would less than thirty years later. Still, the school may have shut down at 1:00 p.m. on school days to save fuel, as Plattsburgh did, and the students furthered the war effort by helping Ellen North's Jam Kitchen prepare ten thousand cans of prune jam ordered by the government. The village offered up approximately fifty men to the army, while the Normal School sent 117 students and graduates, eight of whom lost their lives, and four faculty as "doughboys." One of those faculty members was Robert Greene, assistant in the science department and accomplished puppeteer. He returned to become one of the most beloved College faculty members. The ultimate tribute was naming a building after him for his thirty-eight years' distinguished service.[34]

One aftereffect of the war was the anti-sedition law that Governor Nathan Miller signed in May 1921. Public school teachers, including Normal School faculty, had to submit a certificate obtained from the commissioner of education, stating they were not only of "good moral character," but also loyal and obedient to the laws of the state and federal government. The bill resulted

Ellen North, a rare early-twentieth-century woman business owner, may be one of the women standing on the porch roof of her Jam Kitchen, located about where University Drive and Main Street intersect today. Her factory worked overtime to produce jam for World War I soldiers. (Hans Tanner collection)

from an exaggerated fear of radicalism that gripped the country. (Similar fears led to loyalty oaths again during the Cold War.) Not surprisingly, individuals lined up on both sides of the issue. The *Livingston Republican* editor saw only good in the 1921 law, arguing that as role models for their students, teachers ought to be loyal citizens. Teachers' unions, particularly New York City's, viewed the required oaths as a denial of civil liberties.[35]

Normal School students aided the World War I effort by working on the peach harvest, possibly providing fruit to Ellen North's Jam Kitchen. (*The Lamron, 50th Anniversary*)

Celebrating the First Fifty Years

Nothing dampened the spirits which prevailed when the Geneseo Normal School celebrated its first fifty years. The big celebration in conjunction with graduation began on Sunday, June 19, 1921, with the Baccalaureate Service. It was followed the next day by a picnic at Conesus Lake and a lecture by New York City's associate superintendent of schools. Tuesday, the 21st, was dedicated to rehearsals. The main events were held on the following two days, starting with a baseball game at Kelsey Field at 10:00 a.m. Wednesday, the 22nd. Then, at 2:30 p.m. graduates assembled for "A Pageant of Gifts," the description of which reads awfully quaint today, but it offers a real flavor of the event: "Amid a riot of color, music and dancing, Nature's hosts will present her gifts to Man, and Man receiving will, in turn, present his gifts to the world. The pageant will culminate in an ensemble of eight hundred voices singing 'The New America.'"[36] The pageant, described in glowing detail by the *Livingston Republican*, reads like the script for a Hollywood extravaganza or the National Football League's Super Bowl half-time show, even to the number of participants.

The end of World War I inspired many celebrations, including a Main Street bonfire and this impromptu parade in front of Rector's and the Geneseo building. (Hepler collection)

The evening programs were more subdued. A "Sunset Sing on the Campus" preceded Ohio Congressman Dr. Simeon Fess's lecture. Thursday, June 23, was "Alumni Day," with class reunions, Alumni Association meetings, fraternity reunions, "Teas at Geneseo Homes," and the "Alumni Reception" at 8:00 p.m. The eminence of those on the stage for the following Sunday's commencement attests to the importance of the occasion. Notables included U.S. Senator James W. Wadsworth, Jr., New York State Attorney General Charles D. Newton, and commissioner of education Dr. Frank P. Graves.[37]

To commemorate the occasion, *The Lamron* published a 116-page special issue recalling historic events and persons connected with the school and extolling the school's various educational programs.

On February 18, 1921, Arethusa members performed *Behind a Watteau Picture* with cast members Margaret Murphy, Olive Smith, Ruth Harding, Mae Gross, Helen Razey, Mildred Montgomery, Lucy TenEyck, Mary Hotchkiss, Fern Crowell, Marian Avery, Irene Ransbery, Marie Tolan, and Grace Lowell. (1921 *Normalian*)

Dr. Sturges Terminated

Despite the celebration, all was not well. Within a year the local board had fired three of its most prominent Normal School personnel: the principal, the director of teacher education, and the engineer-janitor. Neither the board's minutes nor newspaper accounts tell the whole story. The saga began at an inopportune time, September 13, 1921, the beginning of a new school year, and, ironically, the anniversary of the College's opening. Principal Sturges was granted a leave of absence because his "unremitting attention to his duties has greatly impaired his health and rendered a temporary cessation of work imperative."[38]

Normal School students staged elaborate productions, such as this Elizabethan pageant in 1916. (*The Lamron, 50th Anniversary*)

LAMRON

50th ANNIVERSARY

COME BACK

JUNE 21 · 25 · 1921 · GENESEO · NEW YORK

GENESEO STATE NORMAL SCHOOL

The *Lamron's* dedicated student staff provided a valuable historical resource when they researched, wrote, and illustrated the fiftieth anniversary booklet. (Roemer House collection)

Dr. Sturges missed the entire school year, but on Tuesday, June 27, 1922 "hearty applause" greeted Acting Principal Anne Blake's report that he had "recovered his strength as to feel sure that he will be able to get back into the harness when the regular session [September] opens." Sturges's "splendid message of appreciation," read at graduation two days later, was warmly received.[39]

Something was amiss, however. Earlier, on January 12, 1922, the local board had advised the commissioner of education about "the very grave conditions now existing in the school [which] should not be allowed to continue." Shortly, the board asked the commissioner to come at the "earliest convenience...to look into the situation." Apparently the "situation" was Sturges. The previous December, the board had "advised" Dr. Sturges, officially on leave, to fire Dr. W. Fowler Bucke, the head of the school's department of education. On December 24, Sturges was said to have complied "with deep regret." But the matter was still unresolved seven months later. In July 1922, just over a month before the fall term began, Miss Blake recommended Bucke's dismissal. (His "services" would "not be required after August 31, 1922.") With one dissenting vote, the board agreed to do so. Clearly the majority wanted to be done with this matter.[40]

At that same July meeting, attended by Sturges, education commissioner Frank P. Graves, and assistant commissioner Augustus S. Downing, by a vote of seven to two the board "regretfully" asked Sturges to resign. (The board had reluctantly consented to Sturges's request to appear and to state his case for continuing as principal, but had made it clear to him that his resignation was required.) In fact, earlier board secretary Lockwood R. Doty had informed Sturges that the board had "a settled conviction" that it had "to terminate a situation which appears to them to be responsible for it [the College's decline]." That is, an "Emergency Administrative Committee" formed during Sturges's absence had failed to manage the school properly.[41]

However, there was something else afoot. By a seven to one vote, on August 30, 1922, with Julian Buckley voting no, the board withdrew an earlier recommendation to hire Sturges's daughter Ruth as a Normal School teacher. Buckley, a relatively recent member of the board, felt the board "had not treated

The 1914–1915 faculty included W. Fowler Bucke (front row, second from left) and Principal James V. Sturges (front row, fourth from left), both of whom were asked to resign in 1922. (*The Lamron,* 50th Anniversary)

Doctor Sturges right as to the principalship of the school." Even less clear, at that July 28 meeting, when Sturges was let go, the board approved acting principal Blake's recommendation to terminate the "services of L. Watson Clark, as Engineer-Janitor" on August 31, 1922. (Considering the difficulties of starting the school year, the timing has to be questioned.)[42]

The case of Clark is especially mystifying. A month later the board voted to continue him until the State Civil Service Commission forwarded a list of eligible candidates to succeed him. Of course, anyone who has parked near or passed by the L. Watson Clark maintenance building near the MacVittie College Union knows the end of the story. "Wat" Clark ably served the College until forced to retire in 1949 at age seventy. Attesting to the affection for Clark, the New York City alumni featured him on their program in 1941, he was fêted at a concert at the College on his sixty-fourth birthday and "Wat Clark Day" was proclaimed on the day of his retirement.[43]

The *Livingston Republican* took pains to praise Sturges and Bucke, especially the former. The editor recalled that Sturges must be credited for the Normal School's attendance increase from a low point of 212 shortly after he arrived to 455 in the 1921–1922 school year, the largest entering class to that time. Bucke was cited for making arrangements between Craig Colony and the Practice School for the new special education program.[44]

There is no way to know whether Sturges was forced out because the school needed a healthier replacement or whether he was to blame for alleged

The *Normalian* lauded longtime janitor L. Watson "Wat" Clark for his "unfailing loyalty and patience," and said that "a janitor with a disposition like Mr. Clark's is not only a luxury but a necessity in a school composed mostly of girls" who considered him a "lifesaver." The administration also appreciated him, naming the 1967 service building after him. (1925 *Normalian*)

irregularities. The firing of Bucke also begs explanation. Had he after seventeen years simply outlived his usefulness? Had he offended enough persons at the school or on the local board to require his dismissal? Was he part of the "friction" that led to Sturges's contract nonrenewal? He certainly had the academic credentials, had organized and directed the unusual, possibly unique, special education program at Craig Colony and had helped initiate the Normal's Teacher-Librarian program.[45]

Ten years later, on January 19, 1932, the school Principal Sturges had guided for seventeen years closed at noon, to honor him after his death the previous day. The faculty, which attended the funeral as a unit, sent resolutions of respect and a blanket of roses. Poignantly, shortly before he died, an appreciative Sturges learned that a proposed dormitory at the corner of Wadsworth and Bank streets would be named for him. That dormitory was never built, but another in 1950 (Blake E) bore his name before the administration-classroom building was renamed in his honor.[46]

****

Despite its proverbial trials and tribulations, Geneseo's Normal School had not only survived; it had prospered over its first fifty years. The villagers who indebted themselves in 1867 were being amply repaid. Many of their youth received their first twelve years of schooling here before going on to successful academic, political, and professional careers. For example, board member John B. Abbott, an early graduate, was a successful lawyer. Another, Austin Erwin, would come to chair the state's most powerful legislative committee.

Students posed on one of Old Main's verandas before the 1913 commencement. This group does not appear to be the graduating class, which was smaller, with only 131 students. (Milne Archives)

The Normal's first graduating class was ten; the 1922 graduates numbered 277, contributing to a total of more than five thousand graduates by this time. Enrollment had risen from seventy-one in 1871 to 847 in 1896–1897 before quotas were instituted. During most of those first fifty years everything revolved around Old Main, which housed classrooms, dorm rooms, and the kitchen. In fact, according to *The Lamron*, for years "the smell of cooked food permeated the entire building. The class in Latin took Caesar across the Hellespont to the accompaniment of boiled cabbage on one day; on the next $x^2 + 2xy + y^2$ was imbibed with boiled onions."[47]

Students worked hard to make Old Main's gymnasium a suitably romantic setting for the last dance in 1911. (Milne Archives)

The faculty had grown from thirteen to fifty-nine by 1922, and the curriculum had been made more rigorous and more professional. By design, the students' social activities continued to revolve around the "fraternities" (the term long applied to both men's and women's societies) that afforded the sense of community the first Milne sought by offering a variety of social and cultural activities. Some College events were spectacular, though none matched the school's celebration of fifty years or possibly the "Carnival of Gymnastics" in 1901.[48]

A 1916 graduate, Mary Caragher, asserted that "it is the cultivation…of the human as well as the academic side of our nature that makes Geneseo unique among educational institutions," but that could have been said about any number of small colleges. Geneseo owed its distinctiveness to something more: its successful graduates and the school's reputation for the Kindergarten-Primary Department and the Teacher-Librarian program. For example, the Library Department proclaimed that a quarter of all New York State school librarians were Geneseo graduates, and the school's library, which supported the Teacher-Librarian program, was the envy of other Normals. In time, special education would receive the same recognition as the library program.[49]

Student Housing

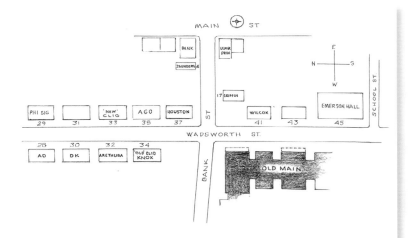

The College had no residence halls until the early 1950s. For many years, Geneseo's students lived on the top floor of Old Main or in approved boarding houses, most of which were located on Wadsworth Street and were later razed to make room for campus buildings such as Bailey, Newton, and Greene. (map by Paul Hepler, locations provided by Ted Bondi)

Emerson Hall, operated by Elbert and Ina Foland, was located on the site of today's Bailey building. (Bright collection)

Bolt House, a former croquet factory at 5 Main Street, is still a student rental property. (Bright collection)

In a postcard mailed to her aunt in 1922, student Dot noted that her friend Hazel lived in Westland House the previous year. (Bright collection)

Ruth, who mailed this postcard of Simmons House in 1916, marked her shared main floor room with an X, just right of the center stairway to the porch. (Bright collection)

D. K. House

Ago House

Arethusa House

Phi Sig House

A. D. House

Clio House

The 1959 *Oh Ha Daih* featured photos of six fraternity and sorority houses. (1959 *Oh Ha Daih*)

FALL BROOK BASIN, GENESEO, N. Y.

Chapter Four

State Normal School
GENESEO, NEW YORK
•
The Expanding Curriculum (1922–1934)

Though calm generally prevailed at Geneseo, it was not un-affected by outside events, including women's right to vote, the advent of radio and talking movies, an historic Atlantic solo flight, and the beginning of the Great Depression.

For example, in 1918, as if anticipating passage of the nineteenth amendment of the U.S. Constitution, the Normal School board welcomed two women, Mrs. Elizabeth P. Wadsworth, wife of the Major, who remained on the board, and Mrs. Bertha Paine Fraser, a former instructor. They and their colleagues, including President James W. Wadsworth, Sr., now in his fifty-first year on the board, faced two serious personnel problems. The first was the board's doing; the second, which arose out of the first, was only partly so.

Elizabeth (Mrs. William Austin) Wadsworth donated a North Street house for use as an infirmary and served on the Board of Visitors from 1918 to 1943. (*The Lamron, 50th Anniversary*)

Another Brouhaha Over the Principalship

On August 22, 1922, after interviewing three candidates, the board offered the principalship to Francis M. Garver, Ph.D., pending the state education commissioner's approval. The forty-eight-year-old

Opposite Page: Students have long enjoyed hiking in the Fallbrook gorge just south of the village. (1932 *Jen-o-see*)

Winfield Holcomb served as principal from 1922 to 1934, when the graduating seniors said they were "particularly proud to have graduating with us our own Principal." (1934 *Normalian*)

Garver, a Mason and Presbyterian with a doctorate from the University of Pennsylvania, seemed perfect for the job. He had taught in rural schools in his native Illinois before graduating from the Indiana State Normal School and had held numerous administrative positions in Ohio, New York, and New Jersey before his elementary education professorship at the University of North Dakota. The *Dansville Express* editor felt Garver's only "failing" was that "he is not a handsome man." However, his "strong, rugged western character" would "inject a little western push into the young easterners who will be under him."[1]

However, a "bombshell was exploded," the *Livingston Republican* editor declared. The Regents rejected Garver, who had already met with the faculty and was planning the opening of the school term. It was rumored that a Regent held a grudge against Garver for supporting one textbook rather than another when he was high school principal at Binghamton previously. At a "hurried" conference in Rochester with state education department representatives, Winfield Holcomb, whom the school and community would come to know well, was appointed acting principal.[2]

Two months later, on November 16, education commissioner F. P. Graves announced that the local board, with his approval, had made Holcomb's appointment permanent. The commissioner praised Holcomb for his "wealth of experience in New York State school matters." A Fredonia graduate, Holcomb was at the time chief of the Bureau of Teacher Certification. For fifteen years he had served as Chautauqua County's school commissioner, moving to Albany in 1906 as general inspector of high schools, rising eight years later to become special inspector of the state's teacher training schools. While in her centennial history Rosalind Fisher believed the board "prevailed upon the commissioner of education to release" Holcomb from his responsibilities in Albany, the decision to make Holcomb principal may have come from Albany's initiative.[3]

It was an inauspicious beginning for Holcomb, who arrived after the school year had started. He found an unsettled campus. Important vacancies had to be filled, and the *Livingston Republican's* editor claimed that "Geneseo has been overrun with rumors." Most troubling was one alleging serious financial irregularities. On October 4, at a meeting in the Normal School's chapel, Holcomb denied that there had been any improprieties. Yes, he noted, the

Clionian sorority members posed in front of the cast plaster friezes in Old Main's library. (1925 *Normalian*)

school's books had been read by auditors, but "usually" all public schools' books were audited annually. Holcomb also tried to put down rumors of more forced retirements of faculty: the local board and commissioner would not "unwillingly release any teacher." Furthermore, "Geneseo has the reputation of having one of the strongest faculties in the state."[4]

While Holcomb was a bit disingenuous, there was nothing directly to suggest the school's problems lay any deeper than the lack of management resulting from Principal Sturges's poor health and leave of absence. Less than three years later, however, Holcomb's words would be thrown back in his face. By an eight to one vote at its June 23, 1925 meeting, the local board fired Dr. Manley H. Harper and Professor Harry B. Smith. When word got out, there was a hue and cry, including attacks on the school by the Rochester papers. Critics of the decision alluded to personal or local grievances against the two, particularly against Harper.[5]

Ironically, three years earlier Harper had been hired by Holcomb to replace W. Fowler Bucke as head of Geneseo's education department. He came with impressive credentials, including a pending doctorate from Columbia University and management of an experimental school run by the university. A Kansan with a bachelor's degree from Kansas State Normal School, Harper had previously headed the Department of Education at Texas State Normal. Psychology professor Smith, who too came with high expectations, had not yet completed requirements for his doctorate at Columbia.[6]

Unlike the courtesy extended to Sturges, the local board refused to allow either Harper or Smith to defend himself and initially offered no explanation for the dismissals. Nor did the commissioner of education find the need to investigate the matter. Nonetheless, given the "newspaper controversy"

over the board decision, Holcomb felt the students deserved an explanation. Shading the truth a bit, Holcomb explained that Smith had simply been filling in for Miss Blanche Fuller, who was returning from a year's study. On the other hand, Dr. Harper had been dismissed "because of his disloyalty to members of the faculty... [and] his having been for two years a source of trouble and serious ill feeling." The school's peace, harmony and "sound professionalism" required his dismissal. The *Livingston Republican* editor summed it up: the two were fired because they "didn't fit the mold."[7]

It is easy enough to gloss over the incident some eight decades later; to call it simply "ancient history" or much ado about nothing. But at the time it split the Normal School faculty and the community and was grist for newspapers near and far. Article headlines blared "Geneseo Quiet on Dismissal of Professors,"

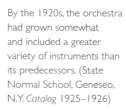

By the 1920s, the orchestra had grown somewhat and included a greater variety of instruments than its predecessors. (State Normal School, Geneseo, N.Y. *Catalog* 1925–1926)

Minerva was not the only artwork in Old Main's library; it also featured ornate friezes, as did other parts of the building. (State Normal School, Geneseo, N.Y. *Catalog* 1925–1926)

"Geneseo Split on Teacher Ousting," "Real Issue Radicalism, Men Assert," "Radical Beliefs Charged Against Faculty Members," "Censorship Charged by Geneseo Pupils...," "Ouster Stirs Storm at Geneseo Normal." The most troubling read: "Geneseo Splits Into Factions; May Lose School."[8]

Virtually all the papers likened the issue to the Scopes trial (whether Tennessee could legally ban the teaching of evolution in its public schools), which had concluded the day before the Geneseo dispute hit the papers. As the Rochester *Journal and Post Express* reporter put it: it was a "battle between educational fundamentalism and modernism." This was clearly the line that Harper and Smith took in their defense. Harper was quoted as saying, "If I did not say a Socialist should be hanged, then I became a Socialist, and if I asked people why they went to church, I was called an agnostic." Smith expressed much the same sentiment in a letter to commissioner Graves.[9]

Harper charged that he and Smith were victims of the school's conservatism. Harper saw a pattern: three of those recently fired (Bucke, himself, and Smith) were psychology instructors. In fact, both Harper and Smith could charge the faculty with being—at the very least—politically conservative and they would have been correct. The faculty resoundingly supported Republican Herbert Hoover's reelection in 1932, voting twenty-seven to five for Hoover over victor Franklin D. Roosevelt. The vote was closer in 1936, with twenty-four faculty for GOP candidate Landon, nineteen for FDR. The split widened again in 1940 with twenty-seven of the faculty identifying themselves as Republicans, eleven claiming to be Democrats. The students' vote was similarly conservative in 1936, with sixty percent supporting Landon and half as many for Roosevelt. (Interestingly, three percent supported either Norman

Hermann Cooper taught at Geneseo for four years before becoming the state's assistant commissioner for teacher education and certification. (1937 *Normalian*)

The Student Co-op bookstore hosted an autographing party for Clayton Mau's 1944 book, *The Development of Central and Western New York*. (Livingston County Historian)

Thomas, a socialist, or William Lemke, a radical North Dakota congressman, for president that year.)[10]

Both Harper and Smith also argued that they were dismissed because they were more popular than most of the remaining faculty. This was supported by a paper's assertion that the two "were hailed by the students as the dawn of a new era for Geneseo Normal." The assertion was based on the fact that 320 out of 383 students signed a petition requesting the local board to reinstate Smith. Further, they claimed they would have supported Harper, as well, had they learned of his dismissal during the school year. Betty Carroll, senior class president, even went so far as to charge Holcomb with intercepting the petition and threatening signers with dismissal. Some students asserted that reports of Harper's and Smith's dismissals were "clipped out of the Rochester newspapers before they were filed in the school library." One newspaper rather uncavalierly charged that Holcomb's degree was only an honorary one, and another paper argued that since the "school is maintained at state expense," only the best faculty ought to be hired and that there ought to be a hearing to clear the air.[11]

For a time Holcomb's and the local board's silence seemed to aggravate the issue, although Holcomb rebutted Harper's and Smith's charges to assistant educa-

Ira Wilson, who taught history and coached for many years, was a dapper young man when he posed with the 1928 basketball team (back row, from left): George Bryant, Wilson, Roland DeMarco; (front): Homer Stuber, James Osborne, captain Howard Schrader, Harold Dowdle. (1928 *Normalian*)

tion commissioner George M. Wiley in a long, detailed four-page letter, asserting that he had no choice but to dismiss Harper. He claimed that Harper had "clearly demonstrated a serious lack of tact and qualities of leadership." Holcomb further charged that Harper was not only "most abusive and insulting" toward an un-named faculty member, he demonstrated "a most violent temper," had been dis-loyal to the school's department heads "to an inexcusable degree," and had aired his griev-ances directly with the local board. On behalf of the faculty Holcomb was "constrained to rec-ommend" Harper's dismissal. Commissioner Graves's refusal to hold a hearing pretty much put the issue to rest. (Harper's dismissal also may have been warranted on grounds that Holcomb could not substantiate or did not wish to divulge.)[12]

Student dramatic productions, such as *Twelfth Night*, have always been an important part of campus and community life. (1927 *Normalian*)

While ostensibly wanting to downplay the unsavory incident, the editor of the *Livingston Republican* derisively charged the Rochester papers with sensationalism, but then took a swipe at Harper and Smith by asking them to "tell us publicly...where they were five years immediately prior to their coming to Geneseo and why they left those positions."[13]

Columbia's eminent psychologist Edward L. Thorndike supplied part of the answer: Harper and Smith had been taking courses at Columbia, which was being unfairly stigmatized as radical. One of his colleagues was more

CRAIG COLONY

A CLUSTER of brick buildings on a rolling hillside, commanding a wide view of the valley below; this means Sonyea to those who have lived there. It is a world in itself with much work to be done. There are busy shops of all kinds with fascinating projects to be carried out. Often the daylight hours are not long enough, and some come back to work in the evening hours, loath to leave unfinished the task they have started. Those who have studied in this atmosphere find themselves giving their best to a cause that challenges their whole interest.

ADELENE TITSWORTH   R. DUDLEY MILLER   DOROTHEA O. SEEGLER

The 1929 *Normalian* featured the Craig Colony at Sonyea and the Geneseo faculty who taught and supervised student teachers there.

blunt: if Columbia was a "hotbed of radicalism," as critics charged, why did Geneseo apply to Columbia for Harper's successor?[14]

Ironically, as Thorndike's colleague asserted, Geneseo replaced Harper as head of the education department and training school with a Columbia graduate, Dr. Hermann Cooper, who was anything but a radical. Cooper, the son of a former University of Iowa president, had obtained his doctorate from Teachers College, Columbia the previous fall. Though Cooper stayed at Geneseo only four years, he would have a profound effect—at times irritatingly so—upon the school into the 1960s.

Two other hires at this time would achieve a measure of fame. The first was Dr. Clayton Mau, who in 1954 would write a brief, unpublished history of the College, though he is better known for his five-hundred-page tome, *The Development of Central and Western New York.* Mau was hired to teach history in the high school in 1923 and was named head of the Normal School history department the following year.[15]

The other was young, vigorous, handsome Ira Wilson, appointed in 1925. He was hired as physical education instructor for the junior and senior high boys and coach of the Normal's basketball team. "Very favorably impressed with Geneseo" on arrival, Wilson remained forty-four years, until 1969, when he retired from the History Department.[16]

STUDENT GOVERNMENT OFFICERS

STUDENT COUNCIL

Women served as the first officers of the student government, established in 1924 just four years after women gained the right to vote. (1925 *Normalian*)

Curricular Changes and Implementations

The biggest challenge for Principal Holcomb and the faculty, beginning in 1922, was to implement the new three-year curriculum, rather than the two, which had existed since the beginning. Students then in the two-year program would have to complete their coursework by January 1924 and would receive only a "limited certificate" good for three years. To obtain a diploma and a life license, students had to finish the new three-year curriculum, first completed by 1925 graduates. Beyond the General Education courses, students had the options of the Kindergarten-Primary, Intermediate, Junior High, Teacher-Librarian, or Education of Exceptional Children programs. Apparently another option was "School Librarian" for those students intending to teach in "third-class cities" or junior high schools. [17]

While the Teacher-Librarian curriculum—expanded to thirty-two hours

In 1936–1937, student government president Sidney Robinson (standing, second from left) posed with faculty advisors (from left) Mary Frances Bannan, Lucy Harmon, R. Leroy Countryman, and Robert Greene. (1937 *Normalian*)

in 1932—deservedly got the lion's share of attention, the new special education program marked a milestone for the school. In fact, six years into existence, it was coming to distinguish Geneseo, just as sister schools claimed specializations, e.g., Cortland, known for health and physical education, and Fredonia and Potsdam for drawing and music. The success of Geneseo's special education program can be attributed to the leadership of Dr. Clarence Lehman, who directed it until the late 1930s when he returned to Potsdam as its principal.[18]

In 1922, *The Lamron* proclaimed that Geneseo was "the only state school in the United States which has the education of any *state institution under its supervision*" [italics added]. The paper was referring to the Normal's connection with the Craig Colony at Sonyea, eleven miles southwest of Geneseo. Once a Shaker settlement, the facility, named for Rochester philanthropist Oscar Craig, had been converted into the only state school in the U.S. for the care of epileptics. Younger patients there were taught academic and vocational courses, with the Normal School students observing and later practicing what they were taught.[19]

This unusual program, begun by Dr. Bucke, was developed to comply with the Stapley Bill, which required special classes for children in each school district with ten or more "subnormal," or unusually retarded, children. Necessarily, teachers had to be prepared to work with "exceptional children." So, the School of Practice and Demonstration at Craig Colony, an extension department, was created to teach teachers of exceptional children. Eight teachers, all women at first, taught occupational and physical therapy, juvenile activities, English, primary education, dramatics, "General Sloyd" (manual training using hand tools, including the Sloyd knife, for wood carving), "Embroidery, Practical and Artistic Sewing and Gardening" and "Manual Training and Joinery." Additionally, these critic teachers oversaw the Normal School students who observed and "practiced" there.[20]

The faculty and student teachers lived and ate meals in the cottages with the Sonyea students and had to take the trolley or drive to campus for meetings and activities. Dr. Gladys Rhodes, who later chaired Geneseo's first separate special education department, recalled that it was "confining" for the faculty and students living there. Not surprisingly, Rochester beckoned the faculty on weekends "for something to do." Equally aggravating, fifty years after her appointment Rhodes still vividly recalled that faculty at the

Carol Holland (front row, left end), shown here with the Carol Choristers and Mrs. Olmsted, was a longtime music department mainstay. (1940 *Normalian*)

Normal School "looked down on" the Craig faculty. (The College's primary connection with Sonyea was severed around 1955, when Rhodes and Dudley Miller went to the main campus.)[21]

Just teaching at Sonyea was a challenge. The K-6 school "was run like a regular school; the same length of day and year," but the faculty and student teachers had to escort the Colony students to and from school, eat with them in the Colony's cafeteria, and teach twenty to twenty-five students in a class without aides. Still, the Geneseo Normal School had created and was implementing a novel program.[22]

"Meeting Individual Responsibilities"

Nearing the end of their time at the Normal School, Principal Holcomb and Dean Blake agreed that the "greatest and most far-reaching change" was organizing the Student Cooperative Government. Put into effect in September 1924, it was "to train students in self-direction and in meeting individual responsibilities." Previously the faculty monitored virtually all student activities. So, students were to govern "such matters as driving after dark, study hours, lighting regulations, control over attendance,

In March 1923, *Peg O' My Heart* was presented by (front, from left): Marjorie Ulrich, E. J. Merchant, Edward Lavery, Katherine Amey as Peg; (back): Sylvia Dates, John Burke, Helen Climensen, Lee Costello. (1923 *Normalian*)

outside dances." Though relieved of some irritating chores, the faculty continued to wrestle with the matter of class and chapel attendance and with appropriate penalties for absences. Absences from class before and after holidays were an especial irritant. (For many years classes were held until 11:30 on the day before Thanksgiving, despite the distance Long Island students had to travel to get home.)[23]

For many years, the baseball team played on Kelsey field near the armory, whose large roof sign served as a navigation aid for airplane pilots. (1933 *Normalian*)

Holcomb had outlined the plan for a student government at the preceding June meeting with faculty department heads, who believed that "in all probability" the students "would react favorably to confidence reposed in them." However, the faculty had asked Holcomb to announce the decision to have a student government at the weekly chapel meeting to offer the students an "open forum...for discussing student problems and matters of literary and civic value." They also wanted an opportunity to remind the students that the faculty "reserved [the] right to take control if [student] gov't did not work."[24]

A survey conducted almost a year later concluded that "on the whole, student government had been a decided success." The only reported problems were those to be expected during the transition. Holcomb confirmed the survey's conclusion: "fewer cases of discipline than ever before...had come before him this year." Three years later, the results of a questionnaire administered to the students were equally, if not more, positive. By a 368 to 44 vote, the students expressed approval of student government, though 81 students would opt for faculty governance "under certain conditions."[25]

The 1932–1933 women's varsity basketball team was composed of the best players from each class's team (front, from left): Jones, McCurdy, Nickerson; (back): Bailey, Hoke, Meagher. Lucille Bailey's mother made the uniforms. Ruth Green Linfoot helped select and coach the players. (1933 *Normalian*)

In 1927, concern for attracting and retaining students prompted another survey; this one asked students why they chose Geneseo. One hundred twenty-three "came because their parents wished it." Almost as many, 120, attended because it was "less expensive than college" [*sic*], while 104 thought they would receive "better preparation than the college [*sic*] course." (Recall that Geneseo offered only diplomas, not degrees which four-year students received.) Ninety-six favored Geneseo because it was "the nearest Normal." Only four were enticed to Geneseo by a better chance of "making" a sorority. *The Lamron* staff poked a little fun at the questionnaire, making up some of their own answers. The reasons why "Girls Go to Normal" were: "To have some fun, To see the world, To have an apartment, To become famous, To get out of work, Because there wasn't any other place to go," AND "Because Dad didn't have the money to send her to college."[26]

Looking back, Dr. Holcomb also believed that the Sigma Pi Sigma honorary society, organized to promote good scholarship, had "proved very helpful to both the school and students." The goal, of course, was "to raise the standards of scholarship." Another innovation that strengthened teacher education was initiating arrangements between rural schools and the Normal's Department of Rural Education for off-campus student teaching, beginning in 1929. Shortly thereafter, sites for "cadet teaching" included Elmira and Gloversville, and five years later expanded to Ithaca, Canandaigua, LeRoy, and Perry schools.[27]

Students demonstrated the various steps used to teach diving skills. (1938 *Normalian*)

Likely, not only the cadet teachers' instruction and behavior, but also attire, was closely monitored. A Plattsburgh graduate recalled that "'While we were pupil teachers our personalities were closely observed, criticized and *recorded*. Our dress was most primitive—long skirts, long-sleeved and high-necked shirtwaists, long hair worn in a twist or bun, colorless nails, etc. Our teachers would have been shocked indeed to [see] such scenes in present-day schoolrooms [1964] as young teachers sitting on top of the desks while teaching classes.'" Likely, we can guess this graduate's reaction to teachers' attire and actions today![28]

In what may have been her swan song, Dean Blake reflected favorably on the student handbook, which was first published in 1927. Beyond the helpful information about the Normal, the handbook offered suggestions for proper etiquette in and out of the school. Perhaps in that spirit, *The Lamron* reminded students that the library is "not a place for promenades, for visiting and confusion." The advice bluntly concluded: "If you can't conform to the regulations which are made in order that other individuals may be able to work efficiently, don't come to the library." Also, although Blake didn't mention it,

Coach Hoover's 1933 basketball team included Jim Dietsche, '33, (front row, second from right) and his brother William (center row, left), who was offered a professional baseball contract but was killed in an auto accident before he could join the team. (1933 *Normalian*)

Students portrayed butterflies in "Nature's Frolic Before the Coming of Man," the first part of an outdoor pageant held on June 22, 1921 to celebrate the Normal School's fiftieth anniversary. (1922 *Normalian*)

beginning in 1934 the students' social life was augmented by the non-denominational Student Christian Fellowship and the Newman Club for Catholics. However, Sunday attendance at village churches by the school's students long remained a staple of community life.[29]

In contrast, the behavior, particularly scholarship, of the high school students frustrated the College's administrators. "Certain high school students not keeping up with their work in this school may be transferred to the Center Street School in charge of Mrs. [Elizabeth V. R.] Shepard," the board declared in May 1926. The board had already restricted admission to village residents, in part because of the concern about the students' scholarship and in part because the Normal school was overcrowded. Earlier the board had shown more leniency toward the students, granting local diplomas to students who "maintained a 75% in each prescribed course." Denying graduation to a student "who has done faithful and acceptable work" but failed the Regents examination was "unfair and unjust," the board believed.[30]

Of far less concern to the board or administration was the intercollegiate sports program that had never recovered from World War I. An attempt to resurrect the football program in 1922 and 1923 failed, as did the fortunes of the baseball team. The disastrous 1923 baseball season was blamed on the fact that "so many of the members have been ruled off because of low marks in their subjects." By comparison, the women's "Play Days," featuring a wide variety of activities, including hiking, horseback riding, skiing, basketball, and swimming, flourished. Competitive events with women from sister schools were also highlights of those years, and in 1931 Geneseo was the host. While a far cry from the successful women's sports decades later, they were important events in those years.[31]

Shabby Buildings

When looking back at his Geneseo tenure, Holcomb conveniently ignored the school's "shabby buildings," a term that was frequently used even into the early 1950s. In fact, not long after he arrived, he had to reassure the students

that there was no danger to them
or to the school. One rumor had it
that the school was in such poor
shape that it was to be replaced on
another site. Holcomb countered:
"There is no more danger that the
Normal School will be moved from
Geneseo than that Conesus Lake will
be moved to Mt. Morris." Holcomb
also wanted to stifle the rumor "that
the walls were badly cracked, the
foundations were insecure, and the
whole building a menace to the
well-being of its occupants...."

Geneseo finally opened its
own junior-senior high school
in 1932. (Bright collection)

This and other rumors were, Holcomb flatly stated, "false." But, he wasn't
completely honest with the students. He, like everyone from the governor down,
knew full well Geneseo at the very least needed to shore up its old buildings and
to build a new practice school.[32]

The buildings were aging, badly deteriorating firetraps. Geneseo mistakenly
believed it was fortunate to escape major fires, which sister schools Oneonta
(1894), Fredonia (1900), Albany and New Paltz (1906), Cortland (1919), and
Plattsburgh (1929) suffered. They got new buildings while Geneseo struggled to
maintain and insure its antiquated buildings. So, in 1923, the board had asked
the village to help pay for insuring the school, and two years later held a joint
meeting with the District No. 5 trustees to examine the "school situation."[33]

The "school situation," labeled "unbearable" by the Normal's board, also
referred to the overcrowding in Old Main. In October 1926, a special committee of the board recommended a new training school to be located south
of the library building. Five months later the board charged that there was an
"urgent need of better quarters." A new heating plant was even more urgently
needed. After waiting another seven years, the board desperately appealed to
the commissioner and the legislature for an estimated thirty thousand dollars
to replace the heating system. The "dilapidated condition of the boilers...and
the imminent danger of complete break-down" demanded immediate action.
It was a disaster waiting to happen. No parts were available for the boilers,
and since the heating system had been installed in 1889, the College had
spent greater than thirty-four thousand dollars ($1,721 per year) on it. In
fact, one section of Old Main was without heat![34]

Grounds for athletics and physical education also were totally inadequate

Generations of Geneseo
children received their
elementary, secondary, and
sometimes normal school or
college education in Old Main.
The boy looking directly at
the camera is Austin Erwin, Jr.
(Roemer House Collection)

for the 430 Training (Campus) School students and the 650 Normal School students. The pressing need for a larger practice school previously had led the local board to obtain an appropriation of eighty thousand dollars from the legislature and to have the state architect draw up plans in 1923. The planning finally came to fruition in 1932. But in true bureaucratic fashion, it came only after other issues, including how to provide for a village high school, were resolved.[35]

In part the resolution came from an arrangement between the Normal School board and the trustees of District No. 5. (The president of the latter was Fred Quirk, father of Joseph Quirk, who would preside over the College Council for many years.) Shortly, the state education department, which earlier had ordered the Normals to close their high school sections, approved construction of both, a tribute to the two boards that had worked hard to obtain that approval.[36]

Another stumbling block was removed at an April 1930 District No. 5 meeting at which Mrs. William A. Wadsworth, Normal School board member and Homestead owner, offered the district almost eighty acres adjacent to the Normal School at a "nominal" one hundred dollars per acre. Three months later District No. 5's voters unanimously consented to buy the land, with the state's "implied obligation" to buy fifty-nine acres from the district later for Normal School use. So, after many agonizing meetings and requests for money, the state gave the go-ahead.[37]

Completing the story, in December 1933 the Normal School board asked the state to buy the land from District No. 5. When the state denied the request, the district gave the land to the Normal School. It appears that at least part of this land was used to build the new campus school just off Route 63 in the late 1960s. Also it appears there was a stipulation about both parcels. That is, if and when the parcels were no longer used as schools, the land would revert back to Mrs. Wadsworth's family.[38]

Thus, despite the deepening economic depression and after agitating since 1915, it looked like the village was going to have its first public high school and the Normal a new training school. Somewhat sadly, with the opening of the new practice school in August 1932, the village's venerable Center Street School—the Cobblestone School—was to be closed (though it would be transferred to the Livingston County Historical Society). So, until 1974, when the K-12 Geneseo Central School admitted its first students, the village elementary students would attend a self-standing practice school. Although at times they felt they were "guinea pigs" for experimental teaching, more than seventy years later many attendees fondly recalled the school. They especially remembered Frederick Holcomb, its first principal, who died at the young age of forty-six after having miraculously survived a near-fatal streptococcus infection eight years earlier.[39]

The Winfield Holcomb School of Practice (now Welles) opened in 1932 and served as Geneseo's elementary school until the new Holcomb School opened in 1969. (1938 *Normalian*)

However, even with state approval, the practice school almost did not come about. The legislative appropriation was $85,000 for the *foundation only*. Another $385,000 for a complete building was diverted to Cornell, the university with a rather anomalous arrangement. Sparing the reader the almost byzantine history of the state's relationship with Cornell, suffice to say that Cornell is a private-public university. Most of the university's departments and colleges are privately funded. However, the School of Industrial Relations and the College of Agriculture and Life Science, including the State Experiment Station at Geneva, are "statutory colleges," funded by the state. Unlike the land-grant colleges in the Midwest, Geneseo and the other Normal Schools have vied with Cornell and the other statutory colleges for funds from the outset, as in 1930 when funds earmarked for Geneseo went to Cornell.[40]

Completion also required overcoming the objections of the state's comptroller, who had fulminated about the waste of state money on buildings, particularly those with "gingerbread architecture" and "Byzantine arches or Grecian columns." Well-lighted, ventilated, heated, and solidly constructed buildings were necessary, but the state's "net funded debt" was $229 million in 1925. Any new construction, even renovation, had to be absolutely necessary—and practical.[41]

Likely, authorization of the new practice school also benefited from the appointment of James W. Wadsworth, Jr., U.S. Senator from New York, 1915–

1927, to the local board in January 1927 to succeed his father, who died in 1926. "The Senator" not only used his influence to obtain needed money for both schools, but he also called upon his son, state assemblyman, later majority leader, James Jeremiah ("Jerry") to help. The appropriation came through in 1934, when the state legislature agreed to demolish the crumbling house Principal Holcomb occupied on Wadsworth Street across from the practice school and provide him with a housing allowance instead. Not until Dr. Moench arrived in the early 1950s was the president again provided a house.[42]

Finally, in mid-October 1930, the money came through and a contract for the Practice School was let. Plans called for the "collegiate Gothic of Virginia Colonial brick" building to have ten twenty-two-foot by twenty-eight-foot classrooms and nine twenty-eight-foot demonstration rooms, a gym, library, assembly hall, science rooms, two kindergartens, and rooms for "subnormal and special classes." Of course, anyone who attended classes in the building knows that it didn't come out exactly as planned. Nor would today's students or visitors get a genuine feeling for the layout of the building, renamed the Welles Building and, since 1969, used for College classes and faculty offices.[43]

Principal Holcomb and Dean Blake Retire

On May 27, 1933 "The Winfield A. Holcomb School of Practice" was dedicated, and a bronze plaque recognizing Holcomb was unveiled on June 11. Festivities included a luncheon, entertainment by an orchestra and glee club, and a speech prepared by Judge John B. Abbott, Normal School class of 1875 and longtime board member. It was fitting to name the new practice school for Holcomb, for it was his most visible accomplishment, although he claimed upgrading the faculty was his most important contribution. "When I first came here [1922], twenty-seven of the teachers held no degree," he recalled. Twelve years later, four of his fifty-five faculty had the doctorate or equivalent, thirty-four held master's degrees, twelve had bachelor's degrees, and only five were without degrees.[44]

In 1930, the science faculty included (from left): J. Louise Moran, Guy A. Bailey, and Robert A. Greene, two of whom were honored by having buildings named for them. (1930 *Normalian*)

Dean Anne Blake, who retired the same year, cited the improvement in student housing standards and supervision, the student government, the student handbook, the social center lounge, freshman orientation, and the "all-school Christmas pageant" as highlights of her seventeen years at the Geneseo Normal School. Sadly, given her vital services, probably she is remembered only by the remaining Blake buildings, if at all.[45]

On April 10, 1934, board secretary Lockwood R. Doty announced a special meeting to be held in Holcomb's office four days hence, a Saturday, ostensibly to discuss his pending retirement letter. On the 18th, the board received Holcomb's resignation and, without giving reasons, agreed to consider only in-state candidates. On April 22, board members interviewed five candidates. (The sixth candidate, Dr. Clarence O. Lehman,

The 1930 English faculty included (from left): Mary Thomas, John Parry, and C. Agnes Rigney. Parry chaired the department from 1922 to 1955 and taught part-time for many years after retiring. (1930 *Normalian*)

Geneseo's Director of Training, apparently did not appear before the board.) Board member John B. Abbott's motion to appoint Academic Department graduate Dr. James B. Welles was seconded, but the board adjourned without action. The absence of board president Wadsworth may explain the inaction, but the month-long delay in making the appointment begs explanation. Finally, on May 27, by the narrowest margin (four to three), Welles was declared the board's choice, pending the commissioner's and Regents' approvals.[46]

****

Geneseo Normal School had profited from Principal Holcomb's steady administration. He inherited and overcame a school suffering from financial irregularities, rumors that the school would be moved, aging facilities, overcrowded dorms and the dismissals of two faculty members, to cite the most obvious. Importantly, he hired Hermann Cooper, whose star was on the rise, and Cooper's successor, Clarence O. Lehman, to help implement needed changes. The school had a more professional three-year curriculum, with a Department of Rural Education offering more realistic student teaching experiences. Its enrollment was up to 707, it had graduated another 2,183 students, and its 55 faculty held more professional degrees than previously. Student housing standards and supervision were improved, and a student government was up and running. Importantly, despite a worldwide economic depression, Geneseo's students were finding teaching positions. And Geneseo had a new practice school. Principal Holcomb and Dean Blake could rightly claim that they were leaving the school in considerably better shape than when they arrived.

Geneseo
STATE TEACHERS COLLEGE
•
The Depression and War Years (1934–1946)

"Brother, Can You Spare a Dime?"—The Economy and the College

Harrison "Flops" Phillips, Class of '42, acquired some handy extracurricular skills at Geneseo under the guidance of "Janitor-Engineer" Watson Clark and custodian Thomas Bovill. It wasn't exactly of his choosing, however. He was simply trying to fund his education at a very difficult time. The Great Depression had taken a toll: an unemployment rate that had topped out at nineteen percent in 1938, unprecedented foreclosures, bread lines, and once-unimagined homelessness. There were also international events that threatened to interrupt Phillips's schooling, including Japan's 1941 attack on Pearl Harbor following its earlier invasion of China and Germany's conquest of Poland and France.

Like Phillips, the College was deeply affected by these events, especially by the dismal state of the economy. By 1932, Geneseo Normal School faculty had already taken a hit. Salaries of all state employees were cut on a sliding scale: from six percent on salaries between two and three thousand dollars a year to twenty percent on salaries over twenty-five thousand dollars. By the end of the decade, budget restrictions would force the Regents to limit Normal School enrollments. Geneseo's

Opposite Page: From 1938 through 1950, the campus consisted of the Holcomb School of Practice (now Welles Hall), Old Main, and the classroom/administration building (later named Sturges). (Hans Tanner collection)

1939 freshman quota was "110 for the three-year elementary teachers curriculum and 35 for the four-year librarians and elementary teachers curriculum...." Further, no freshmen were to be admitted at the beginning of the second semester. With operating budgets based in large measure on enrollment, Geneseo's survival was threatened.[1]

More than a few Normal School students feared that the relief measures from which they had benefitted, including the New York Temporary Emergency Relief Administration (TERA) and the federally funded National Youth Administration (NYA), would be eliminated. The implications were obvious: without those jobs, students would drop out or would never enroll. Harrison "Flops" Phillips and his friend Robert "Jeep" Spencer, '42, who got to know every "nook and cranny" in the administration building, would not have enrolled without the NYA. Washing the building's windows, removing chairs from the auditorium for Friday night dances, and returning them the next morning earned them thirty-five cents an hour. Loose change today, but back then it would more than pay for a fifteen-cent "hot hamburger and gravy dish," Phillips recalled more than sixty years later.[2]

James Welles, a 1905 graduate whose father was in the first graduating class, served as principal from 1934 to 1946. (1943 *Oh Ha Daih*)

Principal Welles at the Helm

Principal James B. Welles could not have anticipated what lay ahead when he arrived in 1934, including a fire that damaged his home two years later. The good news was that he had a new practice school and that a new administration building was in the planning stages. The bad news was that the economy was in the doldrums. Yet it was a kind of homecoming for the forty-eight-year-old Welles. His father was one of the school's first ten graduates and later an instructor, his sister-in-law taught at Sonyea, and a niece was in Geneseo's junior class.[3]

Welles had taken the College Preparatory course, graduating in 1905 (his lowest grade was a ninety), and four years later he obtained an A.B. degree from Union College, where he was Phi Beta Kappa. He received his master's degree at Teachers College, Columbia University, in 1913, and in 1936 Columbia would award him a doctorate. His dissertation was particularly appropriate: "The Development of a Program of Student Adjustment in the New York State Normal School at Geneseo." Following in his father's footsteps, Welles taught Latin before becoming an administrator in numerous New York State schools, including Roslyn Heights, from which he came to Geneseo.[4]

Though Welles was considered a "local boy" and would serve for a dozen years, he was never popular "uptown," according to two faculty members who served under him. The feeling was that Judge John Abbott, the only Democrat on the Board of Visitors (and one of few in the village), had brought Welles here. Welles did not help his cause by seeming "uncomfortable" or insecure in the role of principal. His diffidence and aloofness unnerved the faculty, though he generally "left them alone," and, as a result, he "got along." While most students knew him only from a distance, "Flops" Phillips, who knew every "nook and cranny" in the administration building, found Welles to be "a gentleman."[5]

However, Welles was blessed to have the services of Frances Brown, who served as the school secretary from 1912 to 1954 and was regarded by many as "The College." Lore has it that she did it all. She prepared and filed the principals' papers and monthly reports, sorted mail, answered prospective students' requests, scheduled classes, and even kept the books for some student organizations.[6]

She was, in fact, overworked. In his request for additional staff, Dr.

Frances Brown, seen here with assistant Gladys Westmoreland, may have been the most overworked secretary in college history, since she was the only secretary for many years. (1925 Normalian)

Old Main's inadequacies were clearly evident to students who used this poorly lighted makeshift piano studio in an abandoned stairwell. (*Old Buildings at Geneseo State Teachers College,* 1948, Hepler collection)

Welles asserted that Geneseo exceeded the ratio of students to secretaries of the other state Normals preparing elementary school teachers. With 666 students, Geneseo was the second largest of the nine, but it had only two secretaries. Welles asked for a financial secretary to "centralize all financial matters," a registrar, and a stenographer or clerk. Similar needs applied to janitorial services. There was no one on duty from 5:00 to 10:00 p.m. weeknights or from Saturday noon to midnight Sunday. And, possibly wishful thinking, Geneseo needed three additional instructors: one to handle the increased enrollment in the four-year school-library program, another to teach dramatics and public speaking, and a third to teach foreign languages.[7]

The buildings and grounds too needed attention. Budget requests for 1935–1936 were new boilers for the heating system, money to buy fifty-nine acres District No. 5 had acquired from Elizabeth Wadsworth for athletic fields, removal of the principal's house and Old Main's clock tower, and repair of conductor pipes and gutters. Then, toss in reinstatement of salary cuts and scheduled salary increments. Surprisingly, only the requests to buy the land and repair the conductor pipes and gutters were denied. Fortunately, District No. 5 gave the land to the College.[8]

The Loss of a Familiar Face

The razing of Old Main's historic clock tower in August 1935 is worth noting. It had long been obvious that the "familiar landmark" could collapse at any time, but its demise was widely lamented. Anticipating the event, some daring writers for *The Lamron* opened a trap door and climbed two flights of unpainted wooden stairs into the tower, from which they were rewarded by a magnificent view of the valley and village—and revealing bits of graffiti decorating the tower's walls. Beginning in 1877 seven hardy souls, including the intrepid "Gertrude Sanford, Feb. 1886," had chalked, penciled, painted, or carved their names. The reporters also mused about what the tower had experienced: "'77—President Hayes; '15—WWI; '31—despair with eleven million unemployed; '35—The New Deal, Hitler, Mussolini, Stalin, the tramp of armies once more."[9]

UPON THE FOUNDATION OF THE OLD THE NEW IS BUILT. NOTHING VITAL CAN BE WHOLLY INDEPENDENT OF THAT SOURCE FROM WHENCE IT SPRINGS. A NEW SCHOOL, AS WELL AS A NEW LIFE OR A NEW EVENT, MUST ALWAYS DEPEND UPON THE PAST FOR ITS BEGINNING. LEST WE FORGET, IN CONTEMPLATION OF THE GLAMOUR AND BRILLIANCE OF A NEW TEACHERS COLLEGE REMODELED IN RESPONSE TO THE SPIRIT OF A PROGRESSIVE AGE, LET US HERE PAY HOMAGE TO THE FAMILIAR FACE OF AN EDIFICE WITHIN WHOSE WALLS THE SEED OF THE DEMOCRATIC IDEAL FOR EDUCATION WAS PLANTED MORE THAN HALF A CENTURY AGO.

In 1935, Old Main's landmark clock tower was so badly deteriorated that it had to be razed. The tower had clock faces on all sides, but only the one facing front was a working clock. (1937 *Normalian*)

Obtaining money from the state, as Welles quickly learned, was little better than a crapshoot. The Regents' 1939 report, "The Preparation of School Personnel," candidly admitted that New York State had "literally starved its normal schools." Budget requests had to run the gauntlet from the Normals' local boards, the New York State Education Department, the Regents, and the state legislature to the governor.[10]

Making it worse, three venerable board members would be missed. Distinguished-looking County Judge John B. Abbott, an 1875 Geneseo Normal School graduate, county bar association president from its founding in 1906 and longtime president of the local school district, died at age eighty-one on January 17, 1935. In the dual role of Normal School and District No. 5 board member, his influence was often evident. The deaths of two other longtime board members, Lockwood R. Doty in 1937, and Elizabeth (Mrs. W. Austin) Wadsworth in 1943, also were deeply felt. Doty had served as board secretary for over three decades, while Mrs. Wadsworth was best remembered for having purchased, equipped, and staffed—at her own expense—the Nursing Home on North Street, which served the students from March 1915 until the 1950s.[11]

Particularly problematic for the Normals was that the fiscal crisis of the 1930s was exacerbated by state politics. "Governors and legislators...perennially seemed to favor the state's private colleges and universities—their vari-

In 1937–1938, the new classroom/administration building (later named Sturges) was nearing completion. (1938 *Normalian*)

ous alma maters—or to focus on New York City, with its financial and political influence." The rural areas, where Geneseo and virtually all the Normals were located, tended to lose out. Nor could the Normals count on any sizable private support until well into the 1970s when they were permitted to create foundations and solicit funds. Even then, it was a slow, uncertain process.[12]

Finally, in 1937, the exasperated principals—likely with Dr. Cooper's approval, even urging—drafted a memo to the State Education Department complaining about "inadequate" funding: "less than $2.5 million in 1937 for all the normal schools combined." Student to faculty ratios were as high as 21:1. Money for building maintenance and construction was woefully inadequate. In one regard, however, Geneseo stood out. Its library had twenty-four thousand volumes, "the most" of the Normal Schools.[13]

Geneseo and its sister schools vitally needed new buildings. Dr. Robert Redden, a 1939 graduate who returned to Geneseo as assistant dean in 1962, recalled that Old Main was essentially three "shabby" buildings. On a scale from one to ten, with ten high, he rated Old Main a one. In fact, he believed the condition of the buildings was a metaphor for the school generally. For example, the Holcomb School, the new campus school, had forty students per room. Fortunately, the state legislature had appropriated $475,000 for a new administration-classroom building in April 1934, and construction began in fall 1936.[14]

The proposed 288 by 72 foot, three-story building (four, including the basement)—ultimately the Sturges building—had been in the works for years. The "ground floor" (basement) was to house student and faculty lounges, a bookstore, a cafeteria seating 250 students (with an adjoining dining room for faculty), deans' offices, and student government rooms. The first floor was reserved for administrative offices and twelve classrooms. A soundproof speech clinic would share the second floor with an auditorium, four laboratory rooms, seven classrooms and two seminar rooms for education and social studies classes. Plans for the third floor included a seminar lounge, faculty offices and committee rooms, and a greenhouse with a skylight. The cornerstone laying on Friday, September 30, 1937, was a grand event. It was highlighted by the speech of Congressman and Local Board of Visitors President James W. Wadsworth, Jr. and musical selections by the Carol Choristers. Various items, including the fiftieth anniversary booklet of *The Lamron*, signatures of faculty members, and records from student organizations, were placed in the cornerstone.[15]

Construction of the administration building was only the beginning of a very ambitious program to upgrade Geneseo and the other Normals. Geneseo

The new classroom/administration building was formally dedicated in 1940. (Livingston County Historian)

was scheduled to add three more buildings by 1943. A library was planned to sit "on the site of the original plant," and an auditorium was to be located at the corner of Wadsworth and Bank streets. When these buildings were completed, the campus would have the traditional quadrangle. Finally, the walkway along "the ravine" (south of Sturges) would lead to a "future open-air theater and gymnasium." So much for aspirations. The Milne (renamed Fraser) Library and Wadsworth Auditorium did not materialize for another nineteen years (1955), and it was 1961 before Schrader gymnasium was built. However, $26,440 from the federal Works Progress Administration (WPA) assured graded athletic fields.[16]

Unfortunately, as noted, these and other sorely needed changes depended not only on the economy, but on New York State's politicians and the nearby community, which Geneseo's faculty were not allowed to forget. For example, Principal Welles instructed his faculty "to be nice to Senator Joseph Hanley from Perry." Welles also directed faculty and staff not to be seen on the village streets during school hours, for it was important to get along with those in the village, who, faculty were reminded, "paid their salaries." Dr. Hermann Cooper, whom one former Geneseo administrator likened to House of Representatives Speaker Sam Rayburn, even determined the number of students and faculty per Normal School

The sisters of Arethusa proudly displayed their insignia and sorority sweaters. (1938 Normalian)

per year based on the number of openings for teachers in the field, a tricky balancing act.[17]

While appeals for building updates were longstanding, the nature and intensity of demands for curriculum change were new. The principals and students wanted the Board of Regents to upgrade the Normal Schools to the status of teachers colleges. Students felt discriminated against because they were awarded diplomas rather than degrees, the norm for liberal arts colleges. (The principals, who shared their feelings, also may have been motivated in part by a desire for the more suitable title "president.") But the Regents dragged their feet, arguing that until the Normal Schools had adequate facilities (libraries, laboratories, and additional faculty) they would not be designated as teachers colleges nor be approved to award bachelor's degrees. The principals countered, how could they show adequate facilities without state funding? The best they could do was to prove that their standards were as rigorous as the state's liberal arts colleges purported to be.[18]

The Road to State Teachers Colleges: Tackling the Curriculum

Attaining the necessary rigor, at least the appearance thereof, would take some doing. Two members of Geneseo's faculty in the late 1930s recalled that though the students were "bright" and the school was considered one of the top state schools (below only Albany and Cortland), it was "still a glorified high school" with a "very primitive" curriculum. Beyond the teacher education courses, the students took two years of social studies (twelve credit hours), three years of English (eighteen credit hours), one year (six credit hours) of science (biology), a two-year sequence of "Liberal-Cultural" (ten credit hours), and six hours of electives. Also there may have been a semester of math "taught at a low level," though this does not appear in the 1938–1939 catalog.[19]

A big step, raising admission standards, had already been taken. By 1935, the Normal Schools required a "selective admissions test" at a prescribed test site, a "confidential statement" from the applicant's high school principal, interviews by at least two faculty members, and voice and diction tests. Five years later, forty percent of the applicants' total scores for admission was based on their high school Regents exams, thirty percent on their personal interviews (emphasizing "social adaptability, forcefulness, vitality, temperament, and the use of English") and the remaining thirty percent on their psychological, reading, and English test scores. (Still, on average Geneseo admitted seventy percent of its applicants in the 1930s—apparently reflecting the quotas established by Dr. Cooper's office.)[20]

1939 graduate Robert Redden would later become the College's dean for undergraduate instruction. (1939 *Normalian*)

Nevertheless, Dr. Paul Neureiter, whose first stint at Geneseo was during the 1937–1938 school year, recalled that the students—almost exclusively women—were "high caliber." They simply were unable to afford to attend private schools. The men, at best twenty-five, including future Geneseo dean of instruction, Robert Redden, were "of especially high quality." While students came to obtain teacher certification, some, including Redden, felt deprived of the professional opportunities liberal arts graduates enjoyed. Redden believed that Geneseo was hurt by its image as a women's finishing school. His lasting recall was the teas for which the female students were instructed to wear white gloves. In fact, he claimed a fair share of the women students were from upper-middle-class families, which he felt was borne out by the substantial sorority houses adjoining the campus. He also remembered that at least some of the classes he attended were "men-only," which he assumed was to minimize gender mixing.[21]

However, placement data support Neureiter's assessment that Geneseo's graduates were "high caliber." On December 3, 1940, *The Lamron* proclaimed that eighty-two percent of the August 1939 and January and June 1940 graduates had jobs—ten percent more than had been predicted. Of the thirty-six 1940 graduates who were not placed, six were married (which automatically disqualified women for teaching at the time) and five went on to graduate work. Greater than ninety percent of the graduates found jobs the following year when the defense industry began luring graduates at higher pay than teachers typically earned. Even earlier, a 1938 graduate went to work at General Motors in New York City for a salary of $2,800, more than double

Cothurnus members probably found casting a challenge when World War II left the campus with very few men. Cothurnus traces its roots to 1925, when the Dramatic Club reorganized under a new name. (1944 *Oh Ha Daih*)

COTHURNUS

the highest salaries of his contemporaries, which ranged from $760 (Conesus District No. 7) to $1,300 (Sag Harbor and Huntington, New York) per year. (Although the higher salaries were primarily on Long Island, a junior high school science position in Ripley, New York, near the Pennsylvania state line, carried a salary of $1,200.) School librarians, whose curriculum was already four years, typically drew salaries in the $1,100 to $1,300 range, though one graduate received $1,950 to serve as librarian and second grade teacher in Canandaigua.[22]

A dream of an administrative position (a principalship, later a superintendency) was realized by Ellis Hyde, '36, barely a year after he left Geneseo. A pacesetter, he was the first male to teach in Dansville's elementary school, which would eventually honor him by naming a school after him. He also may be remembered for the advice he offered others about dealing with a troublesome student, namely, "you're not meeting his needs." Over time, popular "Jimmy" Dietsche, Hyde's classmate, obtained a principalship and enjoyed similar faculty and student affection.[23]

In 1937, another requirement for graduation was initiated statewide: a two-part comprehensive examination (short answer and essay) to be prepared by each of the Normals' faculties. The students in the professional-technical and English sequences were to take the exam at the end of their three years. It followed a six-week seminar during which the students worked in small groups with faculty advisors writing term papers to be presented to their peers. The purpose of the exams, according to Dr. Clarence O. Lehman,

The 1937–1938 Faculty Council, which acted "as a benevolent parent" and advised the Student Council, consisted of (front, from left): Clarence Lehman, Lucy Harmon, John Parry, Principal Welles; (back): Mary Richardson, Lena Rogers, Herman Behrens, Clayton Mau, Guy Bailey, Frederick Holcomb, R. Leroy Countryman, and Garretta Seger. (1938 *Normalian*)

Geneseo's Director of Training, was to measure how well the students were "maintaining high scholastic standards."[24]

Another means to upgrade was the Office of Research and Extension, which was developed in 1934 to conduct research "to improve [faculty] instruction" and to create and oversee the off-campus teaching centers, where ultimately all "practice [student] teaching" was to be done. Professor of psychology from 1935 to 1952, Dr. Herman Behrens, a Kansan with a doctorate from Ohio State, directed the office. Ironically, the successful growth of off-campus teaching centers was the Regents' justification for abolishing seven positions in the Holcomb Practice School in 1941. While three positions were added to the Normal Department, it was still a net loss of four faculty.[25]

Tackling the Curriculum: "The Tacklers"

Efforts to improve faculty instruction were ongoing. From its humble beginnings, Geneseo sought the best faculty it could attract. But, good as the faculty were, and had been from the outset, luring quality candidates was a perennial problem. Employment at Geneseo in the 1930s, according to Paul Neureiter, was a "death warrant." That is, faculty could not go anywhere from Geneseo, which was still perceived as a second-rate women's school. Obvious exceptions were assistant education commissioner Hermann Cooper, Dr. Lehman, who in 1939 became president of Potsdam, and Dr. Royal Netzer, Director of Training, who assumed the presidency of Oneonta in 1951.

Overcoming that perception was difficult, even though by 1941 more than half of the faculty had doctorates, compared with just two (including Dr. Sturges) in 1915. By contrast, only three of twenty-seven Plattsburgh faculty members held doctorates in 1937. Geneseo's faculty, including Welles, enjoyed degrees from NYU (four), Cornell (three), Ohio State, Harvard, and the University of Iowa (two each), Columbia, Colorado and the University of Vienna.[26]

The Vienna graduate was Paul Neureiter, who distinguished himself from 1939 to well beyond his retirement at age seventy in 1966. (Approximately six years into retirement, he traveled with other faculty to various sites in the southern tier to teach extension courses. His offerings often proved the most popular then and again in the early 1980s when he taught two math classes on campus.) Then there was dean of students Lucy Harmon, who had a Ph.D. in English literature from New York University. She faced the formi-

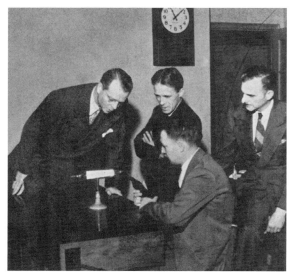

In the late 1940s, the science faculty included William Hamilton (seated), department head Robert Greene, Gerrard Megathlin, and Paul Neureiter. (1946 *Oh Ha Daih*)

dable task of replacing the seemingly irreplaceable Anne Blake when she arrived in 1934, and, in the eyes of many, she did. Robert Greene, a Cornellian along with geology professor Gerrard Megathlin, remained the most popular faculty member into the 1950s. Partly it was due to Greene's love of dramatics, even during science field trips. "Bugs, worms, and eats!" is the way a writer for *The Lamron* described one trip, referring to Greene's instructions to the students to taste some of their finds. "Sticktites on our clothes, burdocks in our hair—and mud on our dirty white shoes....We shudder, we rant, we protest—for a while...." A competitor for the students' and faculty's affection was Gaile Carbaugh, like Behrens, a native Kansan with an Ohio State doctorate, who came in 1937 and served in a variety of positions, including as campus school principal. (A lecture was named for him after his retirement in 1965.) Another newcomer was Louise Kuhl, a champion tennis player, who from 1941 until her untimely death in 1967 headed the health and physical education department and was acting academic dean three times. She was duly recognized in 1973, when Kuhl Gym was named for her.[27]

Some faculty members enjoyed reputations well beyond the campus. The most obvious was Guy Bailey, renowned photographer of birds, including a rare arctic sparrow, and co-author of a biology book. His orchards on what is now Stuyvesant Manor provided specimens for his classes as well as jobs for students at harvest time. Nor should we forget Hazel Hicks, who also taught summer school in the education division of the State School of Agriculture at Cornell. Harrison Phillips "was amazed at how smart" the faculty were compared to his high school teachers and how friendly they were. His favorites included music instructor Lucille Culver (his substitute "Mom"), "Miss" Mary Thomas, "Miss" Agnes Rigney, and, not surprisingly, "Mister" John Parry. (Apparently Phillips had a preference for the English faculty.)[28]

The special class (forerunner of special education) faculty included (seated, from left): department head Mary Boles, Gladys Rhodes, Lillian Hellmich; (standing): Mary Fernan, Josephine Palmer, R. Dudley Miller, and Helen Braem. (1946 *Oh Ha Daih*)

But strangely, the faculty did not wear caps and gowns—a tradition of virtually every college or university—to graduation until 1935.[29]

Despite a buyer's market, Dr. Welles struggled to attract individuals whom he felt would meet the standards for a teachers college faculty. For example he made a particularly determined effort to find a replacement for accomplished Library School head Mary Richardson in 1941. After repeated inquiries, he finally lured Neil Van Deusen from Fisk University in Nashville, Tennessee.

Longtime English faculty included (from left): J. Irene Smith, Mary Thomas, John Parry, and Lucy Harmon. (1946 *Oh Ha Daih*)

Unfortunately, Van Deusen, who held both a doctorate in teacher education and a master's degree in library science, died shortly after he came to Geneseo.

Tackling the Curriculum: Success a Long Time a'Comin'

Persuading the legislature and governor to elevate the Normals to teachers college status and to approve the awarding of bachelor's degrees remained a steep uphill climb. Had there been any doubt, the Regents' critical report in 1939 erased it. Except for Albany and Buffalo State, which offered bachelor's and master's degrees, New York State had "starved" the Normal Schools. The "legacy of inertia" continued.[30]

Those nine elementary education Normal Schools had reason to feel cheated. They had raised admission standards and imposed comprehensive examinations. Additionally, beginning in 1933–1934, students followed a four-year elementary curriculum, including the final year completed by means of extension courses and summer sessions. Along with the required academic coursework, students worked in the practice schools in the freshman and junior years, topped off by four days per week in student teaching the final year. Further, freshmen could opt for a two-year sequence of science or foreign language courses (French, Latin, or German, depending on the budget). In short, in terms of curriculum and admission policies the schools had met what they regarded as the Regents' and legislature's standards for teachers colleges.[31]

Future elementary school teachers were taught by primary department faculty (standing, from left) Ethel Ebrite, Bernice Stroetzel, Florence Nagle, and (seated) Elizabeth Rowles. (1946 *Oh Ha Daih*)

By 1940, Geneseo was partially there with approval to award Bachelor of Science degrees to graduates of its four-year library education curriculum. And the Regents had promised to recommend awarding bachelor's degrees to elementary education graduates of the four-year program. But it was only that, a recommendation to the legislature. Supportive of the desired change, in 1938 Perry's Senator Joseph Hanley sponsored the appropriate legislation, only to have it rejected by Governor Herbert Lehman.

Another legislative attempt failed a year later, despite all-out efforts by students who petitioned the legislature.[32]

Welles and his counterparts wondered what more they could do to justify their schools as teachers colleges. Geneseo had capped enrollment at five hundred students, implemented a program of selective admissions, offered a "well-balanced" four-year curriculum, hired as competent a faculty as it could afford, added two thousand books to Geneseo's library, provided a "well-equipped biology laboratory," and set a schedule for faculty ranks: professors (forty percent), assistants (twenty percent), and in-

Library department faculty included (from left): department head Neil Van Deusen, Alice Damon Rider, Frances Baker, Edna Vickers, C. Elta Van Norman, and Edna Lent. (1946 *Oh Ha Daih*)

structors (forty percent). Also, it had conducted more research and had provided more supervision of off-campus student teaching. The only reward was a statutory raise in salaries in 1939, including increasing salary ranges for "lowest grade" faculty from two thousand to twenty-four hundred and from twenty-four hundred to twenty-eight hundred. Another pressing need went unmet—the need for more faculty—which Dr. Welles duly emphasized in his report to the State Education Department in September 1939: "THIS MAKES A NET INCREASE OF TWO PROFESSIONAL POSITIONS IN THE NORMAL SCHOOL IN TWENTY YEARS" [capitalization in original].[33]

A break came in February 1942, when State Senator Benjamin Feinberg

The Library Club, organized in 1935, promoted books and library work, and sponsored lectures. The Kensett painting was restored and now hangs in the President's home. (1937 *Normalian*)

from Plattsburgh, a one-time teacher, introduced the third bill to convert the Normals to teachers colleges. Two months later the "Feinberg Law" was signed into law by Governor Lehman. Though the law was not effective until July 1, elementary education graduates received bachelor's degrees that June. Success had come after the schools and Regents had upped the ante. Henceforth, students would need to complete 128 credit hours of coursework. That consisted of seventy-seven hours of liberal arts courses, thirty-six of teacher education, and fifteen hours of electives. The liberal arts requirements were twenty-one hours each in English and social studies, eighteen hours of science and mathematics, eight credit hours of fine arts, three of practical or industrial arts, and six hours of hygiene and health. (If this arrangement sounds vaguely familiar to recent graduates, it should, for the balancing of credits between teacher education and liberal arts courses remains generally unchanged today.)[34]

Thus, Geneseo's letterheads now officially read "Geneseo State Teachers College." Fittingly, on Monday May 25, a celebratory dinner at the College

Holcomb School children enjoyed using tools to build useful objects in their manual arts class. (Hepler collection)

The 1942 Faculty Council comprised the principal and department heads (seated, from left): Lena Rogers, Lucy Harmon, Royal Netzer, Principal James Welles, Karl Hartzell, Louise Kuhl, Herman Behrens; (standing): Neil Van Deusen, Gaile Carbaugh, Frederick Holcomb, Joseph Saetveit, Clayton Mau, Robert Greene, and John Parry. (1942 *Normalian*)

was attended by assistant commissioner and former director of Geneseo's education department Dr. Hermann Cooper.[35]

Though elated by the school's transformation to a teachers college, Geneseo's students had to poke some fun by reminding their peers of some unintended consequences. For example, the titles of the yearbook and newspaper, the *Normalian* and *The Lamron* ("anagram for normal," students were reminded) would have to go. Geneseo's campus store, The Co-op, would have to rid itself of its "Normal" pennants, sweatshirts, and similar items. The school's office needed to order new stationery, forms, etc. The constitutions of the student government and the clubs would have to be reworked, the school's songs and cheers revised, and "dear old college" replace "grand old normal."[36]

On the other hand, obtaining accreditation by the venerable American Association of Teachers Colleges, which had visited Geneseo and the other former Normals, was an important recognition. Criteria included admissions and graduation standards, faculty preparation and teaching loads, capacity of the training school, courses taught, financial support, and faculty-student relationship. The efforts to upgrade paid off. Certainly, the time was right.[37]

The "Extra Curriculum"

The accreditation was based not only on the College's quality of instruction, but also on its sense of community. That sense began on students' "Sub-Frosh Day," a day of activities sponsored by the upper classes for incoming freshmen. Alumni of that time, like most of their counterparts today, regard their

Only the floor was left undecorated for this formal dance in Old Main's gym. (Bright collection)

alma mater as a "great place," but it is more than mere nostalgia. Many graduates of the 1930s remained connected long after graduating, thanks to *The Lamron*, which typically devoted two full-page columns or more to alumni news. Marion Higgins, '34, asserted that *The Lamron* "binds alumni to Geneseo Normal." (Maintaining that relationship, as well as strengthening future support for the College, might well have motivated Dr. Welles to formalize the various alumni groups into the Geneseo Alumni Association in 1942 and to incorporate it in January 1943. Annual giving through the Geneseo Foundation today confirms the value of maintaining alumni loyalty.)[38]

With approximately seven hundred students located downhill from the village's Main Street and a good stretch away from Rochester, the College was its own community. Even those commuting from as far away as Batavia (a sixth of the students in 1935 commuted) fully identified with the school. To their credit, despite their relative isolation, the students also were generally well informed. On a standardized Cooperative Contemporary Affairs Test administered by Dr. Behrens, Geneseo's freshmen obtained a median score of 77.11. The median score for freshmen at liberal arts colleges was only 63![39]

In part, the students' awareness of contemporary affairs was due to regularly scheduled events which ranged from symphonies, marionette shows (Dr. Greene's specialty), and the Vienna Boys Choir to informative lectures and talks. For example, over the years noted speakers included Booker T. Washington (1896), Carl Sandburg (1925), Robert Frost (1930), Vilhjalmur Stefansson (1935), Oswald Garrison Villard (1936), Clifton Fadiman (1937), and Bernard DeVoto (1938). Not all were appreciated, however. For example, one student found Dorothy Thompson, journalist, foreign correspondent, syndicated columnist, and then-wife of Sinclair Lewis, "fairly good, but rather boring." Carl Carmer, novelist-poet (and brother-in-law of Guy Bailey) who entertained a children's literature class in 1935, was better received. And in 1937 Normal Hall was sold out for the debate between Socialist presidential candidate Norman Thomas and conservative state assemblyman James Jeremiah Wadsworth, son of the local board president.[40]

Students also were doing their share of reading. According to freshman Helen (Williams) Rogers from Oakfield, the most popular books in 1935 were: Sinclair Lewis's *It Can't Happen Here*, Alexander Woollcott's *While Rome Burns*, Willa Cather's *Lucy Gayheart*, Anne Morrow Lindbergh's *North to the Orient*, and Lloyd C. Douglas's *Green Light*. And they knew the current slang, including "Detroit Disaster" (a Ford car), "Cup Cake" (an effeminate male), "Desert Horse" (a Camel cigarette), "Coffin Nail" (a cigarette), "Pop Quiz" (with which we are all familiar), and a gentle slam against faculty, "Forget Together" (a meeting of professors).[41]

An amateur pedicurist enjoyed a little fun at the expense of Minerva, the statue of the Roman goddess of wisdom, which resided in the library.

Many of New York's normal schools had statues of Minerva, Roman goddess of wisdom, and some of the original statues still exist. Geneseo's Minerva, shown here in Old Main's library, apparently was bulldozed into a ravine when the building was razed. (*The Lamron, 50th Anniversary*)

According to June Mitchell, *The Lamron* reporter, one spring morning in 1938 the "stolid and most conservative" Minerva sported "bright red toenails," administered with nail polish. While the paint job was hurried and the color in bad taste, at least Minerva had been spared eyebrow pencil, rouge, or lipstick. Who perpetrated the dastardly deed between 5:30 and 6:45 p.m. remained anonymous.[42]

It's very unlikely that the culprit was Martha Jane Countryman, daughter of Dr. Leroy Countryman, former dean of men. Dr. Welles had recommended her to Marie M. Duggan, who sought a nanny for Mrs. Nelson Rockefeller's children. The successful candidate had to have an "excellent personality," be willing to work, possess a "sense of humor," and express an "enthusiasm for children" for a salary of $150 a month (almost double most first-year teachers' pay). Whether Welles's flattering recommendation did the trick is unknown, but the fact that Welles was approached might well attest to the caliber of Geneseo's students.[43]

Geneseo's basketball team practiced and played in Old Main's gym, where metal cages protected the lights from shots that missed the baskets. (1940 *Normalian*)

However, Geneseo's basketball record paled by comparison with other students' accomplishments. In 1938, columnist Bill Ferriss of *The Lamron* was pained to write that "the most disastrous basketball season in the history of Geneseo Normal has come to its close....Defeat followed defeat." Despite "creditable showings" and admirable courage, the hoopmen were often "hopelessly" outclassed by physically superior teams. Not even the guidance of James Welch, a Geneseo native, varsity basketball player at St. Bonaventure, and future president of the Genesee Valley Bank and Trust Company, who had substituted for Coach Ira Wilson two years earlier, had helped. But all was not lost. Spring, with the "chirping of the birds," budding flowers, and Kelsey Field's green pastures would soon beckon the baseball team.[44]

Weekends were welcome, as they

are today. "The week-end, ah, the week-end. The flames of the light that guides us through the week; the source of renewed energy and faith; our Shangri La," wrote one of *The Lamron's* columnists in February 1941. With time to herself, she mapped out an ambitious weekend schedule of reading and checked out four library books. However, due to procrastination, she "accomplished nothing." By contrast, Lester "Let" Ferriss, a former contributor to *The Lamron*, had a very different recall of his weekends. In February 1943, then Lieutenant Ferriss, a flight instructor at Bainbridge, Georgia, remembered "dancing and coke [Coca Cola] drinking in a smoky Grill...mild flirtations and more serious love affairs...mad dashes down slippery Bank Street at 10:28 [to meet the curfew], wild but harmless fraternity parties...basketball games that were close but never won...All these and a million more are memories that will always keep Geneseo close to me."[45]

Main Street's Normal Grill was one of many popular student gathering places. (1940 *Normalian*)

While Ferriss made fun of the curfew, abiding by it was irksome at best. "'I am sick and tired of leaving Johnnie standing on the sidewalk in front of the house at 10:25 every Wednesday night while I make a frantic dash for the door because the sorority light went out as we ran down the street,' said an exasperated Senior." Worse, the housemother's clock was set "'by radio time,'" while the senior's watch was set "'by the town clock.'" This student's solution—unbelievably naïve to today's generation—was for dean of women Harmon to have the town clock or village fire department standardize the time![46]

The very notion of a curfew is as foreign to today's students as are rotary phones, phonographs, typewriters, and Nehi orange soda. Students had to be in their rooms by 10:30 on weeknights (retiring by 11:00) and by midnight on

Archery was a popular sport, and tournaments between women's teams were mentioned in several *Normalians*. (1934 *Normalian*)

weekends without prior approval. No men were allowed in women's boarding houses after 8:00 p.m., when "study" or "quiet hours" began. However, men were allowed on porches if they observed "proper conduct." Of course, resourceful students hatched endlessly creative schemes to circumvent the rules.[47]

War Clouds Darken the Horizon

In April 1939, historians Clayton Mau, Ira Wilson, and Benjamin J. Gault engaged in "one of the chief topics of discussion" at Geneseo at the time—the war clouds gathering over Europe. Mau viewed the situation in Europe as "ominous" and predicted that the U.S. would be drawn into a European war. Wilson believed that Hitler's aim, indeed Germany's since long before World War I, was to take Poland as a buffer, then grab Ukraine's and Romania's rich resources. He foresaw the "democracies" procrastinating for two more years. Although opposed to Hitler's persecution of the Jews, Gault supported Hitler's plans to "integrate central Europe economically." Realistically, Geneseo's students, including more than three-quarters of the men, believed that the U.S. would be drawn into the conflict, but opposed entering the war at this time.[48]

Of course, the U.S. entered the war after the devastating December 7, 1941 bombing of Pearl Harbor. Reluctantly, the government had been quietly planning for the likelihood, including instituting the first peacetime draft. On September 16, 1940, the Selective Training and Service Act, introduced into the House of Representatives by Congressman and Local Board of Visitors President James W. Wadsworth, Jr., was approved. A month later, 16,400 males age twenty-one to thirty-five were registered, with the first draftees selected October 29. Over a million troops and eight hundred thousand reserves were trained during the first year of operation. The program was extended for eighteen months the following August by the narrowest of margins in the House, 203-202. While Wadsworth asserted that "all good Americans love their country and are willing to make sacrifices for it," as his son, Reverdy, later did, nineteen draft-eligible males at Geneseo must have been less enthusiastic. They were not as fortunate as students in degree-granting colleges and universities who were deferred through the 1940–1941 school year. Geneseo was still a year away from being a degree-granting college.[49]

While some students joined the military, those on the home front helped the war effort through such activities as selling war bond stamps or sponsoring rummage sales. (Roemer House collection)

Thus began another trying period for Geneseo. Just when the school was about to win the battle to become a teachers college, its survival was at stake because of the loss of students due to the Selective Service Act ("the draft"). Best estimates are that close to 285 students and graduates, including seventy women, served in the military. At least eleven lost their lives. Apparently, the first Geneseo enlistee was Virginia Scott, class of 1938, who left her job at Bausch and Lomb in Rochester to join the WAACs. The first faculty member to enlist (in the WAVES) was Elsa Peacock, health and physical education instructor, to whom the College's 1943 yearbook was dedicated.[50]

Likely, the first to lose his life was Elwood "Fritz" Krisher, '40, from Conesus, who had enlisted July 17, 1941. In the January 16, 1942 issue of *The Lamron*, a photo showing his smiling face and familiar pilot's headgear

The 1943 *Oh Ha Daih* was dedicated to Ensign Elsa Peacock, who left her faculty position to enlist in the WAVES. (1943 *Oh Ha Daih*)

Frank McKibben, a "prominent senior" in 1939, was one of several Geneseo graduates killed in World War II. (1939 *Normalian*)

made the war seem a bit more real. Seven months, fifty flights, and one downed Japanese plane later, it was all too real. First Lieutenant Krisher of the 38th Fighter Squadron was reported missing near New Guinea.[51]

Another who brought the war home to Geneseoans was dark-haired Frank McKibben, '39, a recently married elementary school teacher. One of the "Prominent Seniors," McKibben had been editor of *The Lamron*, Junior Class treasurer, Phi Alpha Zeta fraternity president, Sigma Pi Sigma (academic honor society) member, and number 8 on the 1938–1939 basketball team. Pfc. McKibben, USMC, lost his life in the bloody 1944 Saipan campaign which resulted in 14,111 casualties (killed, wounded and missing). Sergeant William McDonald, an Army Air Force B-24 nose gunner who attended the 1942–1943 school year, went down with his plane on a flight over Linz, Austria in 1945, just weeks before the war in Europe ended. Ensign Clarence Van Der Wall, '39, was killed in action in the Pacific, while Lieutenant George A. Roffe, who had co-piloted a B-24 Liberator, was reported missing in 1943. Still another with a Geneseo connection was First Lt. Thomas Flynn, a US Army Air Force bombardier, who had attended the College during the 1936–1937 school year and was reported missing February 7, 1943. And Geneseo's Veterans of Foreign Wars post is named for Fred Totten, reported "missing in action" shortly after D-Day, 1944. Totten's maternal grandfather was once a College faculty member.[52]

Characteristic of the time, Harrison "Flops" Phillips, '42, who worked his way through school on his National Youth Administration pay, and his buddies Smith Higgins and Jack Goodale were in the military barely eight days after graduation. Higgins and Goodale, who would be in the first wave of landing crafts on D-Day, went into the Navy, Phillips the Army. Fortunately, the three survived the war, and Phillips served in Army Intelligence as regular army and as a civilian for over thirty years.[53]

The Struggle to Remain Open

Enrollment plummeted from a high of 723 in the 1935–1936 school year to 324 in 1943–1944, the modern-day nadir. Faculty jobs were on the line, so having naval and air cadets on campus beginning September 16, 1942 was a real blessing. The first program was the V-1 plan, whereby young men worked toward degrees while receiving two years' training to become naval officers.

The 1941–1942 brothers of Alpha Sigma Epsilon posed with their paddles. Faculty advisors included (back row, second from left through third from right): Dr. Behrens, Dr. Saetveit, Mr. Clark, Mr. Sunter, Dr. Netzer, and Dr. Van Deusen. Harrison "Flops" Phillips is second from left in the second row. (1942 *Normalian*)

The second program of ten-week on-campus classes was offered to Army Air Cadets who received flight training at the Dansville airport. Professors Neureiter, Hamilton, and Megathlin taught the cadets math, physics, and meteorology, while Ira Wilson offered an hour daily of physical training. The latter included calisthenics in the gymnasium beginning at 6:30 a.m. and (local legend has it) "a run around the block": up the hill to Center Street to Highland, down North, and back to the College via Main Street.[54]

Other wartime measures included finding room in Old Main for the county rationing board, which had expanded operations beyond its quarters at the courthouse. The College also rearranged students' schedules so they could help harvest or pack produce for civilian and military consumption. The students were equally committed to save the school in other ways: they formed a "War Council" that organized volunteers to serve as blackout wardens, to collect scrap metals to be melted down for armaments, and to assist the rationing board.[55]

It is hard today to imagine wartime rationing and its effects. It seemed everything was rationed: sugar, gasoline, and fuel oil (the latter resulted in many cold showers), car tires, shoes, meat, ad nauseam. On October 14, 1942, a coed spent three hours fruitlessly searching for her ration book which had

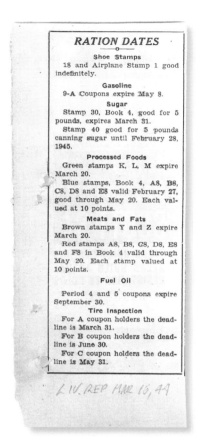

RATION DATES

Shoe Stamps

18 and Airplane Stamp 1 good indefinitely.

Gasoline

9-A Coupons expire May 8.

Sugar

Stamp 30, Book 4, good for 5 pounds, expires March 31.

Stamp 40 good for 5 pounds canning sugar until February 28, 1945.

Processed Foods

Green stamps K, L, M expire March 20.

Blue stamps, Book 4, A8, B8, C8, D8 and E8 valid February 27, good through May 20. Each valued at 10 points.

Meats and Fats

Brown stamps Y and Z expire March 20.

Red stamps A8, B8, C8, D8, E8 and F8 in Book 4 valid through May 20. Each stamp valued at 10 points.

Fuel Oil

Period 4 and 5 coupons expire September 30.

Tire Inspection

For A coupon holders the deadline is March 31.

For B coupon holders the deadline is June 30.

For C coupon holders the deadline is May 31.

L. IV. REP MAR 15, 44

Wartime rationing and shortages of consumer goods often made daily life a challenge. (*Livingston Republican* clipping, Hepler collection)

the valuable stamps entitling her to purchase scarce sugar. Twenty-four hours later she figured she would have to learn to drink sugar-less coffee. (Some substituted syrup for sugar in their coffee and on their cereal.) One night, a blackout (a common measure in war-ravaged England to reduce targets for enemy planes) ruined the co-ed's chance to make her first grand slam at bridge. But there was no joking about the empty chair at the Thanksgiving table, vacated by a loved one for whom the war had a more immediate impact. On the other hand, it is doubtful any applicants complained when the College dropped entrance examinations because of gas rationing.[56]

Yet, even during those war years, much remained the same on campus. There were lectures, student government meetings, horse-back riding, Halloween and Christmas parties, plays, and teas. And there was an evening's entertainment by the Trapp Family singers, led by the Baroness Maria Augusta von Trapp, the subject of the popular musical *The Sound of Music* decades later. The yearbook, which had borne various names, the most recent of which was the *Normalian*, would henceforth be called the *Oh Ha Daih*. Suggested by the Arethusa House to recognize the Native Americans who once lived here, the winning name received 170 votes to 48 for "Gen-O-Scroll" and twenty-five for "Genestate." Also breaking with tradition, just a short time earlier the venerable Delphic fraternity had become a chapter of a national, Alpha Sigma Epsilon.[57]

The war brought other, totally unexpected, events, including a Prisoner of War camp (ten prefabricated buildings) constructed in June 1945 close

Horseback riding was organized as a women's athletic activity in 1930 under the guidance of Captain Miller, riding instructor at the armory. (1934 *Normalian*)

to the Birdseye-Snyder canning factory near lower Court Street and Route 63. (Per contracts with the federal government, the prisoners provided necessary labor for Birdseye-Snyder.) The presence of the camp led to the inevitable. One coed taught a prisoner to use a slide rule (with Prussian-born math instructor Paul Neureiter translating), which evolved into their postwar marriage, and local lore has it that other young women took the POWs for car rides. Ted Bondi, a local boy, learned soccer well enough from the POWs to become a four-time All-American at SUNY Brockport, and Jack Hagen and other farmers contracted with the Livingston County Agricultural Cooperative Association for the prisoners' labor.[58]

The most bizarre incident of the period can be found in the *Livingston Republican's* lighthearted report of an invasion nearby. The gist of the account is that in February 1942, anywhere from a single "Jap" saboteur to more than one hundred parachutists had invaded Hunts Corners, south of the village. Evidence was, it turns out, only a red and black flag the Tennessee Valley Authority had planted to aid a topographical survey. Not surprisingly, alarm spread throughout the area. The article is worth reading in its entirety.[59]

However, there was nothing funny about the 1943 recommendation to

A prisoner of war camp was built in 1945 near a canning factory at the lower end of Court Street. (Bright collection)

transfer Geneseo's special education program to the State Teachers College at Buffalo. The local board's reaction was a given; it petitioned the state education department to oppose the move. Fortunately, nothing came of the recommendation, so the program remains within Geneseo's School of Education today, having achieved recognition many times over the years. Ironically, later Buffalo State lost its certification program.[60]

This World War II plaque honored the students and faculty members who served in the military. (1944 *Oh Ha Daih*)

Post-War Planning

Beginning in 1944, Dr. Welles and his peers were engulfed by post-war planning, which was accelerated by assistant commissioner Cooper's 1945 memorandum to the teachers college presidents alerting them to anticipate major capital construction outlays. Cooper and other higher education administrators throughout the nation were being asked to accommodate a heretofore unknown flood of students. (New York expected to enroll up to one hundred thousand veterans, which turned out to be a gross underestimate.)[61]

Like their counterparts all over the U.S., ex-artillery Captain Robert Redden; ex-Lt. and medic Steve Shepard; ex-First Lt. Corneil Balding, a radio engineer; ex-Captain Lynn Roberts, who had been awarded the Flying Cross for piloting B-25s; and others would return to Geneseo to obtain their bachelor's degrees, while ex-Lt. j.g. Elsa Peacock of the WAVES would temporarily resume her career as a physical education instructor at the College. The veterans were inspired in part by the G.I. Bill of Rights (Servicemen's Readjustment Act), passed by Congress in 1944. By providing up to four years' tuition, fees, books, and living expenses, it promised two things. First, it was to help meet the needs of as many as fifteen-and-a-half million veterans in an economy lacking jobs to accommodate anywhere near that number; second, it meant education for the masses. Schools of every type across the nation would have the unprecedented burden of trying to meet the veterans' educational needs. However, by 1949, when many veterans were about to graduate, Geneseo still had not experienced the expected flood of veterans, which is clearly illustrated by a photograph showing a bevy of females engulfing nineteen males.[62]

Campus planning also included what is now Wadsworth Auditorium (with practice rooms for the Music Department) on the site of Old Main, Milne (later Fraser) Library where it is presently and a gym where the Erwin building is today. (A planned field house was three decades from reality.) However, this would not create the lower quadrangle we know today, for the heating plant was to enclose the north side of the quadrangle, not what became the Blake dorms. Still, housing—make that safe housing—was a pressing need. (A sorority house fire at Cortland in November 1948 had caused the deaths of three and seriously injured another six girls.)[63]

Based on Dr. Welles's study of "living conditions," on April 29, 1944, the board of local visitors met to capitalize on the state legislature's recent

President Moench (right) entertained visiting SUNY executive dean for teacher education Hermann Cooper (left) and SUNY President Thomas Hamilton (third from left) along with College Council members George Newton, Kenneth Willard, Helen Mulcahy, C. Everett Shults, and Alice Benjamin. (Pretzer collection)

creation of the Dormitory Authority, which was empowered to construct and operate dormitories. At that special meeting the board petitioned Assistant Commissioner Cooper and State Senator Austin W. Erwin to "use their good offices" to finance a 150-student residence hall. Appealing to Erwin, who had played a part in authorizing the Dormitory Authority, was a natural. A Geneseo native, he had completed the Classical course at the Normal in 1909 and was the local Alumni Association president in 1925. Additionally, his Republican party controlled the senate and governor's office. The local board also was counting on newly appointed Judson Zimmer, a Union College graduate, president of the Fonda, Johnston, and Gloversville Railroad, and member of the Dormitory Authority.[64]

The specific location and arrangement for the dorms we have come to know was seven years in the doing. A student union (now Blake A) was to face the north end of the administration building. Uphill from the union in order would be residence halls labeled simply B, C, D, and E.

Zimmer reported that initially the Authority had denied Geneseo's petition, then approved it. However, including the student union in the plans had become an issue. The authority decided that a $225,000 student union had to be separated from the residence halls. Only dormitories could be paid from "student funds." The next snag to dormitory construction was obtaining options to buy property near the College for the dorms while maintaining secrecy, so the owners would not raise their sale prices. The optimal site was on Bank Street between Wadsworth and Elizabeth streets, with eight identified properties assessed at $28,700. The first seven options were obtained readily, but an apparent holdout forced the total price to $36,000. Worse, the whole matter seemed moot when the board met in February 1946. The state budget did not include funds for the actual purchases. Board members Zimmer and George Newton underscored the urgency of obtaining the money and the land if Geneseo was to be a successful recruiter. Should Brockport get dorms first, it would have a draw that Geneseo wouldn't.[65]

Concern about student enrollment occupied considerable board time beginning with its June 9, 1945 meeting. Dr. Welles reported that Brockport, Fredonia, and Geneseo had already "mapped out a cooperative program for recruiting students in Western New York." Each school had a "definite territory" for high school visits, starting west of a line running north and south through Geneva and Elmira. Not content, Geneseo also hired Rochester's Rumrill Advertising Agency to produce a pamphlet that was mailed to 4,500 New York State high school students along with three thousand calendars and one thousand souvenir memo books. Alumni association members and Geneseo's school-library graduates were contacted to solicit potential students, while Welles spent a week visiting "key" Long Island high schools. Additionally, on May 4, 1945, the College entertained approximately two hundred prospective students and parents from a fifty-mile radius (limited by "traffic regulations," likely gas rationing). However, there were only ninety-four applicants for the 1945–1946 school year.[66]

After submitting the annual report to the American Association of Teachers Colleges, Principal Welles announced his retirement, effective August 31, 1946. He felt "thirty-seven years of service in Public Education" (of which "thirty-two years have been continuous") was enough. Though he did not say it, twelve of those thirty-seven years (as Geneseo's principal) had been especially demanding. He had suffered extraordinarily lean budgets and had seen enrollments plunge. Nor would he be recognized for almost a quarter-century, when the practice school on Wadsworth Street was renamed the Welles Building to recognize his efforts to transform Geneseo into a teachers college.[67]

At any rate, beginning September 1, 1946, managing Geneseo State Teachers College would no longer be Principal Welles's responsibility; it would be his successor's, the College's first "President."

****

Clearly, this period will best be remembered for Geneseo's having remained open and functional during the depths of the Great Depression and through a catastrophic world war. Not even the deteriorating buildings, the devastating enrollment decline, rationing, and blackouts proved the College's undoing. Importantly too, Geneseo now had degree-granting status as a teachers college. The strengthened curriculum and a quality faculty were factors leading to legislative and gubernatorial support. Another plus was that Geneseo's graduates enjoyed better than expected job placements and, finally, the need for new buildings was acknowledged by Albany. Much still needed to be done, but real progress had been made under Dr. Welles's leadership.

Architect James Gamble Rogers completed designs for new campus buildings in the early 1940s, but World War II delayed construction. Rogers planned an especially ornate Wadsworth Street entrance to the quadrangle that would be formed by the new buildings, with an auditorium on the left of the entryway and a gymnasium on the right. (Milne Archives)

Rogers's aerial view looking south shows three buildings on the site of Old Main: an auditorium, a library between the auditorium and Sturges, and a gymnasium where the Erwin administration building was eventually constructed. The plan also included a decorative Bank Street entrance and a new heating plant. (Milne Archives)

Rogers's planned auditorium and library were built in slightly different form in 1955. The planned gymnasium was scrapped; instead, a new design was created for a site farther downhill, and Schrader Gymnasium opened in 1961. (Roemer House collection)

Rogers's drawing of the southeast corner of the new quadrangle showed the rear view of the planned gymnasium, Wadsworth Street entrance, and auditorium, along with the east end of the library. (Milne Archives)

Right: When the Milne (later Fraser) Library was finally built in 1955, it had a less practical flat roof and only a single arch in the connection to Sturges. The Bank Street entryway was never built, since the new dormitories and College Center (Blake buildings) were built in that location in the early 1950s. (Milne Archives)

Left: Rogers planned a heating plant near the north end of Sturges, roughly where the gazebo stands today. The switchback walkway going down the hill would have been a less direct but less steep route than today's "Cardiac Hill." (Milne Archives)

Chapter Six

tate University of New York

TEACHERS COLLEGE *at* GENESEO

•

The Transition Begins (1946–1963)

The World War II veterans that Tom Brokaw labeled the "Greatest Generation" were returning home, but questions persisted over how to provide housing, jobs, and schooling for them (and to stave off a depression). There was an especially urgent need for colleges and universities to accommodate an influx of veterans expected to attend school under the G.I. Bill (formally, the Servicemen's Readjustment Act of 1944). However, New York's public higher education continued to suffer from the "legacy of inertia" that had proved so disadvantageous over the years. In fact, it was more than inertia; it was benign neglect. With the possible exceptions of Albany and Buffalo State, the teachers colleges were still "poor cousins" to New York's private colleges and universities, with which the Normals were never intended to compete. Designating the Normals as teachers colleges was regarded by many as simply a name change. Even so, the change had been opposed by Albany and Buffalo State, the only previously designated state teachers colleges, and by private schools, especially Columbia University, Syracuse, and Cornell. Cornell, with its state contract colleges, had long benefited from a vigorous lobby and strong contingent of alumni in the state legislature.

Opposite Page: In the late 1950s, business was booming in many Main Street establishments: the Campus Dairy Bar, Geneseo Hardware, Red and White and Market Basket groceries, and the Hotel Geneseo. ("Geneseo" pamphlet, photos by R.I.T. class of 1957)

In 1959, the east side of Main Street was dominated by Minckler Drugs, Folts Jeweler, McDonald's Clothing, and the Hotel Geneseo, some of which later burned. (1959 *Oh Ha Daih*)

Herbert Espy, the first to hold the title of president, served from 1946 to 1952. (Livingston County Historian)

While the state might have been neglecting its teachers colleges, long-serving assistant commissioner of education (and former Geneseo faculty member) Hermann Cooper was not. Case in point: someone privy to the local board of visitors informed outgoing Principal Welles that Cooper had met with the board's executive committee on February 9, 1946, to explain its role in selecting Geneseo's next chief administrator: "The Comm[issioner of Education] must approve and the Regents appoint." However, Cooper "offered to do some 'scouting' if necessary." The informant also wrote that Cooper "has men of the required fitness," whose names he would send to the board for interviews. But the assistant commissioner also warned that "an acting president would be appointed should September 1 find the position unfilled," a reminder of how Winfield Holcomb became Geneseo's principal in 1922.[1]

However it came to pass, fifty-year-old Dr. Herbert G. Espy was appointed president of Geneseo State Teachers College effective September 1, 1946. He came with impressive credentials—an A.B. from Occidental College, Ed.D from Harvard with a dissertation examining liberal arts curriculums, assistant professor at the University of Rochester, staff education officer under General Douglas MacArthur, and chairman of Western Reserve University's division of education. However, he was not prepared for vitally needed, but seemingly unobtainable, changes.[2]

"The Facilities…Are Obsolete, Unattractive, Unsafe, and Inefficient"

Sadly, Espy, Geneseo's first "president," wasn't even installed as such, a tribute that all but one of his successors enjoyed. (Edward Jakubauskas, who decided the expense was too great for the time, also was not formally installed.) Worse, Espy had to deal with low enrollment, housing shortage, building demolitions, woeful facilities, and faculty recruitment. So, it is not surprising that his was the shortest tenure of any of Geneseo's first five full-time school heads.

Complaints in annual reports from 1946 through 1952 seem repetitive. In 1949, for example, President Espy wrote, "The auditorium, the library, the facilities for health and physical recreation, the offices, the conference rooms [*et al.*]…are obsolete, unattractive, unsafe, and inefficient. Because they were condemned before the war, these structures have not even had the repairs, which would have preserved them in their former state of dilapidation. Time, use, and the elements have brought these old structures to a very shabby, worn-out, useless state."[3]

The only "satisfactory remedy," Espy concluded, "is their elimination and replacement." Espy was not exaggerating. At the time Geneseo "had props up in the halls holding the ceilings up," according to Charles Foster, State University of New York's first vice chancellor for business. Poking fun at Old

In the early 1950s, faculty parking was conveniently located on the quadrangle. The old heating plant at the left was razed to make way for the new library (now Fraser). (1997 *Oh Ha Daih*)

141

In the late 1940s, people attending Artist Series programs in Old Main walked past beams that shored up the ceilings. Dr. Paul Neureiter is on the right. (*Old Buildings at Geneseo State Teachers College*, 1948, Hepler collection)

Main, *The Lamron* recalled "the musty odor that is part of the library…the pools of water that accumulate on the second floor in the spring and fall and most of the time in between those two seasons… the bucket…put up on the second floor to catch the drip…the top floor of Old Main where the plaster has departed from the walls and the floor boards have separated…." (Ironically, the destructive fires at Geneseo's sister schools may have been a blessing in disguise, for they led to new buildings.) Of course, razing Old Main meant that from September 1951 to October 1955 virtually everything had to be concentrated in the administration-classroom building, an even greater inconvenience. For example, "a human book brigade" of faculty and students formed in groups of hundreds to move books from Old Main to the administration-classroom building and a few years later to the new library.[4]

Valley Hall An Expedient

Valley Hall may well symbolize President Espy's era. In his report deploring the physical plant, Espy lauded the new "temporary dormitory" ("Valley Hall" to the students). In fact, he proclaimed that it "has also been successful beyond all expectations. In spite of meager space and very modest comforts the students living in the dormitory have had a very successful year." But, in a classic case of understatement, he confessed that credit was due to "the cooperation among all the interested groups." A former administrator rather sheepishly admitted that he did not want to remember the building and confessed that the administration at the time was "eager to get it down."[5]

Located behind the administration-classroom building—approximately where the MacVittie College Union is now—the "temporary dormitory" was accessible by a long, sloping walk that was very slippery in the winter. It was simply a long, tan-colored, one-story, army surplus barrack, which housed a "house mother," more formally "social director," eleven upperclassmen

advisors ("big sisters"), and seventy-seven freshman "girls" in eleven rooms separated by a middle room, labeled a "lounge." Each room was furnished with four bunk beds, four end tables, four dressers, and a large table in the center of the room. Sharing was the name of the game, including a bathroom for the eight roommates and a wardrobe, not a closet, wherein one roomer's clothes were on top, the other's on the bottom. Elizabeth Horek (Anderson), '50, who served as Room 3 advisor, attested to the spartan conditions when she assumed that there were eight chairs per room, "although I'm not sure about that."[6]

Associate Dean Rosalind Fisher claimed that the College "stacked students like cord wood." Yet, looking back some fifty years, some of the Valley Hall dwellers fondly recalled their stay there. For example, on the walkway leading to the McClellan House on Main Street there is a brick inscribed: "1948, Room 3, Valley Hall," memorializing those dwellers.[7]

Fortunately, Geneseo's students, such as the Valley Hall residents, generally took things in stride. Two contemporaries of the Valley Hall coeds admitted that the condition of the campus really didn't faze them all that much: "We didn't know any better." College life was new to them and this was post-war, post-Depression, so they pretty much accepted what they were given. That included living on the top floor of the administration-classroom building, to which Lois Ann Klehamer, '53, was assigned, and for which she paid $160 per year.[8]

It may well be that many of the students in this era were, in Dr. Walter

By 1961, the new library (now Fraser) was becoming crowded, as shown by the bookshelves wedged between the window and doorway. The staff included (from left): Miss Altmeyer, Mrs. Bancroft, Miss Glasgow, Mrs. Egan, Mr. Patall, Miss Fedder, director Dr. Eberhardt, and Mrs. LaVerdi. (1961 *Oh Ha Daih*)

The temporary Valley Hall dormitory, located just north of the heating plant, provided no-frills housing to female students whose fond memories moved them to dedicate a McClellan House brick in its honor. The building also served briefly as an infirmary. (Milne Archives; inset Wayne Mahood)

Harding's words, "provincial." (Harding had just come from a teaching stint at the University of Virginia.) To make his case, he might have cited *The Lamron's* failure to mention the Soviet Union's launching of Sputnik in October 1957, an event that caused considerable consternation in the U.S. As good as some of the faculty and students were ("a nucleus of good, even superior, students," per Harding), they suffered by comparison with many private school faculty and students then, as well as with today's students. [9]

Replying to Espy's plea for help, Cooper wrote that he was "not too pessimistic about the future of the teachers colleges...Steps have already been approved" to remedy the situation. "Unfortunately [too many persons think] it is buildings, attractive campuses, and good athletic teams that make a college." Cooper went on to assure Espy that it would be easier to recruit students and faculty when Geneseo "gets its new [physical] plant and its dormitory."[10]

Espy was not so easily persuaded. Responding almost immediately, he also lamented the low salaries and lack of promotions which were chasing away current faculty and likely candidates. Again, Cooper's response was to allude to some major changes that were forthcoming, though it is unlikely that he could have predicted how extraordinary those changes would be.[11]

Between the time Old Main was razed and Schrader gymnasium opened, physical education faculty had to be creative in finding places to hold class. Myrtle Merritt led two class groups simultaneously on Elizabeth Street, roughly in the area between today's Steuben and Livingston residence halls. Valley Hall and the heating plant are in the background. (Bright collection)

The Creation of the State University of New York

Changes were inevitable, given the turmoil that characterized the period from 1943 to 1947. Existing facilities in higher education throughout the nation could not accommodate the dramatic projected post-war enrollment increase. Yet, the timing represented an unprecedented opportunity to expand and to move in new directions. That opportunity became the creation of the State University of New York, a long, convoluted story for which a brief summary must suffice.

The 1959–1960 English department included (from left): Hans Gottschalk, Rosalind Fisher, James Scholes, Lucy Harmon, Walter Harding, Emanuel Mussman, Gerald Smith, Rose Bachem (later Alent), William Orwen, and J. Irene Smith. (1960 *Oh Ha Daih*)

The State University of New York, created in 1948, moved its headquarters to Albany's former Delaware and Hudson Railroad, *Albany Journal*, and Old Federal Building complex in 1978. The building was a copy of the Cloth Guild Hall in Ypres, Belgium. (State University of New York, *The News*, September 1978)

In his annual message to the legislature on January 9, 1946, Governor Thomas E. Dewey cited the need for a state university "to equalize opportunities throughout the State…." (Dewey not only anticipated a run for the presidency against incumbent Harry Truman, who had already indicated his support for extended higher education, he was being pressured to do something for veterans wanting jobs and schooling.)[12]

However vaguely stated, Dewey's goal for the state's higher education addressed a potentially divisive problem for New York State. Syracuse University Chancellor William P. Tolley probably spoke not only for himself but for other private university presidents and many of the state's Regents when he warned against any new state schools "becoming permanent," because he did "not want an embryo of a state university." Paradoxically, the legislative outcome was the creation of what has become the largest state university system.[13]

Less than a month after his address to the legislature, Dewey created the New York State Temporary Commission on the Need for a State University, which was chaired by former General Electric chairman and Regent, Owen D. Young. In announcing the commission, Governor Dewey focused attention on some of the state's public higher education problems. First and foremost, the private colleges and universities could not accommodate the post-war veterans, however much they might want to keep them away from the public schools. Second, downstate legislators (New York City and Long Island particularly) wanted universities and colleges for their constituencies because they would generate considerable business. Third, Dewey promised to fulfill the historic desire, not always articulated, to have a "people's university" with access to all, not unlike Midwestern land grant colleges. A problem conveniently brushed under the rug was whether this was to be a centralized or decentralized university, leading to a debate that surfaced later. The immediate issue, a statewide system, was resolved by retaining the state's local colleges, but not without some bruising battles in the legislature and behind the scenes. Clearly, this new entity was "to supplement, not supplant" New York's private higher education, a refrain repeated endlessly over the years.[14]

The New York State legislature passed the bill authorizing the State University of New York in mid-March 1948, Governor Dewey signed it into law April 4, 1948, and SUNY's first president, Dr. Alvin C. Eurich, was appointed January 1, 1949. Observers questioned whether this new entity would ever get off the ground. It was a "hodgepodge." Individuals invited to join SUNY were warned by friends not to touch it with a ten-foot pole; it was a dead end, reputedly reflecting Governor Dewey's true feelings. Before being moved to the state capitol later that year, SUNY Central offices were in the basement of the state education building. It was so bad that Charles Foster, the first vice chancellor for business, recalled that his "office was a table and pull-chain light under the stairs" leading up to the second floor. Worse, he had to walk through the office of President Eurich to get to his table.[15]

After serving as U.S. Army paymaster during the Nuremburg trials, Howard Erwin was appointed financial secretary in 1953 and controlled the College's finances for many years before serving as personnel director. (1959 *Oh Ha Daih*)

One of the first challenges to the new university system resulted from the Trustees' initial budget request. The Trustees sought $10 million for the medical schools, four-year colleges, and graduate and research facilities, and $2 million for community colleges, with a subsequent five-year projection (1949–1954) of $67.5 million. The antagonistic Regents immediately attacked the powers of the Trustees. Using his considerable influence, Governor Dewey persuaded the Republicans, who generally opposed any dilution of the private schools' responsibilities for higher education, to pass a budget. Thus, the teachers colleges could address the prewar recommendations for improvement. Although the new university would flounder for some time, it was believed to have the potential for excellence.[16]

For much of the mid-twentieth century, the Wadsworth Memorial Fountain, a former horse watering trough, served as a traffic control device complete with signs and flashing lights. (Roemer House collection)

Favoring New York's teachers colleges was a report that its students had been found "notably superior" on a test administered to students at seventeen unidentified teachers colleges with selective admission policies. But the schools themselves, including Geneseo, fared poorly compared to "better teachers colleges" out of state in terms of student housing, libraries, and professional preparation. To improve, New York's public colleges had to specify duties, selection, and promotion criteria and a retirement plan for faculty and staff. More student housing, too, was a must. The Postwar Public Works Planning Commission had allotted planning money to the newly-created Dormitory Authority. Now the Authority had to act. Meanwhile, Cooper reminded the teachers colleges' presidents that curriculum was more than courses. The colleges had to "play a much larger role" in developing their curricula to meet students' needs. Finally, faculty-student ratios had to be reduced from 1:26 to 1:15 to approximate the ratios at the private liberal arts and science colleges.[17]

How Would Geneseo Benefit?

Though Espy knew Cooper was the teachers colleges' most ardent supporter, he must have wanted to say "Show me the money!" For example, an additional 600 beds and 450 dining room seats would be needed by 1963 to accommodate a projected 1,150 students. Until dorms were built, the College's disapproval

Freshmen T. Pierce, B. Carls, R. Dalton, and K. Schussele wore their beanies while shopping for textbooks and supplies in the Student Co-Op. (1961 *Oh Ha Daih*)

Group photographs of the entire maintenance staff are rare. Shown here are (seated, from left): Tony Jacuzzo, Joe Least, Thomas Bovill, Louis Least; (standing): Howard Tuttle, Carroll DeMocker, Joseph Bovill, John Kyle, Homer Wilcox, and Archie McCurdy. (1950 *Oh Ha Daih*)

of any off-campus boarding houses, however inadequate or fire-prone, would exacerbate the problem. Repainting war surplus beds gray or brown, sewing muslin curtains (faculty wives' contributions), and converting rooms in Old Main, the administration-classroom building, and one of the private homes would make ninety-six students more comfortable, but that was not the solution either.[18]

Construction of new facilities was long overdue. In his annual report for 1950–1951 Espy recalled that "the necessary authorizations and the budget allocations for the library and the auditorium were made many, many months ago." In fact, plans for those buildings as well as a gymnasium had been approved in 1944, seven years earlier. The Trustees needed to "insure immediate action," Espy asserted. Inadequate facilities only compounded the "uncertainties," including the Korean War (and inflation, Espy could have added), which portended another drop in male students and faculty. Additionally, the mid-year departure of Dr. Royal Netzer to take the helm at Oneonta had left the College with an acting dean and director of training. Then, as Espy claimed in his annual report, new faculty "simply refuse to move here" because of lack of housing, while current faculty complained about heavy workloads and low pay.[19]

However, in 1951, Espy had some good news: the College had awarded its first master's degrees to library education graduates, had been authorized to offer a speech and dramatic arts specialization, and had seen its enrollment

From Old Main's 1951 razing until the opening of Schrader gymnasium, the College's basketball team played in the high school (now Doty) gym. (Bright collection)

pick up. With a total of 680 undergraduates, excluding summer school, Geneseo had experienced a 122 percent gain over the low point of 324 in 1943. Freshman enrollment alone was up 79 students over the previous year's class, with the male enrollment almost doubling.[20]

Two of those males in the early 1950s, James Thomas "Tom" Conlon and Robert Meyer, were not only successful athletes but successful faculty later. Another, Fred Brown, '55, would make his mark as a soccer player, teacher, and businessman. Conlon, '52, a Mt. Morris native and 1952 Winter Carnival King, once scored fifteen points in a basketball game against Utica College. Meyer, '53, a "lanky, right-handed hurler from Wellsville," got shelled in his first stint as a pitcher, but in a two-week period the next season he pitched a seven-hit win over Rochester's School of Commerce and a six-hit victory over Roberts Wesleyan. Meyer also excelled as a halfback on the soccer team.[21]

Both Conlon and Meyer returned to their alma mater in the 1960s. Conlon was a campus school teacher before heading the student teaching office and retiring in 1991. Meyer was a mainstay in the special education department until his 1992 retirement.

The third student-athlete was Avon's Brown, an elementary education

major, outstanding basketball player, and member of Geneseo's 1954 undefeated soccer team. In 1980, he was named to Geneseo's Sports Hall of Fame. In 2003, he received the Geneseo Foundation's Meritorious Service Award, and two years later, a half-century after graduating, he was inducted into the prestigious Society of Old Main.

Part of the athletes' successes must be attributed to Dr. Frank Akers, who had just replaced Morton Thau, who, in turn, had briefly replaced Ira Wilson as a physical education instructor. Shortly, the twenty-nine-year-old Akers, who had played in the Brooklyn Dodgers farm system before and after his military service, made the first page of *The Lamron's* June 1, 1951 issue. The editors were "intoxicated with joy, pride, and admiration" over Akers's success as a soccer, basketball, and baseball coach.[22]

Mention of Morton Thau irresistibly leads to Dr. Wilbur Wright's recall that at one time physical education faculty names read like a weather report: Kuhl (Louise), Snow (Barbara) and Thau (Morton).

However, there was nothing humorous about threats to the College resulting from an enrollment decline. After a steady rise, in 1953, enrollment dropped nearly ten percent. President Espy, the faculty, and the students again feared that Geneseo, the smallest of SUNY's teachers colleges, might be closed. Barely five years earlier, a state commission had recommended cutting the eleven colleges to five or six while enlarging the others. (A state college was to be established in Rochester to replace Geneseo and Brockport.)

Frank Akers's 1954 soccer team included several Korean War veterans and went undefeated, ranking third in the state with seven wins and one tie. (Roemer House Collection)

Wilbur H. Wright joined the College in 1949 and served in a variety of administrative and teaching posts until his 1977 retirement. (1959 *Oh Ha Daih*)

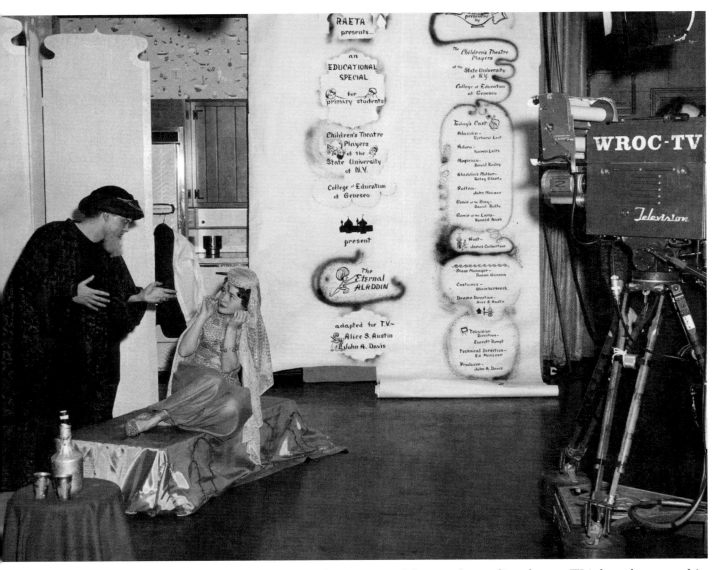

In the mid-1960s, Rochester's educational television station RAETA (now WXXI) aired Alice Austin's Children's Theatre Players' production of *The Eternal Aladdin.* (Milne Archives)

Fortunately nothing came of that or the earlier threat. Wright, who served in a variety of roles at Geneseo between 1949 and 1977, credited State Senator Austin Erwin, College Council chairman from 1954 to 1957, with saving the College. A brief digression is in order to tell the story.[23]

As chairman of the state Senate Finance Committee, "the most powerful committee in either house of the legislature," Erwin apparently used his clout. Likely, he was helped by Mark Welch, a local lawyer and chief counsel to the senate majority leader, and possibly by Hermann Cooper. Erwin, who completed the Normal's classical course in 1909 and who gave his name to Geneseo's present administration building, is also credited with securing money to build Schrader gymnasium. Reputedly, in 1957 he insisted that a gymnasium for Geneseo had to come out of a $250 million bond issue SUNY wanted to float.[24]

That is only part of the story, of course. Selling Proposition 1 of the bond issue (for capital improvement of the SUNY units) required a huge commitment across the state, including at Geneseo. In 1957, newly installed President Francis Moench and faculty members were expected to deliver the message throughout the valley, and school-community committees were expected to raise almost three thousand dollars to campaign for approval. Moench first had to sell the faculty and students by trumpeting how Geneseo would benefit. The main addition would be a new health and physical education building with a twelve-hundred-seat capacity gym, swimming pool, four bowling alleys, squash and handball courts, and a dance studio. More residence halls for six hundred students and a dining hall seating two hundred were also part of the plans. President Moench also hoped that there would be money to build a new campus school and convert the Holcomb School into College classrooms. (It was another dozen years before the latter was realized.) Dr. Paul Hepler, a new art department faculty member at the time, attributes the success of the bond issue in part to Bertha Lederer, the art department head who directed him and the students to create "big signs" to post all over the village—virtually overnight. In 1981, Lederer was honored for her thirty-five years of service when the art gallery in Brodie Hall was named for her.[25]

Proposition 1 of the bond issue passed by an almost two-to-one majority, which was reflected in the vote in the immediate Geneseo area. Dr. Moench was quick to thank the community on behalf of the College Citizens' Committee, the faculty and the students.[26]

But this lay ahead. Dr. Espy was still struggling just to keep the College going. In fact, when he must have wondered what else could go wrong, he lost the services of longtime chairman of the local board, James W. Wadsworth, Jr.

In 1981 (from left) Paul Hepler, Alice Austin, architect Edgar Tafel, Bertha Lederer, and President Jakubauskas celebrated the renaming of the Brodie Fine Arts Gallery in honor of Lederer. (Hepler collection)

Wadsworth officially retired from public life on December 31, 1951, when he was honored by over 850 persons who attended a testimonial dinner. (He died just over six months later, and his son Reverdy took his place, maintaining the Wadsworth connection to the College, though the son would not prove to have his father's influence or longevity).[27]

Then Espy was hit with two state mandates that had a more immediate impact. The first was a ruling by the Anti-Discrimination Commission barring the use of photographs by applicants for teaching positions. Espy's response to Hermann Cooper revealed a delightful sense of humor: "Hermann, I can almost believe that the Lord has decided He doesn't like public education or that He doesn't want it to be at all attractive. For my own part I have never thought it made very much difference whether high-school teachers were ugly or beautiful and I have always hoped that it didn't make any difference whether college professors and presidents were ugly as the dickens to look at. But I have sincerely believed that kindergarten teachers ought to be beautiful." If Cooper could do nothing to change the ruling, Espy would. "By golly, when I go to the synagogue on the Sabbath I am going to cry out to Javeh [sic] to appoint an Anti-damn-foolishness Commission."[28]

The second mandate was even less to his liking. Teachers college advocate Senator Benjamin Feinberg dropped a bomb when his Anti-Communism bill became law in 1949. It called for the "disqualification and removal of school employees who advocate the overthrow of the government by any means." This included those who belonged to any organization found by the Regents to "advocate, advise, teach, or embrace the doctrine that the government should be overthrown by force or violence." Membership in any such organization

Art professor Leonard Barkin advised the Hillel Club, founded in 1952. The group held services every Friday night in St. Michael's Episcopal Church chapel. (1960 *Oh Ha Daih*)

was "prima facie evidence" of guilt. To be employed, faculty and staff of New York's public schools had to sign an oath that they did not belong to a subversive organization.[29]

As it was after World War I, the nation was caught up in another "Red Scare," stemming from what businessman-statesman Bernard Baruch labeled a "Cold War." The law's rationale was that public agencies offered perfect avenues to undermine the United States. Subversives had to be rooted out. Strangely, there appears to have been little or no discussion of the law or its effects at Geneseo, though the law was challenged in the courts and struck down by the United States Supreme Court in 1967.

Some Good News for Geneseo

Although President Espy rightly railed against the problems facing Geneseo, he enjoyed some minor successes. Yes, he lost Dr. Herman Behrens, his number two man, who followed Dr. Netzer to Oneonta. Also he saw Barbara Frey, a Geneseo graduate and campus school teacher, move to Buffalo State where she enjoyed a long, successful career. However, he was able to lure a number of faculty who would play key roles well into the future, including Dr. Hardy Wahlgren, who came in 1948 and helped establish the psychology department. Dr. Myrtle Merritt, an Iowan who arrived in 1952, held a number of College and statewide offices and was a major College benefactor, for which she was finally recognized when the Alumni Field House was named for her in 2004. Dr. Gerald Saddlemire, who came in 1953, was dean of students

In 1949–1950 the education faculty were (standing, from left): Wilbur Wright, Bess Johnson, Bruce Moore, Helen Glynn, Gaile Carbaugh; (seated): Hardy Wahlgren, Hazelle Berkness, Herman Behrens, Helen Boyd, Gladys Rhodes. (1950 *Oh Ha Daih*)

for years. Dr. Stanley Rutherford, hired that same year in the new speech and dramatics department, retired as speech communication department chairman more than twenty-five years later. Dr. Loren Woolston, who preferred to be called "Doc," came from Rochester's Madison High School to teach in the social studies department along with Richard Howe, who held a master's degree from Western Reserve.

Another big catch was Rosalind Fisher, "a vivacious person, with a quick smile and a ready wit," who, of course, was author of the College's centennial history, *…the stone strength of the past…*. Fisher, who arrived in 1950, had a big job replacing—if anyone could—Dr. Lucy Harmon. Harmon was "one of the real characters here," Dr. Walter Harding, a future star at the College,

In 1959, the social studies faculty included (seated, from left): department chair Martin Fausold, Kathryn Beck, Ira Wilson; (standing): William Derby, Philip Johnson, Richard Howe, and Loren Woolston. (1959 *Oh Ha Daih*)

recalled. "A colorful old gal…[Harmon] loved to dress in purple, purple hat, purple coat, purple dresses, anything so long as it was purple." Imperious, she forbade coeds to wear red for fear of exciting male students. But Miss Fisher, who came with a khaki field jacket bearing service insignia from U.S., British, and Canadian servicemen whom she had met as a program director for the Red Cross in England during World War II, immediately established herself in her own right. Her nine years as associate dean before joining the English department full time were marked by some major changes at the College, including opening the new residence halls in 1951, which she handled admirably.[30]

Others who came at this time include Ms. B. J. Keller, publications and

English, Dr. Kenneth Riesch, director of elementary education, Dr. Gerald Smith, English, and Dr. Kathryn Beck, history. Robert Sinclair, who arrived in 1950, not only was "a hell raiser," he had an immense influence on the school's culture with the plays he presented. His productions were "fantastic dramas, phenomenal shows," a faculty member recalled decades later.

Groundwork for Sinclair had been laid by Geneseo's speech and drama pioneer Alice Austin and by an underreported event in March prior to Sinclair's arrival. Miss Austin, President Espy, Paul Neureiter, English professor Mary Thomas, library school director Harold O'Neal, and students Joan Mark and Robert Hall (one of the outstanding seniors) had founded the Geneseo Community Players. It debuted with Robert Sherwood's *There Shall Be No Night*, with the retiring Dr. Robert Greene and longtime Board of Visitors member Mrs. W. A. Wadsworth in the cast. Of course, the consummate Cothurnus remained the primary source of on-campus plays, readings, and workshops, including putting on *Bell, Book and Candle* in November 1954.[31]

In 1952, Espy also derived satisfaction from receiving the College's first accreditation by the venerable Middle States Association, from achieving approval to offer the M.S. in Library Science certifying public librarians, and from awarding the College's first Distinguished Service Award to Dr. Robert Greene in July.[32]

A particularly big affair to celebrate completion of the College Center (Blake A) was the 1951 Christmas dinner. Intended "to impress townspeople," it did not quite come off as expected. The potato masher "went berserk and sprayed potatoes all over the spanking new equipment," according to B. J. Keller, journalism and English instructor. Importantly, until the Robert W. MacVittie College Union was opened in February 1970, the College Center Snack Bar was **the** meeting place for students and faculty, a genuine campus hangout. It was supervised by the year-old Student-Faculty Service, which evolved into the Faculty Student Association (FSA) and more recently into

Education division faculty in the late 1950s included (left photo, seated, from left): Truman Hall, Jane Stare, Beulah Lafferty, Helen Vance (later Foster), Gaile Carbaugh; (standing): Kenneth Riesch, Richard Bloomer, Richard Stolper; (right photo, seated, from left): Helen Boyd, R. Dudley Miller, Gladys Rhodes, Hardy Wahlgren; (standing): Norman Lyon, Merrill Murray, William Cotton. (1959 *Oh Ha Daih*)

Festive Christmas pageants were popular for many years. President Moench (standing) presided, surrounded by his court (from left): Mrs. Saddlemire, Mrs. Moench, Dean Gerald Saddlemire, and Robert Sinclair. The third student from the left is Mary Jo Armstrong Johnson, '58. (Milne Archives)

Campus Auxiliary Services (CAS).[33]

President Espy also hailed the opening of four residence halls. The first, Sturges (Blake E), admitted residents on November 11, 1950, followed by Fraser (Blake C) after Thanksgiving, and Bailey and Blake (Blakes B and D) after Christmas. The new, safe housing honored a former president (James V. Sturges), local board member (Bertha Paine Fraser), biology professor (Guy Bailey), and dean (Anne Blake).[34]

While the residence halls were far from luxurious, the buildings, housing two hundred students, offered three floors (including the basement rooms) of two-person rooms with communal lavatories and shower rooms on each floor. *The Lamron,* sounding like a real estate ad, proclaimed the dorms had "large and airy" rooms that accommodated "Simmons beds with dust proof chests underneath, two kneehole study desks with chairs, two lounge chairs, two clothes closets, floor lamps, and window hangings." Topping it off were reception and game rooms plus a "modern automatic laundry with washers and dryers." Students paid $145 per ten-week quarter for board and room. It was first-come, first-served, with a block of rooms already reserved for Clio sorority, which was unable to use its house for the following year. (Later these dorms would serve as faculty offices with gray or green metal army surplus desks and file cabinets and makeshift book shelves.)[35]

Razing Old Main, beginning with the north wing in May 1951, however, was a different matter. It had to go, but with its demise went eighty years of history. It had housed the entire school at one time. In addition to the library, classrooms, student housing, and faculty and administrative offices, major events were held in the auditorium, including freshman convocations and the

Students and townspeople gathered at the decorated fountain to sing Christmas carols, a tradition that continues today. The Riviera Theater and Minckler's Drugs are in the background. (1960 *Oh Ha Daih*)

annual Christmas pageants. To most graduates up to then it was the symbol of the College, however bad its condition. In fact, induction into the Alumni Association's Society of Old Main is one of the highest honors for an alumnus, and was first conferred on "Jimmy" Dietsche, '36. However, Board of Visitors chairman James W. Wadsworth, Jr. had no qualms about razing the venerable

Old Main, seen from the rear (west) side, was razed in 1951. The north wing was leveled first, to make way for the new dormitories (Blake buildings). (Alumni Office)

old building; on one visit the former senator knocked "down a portion of the ceiling and walls with his cane to emphasize his support for…constructing new buildings."[36]

What would replace it? Nothing would immediately. Instead, faculty, students, alumni, and the community had only an architect's wonderful drawing of the new library, auditorium, and gymnasium, which was the centerpiece of the College's 1946–1947 catalog. However, hope springs eternal. It was vital, for after the razing of Old Main the first commencement was held in the Armory, "which leaked during a rainstorm that left proud parents hopelessly mired in the mud of the parking lot." Another graduation in Parking Lot "C" was marred by a "terrific wind storm" that threatened to blow away the tent anchored by cars brought in for the emergency.[37]

President Espy would not celebrate the opening of Old Main's much-needed replacements. Instead, he resigned somewhat unexpectedly at the end of 1952 to become Maine's superintendent of public instruction. Walter Harding claimed that individuals at the College asked the SUNY Central administration to remove him. Paul Neureiter recalled that Espy "made one mistake after another," the biggest of which was his failure to appoint Dr. Herman Behrens director of education.[38]

Sadly, Espy is little remembered. Changes he had sought so fervently eluded him, and he had been beset with seemingly insoluble problems. To his credit, the College survived threats of closing, and its enrollment hit 774 in 1950–1951, exceeding its pre-war peak. The College Center and four new residence halls had opened, and he had helped set the College on

Phi Sigma Epsilon's Yogi Bear snow sculpture won first place in the 1962 Winter Weekend competition. (1962 *Oh Ha Daih*)

a construction spree. These accomplishments are his legacy.

Espy was succeeded temp-
orarily (from January 1953 to June
1954) by Dr. Kenneth H. Freeman,
the third dean during the 1951–
1952 school year. Freeman had replaced Acting Dean Dr. Louise Kuhl,
who had replaced Dr. Royal Netzer
when he left mid-year to become
Oneonta's president. Freeman, former head of the department of elementary education at the University

Mrs. Moench watched a
formal gift presentation
between Kenneth Freeman
and President Moench.
(Pretzer Collection)

of Nebraska, had received his doctorate from the University of Missouri.[39]

The Transition Begins

Changes affecting the College came in rapid order. One was the State University
of New York policy banning fraternities and sororities from affiliating with national
organizations to prevent racial, color, religious, creed, or ethnic discrimination. (National organizations dedicated solely to academic achievement were
exempted.) Another change—only rumored—was the SUNY Trustees' intent to
charge four hundred dollars in tuition. (The rumor came true in 1963.) Espy,
as would his successors, had adamantly opposed it, fearing it would reduce enrollment "qualitatively and quantitatively." Also, beginning in July 1954, the
governor was empowered to appoint members of College Councils (no longer
Boards of Visitors) for nine-year, staggered terms. Senator Austin Erwin was
appointed chairman of Geneseo's council in 1954 for a three-year term by outgoing Governor Dewey. Four years later, thoroughly Republican Geneseo got a
Democrat chairman, Joseph Quirk, whose father had headed Geneseo's District
No. 5 school board, and whose grandfather had helped build Old Main.[40]

Of more immediate importance to Geneseo was the 1954 appointment of Dr.
Francis J. Moench, the first individual to be formally installed as president of
Geneseo. A native of Sag Harbor, New York, Moench was one of the outstanding graduates of Cortland Normal School in 1916. After service in WWI he received his bachelor's degree in physical education from Springfield College and
his master's and doctorate from New York University. He returned to Cortland
in 1923 as a faculty member and later chaired the men's physical education
department before serving as dean for two years prior to coming to Geneseo.[41]

Critics of the appointment complained that at fifty-seven, Moench was too

President Moench's wife Katharine, a 1919 alumna and sister of local druggist Harold Ulmer, was a gracious hostess at many events. (Pretzer collection)

old, that his background was physical education (not an "academic area"), and that he was too inexperienced, having been made dean at Cortland only to enable him to become a college president. (On the other hand, some locals justified his appointment because his wife was an alumna and her brother was Geneseo pharmacist Harold Ulmer.) It may be that Dr. Moench was expected to be an interim president to stabilize the College after Espy's abrupt departure. However, during his nine-year term he was anything but a caretaker.[42]

He was immediately reminded—if necessary—of the College's unfinished campus when he had to raise a tent for the 1955 commencement and again for his precedent-setting installation on October 13, 1955. The first went without incident; not so the latter, when rain fell. But each came off with the appropriate ritual. Ironically, in the 1960s, Geneseo students, merrily unaware of earlier disasters, argued successfully for outdoor graduations. That arrangement lasted until 1972, despite a horrendous May 1970 rainstorm that drowned graduates and families, including Geneseo associate librarian Joan Cottone, '70. (The speaker was asked if he "had a ten-minute talk" and responded "How about three?") The ceremonies then were held in the Wilson Ice Arena from 1973 until the students succeeded in having their commencement outdoors again, beginning in 1999. First held outside behind Letchworth Dining Hall, in 2004 ceremonies were moved to Parking Lot B with rented stadium seating.[43]

Dr. Moench established himself in short order because his style was "this is my college and I am going to run it." "He had to run things," according to Theodora ("Theo") Greenman, Moench's secretary starting in 1955. "He had his finger on everything that was going on, on the campus." It was not only his style; it may have been necessary, Miss Greenman believed.[44]

He had scarcely arrived—in fact, he was living in the apartment in the College Center—when he presided over the cornerstone-laying ceremony for the Wadsworth Auditorium-Milne (later Fraser) Library. The principal guests were Governor Thomas Dewey, SUNY Chancellor William Carlson, and Senator Austin Erwin. Governor Dewey presciently labeled the occasion part of a "Golden Era" in education. The next dozen years would bear him out.[45]

The College purchased 15 Main Street in 1955 for use as the President's residence. (Fred Bright)

While President Moench missed Geneseo's first homecoming October 16–17, 1953, which drew James Snyder, '86, the oldest graduate, and James Walton, '97, who came the farthest (from Cheyenne, Wyoming), he would be party to a number of major events. In short order Moench dedicated a new heating plant (1953); the auditorium-library (1955); three dorms, [Dean Lydia] Jones (1958), Livingston (1959, named for the county), and Monroe (1961, the neighboring county); Mary Jemison Dining Hall (1960, named for the "White Woman of the Genesee"); and the long-awaited and much-needed $1.8-million Schrader Health and Physical Education building (1961). (The latter was named for Carl Schrader, whose "Carnival of Gymnastics" in 1901 was such a success.) Further, enrollment nearly tripled (rising from 783 in 1953–1954 to 2,262 in 1962–1963). On the other hand, special education's half-century connection with Sonyea was severed by the state in 1955. This event went virtually unnoticed, though the special education faculty were happy to be on campus.[46]

Of all the events in the Moench years, two deserve special mention. The first is the long-awaited opening of the first Milne Library (later renamed for former faculty and local board member Bertha Paine Fraser) and the thousand-seat Wadsworth Auditorium. Ironically, Republican Governor Thomas Dewey laid the cornerstone for the auditorium on October 12, 1954, while less than two years later Democrat Governor Averell Harriman helped dedicate the buildings. But it was former first lady Eleanor Roosevelt's speech in Wadsworth Auditorium on February 13, 1956 that stuck in the minds of many. It was also memorable because the State Department of Public Works had to approve occupancy of the still-unfinished building. Others found it ironic that Mrs. Roosevelt was the guest of Board of Visitors chairman Reverdy Wadsworth, the son and grandson of two chairmen of the local board, representing three generations of staunch Republicans.[47]

Governor Thomas Dewey wielded the trowel for the October 1954 Wadsworth Auditorium cornerstone-laying, observed by (from left) state senator and College Council chair Austin Erwin, Sr., President Moench, and SUNY President William Carlson. (*Geneseo Compass*, April 1983)

Geneseo's first homecoming was held on October 16–17, 1953. While waiting for the parade to begin, Queen Stephanie O'Hara and Acting President Kenneth Freeman chatted with Dean Rosalind Fisher, general chair of the parade. (Milne Archives)

Aiding the Transition

While it was still too early to judge the effects of creating the State University of New York, one positive result was faculty recruitment. In no time, it seems in retrospect, Geneseo attracted faculty and staff who would establish themselves as major players. One was Dr. Lawrence Park, who came as dean in 1957, replacing Dean Kenneth Freeman, who left to become president of Christian College in Columbia, Missouri, at the beginning of that year. For twelve years Park, a New Paltz graduate with a master's and a doctorate from NYU and a former faculty member at Pennsylvania State University, would be the right-hand man of Presidents Moench and MacVittie.[48]

After more than a decade without a gymnasium, the health and physical education faculty celebrated the Schrader cornerstone laying. From left are: Betty Jo Fuller, Myrtle Merritt, Louise Kuhl, Frank Akers, David Carrington, Barbara Snow, Robert Durkin, Mary Breid, and Ira Wilson. (Bright collection)

Among those who came in 1956 and would play key roles was Dr. Rose Bachem Alent, unforgettable for her legendary enthusiasm for teaching, her indomitable spirit, her sheer presence and her elegant parties during the forty years she served the College. Another was Dr. Walter Harding, the College's first University Professor and first Geneseo emeritus to be awarded a SUNY Honorary Doctor of Letters degree. Harding, who taught at Geneseo for twenty-six years, was regarded as the "world's leading scholar on nineteenth-century author Henry David Thoreau." Dr. William Cotton, a Fredonia and Teachers College, Columbia University graduate, was named director of the education division to succeed Kenneth Riesch, who remained on the faculty. Cotton, who became well known throughout the state, served as director until 1971 and remained as a faculty member another dozen years or more.[49]

Lydia Jones served on the faculty from 1904 to 1922 and was the namesake of the only current residence hall not named for a county. (Livingston County Historian)

Still others who made their mark were Paul Hepler, Daryl Hanson, William Orwen, and Charles Miskell, followed shortly by William Derby, John Black, Martin L. Fausold, John Paul, James Scholes, Wendell Rhodes, Harold Starbuck, Josephine Mills, and Helen Vance Foster.

Hepler, who earned a doctorate at Teachers College, later chaired the art department and taught part-time into the twenty-first century. Hanson ably led the music department, while the quiet Orwen became a Thomas Hardy expert over his nearly three decades at the College, and Miskell became a mainstay of the chemistry department when it was formed in 1965. Orwen's brother, Gifford, chaired the foreign language department when it was created in 1962.

Derby, who arrived in 1957 with a history Ph.D. from the University of Wisconsin, chaired the history department and Faculty Senate before retiring more than three decades later. Dr. Martin L. Fausold came in 1958 from sister school Cortland to direct the College's social science division. A prolific author, including a biography of Board of Visitors president and U.S. Senator James W. Wadsworth, Jr., Fausold was the guiding spirit behind the memorable "Valley, Village and College" display in Newton Hall. One of Fausold's first hires was Dr. Wendell Rhodes, a Syracuse University (Maxwell

Former first lady Eleanor Roosevelt was the first person to appear on the stage in the new Wadsworth Auditorium in 1956. (Bright collection)

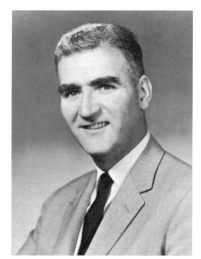

Lawrence Park was appointed chair of the elementary education department in 1955 and soon became Dean of the College. (1958 *Oh Ha Daih*)

1930 alumnus John Black was appointed Holcomb School principal in 1957 and later served on the education faculty. (1959 *Oh Ha Daih*)

School) graduate, like Fausold, and one of five at Geneseo simultaneously. Rhodes later chaired the anthropology department and was recognized for his research. James Scholes, who arrived in 1959, subsequently headed the English department and was a remarkably talented actor well into his—and his students'—retirement. Alumna Josephine Mills, '49, joined the Library School faculty and bridged the old and new curricula in her long and successful career here. Helen Vance Foster came to the College as a Holcomb School teacher in 1957 and retired approximately four decades later after twice chairing the special education department.

In 1957, Dr. John Black, a 1930 Geneseo Normal School graduate with a Teachers College, Columbia University, Ed.D., left the principalship of the Oneonta Campus School to head Geneseo's Holcomb School. Joining Black were Geneseo graduates Ruth Coffin Underhill and Anna Marie Biondollilo Loncao, along with Ruth Rodamaker and Mary Grove. Mrs. Grove was hired to replace another Geneseo graduate, Eleanor Woelfel Roodenburg, '53, who was named music supervisor. "Lennie," a contralto soloist who had studied at Oberlin's music conservatory, had already distinguished herself in December 1947 when she sang three songs from Handel's *Messiah* in Old Main. Shortly, Frances Willey Lipson, '52, and Mary Parent joined them. All remained until the Holcomb School was closed in 1981.[50]

Two others hired at this time deserve mention. Dr. Julia A. Delehanty, M.D., who had a Geneseo Normal School diploma, returned to the College in 1956 as a part-time physician. She is recalled fondly by more than a few students and faculty because of her availability and care. The other, Victor Raschi, wore one of five consecutive World Series championship rings earned by his successful pitching for the New York Yankees. Raschi, "the Springfield Rifle," was hired in 1959 to teach physical education, coach basketball and baseball (filling in for Frank Akers, who was on leave), assist with soccer, and handle the vital intramural program. Later, for a short time, he taught physical education at the campus school.[51]

State University College of Education

Just as the journey from Normal School to Teachers College was not without mishaps, the rest of the trip has been bumpy. Recall that in 1951 the SUNY Trustees informed Geneseo and its sister schools that they had to convert to liberal arts colleges, but they were given a ten-year grace period. At a meeting with Geneseo's College Council in October 1961, Hermann Cooper reminded the attendees that the time was up; Geneseo was to be a multipurpose college. Juniors and seniors could elect liberal arts majors beginning in 1962; the freshmen two years later. Two SUNY colleges at a time had to submit master plans for the change to liberal arts status. And the Trustees had changed the colleges' titles. So, the former Teachers College was now State University of New York College of Education at Geneseo.[52]

Art faculty Paul Hepler, Elizabeth Hakes, and Bertha Lederer had a combined total 47 years of art department leadership and 103 years service to the College, spanning from Hakes's 1923 appointment to Hepler's 1992 retirement. (Hepler Collection)

Anticipating the mandate, Geneseo had already added a graduate program in library education, had created an early secondary social studies education program (N-9), and was developing a Master's program in speech and hearing.

Building on its reputation as a pacesetter and with a new building in the works, in 1951 the library school became a college division. By 1959, with

210 students enrolled, it was the second largest specialization on campus. (Elementary education remained the largest.) Importantly, before the "legendary" Alice Damon Rider retired in 1961, Geneseo also had instituted a graduate library science program in school librarianship. Ms. Rider's prescience was clearly illustrated by the following anecdote: "In 1957, when filmstrips were rather revolutionary, she wrote on the green board—CYBERNETICS. We were mystified. She warned us, 'You can't spell it. You can't pronounce it. You don't know what it means. But you better find out. It is how you will do your work before you leave the profession.'"[53]

The N-9 social studies program, begun in 1959, was to prepare those who intended to teach elementary through junior high school social studies. Students were required to take twenty-seven semester hours of coursework in the social sciences along with the regular elementary program. Secondary teacher education programs in English, the sciences, and mathematics, which

The 1958–1959 Holcomb School faculty included: (left photo, seated, from left): Mrs. Rodamaker, Miss DeCarne, Miss Adam, Miss Coffin, Mrs. Loncao, Mr. Bronfeld; (standing): Mrs. Richardson, Miss Besser, Mrs. Lynch, Miss Klapper, Mr. Forrester, Mr. Zufelt, Miss Knight, Miss Barry; (right photo, seated): Mrs. Grove, Mrs. Schilling, Miss Woelfel, Mr. Schlageter, Mrs. Sheppard, Miss Allewelt; (standing): Miss Salter, Miss Ledoux, Mrs. Stroetzel, 1953 alumnus Robert Meyer, Gloria Mattera (who later headed the Migrant Center), Miss Herrala. (1959 *Oh Ha Daih*)

Left: 1921 alumna Dr. Julia Delehanty was appointed the first college physician in 1956. (1959 *Oh Ha Daih*)

Right: The 1959–1960 Lettermen's Club included (standing, from left): J. York, R. Nodar, J. Reed, three-letter man and later placement director Jim Allan, J. Cook; (seated): C. Lewis, R. Bergman, R. Moldram, W. McQuilkin, V. Laurini, H. Allan, M. Hart, coach Vic Raschi, coach Durkin, F. Smokoski. (1960 *Oh Ha Daih*)

demanded greater subject matter specialization, were added in 1960–1961. (Mathematics had become a separate department on September 1, 1958.)

The speech and hearing program too had come of age. Three years after arriving as an assistant professor of English in 1936, farsighted C. Agnes Rigney initiated the speech and hearing program. Six years later she oversaw the graduation of Mrs. Patricia Brown Kaul, the program's first major. By 1955, with a faculty of five, the program's clinic was serving more than 150 children a week, drawn from a seventy-five-mile radius. (Enrollment in speech communication, which included a speech course required of students certifying to teach, previously had reached the point that the state approved a separate department.) In 1958, anticipating the need for an audiology clinic, Rigney brought Dr. John Paul to the campus to succeed her on her pending retirement. Paul, with a Ph.D. from Purdue, had headed the University of Alabama's speech and hearing center. In turn, he lured his Purdue graduate school friend Harold Starbuck to develop a summer clinic for stutterers, like Starbuck himself. (Fully operational by 1963, Starbuck's clinic garnered international recognition.) Miss Rigney's goal to have a master's program in speech and hearing was achieved in 1960, a year after she retired and five before she died.[54]

But the full impact of Geneseo's transition to a multipurpose school would not be felt for another two decades. In fact, a key participant in SUNY's earliest days believed the university's reputation at this time was still "zilch."[55]

"Zilch?" Not so, if we look at some of Geneseo's students at this time. For example, Donna DeSeyn, *Who's Who in American Colleges and Universities* and the 1955 *Oh Ha Daih* editor-in-chief, later chaired the science department at Fairport and assisted Geneseo's education faculty to write new programs in the early 1970s before her untimely death. Joseph Shubert began his ascent to New York state librarian and assistant commissioner for libraries at Geneseo in 1951. Joyce Tiffany (Zobel), one of the "Prominent Seniors" in 1952, ably served the Williamsville school district as a librarian for many years. Mt. Morris's Fred Barraco, '52, became a school administrator, as did Lima's Walt Pennington, a Geneseo soccer and basketball player. Ray Sciarrino, '55, elementary education, built a successful law practice in his Mt. Morris home town after graduating. Rochester's Jim Allan, '61, a "speedy base runner" on the baseball team and stalwart on the basketball team, returned to his alma

In 1958–1959, the library education division was the College's second largest division with 211 students, and faculty included (from left): Richard Reynolds, director Alice Damon Rider, C. Elta Van Norman, Edna Mack, and Leslie Poste. (1959 *Oh Ha Daih*)

mater and later became Dr. Allan, director of career services. Upon graduation, Robert Freiburger, '61, relinquished his part-time job as "cub reporter" for Rochester's radio station WHAM to earn his M.S. in audio visual communication and radio and TV education at Indiana University. He returned to Geneseo two years later as an instructor, and after a decade, Dr. Freiburger was appointed coordinator of instructional resources. Another "star" from this period is Dr. Thomas J. Sergiovanni, Lillian Radford Professor of Education and Administration at Trinity University in San Antonio, Texas. A 1958 elementary education graduate, Sergiovanni is internationally known for his work regarding successful school leadership.[56]

Perhaps the most successful alumnus of this period was a Geneseo native, Roy McTarnaghan, a 1954 speech communication major. He earned a doctorate at Michigan State University in 1962, returned to his alma mater for a short time, including serving as acting vice president for academic affairs, before becoming executive vice chancellor of the State University System of Florida (1989 to 1993) and founding president of Florida Gulf Coast University (1993 to 1999). Not satisfied with retirement, he was induced to serve as interim president of California State University, San Marcos, 2003–2004.[57]

Geneseo native Sam Orlando, who had returned from almost four years in the navy to complete his Geneseo education, was the first of three brothers to receive bachelor's and master's degrees at Geneseo before teaching in area public schools. The three (Sam, Nick, who subsequently taught at Rochester Institute of Technology's National Technical Institute for the Deaf, and Carmen) also distinguished themselves by serving simultaneously as town or village justices.

The 1958–1959 speech department included faculty who would later form the separate departments of speech communication, speech pathology and audiology, and drama. Seated, from left are John Paul, Alice Austin, Dorothy Lynds, Robert Sinclair; standing: Stanley Rutherford, Roy McTarnaghan, and George Haspiel. (1959 *Oh Ha Daih*)

Wearing the Beanies was the Secret to Success

Maybe their Geneseo initiation paid off. As freshmen they learned to wear their "beanies" ("dinks") for their first fourteen days or pay the price: "Kangaroo Kourt." Befitting their status, the beanie was their "badge of ignorance." Their lowly status was reinforced by their having to be "at the beck and call" of any upperclassmen.[58]

Leo Marks, a beanie wearer in 1956, had taken a very circuitous route to Geneseo. It took him from his Romanian birthplace to Czechoslovakia, Poland, Germany, and finally to Perry, New York, barely four months before he found the campus. Tipping his beanie to *The Lamron* interviewer, he acknowledged he was becoming acclimated to the "girls in shorts—and pretty short shorts!" and to playing on the soccer team. While he hoped to teach German and Russian, instead, he headed the mathematics department at Dansville High School for many years.[59]

But the beanie wearers were also exposed to cultural events that tended to belie the notion that Geneseo was just some rural outpost for "provincials." For example, John Sargent, later an administrator in Rush-Henrietta, was in the cast of Arthur Miller's *The Crucible* in 1956. Lawrence "Butch" Mothersell, who became a professor at Rochester Institute of Technology's National Technical Institute for the Deaf as well as an Episcopal priest, played a major role in Ago-Phi Sig's rendering of *The Mikado*.[60]

If they didn't participate directly, the students

One of stuttering clinic director Harold Starbuck's students was Pat Sacco, who would later head the clinic. (1962 *Oh Ha Daih*)

Radio club members entertained the campus and gained practical experience by operating WGTC for forty-two-and-a-half hours over a six-day week. Club president Bob Freiburger (at microphone) later directed the College Instructional Resources Center. Advisors John Davis and Robert Sinclair are at the right. (1960 *Oh Ha Daih*)

benefited from Cothurnus productions of *The Skin of Our Teeth* and *Death of a Salesman* or the music department's *Amahl and the Night Visitors* and *The Promise*. Or they enjoyed hearing the George Shearing Quintet, pianist Eugene List's first U.S. concert, and Eastman School of Music graduate, William Warfield. And they appreciated the fifty-five-piece College Wind Ensemble concert, directed by Professor Daryl Hanson in 1958. A particular treat was the appearance of the Metropolitan Opera's mezzo-soprano Risë Stevens, who opened the 1958 season's Artist Series, followed by Maurice Evans's performance in February 1959.[61]

The three fraternities and four sororities, with their sponsored dances, parties, homecoming floats, rushing, hazing, and "pinning," also played a big role in campus life. "Night life" often included a trip down Court Street to the "M & B" (today's Statesmen), where a jukebox alternated with a live band enabling students to do slow dances or jitterbug before the twist became the fad in 1961. And it was relatively cheap to attend Geneseo: $75-125 per year for books, $280 for off-campus housing, $400-440 for meals and $146 for student fees. What's missing? Tuition, of course. It was still $0.[62]

Students still conformed to a dress code—no jeans or sweatshirts in class, the library, or cafeteria for guys, while skirts or dresses were required of the female students. The policy was minimally loosened after May 14, 1962, when library head James G. Eberhardt allowed men the same privileges as the women: they could wear Bermuda shorts and slacks in Milne "after the dinner hour" and on Saturdays. However, students were reminded that "BERMUDA SHORTS [capitalization in the original] are shorts that are no more

The Blake A College Center lounge, redesigned and decorated by Paul Hepler, was enjoyed during a 1965 Homecoming coffee hour by (from left): Gaile Carbaugh, Paul Neureiter, Roy McTarnaghan, '54, Beverly Boyce McTarnaghan, '54, Ira Wilson, and Clayton Mau. (Roger Smith photo, *Geneseo Alumni News*, May 1966)

than two (2) inches above the knee…," and "T-shirts are not permitted at anytime." Punishment for "continued and consistent" violations was cancellation of library privileges. In March a year later, male students were permitted to wear blue jeans and sweatshirts in the library and cafeteria, but on March 9, *The Lamron* editor disapproved: "Professional people from other colleges are frequently seen around campus. Do we want them to get the impression that our men are nothing more than what you would see in high school or on a street corner?…We are sure that the Geneseo men can be just as comfortable and look much better in a sports shirt and slacks."

Art professor Hepler recalled another reluctant loosening of the dress code when he faced Associate Dean Evelyn Nicholson to explain why female students should be allowed to wear slacks rather than skirts to his Design in Wood [woodworking] studio class. Encountering the dean, "small of stature, muted voice and steel-gray hair," Hepler felt like he was in his "high school principal's office…all over again." Imagine how the students themselves felt![63]

Reflecting the greater affluence of the time, there were other complaints. With just 145 parking spaces in three lots, decals had been issued only to "essential drivers" for fall semester 1956. While those without the decals were complaining, that's the way it had to be, a member of the parking committee explained in a letter to *The Lamron*. Also, a student took the faculty members to task for their apparent disinterest in many of the student-sponsored social and extracurricular events. By comparison, the letter writer pointed

The cast of *Look Homeward, Angel* included (front row, from left): D. Brode, G. Kellogg, C. Marchewska; (back): S. Singer, S. Fawcett, D. Ruffo, C. Culver, B. Brown. (Milne Archives)

out, the faculty showed up in force to hear Minnesota Senator and future Vice President Hubert Humphrey speak on March 24, 1959. Showing their interest in politics—and conservatism—a student straw vote gave 1960 GOP presidential candidate Richard Nixon a 335 to 226 plurality over eventual winner John F. Kennedy.[64]

Despite a seeming naïveté, students of these expansion years were increasingly iconoclastic. Consider the Pete Lagootie story. Charles "Dutch" VanRy, '64, says that the elusive Lagootie first "appeared" on campus Spring 1961. "Pete," who allegedly registered himself using official registration forms, was rumored to have flunked out, but popped up at various times as a candidate for office or as an exhibitor in an art show. He was even invited to join a fraternity and may have "hung around" until the mid-sixties, when he "disappeared" as mysteriously as his creators. Other bored students bet on the number of times an instructor repeated a particular phrasing. The student who correctly guessed was amply rewarded after the class.[65]

The 1959 music department faculty included (from left): John Kucaba, Daryl Hanson (standing), and department chair Gordon Goewey. (1959 *Oh Ha Daih*)

The Hoax

Another manifestation of the emerging iconoclasm was the November 1962 Thanksgiving vacation hoax. It occurred after a sophomore (aka Dr. J. Peter Gregoire, '63) talked a friend (aka Dr. George Wilkerson, '64) into abetting

Phi Sigma Epsilon fraternity's "Bridge on the River Kwai" float took top honors in the 1958 homecoming parade. The brothers walked behind the float whistling the movie's theme, "Colonel Bogey March." (Milne Archives)

Before the drinking age was raised, the Village Taverne was one of many popular student gathering spots. The building later housed Pauper Jack's restaurant and Pictures and Presents. (Roemer House collection)

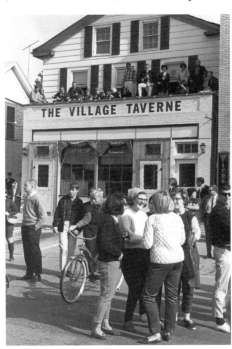

him. Gregoire had obtained one of the dean's letterheads on which he typed the announcement that "'due to unforeseen circumstances' Thanksgiving [will] begin one day earlier than usual." Using a purloined key, Gregoire stuffed the fake announcements in the students' mailboxes in the dorms while Wilkerson played the pianos in the common areas to divert attention from his fellow conspirator. The next morning the students frantically changed their travel plans.[66]

When the administration announced that the memo was a hoax, allegedly half of the students, having changed travel plans, walked uptown to Dr. Moench's house to protest. A compromise was struck: school would be in session, but students who missed classes would not be punished. However, the dean, intent on punishing the perpetrators, called in Wilkerson, who had been identified as one of the culprits because he was well known for his acting and writing talents. "Playing it tough," Wilkerson refused to "rat" on Gregoire. The dean called his bluff: "You're out. You pack your things and be off this campus by noon tomorrow." The stunned Wilkerson "gulped." His friend Charles "Dutch" VanRy suggested he talk with someone. That someone turned out to be Robert Sinclair, drama instructor and Wilkerson's mentor, who shortly informed Wilkerson "It never happened." Relieved, Wilkerson attended classes until noon Wednesday, then blithely went home for vacation.

As part of the 1962 Thanksgiving vacation hoax, prankster J. Peter Gregoire stuffed mailboxes similar to these. (Roemer House collection)

But that was not the end of the hoax. Upon his return, co-conspirator Gregoire, head down and accompanied by dorm counselor John Meuser '63 (aka "Captain Goody Twoshoes"), admitted that he had confessed to the dean; he'd told the whole story. Alas, both he and Wilkerson were to be suspended. Unprepared for this, Wilkerson could only mutter to himself. Nor was he entirely relieved when Gregoire and Meuser broke out laughing and admitted they were teasing. Wilkerson could see Gregoire pulling this dirty trick, but not "Teddy Bear" Meuser. Sadly, the late Meuser, who became a dean at Finger Lakes Community College in Canandaigua, cannot verify his role, and Wilkerson, later a dean himself at Texas's Austin Community College, still vows revenge on Gregoire.

Jim Brunner, '62, claims to have spared President Moench another surprise march on his house after discovering the students' uproar over the closing of the College Center's cafeteria not long before the hoax. The way Brunner tells it, the cafeteria was closed because students had left an awful mess. They intended to retaliate by visiting Moench while he hosted a dinner party. Brunner, Moench's gardener for all four years as an undergraduate, claims to have run cross lots to warn the president who, because of the timely warning, quickly defused the situation—and reopened the cafeteria.[67]

Although these pranksters, their cohorts, and their professors didn't realize it, they were a transitional "generation." Their successors and the small, intimate, tuition-free campus were about to change dramatically.

Cothurnus productions included *Aladdin and his Wonderful Lamp*, featuring (front, from left): B. Glantz, R. Lent; (standing): K. Leith and John Meuser, who also played a role in the 1962 Thanksgiving hoax. (1961 *Oh Ha Daih*)

The Espy-Moench Years

In many respects this period was as difficult as any in Geneseo's history. As President Espy wrote to Assistant Commissioner Cooper, with the exception of the administration-classroom building and the campus school, the facilities he inherited were "obsolete, unattractive, unsafe, and inefficient." Student housing was insufficient or unsafe or both. Faculty recruitment was even more difficult than student recruitment. Though the various curricula had served well, changes were needed. And necessarily, but sadly, Old Main had fallen to the wrecking ball.

Though not intended directly, creation of the State University of New York would counter the "inertia" that had dogged the Normals and the teachers colleges. If money followed, the problems Dr. Espy faced would not go away directly, but they would be greatly ameliorated. And in the future, the SUNY system would help solve many of the problems he faced. But after engaging in unending planning, which taxed his physical and mental endurance, Espy took his leave. He had laid the groundwork, including obtaining approvals for long-overdue buildings, for his successors.

Importantly, he had obtained Middle States accreditation, had awarded the first master's degrees and had opened much-needed residence halls and a college center.

His successor, Dr. Moench, reaped the harvest in terms of dedicating new buildings. His style, having his "finger on everything that was going on, on the campus" may well have been necessary. Without Old Main, initially he had to cram everything into the administration-classroom building and then had to oversee construction of the library-auditorium, three dorms, a dining hall, and the health and physical education building. Increased enrollment necessitated faculty recruitment, which meant beating the bushes. But Moench was helped by the new look of the College, increases in faculty salaries, and newly permitted Social Security contributions. He had relied on distinguished faculty such as Agnes Rigney, Alice Damon Rider, and Paul Neureiter, and administrators, including Louise Kuhl, Wilbur Wright, Gerald Saddlemire, and Lawrence Park and their colleagues, who wanted their college to prosper. Likely, also he was aided by federal programs, including the newly created National Defense Education Act, which, in response to the USSR's 1957 launching of Sputnik, supported curricular reform and teacher education.

Unlike Espy, Moench was generally well liked. Paul Neureiter, who served under four Geneseo presidents, felt that Moench turned out to be an "excellent president….Most successful….Energetic, decisive, yet left faculty alone. Eloquent." By contrast, his critics may have felt threatened by the new emphasis on the liberal arts.[68]

When Moench retired at the end of the 1962–1963 school year, he left the College in much better shape than he found it. On December 4, 1962, reflecting on Moench's announced retirement, *The Lamron* lamented "Geneseo to Lose Good Friend."

Francis Moench served as president from 1954 to 1963. (Roemer House Collection)

Twenty Years of Campus Growth

Between 1950 and 1970, Geneseo's campus experienced its most dramatic growth. During that time, more than thirty new buildings were constructed.

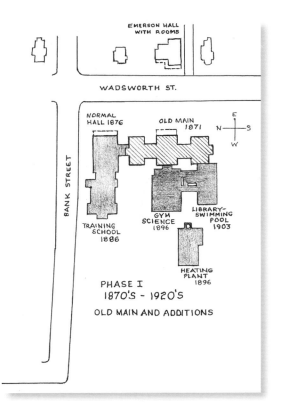

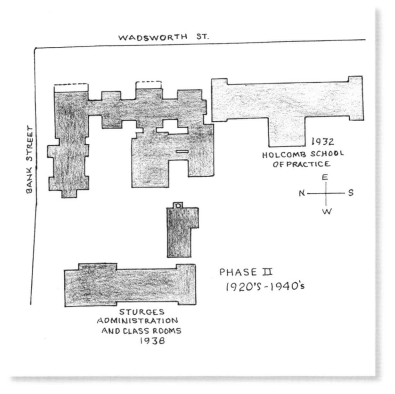

Old Main's original sections and additions, with construction dates, are shown in the Phase I map. Phase II shows Old Main's location in relation to two familiar buildings, Sturges and the Holcomb School (now Welles). Emerson Hall was a popular student boarding house. Phase III depicts the campus in the early 1960s. (Redrawn by Paul Hepler from maps in *Recommendations for Landscape Management for SUNY College of Arts and Sciences at Geneseo*, prepared by SUNY College of Environmental Science & Forestry Landscape Architecture Faculty, 1986)

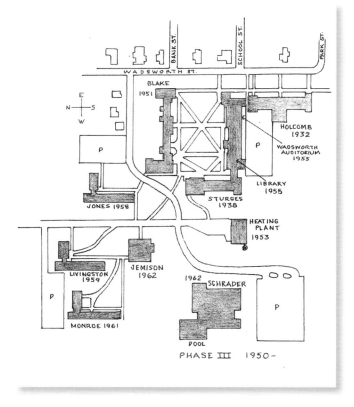

In 1951, the campus consisted of the classroom-administration building (now Sturges), the Holcomb Campus School (now Welles), the College Center and new residence halls (Blake), and Old Main, which had already lost part of its north end to the wrecking ball. (Facilities Planning Office)

In 1950, the College's first residence halls (Blake) were being built near the north end of Old Main, which would soon be razed. (Charles Beebe photo, Livingston County Historian)

The new College Center (Blake A) opened in 1951, and the four new residence halls opened in late 1950 and early 1951. Blake D and E (right end of building) have been razed. (Hal Campbell photo, Milne Archives)

The old heating plant, near the south end of Sturges, was razed to make way for the new library (now Fraser). The Holcomb Campus School (Welles) and Geneseo High School are in the background. (Milne Archives)

In 1953, all classes were held in Sturges. A new heating plant had been built near Sturges's southwest corner, and the old plant had not yet been razed. Note Valley Hall just behind Sturges and the prisoner of war camp in the background. (Facilities Planning Office)

By 1956, Wadsworth Auditorium and Milne Library (now Fraser Hall) had been built on the site of the south end of Old Main and the old heating plant. (Henry DeWolf photo, Livingston County Historian)

Construction crews worked on the interior of Mary Jemison Dining Hall as Schrader Gymnasium took shape in the background. (Milne Archives)

Mary Jemison Dining Hall looked like this for many years but has been dramatically remodeled after being closed for several years. (Hal Campbell Photos, Milne Archives)

By 1962, the campus had added three residence halls (Jones, Livingston, Monroe), Mary Jemison Dining Hall, and Carl Schrader Gymnasium. Geneseo High School is in the foreground. (Wahl's Photographic Service, Bright collection)

In the early 1960s, Wadsworth Street still extended to Park Street, and Elizabeth Street ran from Court Street to the heating plant. The Wadsworth Homestead and grounds are near the upper left corner. (Facilities Planning Office)

In 1962, Jones and Livingston residence halls faced each other across Elizabeth Street. By the middle of the decade, the College acquired all the property on that street and razed the houses to make way for additional residence halls (Steuben and Erie) and parking lots. (Wahl's Photographic Service, Bright collection)

President Francis Moench spoke at the groundbreaking for the new science building, later named for longtime science professor Guy A. Bailey. (Little Studio, Milne Archives)

By the mid-1960s, the Bailey Science Building had been built on the site of the Emerson Hall boarding house, Steuben Residence Hall had been built, and Letchworth Dining Hall and four residence halls (Allegany, Genesee, Ontario, Wyoming) were under construction. (Facilities Planning Office)

While the Bailey Science building was being constructed at the intersection of Wadsworth and School Streets, the campus had a good view of Main Street buildings including the bank (far left) and Geneseo building (far right). (Ron Pretzer collection)

This view provides a closer look at the mid-1960s residence hall construction project. (Wahl's Photographic Service, Roemer House Collection)

Lauderdale Infirmary, shown under construction in 1965, opened in 1966. (Milne Archives)

In December 1965, Erwin Administration Building was beginning to take shape next to Wadsworth Auditorium, at the north end of the site of Old Main. A crane and the Milne Library construction project are seen at right. (Norman Miller photo, Milne Archives)

This 1966 photo shows progress in constructing the Clark Service Building, named for longtime janitor L. Watson Clark. (Little Studio, Bright collection)

This 1968 photo shows the old and new administration buildings, Sturges and Erwin. (Milne Archives)

Erie Residence Hall was built along the former Elizabeth Street. (Roemer House Collection)

Newton Lecture Hall, shown under construction in June 1966, opened in 1967. (Norman Miller photo, Milne Archives)

Newton's large lecture halls were built with state-of-the-art instructional technology such as multiple rear-screen projection systems. (Milne Archives)

Beyond the new Holcomb Campus School, new residence halls were constructed in the late 1960s and early 1970s. Students who had to hike across the windy "tundra" to their dorms dubbed the area "East Cuylerville." (Milne Archives)

In March 1968, construction continued at the new Holcomb Campus School, which opened in 1969. (Norman Miller photo, Bright collection)

The Fine Arts Building, later named for William Brodie, opened in 1967. (Roger Smith photo, Hepler collection)

This beautiful stained glass window was not part of the original plans for Brodie, but architect Edgar Tafel's careful management of construction funds enabled its creation and installation. The stairway was later enclosed to comply with fire regulations. (Roger Smith photo, Hepler collection)

Brodie Fine Arts building's Alice Austin Theater (earlier named Fallbrook Theater) has been the scene of many dramatic and dance performances. (Johnnie Ferrell)

The exterior of Greene Science building neared completion in November 1968. Bailey Science Building is seen in the right background. (Norman Miller photo, Facilities Planning Office)

Greene Science Building, named for popular science professor Robert A. Greene, opened in 1970. (Roemer House collection)

Student-decorated board fences surrounded the Alumni (now Merritt) Field House construction project. The heating plant is in the foreground. (1972 *Oh Ha Daih*)

State University of New York
COLLEGE *at* GENESEO
•
Curriculum, Construction, Conflict (1963–1971)

By any standard, the 1960s were a tumultuous time. Dr. John Black, a Geneseo native, 1930 graduate, and faculty member at this time, did "not recall any earlier tenure of any Administrator to and including Dr. Jas. V. Sturges, which has been so turbulent for causes not related to the administration of the Institution!"[1]

Yet, the decade was ushered in by a deceiving calm. For example, when it opened, the Geneseo campus still observed a conservative dress code and restrictive visiting hours in dormitories. Geneseo's Main Street also reflected that time:

> Ulmer's Drug Store [across Bank Street from the bank] still had its marble soda fountain. Manager Harold Meyer of the A & P grocery store…still pulled items for sale off the top shelf with his stretch pole. Bank president James Welch continued to work from a desk up front in the Genesee Valley National Bank and Trust Company. Realtor Ben Linfoot advised newcomers where to live. Elderly ladies in the village still dressed up and put on white gloves to call on newcomers.[2]

Longtime mayor George Scondras posed outside his popular Main Street ice cream shop, whose ads noted "the doorstep says 'Normal' and the clock says 'Take Your Time.'" (1964 *Oh Ha Daih*)

Opposite Page: One of the most impressive results of the late 1960s and early 1970s construction surge was the fine arts building, featuring a music wing on the right, art wing on the left, and drama/dance wing dominated by a theater with a professional-grade fly-loft area that was three scenery changes high. (Roger Smith photo, Hepler collection)

When the decade closed, students had been stunned by the assassinations of President John F. Kennedy, his brother Robert, and Dr. Martin Luther King, Jr.; baffled by the deadly urban riots; energized by civil rights demonstrations; awed by Neil Armstrong's walk on the moon; and had engaged in a variety of protests.

Above all, like their counterparts on other campuses, the Geneseo students were different from their predecessors. They were more diverse, more sophis-

In 1965, the signs marking Geneseo's village limits boasted the College's presence and dated its founding as 1867, the year townspeople voted to tax themselves to support a Normal School. (Livingston County Historian)

The brothers of Sigma Tau Psi fraternity posed around the Wadsworth Memorial Fountain, possibly smiling at thoughts of student lore about the bear, a sculpture attributed to Antoine-Louis Barye. (1966 *Oh Ha Daih*)

ticated, more demanding, and more iconoclastic than their predecessors, if the Class of 1967's recall is any indication:

Remember when:

—the fraternities took over the horticulture and painted the tree on the quad to keep the sap from running.

—President MacVittie entered the Song Fest and sang, "I've Got a Loverly Bunch of Coconuts" and dedicated it to the entire staff.

—the Year Book Staff tried to give DELL comic books a run for the money.

—Walt Hover [head of food services] went on a Hunger Strike after eating in M. J. [Dining Hall].

—everyone wanted to abolish the dress code…I don't know what all the fuss was about. Mr. [Ira] Wilson did that a long time ago.

—the girls put Geneseo on the map by initiating BVD raids as retaliation for panty-raids.

—our freshman float sailed down Main Street [during a rainy Homecoming parade] and sank!

—the infirmary's [doctor]…prescribed and administered enemas as cures for earaches.[3]

Strangely, the class chroniclers said nothing about campus construction, the controversial talk by American Nazi Party leader George Lincoln Rockwell, a threatened 1963 boycott of village businesses that discriminated against African-Americans, the ambitious 7 a.m. to 11 p.m. programming on WGSU-FM and the "Blizzard of '66," which dumped more than twenty-eight inches of snow between January 29 and February 2. The last was certainly memorable. With the College closed for three days and travelers stranded here, the faculty (particularly the HPE faculty), administration and staff were forced to use their ingenuity. Students and stranded visitors partied, danced, swam in the pool, and bowled in the Schrader building. But the class's recollection of their four years at Geneseo was meant to be—and was— simply a lighthearted piece.[4]

Phi Sigma Epsilon fraternity's Center Street house was new to them when they won the winter weekend snow sculpture contest with a life-sized chess set designed by Fran Johnston. (1964 *Oh Ha Daih*)

While *The Collector* played at the Riviera, Geneseo collected mounds of snow, thanks to the blizzard of '66. (1966 *Oh Ha Daih*)

Geneseo Gets a New Leader

While dedicated to making the teachers colleges "multiple purpose," the College Council and SUNY Central Office dipped into the ranks for a teachers college, rather than liberal arts, graduate, to lead Geneseo. In fact, the two frontrunners were both products of teachers colleges.[5]

Robert MacVittie served as president from 1963 to 1979 and returned as interim president in 1988–1989. (Roemer House collection)

The choice was forty-three-year-old Dr. Robert W. MacVittie, who assumed office September 1, 1963. Like the nation's equally youthful president, MacVittie, an Oneonta and New York University graduate and former Buffalo State dean, issued a challenge in his inaugural address the next April. Titled, "The Lamp of Knowledge Needs Wiring," MacVittie's speech recalled that the "characteristic symbol for knowledge or learning has been a lamp of very ancient vintage…." But a new type of lamp was needed. Quoting freely from a variety of scholars, MacVittie laid out Geneseo's future. The school was to be "multiple purpose." He counted on the collective energy and competence of Geneseo's faculty and staff—some of whom he suspected might not be pleased with what lay ahead—to carry out the necessary changes. While he emphasized that the education of teachers and librarians would continue to be the College's "main function," it would be in the context of a strong liberal arts curriculum.[6]

Anticipating his official duties, on July 15, 1963, Dr. MacVittie asked secretary Theo Greenman to provide him with lists and termination dates of the College Council members, of the College's twelve-month administrators, and of the teaching faculty. Nor did he forget to ask for a key to the administration building and his new office.[7]

We'll have to assume he got the lists and keys, but this did not assure that his orientation went smoothly. For example, shortly after he arrived, he discovered one of the Sturges building's outside lights was burned out. The next morning he asked the building's custodian to replace the bulb. The custodian, who barely came up to MacVittie's shoulder, perceived the newcomer as another arrogant faculty member and responded, "Do it yourself." After pausing to appreciate the irony, MacVittie introduced himself as the College's new president.[8]

President MacVittie delivered his inaugural address in Wadsworth Auditorium. (May 1964 *Alumni News*)

In short time MacVittie would make himself known to others, aided, fortuitously, by Governor Nelson Rockefeller, whose ambitions matched his personal wealth, and by the recent appointment of equally ambitious Dr. Samuel Gould to head the State University of New York. The rare combination of Rockefeller's and Gould's personalities and ambitions would transform SUNY. A "megalomaniac" to one critic, "incorrigibly optimistic" and gentle-mannered to others, Gould fit into Rockefeller's scheme to put SUNY on the map.[9]

Gould, who on September 1, 1964, became SUNY president (later retitled chancellor), promptly made a statement not only by his impressive installation but by completely revising the university's master plan. He sought more library resources, programs for the disadvantaged, greater use of instructional technology, doctoral programs at the university centers, two additional arts and science colleges, SUNY Press, more community colleges, a research foundation, and a medical center at Stony Brook. The immediate reaction to Gould's ambitions for SUNY was that he was infusing a "sense of pride," which may have led to his appearing on the January 12, 1968 *Time* magazine cover. However, a "veteran administrator"

President MacVittie was aided by a capable staff (from left): Lenora McMaster, Fred Bennett, and Theodora Greenman. (1968 *Oh Ha Daih*)

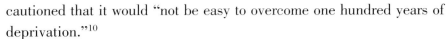

Governor Nelson Rockefeller's budgets provided generous funding for SUNY, facilitating dramatic growth during the 1960s. (1967 *Oh Ha Daih*)

From 1965 to 1980, campus photographer Roger Smith seemed to be everywhere, always wearing and carrying several cameras. He provided a major visual legacy, including many yearbook and other photos that were not specifically credited to him. (1972 *Oh Ha Daih*)

cautioned that it would "not be easy to overcome one hundred years of deprivation."[10]

Nonetheless, that was what Rockefeller expected Gould and SUNY administrators, including MacVittie, to do.

Building the Curriculum and Recruiting Faculty

There were three phases to the revised SUNY Master Plan: teacher education was to be broadened by introducing more liberal arts courses, by starting liberal arts transfer programs at community colleges, and, beginning in 1964, by awarding liberal arts degrees. Offering liberal arts programs would have a profound effect on Geneseo and its sister schools. Teaching would be just one, not the only, option for students. However, implementing those options would cost more, beginning in September 1963, when a four-hundred-dollar tuition was imposed.[11]

The tasks of developing appropriate programs and responding to faculty needs were first addressed during four-week on-campus workshops sponsored by Dr. Harry Porter, SUNY's first provost. "This was," MacVittie recalled, "when I believe SUNY began to move ahead as a university."[12]

Consequently Geneseo, too, began to take on a new identity, illustrated by the awarding of the first liberal arts degrees in June 1964. Beginning in the 1962–1963 school year, all but freshmen could major in biology, chemistry, English, history, mathematics, economics-political science, or sociology-anthropology. Or they could opt for secondary education (7–12) certification, which was added to the more familiar teacher certification programs. (In 1964, freshmen were permitted to register for the liberal arts degree.) Master of Arts programs in English and mathematics began in Fall 1967. That same year the M.L.S. program, offered by the School of Library Science—the first SUNY library school to have one—was fully accredited by the American Library Association. A year later the M.S. in Deaf Education was initiated.[13]

Anticipating the liberal arts transition, in 1962 President Moench had directed an organizational change by creating the Division of Natural Sciences, which included biology, mathematics, and the physical sciences (chemistry, earth science, and physics). Two years later President MacVittie established the Division of Fine Arts (art, dramatic arts, and music departments, with dance added in the 1965–1966 school year). The divisions of speech, humanities (departments of English, foreign language, and philosophy), social sciences (sociology-anthropology, economics-political science, geography, history, and psychology) and health and physical educa-

In the mid-1960s, Holcomb School students were taught by (front row, from left): D. Marshall, M. Giles, M. Isgro, S. Barry, R. Pyper, C. Weekley; (center row): 1952 alumna R. Coffin (Underhill), 1951 and 1968 alumna M. Vangalio, D. Gordon, J. Besser, 1951 alumna A. Loncao, M. Parent, 1950 alumna E. Roodenburg, M. Grove, B. McCaffery; (back row): A. Ryan, R. Isaf, J. Forrester, H. Lynch, R. Funnell, 1952 alumnus T. Conlon, J. Youngers, R. Hughes. (1966 *Oh Ha Daih*)

tion came the following school year.

Necessarily, Geneseo sought faculty with specialized training more appropriate to the College's new mission. However, it still struggled to attract faculty because of low salaries, lack of fringe benefits, and a state retirement system with limited appeal. Fortunately, SUNY's agreement with TIAA-CREF's retirement system helped break the "recruitment log jam," according to MacVittie.[14]

"We," Dean Park wrote in an undated letter to retiree Martin Fausold, "wanted people with doctorates from respectable universities." Presidents Espy and Moench had begun the process, but now money flowed into SUNY as never before. MacVittie and Park beat the bushes all the way to California. Each spent a week at a time recruiting. Park took "a southern route...through Texas...." MacVittie went more northerly, through Michigan to Denver, Colorado, where he hosted a luncheon to explain what SUNY and Geneseo were and where they were located, complete with photos of buildings.[15]

Faculty numbers tripled in just four years (1963–1967). Among new faculty were Dr. Fred Fidura, acting provost in the 1990s; Dr. Donald Watt, later English department chairman; and Dr. Rita Gollin, who with Dr. Srinivasa

Former President Moench and fine arts division chair Bertha Lederer celebrated the 1971 dedication of the Holiday Inn's Presidents' Corner, created by art professor Michael Teres. (Ron Pretzer collection)

In the late 1960s and early 1970s, the south end of Milne Library's main floor housed tables full of print indexes, current periodicals, and pamphlet files. (Milne Archives)

G. Leelamma (1968), was named Distinguished Professor in 1995. Fortunately MacVittie and Park also inherited a solid nucleus, including Dr. Robert Isgro, who directed the acclaimed Chamber Singers in performances all over the globe. Another was Dr. Robert "Duke" Sells, who was enticed to leave Rutgers to head Geneseo's infant physics department just prior to MacVittie's arrival. Sells, coauthor of a leading college-level physics text and Geneseo's first Distinguished Teaching Professor (1973), was encouraged to upgrade the department and pave the way for other science specialists who valued teaching and research. The results were Sells's former Rutgers graduate student Dr. Phillip Alley; Kenneth Kinsey, a University of Rochester Ph.D. (1966); Dr. Douglas Harke; Distinguished Teaching Professor Dr. Jerry Reber (1969); and astronomer Dr. David Meisel (1970), Distinguished Professor and 2004 commencement speaker.[16]

Anthropology professor Wendell Rhodes led students in many archaeological digs at the Macauley complex south of Geneseo. (Roger Smith, Roemer House Collection)

Like Sells, other department heads reflected the specializations demanded of a liberal arts school. Edward Ritter, with an Ohio State doctorate, would chair biology; William Small, a University of Rochester Ph.D., chaired the mathematics department; and Richard F. Smith, another University of Rochester Ph.D., headed the nascent chemistry department. The geography department was chaired by Donald Q. Innis, a Canadian with a doctorate from the University of California-Berkeley and a distinctive laugh. Frank Scholfield, a Ph.D. from the University of Colorado, chaired sociology-anthropology, and David A. Martin, who directed the economics-political science department, had a doctorate from Syracuse University's Maxwell School. Robert Roecker, a zoologist with a Cornell Ph.D., was lured from the New York State Department of Conservation and created the vivarium, which he maintained long after he retired in 1983.[17]

The 1963 math faculty included William Small (left), who chaired the department for many years, and Clarence Stephens. (1963 *Oh Ha Daih*)

In retrospect these were "the glory days" for faculty. SUNY was, in the words of contemporaries, "flush with money." Salaries jumped, and for a time SUNY was a magnet for aspiring faculty.

Ironically, President MacVittie also benefited from passage of the Taylor Law in New York in 1967, which permitted public employees, including college faculty, to engage in collective bargaining. Thus, faculty, wanting to exercise more control over their academic lives, found SUNY schools more to their liking than formerly.[18]

A year later the New York State Center for Migrant Studies was created and housed at Geneseo, resulting in good press for the village and the College.

Migrant Center founder and longtime director Gloria Mattera (left) was a dedicated supporter of migrant workers' rights and education. Meeting with Mattera are (from left) vocational education development coordinator Arthur Nowak, workshops coordinator Steve Weisbrod, '72, research director Theodore Stovall, and state senator Mary Ann Krupsak. (Roger Smith, Milne Archives)

Above left: Student Robert Lynch, '73, seen here with migrant workers' children, later became director of the Migrant Center. (Roger Smith, Milne Archives)

Above right: Art instructor and Public Information Office designer Richard Beale presented President Moench with his 1964 design for a college seal. It was replaced by the present seal (inset) in 1968. (Little Studio, Hepler collection; inset, 1971 *Oh Ha Daih*)

Initiated by President MacVittie, headed by education professor Dr. Gloria Mattera and funded in part by the Migrant Education Office of the state education department, it was designed to offer studies on the migrant culture, consult with communities assimilating migrants, serve as a coordination and information center, and write and test teaching materials for migrants. Over its lifetime it has received numerous awards, in no small part due to Mattera's untiring efforts.[19]

Reflecting Geneseo's changing mission and title change to State University College of Arts and Science at Geneseo, President MacVittie wanted a new College seal. In 1968, just four years after art professor Richard Beale had been directed to design a more traditional seal using the SUNY symbol, MacVittie hired the New York City firm of Martin Moskof and Associates to

President Robert MacVittie, Paul Hepler, and Dean Robert Redden dedicated the case Hepler created to hold the ceremonial mace and presidential medallion crafted by Willard Peterson. During a campus protest, students caused minor damage in an unsuccessful attempt to break into the case and steal what they considered symbols of authority. (Roger Smith, Hepler collection)

design a successor. The new emblem featured "a yellow flame from the torch of knowledge surrounded by leaves symbolic of the bucolic setting of Geneseo State. Both of these are atop waves symbolizing the historic Genesee River. Both the leaves and waves are blue." (Actually, the leaves are green.)[20]

With liberal arts majors and a more specialized faculty, the foundation for a multipurpose college was laid, but the expected changes were temporarily sidetracked by outside events.[21]

Noise, Dust, Mud, More Dust, and More Mud

Construction, begun under presidents Espy and Moench, took on greater urgency now. A multipurpose college with a growing enrollment required appropriate facilities: upgraded science labs, an expanded library, a state-of-the-art communications and lecture hall, more residence halls, an infirmary, and a new administration building.

On February 6, 1964, even before his inauguration, Dr. MacVittie announced that the Trustees had approved a "Comprehensive Campus Development Plan." In the past decade Geneseo had grown from a headcount of 884 students and 75 faculty to 2,724 students and a faculty of 204. Ahead was the task of preparing for 3,400 full-time students and "a corresponding growth in faculty and staff."[22]

The College had to acquire land, which meant dislocating families, including at least one faculty member and his family, and removing proper-

President Robert MacVittie and Vice President Lawrence Park headed the procession as faculty lined up west of the College Center (Blake A) for commencement in 1966. (1966 *Oh Ha Daih*)

ties from the tax rolls. MacVittie had to become a skillful negotiator. Sixteen lots on Elizabeth Street, running from Court Street to the present University Drive, and another thirteen on Court Street, plus a corner lot on Elizabeth and Court streets, had to be purchased. Similarly, Franklin Street, parallel to Elizabeth, had to be emptied and Wadsworth Street truncated. Even the Clionian sorority had to relinquish its property. Land for athletic fields had to be acquired from the Union Free District No. 4 (forty-two acres), from Geneseo Central School District (thirteen acres), and from contractor Joseph Vitale (thirty-five-and-a-half acres).[23]

Campus expansion displaced many village residents, college sororities and fraternities, and student boarding houses. These two photos capture the last moments of one of several Wadsworth Street homes razed to make way for Newton lecture hall. (Milne Archives)

Obtaining money for such purchases during Governor Rockefeller's term of office was no object; acquiring the properties was a different matter. "Letters of Intent" mailed out to thirteen property owners brought expected reactions and at least one lawsuit. The Disparti sisters, an occupational therapist and a teacher, were asked to give up their 120-year-old, recently repaired and neatly landscaped house at 37 Court Street—the house in which they were born. They readily admitted they were "too sensible" to try to block wrecking crews, but they complained that they didn't "feel the village is ours" anymore. Another former owner, despite the attractive new home she had built in another part of the village, long lamented the loss of her home on Elizabeth Street.[24]

Construction also meant removing large old trees, noise from huge cranes and earthmoving equipment, swirling dust, more parking woes, and mud.

Newspaper headlines regularly proclaimed "College Growth," "Geneseo Breaks Ground," "Officiate at Rites," and "Work Starts on New Group of Buildings Soon." But nothing matched the September 1966 sixteen-page Sanders Supplement proclaiming "Geneseo State—Great Today, Even Greater in the Future." A virtual paean to the College, it extolled the expansion ("brings prosperity") and the faculty being recruited.[25]

Between 1963 and 1971, ten residence halls and two dining halls were built. Bailey Science (1965), Clark Service building (1967), the new Milne Library (1966), Lauderdale Infirmary (1966), Newton Hall (1967), Erwin administration building (1967), the new Holcomb Campus School (1969), and the College Union (1969) also were opened. The construction cost in 1964 alone was a staggering $7.95 million; it rose to $13 million the following year.[26]

The most distinctive buildings—Fine Arts, Red Jacket, and the College Union—were designed by Edgar Tafel, a former apprentice of Frank Lloyd Wright. The Tafel-designed campus of 1970 reflected Wright's "Prairie School" of architecture: two-level (above grade) buildings which blended well with the landscape, avoided the need for extra village or College fire equipment, and offered a human scale appropriate to an undergraduate campus. There is no imposing "power tower," unlike some built on other SUNY campuses of the time. Instead, the president's second-floor office in Erwin Hall is no higher than any other office on campus.[27]

College officials struggled just to name the buildings. Following recent tradition, they named the residence halls after the home counties of many students: Allegany, Erie, Genesee, Ontario, Onondaga, Nassau, Niagara, Steuben, Suffolk, Wayne, and Wyoming. Letchworth and Red Jacket dining halls recalled local history, while the academic and administrative buildings bore the names of prominent persons connected with the

The gazebo, a favorite place for enjoying sunsets, was created by architect Edgar Tafel. (Roger Smith, Roemer House collection)

College. The two science buildings (1965 and 1970) honored longtime faculty members Guy Bailey and Robert Greene. The new administration building recognized former state senator Austin Erwin, a graduate and College Council chairman. The new Milne Library too was a natural, and Newton

The 1970 College Council members were (seated, from left): Frances Dew, C. Everett Shults, chair Joseph Quirk, secretary Theodora Greenman, Reverdy Wadsworth; (standing): Kenneth Willard, Lillian Black, E. Stanley Copeland, John Kelly, and President MacVittie. (1970 *Oh Ha Daih*)

Judge George Newton participated in the groundbreaking for his namesake building. (Hepler collection)

Hall, an octagonal building with state-of-the-art audio-visual equipment and large (up to five hundred seats) and small (sixty seats) instruction rooms, remembered local and state supreme court judge, George D. Newton.

MacVittie has rightly been labeled the "Master Builder." By 1971, less than

The Orchesis dance ensemble originated under the guidance of the physical education department. Dance was later moved to the fine arts division. (1966 *Oh Ha Daih*)

ten years into his administration, the campus had a distinctly new look. Only Sturges, the first Holcomb School (now Welles), Wadsworth Auditorium, the earlier Milne (now Fraser) Library, the Blake buildings, and Jones, Monroe, and Livingston halls recalled the teachers college past.

"Don't Trust Anyone Over Thirty!"

Along with new buildings, there was a new student culture on campus. It was illustrated by a minor matter early in President MacVittie's tenure. On March 29, 1965, art professor Willard Peterson wrote the president that "no qualified students…are willing to accept editorial responsibilities" to put out the 1966 *Oh Ha Daih*. Whatever recognition and personal satisfaction past editors enjoyed was insufficient to compensate aspiring ones for the expected grade point drop due to the work of putting out a yearbook. Alternatives were to pay the editors, allow them course credit, or hope that individuals would come through under the "current system." MacVittie advised Peterson to expect volunteers. Fortunately, enough appeared.[28]

President Robert MacVittie and 1964 homecoming queen Carol Lanphear led the festivities on the quadrangle. (Milne Archives)

Before the decade was out, Dr. MacVittie would gladly have settled for such easily solved problems. The "Silent Generation" had given way to a more raucous one.

These students were more likely to be males, to come from cities and suburbs, and to be more affluent than previously. The proportion of males at Geneseo almost doubled between 1962 and 1970, to forty percent. (One explanation was that satisfactory college attendance could qualify for exemption from the military draft. Another was the College's effort to attract males.) Compared with their predecessors, more students reported both parents "had some exposure to college," were more affluent, and had higher secondary school averages (eighty-seven versus eighty in 1962). Moreover, not only did fewer want to teach, more intended to pursue postgraduate degrees. A larger percentage of the students "discussed politics" and had more liberal attitudes toward abortion, divorce, capital punishment, legalization of marijuana, and gun control. Their instructors' credentials were changing as well. In 1960 only forty percent of the Geneseo faculty had attained the highest degree in their fields. A dozen years later almost sixty percent had.[29]

Left: Robert Sinclair, namesake of the current black box theater in Brodie, watched in the background as student actors performed in the original black box, located in the basement of Welles. (Milne Archives)

Right: The College band, directed by Daryl Hanson (not shown), was a parade highlight for many years. When their marching days ended, their uniforms were donated to Geneseo's high school. Sample uniforms are in the College Archives thanks to former librarian Anita Whitehead, who rescued them when the high school discarded them. (Roemer House Collection)

Gradually, these demographic changes were reflected in student behavior, although Geneseo remained a relatively conservative campus, even apathetic, to critics. For example, in 1967 the newly appointed editor of *The Lamron* announced he was transferring to SUNY Buffalo for his senior year to find "students who can challenge you" and were willing to do something to achieve "more freedom." Not even the mid-sixties campus appearances of Robert Welch, founder of the ultraconservative John Birch Society, and of George Lincoln Rockwell, founder of the American Nazi Party, resulted in genuine disturbances. This may have shown the influence of an administration that generally was open to change, including to student grievances over dorm hours, dress codes, and student fees. But protest was in the air, producing in the words of an alumna, a "discordant sound…as clear as some of the Beatles or Monkees songs."[30]

The watershed year was 1967, when campus demonstrations gained steam.

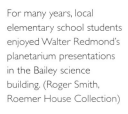

Students protested American Nazi Party founder George Lincoln Rockwell's campus appearance. (1967 *Oh Ha Daih*)

A January article in the *Livingston County Leader*, signed by "a Freedom Fighter," a member of the newly formed Students For Freedom (SFF), set the tone: "Geneseo Women Demand Freedom-Equal Station." While focusing on discrimination against women students, the group, led by Jay Coughtry, objected "to all suppression of student rights." Directly challenging midnight curfews, the SFF called for students to demonstrate on the quadrangle at midnight, Saturday January 21.[31]

Responding almost immediately, MacVittie met with "a five-member

For many years, local elementary school students enjoyed Walter Redmond's planetarium presentations in the Bailey science building. (Roger Smith, Roemer House Collection)

student delegation" the following Monday and agreed to "some modification" of the rules. However, he reminded the students that the changes had to be approved by the Faculty Senate and passed on to the College Council for final approval. It turns out this was only the opening salvo. Dr. Richard Roark, who chaired the Faculty Senate Student Affairs Committee, was alarmed by an SFF "Position Paper" that he regarded as inflammatory and promptly forwarded to MacVittie.[32]

Two weeks later a local reporter for a Rochester newspaper hyperbolically reported that the SFF had "exploded…into a slashing, all-out attack on the way the college is run and the educative job it is doing." At a "teach-in," a phenomenon new to Geneseo, the students were joined by seven faculty members, including biology professor Dr. Herman Forest, who readily admitted that he was critical of the education the students were getting. The students' real objection, shared with thousands of other students, was to the College's *in loco parentis* (acting for a parent) policy. Assistant professor of English William Slavick, whose contract had not been renewed and who would become one of the leading critics of the administration, called for "student power." If the students did not act, he proclaimed, they would be as "dead as the Geneseo faculty."[33]

A Rochester *Democrat and Chronicle* editorial skewered the students,

The Hotel Geneseo, located just north of the entrance to the village parking lot, was popular with students until fire destroyed it on May 10, 1967. (Pretzer collection)

claiming they wanted headlines more than relief from administrative strictures. It noted that MacVittie had regularly held monthly meetings with students, so there were opportunities to resolve issues. As if proving the point, on February 15, the Faculty Senate voted to extend the dorm hours on a trial basis, and the College Council approved.[34]

But protests continued. Slavick, English professor Dr. Leo Rockas and assistant professor of sociology Joseph P. Lonero argued that at a true liberal arts college "Unrest Is Healthy, Not Disruptive." In early March 1967, a four-person panel took up the various issues before about two hundred faculty, in what a reporter labeled a "stormy" session. Dr. Jerome Nadelhaft, assistant professor of history, began by arguing for "faculty dissenters." Dean Park, who followed, made it clear he would not "sit by idly" and watch the College torn down by "forces of destruction." Approving the fervor at the College, University Professor Walter Harding argued that "there is no intellectual desert on campus." Finally, David Martin, newly appointed chairman of economics-political science, felt the College lacked "a dynamic student and faculty government" and prescribed a number of changes necessary to reform the College, though he doubted they would occur "in the near future."[35]

At a subsequent colloquy with MacVittie on March 15 "the hard-core" dis-

Students demonstrated their displeasure with President MacVittie after English professor Leo Rockas left the College. (Roger Smith, Roemer House collection)

senters—professors Nadelhaft, Slavick, Rockas, Lonero, and George Mower (English)—"found it almost impossible" to get the president to focus on "the real issues: the academic quality of the institution, hiring and firing policies, the role of dissent, and student rights." The rest of the faculty was divided about whether existing channels to pursue dissent were adequate and quiet might prevail.[36]

Apparently the "channels" were not adequate. The next campus protest focused on whether student activity fees should be mandatory. Supporters argued that students should have the right to tax themselves. Critics argued that mandatory fees were an arrogation of administrative power and threatened to go to court to fight it even if students voted for mandatory fees. This was no small matter. Fees supported athletics, cultural events, student publications (*The Lamron* and *Oh Ha Daih*), and campus speakers, to name the most obvious items. The students did approve mandatory fees by a 694 to 283 vote, and there was no lawsuit. Nonetheless, President MacVittie decided to continue the voluntary fee payment policy while awaiting a SUNY-wide policy.[37]

MacVittie resolved one issue—serving alcohol on campus—quite amicably in the spring of 1969, when the Rathskeller opened in the basement

The 1966–1967 Chamber Singers included (front, from left): Laura Marcy, Bob Rich, Sherry Smith; (center row): Meredith Thompson, Jackie Palladine, Martha Wilbert, director Robert Isgro, Cathy Farrell, Paul Weller; (back): Jeanette Shady, Bob Jaquay, Nancy Smith, Jim Domm, Sue Stratton, Penny Beebe, Joe Thoman, Ysaye Barnwell (founding member of Sweet Honey in the Rock and 1998 honorary degree recipient), Jill Meisenheimer, Ken Roberts, Mark Dievendorf. (1967 *Oh Ha Daih*)

Despite protests, the majority of students voted for mandatory fees. (1967 *Oh Ha Daih*)

The Rathskeller in Letchworth Dining Hall's basement was a popular alternative to uptown bars from 1969 to 1982. (1971 *Oh Ha Daih*)

of Letchworth Dining Hall. (The issue arose again in 1982 when the Rathskeller closed, because New York's drinking age was raised from eighteen to twenty-one.)

However, MacVittie faced other protests that stormy spring, including one on May 24 that "differed markedly from other incidents there [at Geneseo] this semester," according to the Rochester *Times-Union*. Led by sociology chairman Dr. Frank Scholfield, twenty-five "faculty members, including five department chairmen, and about one hundred students...slowly and quietly" walked around the quadrangle for approximately an hour to protest the dismissal of associate art professor Glen E. Howerton. Despite a petition signed by forty-seven faculty members supporting him, the dismissal stood.[38]

That was not the end of faculty protests. After the semester ended, six faculty, including Nadelhaft, Mower, and Rockas, who left the College, sent an "open letter" to Chancellor Gould condemning his support of President MacVittie. They disagreed with a SUNY subcommittee report, based on interviews with approximately fifty Geneseo faculty, that praised MacVittie for affording "a very full measure of academic freedom." MacVittie retorted that he intended to protect "the rights of the majority" (presumably non-protesters) in whom he had faith.[39]

MacVittie cited the College's openness, recalling inviting speakers who represented various views, including George Lincoln Rockwell and a forthcoming program on the "God is Dead" school of theology. But he preferred to talk about the College's curriculum changes: the recent approval of an M.A. in mathematics, which he identified as the first among the SUNY schools, the proposed M.A. in English, and additions to the international study program.[40]

Biology professor and village resident Dr. Elwood B. Ehrle wrote a long letter to the editor of the Rochester *Times-Union* condemning the paper's "local representative" [Robert Bickel]. Ehrle accused Bickel, a Geneseo resident and supporter of the College and village, of "yellow sheet journalism." (Bickel, who wrote most of the articles about the protest, was not averse to using rather inflammatory and controversial phrasing.)[41]

President and Mrs. MacVittie were among the many who enjoyed the March 1968 Hudson River School art exhibition in what is now Lederer Gallery. The gallery's inaugural exhibit was attended by *New York Times* art critic John Canaday, whose review was published on March 24. (Hepler collection)

With the end of the school year and the departure of several faculty protest leaders, President MacVittie must have savored "A Pat on the Back" from the Geneseo Town Board for the "fine job" he was "doing under the difficult conditions of rapid growth...."[42]

However, he was not out of the woods and may have been helped to understand the changing climate by a timely article Rosalind Fisher shared with him. Written by Seymour L. Halleck, the director of psychiatry at the University of

Students William Lupardo, '71, Alice Grow, '70, and Susan Bookman, '68, supported Eugene McCarthy's unsuccessful bid for the 1968 Democratic presidential nomination by selling buttons and bumper stickers and collecting signatures on a petition urging Robert Kennedy to support McCarthy instead of seeking the nomination. (Milne Archives)

Student protests of the U.S. invasion of Cambodia and Kent State shootings led to a relaxed final exam policy in May 1970. (1970 *Oh Ha Daih*)

Wisconsin, the article examined student unrest, which baffled many at the time because the protesters were a "privileged generation." Admittedly a minority of students, the protesters tended to come in two varieties. The "hippies," however "tolerant and friendly," flaunted convention, focused only on the present, and found "solace in aesthetics." "The politicals" were attracted to causes, but were "discouragingly incapable of sustaining commitment." Colleges and universities needed to offer students "realistic prerogatives" and inform them of the "serious obligations in decision-making."[43]

Protests Take a Different Direction

While earlier protests reflected discontent over relatively resolvable student rights, campus protests over the Vietnam War took a more ominous turn. They began with teach-ins in May 1965. The first to draw attention here was held in the College Center. Panelists were geography chairman Dr. Donald Innis, historian Dr. Henry Holland, English professor Gilbert Davis, and author-in-residence William Kelly. The first outright demonstration was April 14, 1968, followed by a pause until September 27. The pace picked up a year later, with five demonstrations. More were to come, with greater intensity and effect.[44]

Articles, letters, and op-ed pieces in *The Lamron* illustrate the tenor of the protests. By history professor James Somerville's count there were approximately

Geneseo owed its longtime reputation as a "suitcase college" to students like these, waiting in front of Dwyer's for the northbound Trailways bus. (1966 *Oh Ha Daih*)

120 war-related items in *The Lamron* between October 23, 1964 and February 2, 1973. While Jerry McCarthy, '73, a veteran, may have been the most critical, the greatest single contributor was Paul Scipione, a 1968 graduate and draftee who penned letters from Vietnam where he was an administrative specialist for the 101st Airborne.[45]

On October 3, 1969, one thousand students signed a petition calling for classes to be cancelled on the 15th, but Dr. MacVittie refused to do so. A rally the next day involved faculty, including professors Walter Harding, S. Jay Walker, Richard Roark, and Frank Scholfield; the Reverends Harold Babb and David Carter, representing the Campus Ministry; Father Thomas Statt, Newman Foundation Chaplain; and Reverend Fred Yoos, Central Presbyterian Church pastor.

Accompanied by newly appointed vice president for academic affairs Dr. Thomas Colahan, MacVittie walked down to the student demonstration in Schrader Gym and took a seat in the bleachers. After he had "heard enough nonsense," the president walked up to the microphone and told the speaker, Charles Daniels, an officer of the Geneseo Afro-American Student Society, he wanted to say something. Daniels said MacVittie was not invited. MacVittie countered that he had invited himself. Daniels then asked the attendees whether they wanted to hear the president. Their applause persuaded Daniels to turn the microphone over to MacVittie, who read a prepared statement, which drew more applause and led to the students' orderly departure. Thirty years later. acting vice president for college advancement and loyal alumnus Dick Rosati, '71, dubbed this President MacVittie's shining hour.[46]

President MacVittie asked for an opportunity to speak when he and Vice President Colahan attended a student protest rally. (1970 *Oh Ha Daih*)

The president, with the help of Colahan and vice president for student affairs Dr. David A. Young, had correctly judged the students' radicalism—or lack thereof. Attendance at the October 15 moratorium was disappointing. Only three hundred of the school's thirty-five hundred students showed any interest, according to *The Lamron's* October 31 editorial. Some students claimed they had no time. Others admitted that they didn't want to get involved. Still others regarded the protesters as "a bunch of radicals."

But MacVittie was uncomfortable with the protests and *The Lamron's* reporting of campus events. So, in 1970 he established the *Geneseo Compass* as the school's official news organ. ("Rumor control" is how

R. Buckminster Fuller spent a full day meeting with classes when he was on campus for a lecture. (1967 *Oh Ha Daih*)

Students presented Lillian Hellman's *The Lark* in March 1966, with Ann Bergstrom starring as Joan of Arc. (Milne Archives)

Governor Nelson Rockefeller spoke at the Livingston County Republican party's 1970 fundraising dinner in the College Union ballroom. (1970 *Oh Ha Daih*)

Art faculty in the early 1970s included H. Gordon Miller and Willard Peterson. (1963 *Oh Ha Daih*)

some faculty and students at the College viewed the new publication.)[47]

The U.S. military invasion of Cambodia in April 1970 led to stepped-up protests across the nation, climaxing in the killing and wounding of students at Ohio's Kent State University on May 4 and at Mississippi's Jackson State ten days later. After Kent State, a group of Geneseo students sought approval for a three-day strike to protest the war, which the College granted. The group's request forced the faculty and administration—after almost around-the-clock meetings for days—to allow students to opt out of final exams, thus momentarily calming the situation. But it had been a difficult time for Faculty Senate Chairman Bill Derby and the Faculty Senate Executive Committee.[48]

The last protest of the year occurred May 15 at the annual Livingston County Republican fundraiser in the new College Union ballroom with more than eight hundred attendees. Governor Nelson A. Rockefeller, the guest speaker, was interrupted by approximately twenty protesters carrying what Ray Sherman, the *Livingston Republican* owner-editor, described as "obscene signs" and making "obscene cat-calls." Another group of protesters, "many of them students," staged a "silent protest."[49]

Sherman, a Rotary Paul Harris honoree, World War II veteran, and longtime resident, lambasted the protesters in an editorial. Paul Neureiter, by then a revered emeritus professor who knew authoritarianism firsthand in his native Austria, took Sherman to task. To Neureiter, pursuing the war was immoral; protesting it was not. Other letters reflected the division of opinion.[50]

Despite the seriousness of the decade's protests, there were some lighter moments. For example, geography chairman Donald Innis calmly walked out of a meeting with an administrator in the Erwin building and promptly joined a protest march. Martin Fausold, following some "crazy sociologist" who was leading a demonstration, heard history colleague Randy Bailey ask, "Should we be doing this?"[51]

The Greek Tree and Other Antics

For all the uproar in the papers, the 1969–1970 *Oh Ha Daih* pictured a campus little changed from earlier years. In many respects, the social life wasn't different. For example, the dedication of the much-sought, nondenominational, Tafel-designed Interfaith Center on November 2, 1969, was well attended (Bishop Fulton Sheen was a guest), as was the dedication of the new state-of-the-art Holcomb Campus School downhill a month earlier. (The former campus school building was renamed to recognize Geneseo Principal James Welles, who had died that February).

During the decade, the students had enjoyed a variety of entertainers, including talented actor Theodore Bikel; presidential aide Theodore Sorensen; Pulitzer Prize-winning historian Arthur Schlesinger, Jr.; Russo-Chinese relations expert Harrison Salisbury; Bel Kaufman, author of *Up the Down Staircase*; Tex Ritter (actor John Ritter's father) with the Grand Ole Opry; civil rights activist Julian Bond in 1968; and consumer advocate Ralph Nader two years later.[52]

Neither classes nor protests interfered with the painting of "the gnarled tree," familiarly known as the "Greek Tree," fronting Blake A (formerly College Center), "the last remnant of the original campus." The tradition appears to have begun in the 1960s with fraternities vying to be last to paint the tree before daylight (thereby avoiding possible punishment and abiding by the Greeks' unwritten rules). Bill Brewer, '69, recalls painting the tree "in the early hours" in 1967, along with fellow DKT pledge Cal Brown, '70, before a pledge run. Barbara Finkle, '68, believes she was the second to paint the tree in 1965 when she was a new member of Arethusa. Doug Brode, '65, thinks the first painting, which caused a "big to-do," occurred in the 1961–1962 school year.[53]

Brode also believes he may have introduced "traying" to the campus. After Christmas 1962, he bought a "flying saucer," a fad at the time, and slid downhill toward Sturges, but the saucer "smashed to bits" when it hit the College Center. So, he improvised; he took a tray from the cafeteria and whizzed downhill, which was imitated shortly, causing a shortage of trays.

Diver Dave Krumrine showed winning form in a 1968 meet against SUNY Potsdam. (Bright collection, identification by Duncan Hinckley)

Painting the "Greek tree" in front of Sturges is a long-standing tradition. (1970 *Oh Ha Daih*)

Coach Duncan Hinckley's swimmers won their first SUNYAC title in 1976. Shown with Hinckley are senior co-captains (from left): Jim Hadley, Tim Gillam, Steve Karnath, and Morgan Smith. (Roger Smith, Roemer House collection)

The Sports Scene

Athletics, which had suffered for close to ten years from lack of facilities, took on a new look in the 1960s with the opening of Schrader gym and the hiring of more HPE faculty with coaching specializations. Gone were the days when one person coached all the men's sports. The first new hire was soccer coach Carl Witzel in 1963, known for his play on the famous Kodak softball team; followed in rapid order by Shirley Toler (1963), whose synchronized swimming teams earned a number of awards; Fred Bright (1964), who coached men's tennis from 1975 to 1980, and after initiating the women's soccer team, guided it to an NCAA Final Four in 1994; Dr. Martin Kentner (1966), whose cross country teams' successes were a marvel; Duncan Hinckley (1967), five-time SUNYAC swimming coach of the year; Joyce Wechsler (1969), who produced competitive women's volleyball and basketball teams; Thomas Pope (1969), who brought his winning ways from Arcade High School to Geneseo; and Paul Rose (1970), who led Geneseo's lacrosse team to its first ECAC championship. The promotion of Robert Riedel from associate director of admissions to athletic director by influential HPE division chairman Dan Mullin in 1967 signaled that athletics would enjoy successes that harkened back to some of the early days at Geneseo.

Joe Rebisz (24) went for the shot while Dick Woodward (32) remained alert for a possible rebound. (Bright collection)

Coach Carl Witzel gave his soccer team a pep talk during halftime in 1968. (Bright collection)

Whatever Happened To...?

1967 protest leader Jay Coughtry became Dr. Coughtry, Associate Professor of History at the University of Nevada-Las Vegas. Dr. Bruce Godsave, '65 (7–12 math certification) returned to his alma mater eleven years later to teach deaf education. Student Association president Ron Cicoria, '65, served three ten-year terms as Livingston County judge before retiring in 2005. Paul Scipione, '68, obtained a doctorate at Rutgers, was a marketing professor at Montclair State University (and adjunct at Geneseo), and published *Shades of Gray* (1989), a novel based on his Vietnam experience. Alfred Sciarrino, '69, also described his military experiences in a book after a very circuitous route to a faculty appointment at his alma mater. Bruce Jordan, '66, co-wrote, co-produced, and directed *Shear Madness*, which claims to be "the longest-running [off-Broadway] play in the history of the American theatre." And Marion Vosburgh-Canedo, '65, second-grade teacher at Buffalo's Waterfront Elementary School, was named the state's "Teacher of the Year" by the Board of Regents in 1979.[54]

****

Unprecedented growth and protests distracted the College from achieving real curriculum reform, but halfway through his tenure MacVittie already had made an impact. University Professor Walter Harding asserted "the [College's] real turning point was between Dr. Moench and Dr. MacVittie." Though Harding did not mean to "belittle" the likeable and re-spected Moench, he found Moench "old school," i.e., too controlling. MacVittie was "new school." He had successfully handled a doubling of the student popu-lation (from 2,370 in 1962–1963 to 5,408 in 1970–1971) and an increase in the number of faculty from 204 to nearly 350, had seen the physical plant mushroom—adding ten residence halls, an infirmary, two dining halls, five academic buildings, and a college union—and had overseen Geneseo's ex-panded academic program. Unfortunately, ahead lay severe budget cuts and an enrollment crisis.[55]

Delta Kappa Tau's 1965 Homecoming float depicting the first movable microscope was towed past what is now McClellan House, home of the Alumni Center and Lockhart Gallery. (1966 *Oh Ha Daih*)

State University of New York
COLLEGE *of* ARTS *and* SCIENCE *at* GENESEO
The Liberal Arts Transition (1971–1979)

Geneseo Turns One Hundred

The College began its centennial year of 1971 with high hopes. In the May 1970 *Geneseo Alumni News*, Dr. David Manly, chairman of the Centennial Board, described ambitious plans to celebrate the historic occasion, and *The Lamron's* first issue in September 1971 was devoted almost exclusively to the College's history. Photos of Old Main sharply contrasted with the newer buildings. All former principals and presidents were pictured, and a brief history of the College was offered. The College had gone from one building to thirty-eight, seven acres to 220, thirteen faculty to more than three hundred, seventy-one students to greater than five thousand, and a two-year to a four-year curriculum.

The opening convocation on September 13 had all the hoopla appropriate to the occasion. President MacVittie was joined by SUNY Chancellor Ernest Boyer, who gave the main address; by MacVittie's predecessor Francis Moench; by former dean and acting president Kenneth Freeman; and by retired assistant commissioner of teachers colleges Hermann Cooper. Two months later associate professor of English and former dean Rosalind Fisher signed copies of her legacy, *...the stone strength of the past...*, in the Hunt Room of the new College Union.

Opposite Page: On November 15, 1972, fire destroyed several businesses on the west side of Main Street, the site of devastating fires a century earlier. (Roger Smith, Milne Archives)

The then-current president, a former acting president, a former College and SUNY administrator, and a former president posed together in the 1970s. From left are: President and Mrs. Robert MacVittie, Dr. and Mrs. Kenneth Freeman, Dr. and Mrs. Hermann Cooper, and Dr. and Mrs. Francis Moench. (Pretzer Collection)

Fortunately, many of Dr. Manly's plans, begun four years earlier, were realized. Centennial lecturers included SUNY at Buffalo Nobel Prize neurobiologist Sir John Eccles and University of Illinois educator Harry Broudy. Thirteen "County Days" recognized the counties after which the residence halls had been named. Popular Rochester musician Chuck Mangione entertained twice with concerts, and an eight-day Caribbean Cruise came off as anticipated.

However, the centennial celebration never matched the fiftieth. Debilitating budget problems were surfacing, and protests against the Vietnam War and the military draft continued. A riot at nearby Attica Prison and charges of racism at the College led to more campus protests. Vexing construction delays created problems. President MacVittie was chosen to start an upper division college at Utica-Rome, which led to uncertainty about Geneseo's leadership. Most troubling, before the decade was out, an enrollment shortfall threatened Geneseo's future. Troubling events beyond the confines of the College also intruded, including protests over the U.S. Supreme Court's *Roe v. Wade* abortion decision, the unprecedented resignations of the country's president and vice president, and sixty-three Americans taken hostage by Iranian militants.

The College erected commemorative road signs as part of the celebration of the centennial of its opening. (Roemer House collection)

Further, the centennial celebration had barely begun when, on November 1, Dr. MacVittie announced his resignation to head the SUNY Utica-Rome upper division college. The SUNY Trustees' choice among 150 candidates to head the new school, MacVittie made it clear that he had not applied for the position, but had been asked to interview. The announcement brought the expected reactions and an unexpected one.[1]

On October 13, student Mark Blakely wrote MacVittie wishing him good luck and asked whether "it would be all right if I begin parking" in the spot MacVittie was relinquishing, for it was "directly adjacent to most of" Blakely's classes. Two days later the sympathetic president answered Blakely that acting president Colahan would need the parking space.[2]

As it turned out, Colahan would not need it for long. Three months after MacVittie departed, the Rochester *Democrat and Chronicle* announced that he would return to Geneseo on February 10, 1972. (The fledgling SUNY unit, which occupied an old mill factory in Utica, was then more dream than reality.) Encouraged by support from subordinates and welcome-back letters from faculty, College Council members, and the larger community, MacVittie resumed his post to attack the twin problems of bolstering Geneseo's curriculum and managing the College through a budget crisis.[3]

Thomas Colahan served as vice president for academic affairs from 1968 to 1989. (1970 *Oh Ha Daih*)

Finishing the Job: Curriculum Revisions

The task of curriculum reform was assigned to Dr. Thomas S. Colahan, vice president for academic affairs, "the main architect in Geneseo's transition" to a multipurpose college. Colahan, the former vice dean for academic affairs at Columbia University, had replaced alumnus Roy McTarnaghan, who had temporarily replaced Dr. Park. (Park, who left to become president of Pennsylvania's Mansfield State, recognized that he and MacVittie "were too similar in background for the good of the college." To fully implement the liberal arts programs, another second-in-charge was needed.) Colahan had the needed academic background:

Alumni Association director Angie Saunders, Irvin Underhill, President MacVittie, and library director Richard Quick perused some recent additions to Milne Library's collection. (Milne Archives)

a doctorate (sixteenth to seventeenth-century British history) from Columbia University and administrative experience. However, despite his credentials, some faculty questioned whether Colahan, born, bred, and educated in New York City, would fit in this rural setting, which he typically referred to as "Happy Valley."[4]

The November 1976 dedication of Milne Library's Wadsworth Family Papers Collections was celebrated by (from left): Judge Robert Houston, William P. Wadsworth, Penelope Wadsworth, librarian William Lane, library director Richard Quick, and President MacVittie. Library crowding later forced the collections to be moved to two former listening rooms. (Roger Smith, Milne Archives)

President MacVittie had charged him with making Geneseo "identifiably an arts and science college" without abandoning teacher education. However, Brockport history professor Dr. Bruce Leslie claims that SUNY, following Chancellor Gould's 1964 Master Plan, was, in fact, "running away" from teacher education, traditionally the dominant component of its former teachers colleges.[5]

Curricular changes depended on Colahan's ability to get a handle on how SUNY Central and the College worked. He had a site plan, a very ambitious one, from which to work. It called for increasing enrollment to 8,300 (6,000 of whom were to be full-time students), boosting library volumes from 162,000 to 350,000, developing more liberal arts majors and graduate programs and adding 492 parking spaces for faculty and 2,249 for students. (Students and faculty are still looking for those parking spots.) Even horseshoe pits were envisioned. All of this was to be done by 1974, five years from the date of the report. Immediate questions for Colahan were: what budget constraints did he face? Who and what did the faculty lines represent? What were the staff allocations? And to what extent could he shift monies and lines? While the College's budget was a determinant, the key to real change, Colahan believed, was the faculty.[6]

The Faculty

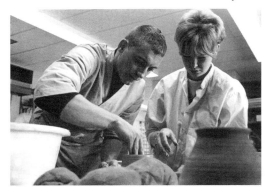

The Brodie Fine Arts building includes a well-equipped ceramics studio, where Carl Shanahan has instructed students for over forty years. He also chaired the department from 1996 to 2002. (Roger Smith, Hepler collection)

Dr. Colahan inherited and added a number of faculty consonant with his expectations. Preceding him in 1967 were Dr. Edward Janosik to chair political science (newly separated from economics); Dr. Valentin Rabe, a Harvard Ph.D. and future history department chairman; and Carl Shanahan, who later chaired the art department. The following year the College attracted Drs. Charles S. Goetzinger, a language specialist, as speech department chairman; James Wilbur, a Columbia Ph.D., as philosophy chairman; James "Fred" Gillen, future history chairman; Kevork Nahabedian, chemistry chairman; Donald DeMott in psychology; and Daniel Fink, whose book, *Barns of the Genesee Country, 1790–1915*, marked his excellence in photography and art history. Of the "Class of 1968," few have had the impact on the community of Dr. Richard Hatheway, one of the longest serving village mayors, while also heading the geology department. (He succeeded the late Robert Eaton,

'60, Geneseo Central School social studies teacher and village mayor from 1982 to 1986.) In 1969, the College welcomed William Edgar and Ronald Herzman, philosophy and English, who in 1979 and 1989 were named Distinguished Teaching Professors; Kathy Trainor, longtime assistant director of the College Union; George Mazuzan and Richard Salisbury in history, and 1968 alumna Marjorie Deal Lewis, Holcomb Campus School.

The "class of 1970," Colahan's first, included William Cook (history), Distinguished Teaching Professor (1984) and CASE Professor of the Year (1992); punster John Barrett, replacing, if possible, Alice Austin as head of the drama department; Joseph Zaremba, economics; Harold Battersby, anthropology; Henry Latorella, biology; Bhairav Joshi, chemistry; Alan Shank, later political science chairman; Vince Keane, future speech pathology and audiology chairman; Ronald Sitler, Keane's successor; Norma Scavilla, sociology; Herbert Leventer, history; and Distinguished Service Professor James Walker (1992), music.

Geology professor and chair Richard Hatheway was elected Geneseo's mayor in 1986 and served for over twenty years. (Roger Smith, Roemer House Collection)

Making the Changes

During his first two years, economics chairman David Martin helped Colahan navigate the SUNY bureaucracy, particularly on budget and staffing needs. But Colahan realized he needed full-time assistants if Geneseo were to make the requisite changes to compete with colleges like Hobart and William Smith, Colgate, and his model of a quality public higher education institution, City College of New York (CCNY). He appointed political science's Virginia Kemp and graduate dean Bruce Ristow (a former chemistry professor) assistant vice presidents, and the math department's Joan Schumaker assistant dean for undergraduate instruction.[7]

In accordance with SUNY's Master Plan, Geneseo had already initiated a management science program, a 3-2 engineering program (three years at Geneseo, two at the SUNY Buffalo), and master of arts programs in chemistry, mathematics, and physics. But Colahan envisioned more—a curricu-

The physics department enjoyed a bit of scientific humor: (front, from left): Phillip Alley, Robert Sells, James Chen; (back): David Meisel, Kenneth Kinsey, G. Bradley Huff. (1976 *Oh Ha Daih*)

Jewelry and metals professor Willard Peterson (second from left, rear) worked in Brodie's metal studio with students. (Roger Smith, Hepler collection)

lum built on four-hour humanities courses, analogous to those at St. John's at Annapolis, Columbia College, and the University of Chicago, but conducted in only two terms. (Four-hour courses would be a departure from the traditional three-hour Carnegie unit upon which Geneseo and most higher education institutions relied.) He had to persuade the larger departments that would be affected, primarily English, to help teach the interdisciplinary courses. Readily acknowledging such courses were "elitist," the new vice president argued that higher education was supposed to be "elitist." However, even with the help of department chairmen to his liking and Dr. Kemp, it took until 1979 to accomplish his goal (two four-hour humanities courses, familiarly "Hum I" and "Hum II"). He also asked department heads to cull "unnecessary" electives.[8]

To fully achieve his goals, Dr. Colahan felt he had to wrest control of programs from teacher education. The president indicated his support when he announced a "major" step: "the complete restructuring of the Education Division" and promised a new building to house a School of Education. (It would be another decade-long wait for the "School of Education" and the passage of a decade-and-a-half and two presidents before the promised building was a reality.)[9]

Colahan and MacVittie were helped by a skirmish that originated with faculty eager to make the transition to a liberal arts curriculum. In Fall 1969, the history department withdrew support for the secondary education social studies program to which it had agreed the preceding spring. Shortly, the other social sciences followed suit, arguing that teachers needed an academic

For many years, faculty such as Phyllis Thompson (geography) and Herman Forest (biology) benefited from the Instructional Resources Center's state-of-the-art media production services. (Roger Smith, Roemer House Collection)

major (a B.A. degree) with teacher certification, not the other way around. The social sciences had thrown down the gauntlet.[10]

Before the school year was out, the Faculty Senate approved a new 7-12 social studies program, whereby students certifying to teach secondary social studies had to earn a bachelor's degree in a social science with coursework in teacher education. The next step was the appointment of Dr. Nicholas LaGattuta as dean of the restructured Division of Educational Studies, albeit after an administrative intervention in the search process and over the objections of many of the education faculty.

Not surprisingly, Geneseo's new B.A. or B.S. with certification pattern was met by mixed reactions across the campus: liberal arts faculty were supportive; the teacher education faculty were opposed.

Distractions

However, before the administration could fully implement the desired curriculum changes they had to contend with student demands for less strict disciplinary policies and a shift in interest in majors. A large increase in sociology majors and a precipitous decrease in foreign language and history majors had baleful effects on faculty in those departments. The decline in foreign language enrollment is partly explained by SUNY Central's permitting its colleges to drop the foreign language requirement. The increase in sociology (and psychology) may be explained by greater awareness nationally of societal problems, a response to the sixties' protests which carried over into the seventies.[11]

A carryover from the sixties was some racial tension and reports of physical and verbal assaults. In Fall 1970 an African-American student working in the College Union charged that a drunken white student had thrown a chair at her. Shortly there-after, five African-American students were attacked by an equal number of whites near Main Street, and village police were called to break up two altercations during intramural football games between blacks and whites. A forum on November 4 in the College Union and an editorial in *The Lamron* called for calm, but cartoons *The Lamron*

The Panthers, 1973 champion intramural basketball team, consisted of (front, from left): Donnie Powell, Vernon Duncan; (back): Pete Turner, Harry Ward, Keith Todd, Monty Brooks. Turner and Ward had previously been members of the varsity team. (Bright collection)

ran the day after the forum, meant to focus issues in a humorous way, back-fired. The climax occurred on December 3, 1970, when twenty-five African-American students occupied the lounges in Wyoming and Genesee residence halls (a "sleep-in") to express dissatisfaction with the administration. While MacVittie's decision—supporting vice president David Young's recommendation to suspend the students for blocking other students from entering their residence hall rooms (rather than getting caught up in the issue of civil rights)—was upheld by the U.S. Court of Appeals in 1973, few regarded it as satisfactorily resolving the issue.[12]

Isom Fearn, shown here with Educational Opportunity Program staff members Nancy Ives and Paula Adwell, inspired and motivated students from 1974 to 2005. (Ken Heskestad, Roemer House collection)

In addition to the never fully subscribed Black Studies program begun in 1970, another initiative to deal with charges of racism was the federally funded Educational Opportunity Program introduced in the 1968–1969 school year. Intended to fos-ter more college attendance and success by economically disadvantaged students, including many African-Americans, the hope was that it also would defuse racial tensions. Admitted students would receive financial aid, tutorial help, and counseling and a reduced course load to start. Rather than "some educational giveaway scheme," the program was to help disadvantaged students earn a college education. First headed by alumnus Sam Green, '69, its success is attributed to Isom E. Fearn, Jr., who, stressing academics, arrived in 1974 to direct the program.[13]

Few faculty have received the praise that Fearn did in the November 24, 2005 Rochester *Democrat and Chronicle*. Former EOP student Terrence Brown-Steiner, '82, wrote: "While I struggled, Isom Fearn was always there, with a confident smile and gentle pat on the back….Without Isom Fearn, I would not be me…I would not be an attorney." Moreover, Brown-Steiner believed that his story "is typical of the hundreds, if not thousands of EOP students who have reached their potential…."

While tension eased on one front, protests over the Vietnam War continued, exacerbated by President Nixon's extension of the military draft because of the likely escalation of the war and the tripling of call-ups. A particular objection was to the draft lottery, whereby eligible males were randomly selected by birthdates. The first 122 who were selected had a "high probability" of being drafted in 1970. The next 122 (123 to 244) had an "average probability," and the final 122 a "relatively low probability."[14]

Student protesters called for Nixon's impeachment in October 1973. (1974 *Oh Ha Daih*)

Nor was the College spared the bomb scares that seemed a part of that time period. The first was on March 8, 1973, when seven threats were called in, beginning at 10:10 a.m. All seven threatened buildings were evacuated for the state-mandated twelve hours, no small problem. The first threat the next day was called in to Blake A at 6:23 a.m., followed by a call to Sturges just after noon and a third to Newton at 2:07 p.m. The final call was at 7:29 a.m. a week later, when Welles was threatened. Campus Security reminded students of the seriousness of bomb threats and the prescribed punishment. *The Lamron* reinforced the message by printing the College policy and by warning students that the semester might be lengthened to make up for lost instructional hours.[15]

In 1976, MacVittie and Colahan faced one last spillover from the sixties, which, along with budget cuts, further distracted from curriculum revision. On Friday April 30, approximately 110 students (the number varies according to the reporter) occupied the Erwin administration building following a larger group demonstration outside. They were protesting local conditions

The Idle Hour on Center Street has long been one of several bars popular with students. (1978 *Oh Ha Daih*)

(lack of representation on faculty tenure committees, mandatory activities fees, the price of meal tickets, etc.) and statewide policies (budget cuts, etc.). A sympathetic president met with the students late that day after returning to campus from Buffalo and allowed the students who were in the building to remain. (MacVittie, who charged the security officers with guarding the building before he went home for the night, even allowed the demonstrators' friends to bring in food.) Alumnus and career services director James Allan recalled that "probably half" of the students left later that night because of "cigarette smoke and lack of air-conditioning!"[16]

Another version is that on Saturday morning, after President MacVittie and Central Council chairperson Steve Allinger came to an agreement about which demands could be met, the protesters vacated the building. Dr. Colahan was impressed by how well "the Grey Fox" (MacVittie) simultaneously handled this incident and maintained positive community relations. For one thing, the president decided that the College would not have to discipline any students if he gave them permission to obstruct, which took some of the steam out of their protest. Secondly, vice president Young and some members of his staff walked among the protesters, thereby showing interest without threatening, while identifying the ringleaders for any disciplinary action, if necessary. On the other hand, MacVittie credited the "good students and faculty leadership." Characteristic of the Geneseo students at the time, little damage was done to the building or contents.[17]

Still another sit-in may be even more revealing of the students at the time. English professor Harding recalled that it occurred in the old cafeteria. Cleaner Sally Malson, who apparently had had enough, hollered, "'Hey, you guys and gals. You're making a mess of this place. You, get that broom and sweep this room up. You, empty that wastebasket.' The sit-down strike came to an end."[18]

Beer and barely floating boats were part of the fun of SigTau's Junk Yard Regatta at Hemp's Pond near Route 63. (1974 *Oh Ha Daih*)

College Tightens Belt

Curriculum building also was complicated by Governor Rockefeller's forecast that the 1971–1972 year would be one of "austere operation." As if on cue, that school year Geneseo added fewer than twenty faculty, a sizeable drop from the fifty to sixty to which the College was accustomed, because SUNY was experiencing a "growth curtailment." Plans for more than 250 SUNY building projects costing $340,000,000, including $9,300,000 at Geneseo, were suspended. Dormitory and classroom construction to accommodate the eight thousand students anticipated by 1980 was out of the question. Likewise, plans for a new education building (projected for 1973 completion), a library addition (also 1973), and conversion of the old Geneseo Central High School to college use (1974) were shelved. (The old high school with its leaking roof, purchased from the state for $1.1 million in 1974 and renamed the Doty building, temporarily substituted for the scrapped education building. But faculty offices remained in the Blake buildings, the former residence halls, for another twenty-five years.) Married student housing off Court Street, an art building annex, and a tiered parking lot between Park and Bank streets also became only wishful thinking. Unfortunately, this was only the beginning of difficult times for Geneseo and its sister schools.[19]

Health, Physical Education, and Recreation Department chair Daniel Mullin spoke at the 1973 Alumni Field House dedication. Others on the platform included Ira Wilson (extreme left), President and Mrs. MacVittie (right of lectern), Mayor Ann Duff (second from right), and athletic director Robert Riedel (extreme right). (Art Hatton)

In 1973 President MacVittie protested a budget that "decimated" allocations to the College. A year later the picture was even bleaker. At the school's 1974 convocation MacVittie declared that the state education department predicted dramatic public school enrollment declines for the next decade and a half because of the decline in age cohorts. Even more severe budget cuts followed newly elected Governor Hugh Carey's characterization of the state's finances in his January 1975 inaugural address: "The days of wine and roses are over." The state's debt had quadrupled over the previous ten years, its economy had steeply declined, and its major city was headed for bankruptcy.[20]

While Geneseo was one of the few SUNY units to maintain its enrollment, this latest threat put more pressure on the faculty and staff. A primary target for cuts was the Holcomb Campus School, but in March 1975, SUNY responded to Dr. MacVittie's appeal by promising to maintain full funding for it. (This was a real concession, for in September 1974, Geneseo Central

A dedicated student took advantage of the early morning quiet to study in Milne Library's bound periodicals section. (1972 *Oh Ha Daih*)

School enrolled half of the total elementary age students in the village's first consolidated elementary school.) However, extending Holcomb's funding proved only a reprieve. A projected twenty percent cut in funding over the next two years meant eliminating nine Holcomb teachers in the 1975–1976 year. (It offered "a grim outlook" for the state's campus schools generally.) Geneseo was spared again in 1976 (although at a reduced spending level) after another appeal by MacVittie, which drew appreciative phone calls from locals. Two years later, September 1978, education professor Manly was appointed director of the "Holcomb Learning Center." His task was to foster the new goals and learning experiences that President MacVittie promised when arguing for the school's continuance.[21]

Geneseo Responds

Complying with SUNY's charge to each campus to submit a master plan from

Michael Teres has taught photography at the College for over forty years. (Roger Smith, Hepler collection)

which SUNY would develop its statewide five-year plan, in 1975 President MacVittie appointed a fifteen-member steering committee and three separate task forces. The task forces were to examine instruction and personnel, research, and public service. A projected enrollment decline of at least seventeen percent between 1980 and 1990 meant Geneseo could lose more than thirty faculty by 1984. Faculty were asked to help plan those cuts if the worst scenario were realized. (Losses ultimately totaled sixty-five, increasing student-to-faculty ratios from 15:1 to 20:1. The foreign language department lost fourteen faculty lines between 1970 and 1976; education, not counting the Holcomb School, ten; English, five; and history, three.) The College's mission had to be reexamined and appropriate plans made. Increasingly MacVittie and vice president Colahan relied on Dr. James McNally, director of institutional research, to supply data to make critical decisions.[22]

A particularly sensitive task for Colahan was allocating faculty lines, especially when enrollments in programs and departments fluctuated, as they are prone to do. Sociology and psychology were in demand; foreign languages and history were not. Beginning in 1973, the art department began to sustain losses from which it has never recovered. Across the College, vacant lines were not filled, and untenured faculty, despite quality teaching and scholarship, were not renewed. This led to a "Bad Tom" Colahan reputation among many faculty members, which took the pressure off of "Good Bob" MacVittie. Yet, Colahan argued that a balance had to be struck to assure turnover and hiring flexibility. Granting tenure was a "thirty to thirty-five-year gamble" as to whether a faculty member would remain a lively scholar-teacher for an entire career.[23]

Among the losses were history professors George Mazuzan, who had been nominated for the Excellence in Teaching award; Herbert Leventer, an accomplished teacher-scholar; and Richard Salisbury, who received the Chancellor's Award for Excellence in Teaching in the second year the award was given. Only Salisbury left of his own accord in 1976 after seeing the pattern of cuts.

Faculty who retained their jobs were also put on notice. Course syllabi had to list objectives, offer an overview, provide an updated bibliography, and assure a fit with the "general aims" of the College. Further, faculty had to prove themselves, a process that had already begun. In Fall 1969 the Student Senate initiated a means to obtain student reactions to faculty instruction, using a thirty-one-item form that was distributed to faculty volunteers. The resulting

The brothers of Phi Sigma Epsilon created this Homecoming float featuring characters from classic children's books. (Roemer House Collection)

publication, unfortunately titled Course-Teacher Evaluation, drew the expected challenges from faculty and led to joint student-faculty revisions that continue today. One of the most significant revisions was changing the name of the instrument to Student *Opinion* [italics added for emphasis] of Faculty Instruction, or SOFI, in Spring 1982. (An earlier faculty vote to discontinue the practice because of objection to the term "evaluation" was overruled by President MacVittie.) Not surprisingly, at the end of each semester faculty still warily look at the SOFIs and the summary reports of the SOFIs published in *The Lamron*.[24]

Meanwhile, with Dr. Colahan's encouragement and after considerable give-and-take, in 1973 the Faculty Senate created a five-person Faculty Personnel Committee, which sidestepped a student initiative to be part of the tenure decision-making process. Made up of full professors, the committee was established to review materials submitted by faculty seeking tenure and/or promotion. According to the first committee chairman, Dr. Gerald Smith (English), it provided "an independent channel between the candidate and the president." Beginning with the 1973–1974 school year, this reduced some of the pressure on the president, who had to make the final decisions. However, to work as he and Colahan wanted, departmental committees and chairpersons needed to take a hard look at their colleagues, which Colahan felt had not been customary.[25]

By 1974, the College had three distinguished professors (from left): University Professor Walter Harding (English) and Distinguished Teaching Professors Richard F. Smith (chemistry) and Robert "Duke" Sells (physics). (Roger Smith, Alumni Office Collection)

SUNY tossed out a carrot to faculty beginning in 1972, with the Distinguished Teaching Professorships and Chancellor's Awards for Excellence in Teaching. The first campus committee, ably chaired by a demanding Dr. James Scholes (English), recommended to MacVittie three faculty for the Distinguished Teaching Professorship. In turn, he submitted the name of physics chairman Dr. Robert L. "Duke" Sells, who became Geneseo's first and one of SUNY's first Distinguished Teaching Professors (DTP). The following year Dr. Richard F. Smith (chemistry) became Geneseo's second DTP, while Drs. William Cook (history) and John Kucaba (music) were recognized as the College's first Excellence in Teaching awardees. In 1975 Dr. Rose Bachem Alent was designated DTP, while Drs. Lawrence Casler (psychology), H. Gordon Miller (art), and Richard Salisbury (history) received Excellence in Teaching awards. The next year Drs. William Edgar (philosophy), Ronald Herzman (English), Joseph Dechario (music), and Wayne Mahood (education) were honored by Excellence in Teaching awards. Edgar and Herzman later were named DTP. (As if competing with her husband, Dr. Stacey Edgar (philosophy) received the Chancellor's Award for Excellence in Teaching a decade later.)[26]

Enrollment Crisis

Among the obstacles to curricular changes, likely the biggest blow was that the significant enrollment decline that SUNY Central had projected hit Geneseo not only earlier than expected, but harder. Coming after an enrollment decline the two previous school years, the College was threatened by a disastrous loss of between 450 and 500 students from the 5,300 headcount projected for 1977–1978. Given an eighteen percent decline in freshman applications, MacVittie feared that the College would open in fall 1977 with seven hundred fewer students than the previous year. The College could lose up to thirty-one full-time equivalent faculty (FTE), coupled with the loss of tuition money.

Geneseo was already coping with a sharp spike in oil and gasoline prices beginning with the Arab oil embargo in 1973. Then during the 1976–1977 school year Geneseo and other state agencies observed mandated conservation measures. (Cold faculty offices on weekends and early Monday mornings tried patience and commitment.)[27]

Music faculty (from left) James Walker, John Kucaba, Robert Isgro, William Leyerle, Ruth DeFord, Joseph Dechario, and James Willey gathered around Bill Shipman's sculpture, which later disappeared. (1976 *Oh Ha Daih*)

Fortunately, the enrollment crisis in Fall 1977 was temporarily ameliorated when the governor and SUNY Central office gave Geneseo a one-year reprieve from staff cuts. In part this rewarded MacVittie's stewardship, which had been recognized recently when SUNY renewed him. But the underlying problem remained.

Geneseo's response was to launch a three-pronged attack on its sagging enrollment. First, plug the hole in the dike by lowering admission criteria and admitting as many applicants as possible (resulting in an eighty-eight percent acceptance rate). Second, establish a task force to study and improve the College's recruitment practices. Third, establish a committee to recommend long-term College priorities. The first prong was a temporary expedient, but the recruitment committee eventually set Geneseo on a path that led to national prominence.[28]

In July 1977, presidential assistant Dr. Frank Kemerer was named director of college enrollment policy and planning to examine current recruitment practices, suggest new strategies, and recommend "a realistic enrollment

William Caren's leadership
was instrumental in
improving the student
admissions situation
in the late 1970s.
(1972 *Oh Ha Daih*)

Health and physical education
faculty in 1976 included
(seated, from left): Daniel
Mullin, Shirley Toler, Myrtle
Merritt; (standing, foreground):
Fred Bright; (standing, center):
Joyce Wechsler, Martin
Kentner, Jim Fitzgerald;
(standing, back): Paul Rose,
Frank Akers, Robert Riedel,
James Ward, Carl Witzel.
(1976 *Oh Ha Daih*)

goal." Kemerer recommended consolidating admissions, financial aid, and career planning under one administrator (ultimately vice president David A. Young) who would report to the president. This was followed by a retreat ("College Planning Workshop") at Rensselaerville, New York, where a month later forty-two faculty and administrators examined what the College was doing and where it was going. Back on campus that September, a college-wide faculty meeting focused solely on the College's mission. Should Geneseo be "pure" liberal arts? Should there be more "career-oriented options?" Or was the answer more "minors?" Marketing Geneseo was central to discussions. However, the immediate task was recruitment. Kemerer, acting director of admissions William Caren, and then-director of college relations Arthur Hatton were charged with engineering the turnaround.[29]

Their "very extensive" plan (per Hatton) began with a seemingly mundane decision by MacVittie to assign four state cars to the admissions office for October–December and March–May. (One of those cars was a six-cylinder Dodge Dart with seventy-five thousand miles on it.) A second step was finding money to make long-distance phone calls. Next, the admissions office, traditionally a two-person operation, was beefed up. Student Association money underwrote "modest" four-color recruitment brochures; computers drafted "personalized" letters (rather than having a secretary type dictated letters all day long); faculty and administrators visited schools with an intensity equaled possibly only during the administrations of Drs. William Milne and James Welles; and high school students were encouraged to visit the campus. (Almost twice as many students were interviewed in October 1977 than the year before.) Still, more was needed, which Caren dubbed "hyperbole." Geneseo had to make the case that it was special. Broadcast that the newest entering class had a higher secondary school average than last; that Geneseo was becoming selective. In short, Geneseo would adopt the trappings of selective private colleges. It was an audacious move by MacVittie.[30]

The third prong to attack the enrollment crisis was a priorities committee. Created by MacVittie in 1977, it was to draft a plan for reducing faculty, should it be necessary. The "hatchet committee," as many viewed it, submitted a draft proposal February 18, 1978, recommending six levels of cuts. Assuming the rosiest scenario, Geneseo would lose five faculty; the bleakest scenario would mean a reduction of thirty-five faculty, with English and education slashed the deepest (four and five and a half lines respectively). The maintenance staff would take a real hit also. Judgments about faculty were based on three principles: cut departments with teaching loads of nine, rather than twelve, hours (or where the student credit-hour production was below the College average), maintain all academic departments, and reduce no department below five faculty. Fortunately, Geneseo reached its enrollment targets in the ensuing years, rendering the bleakest scenarios moot.[31]

Even earlier, anticipating the state's diminished funding—which still declines—President MacVittie saw the need for outside funding, upon which private colleges and universities rely. In 1971 he created the Geneseo Foundation, followed eleven years later by the President's Donor Recognition dinner. The former was to solicit money for student scholarships and faculty research; the latter was to thank donors of money or services. The Foundation has proved its worth many times over, because of thirty years of dedication by vice president for advancement Arthur Hatton. (As of 2004, the Foundation had provided over one million dollars a year in support of faculty and student projects.)[32]

Arthur Hatton served as vice president for college advancement and director of the Geneseo Foundation for more than thirty years. (1983 *Oh Ha Daih*)

It remains that the success of the College depended on the caliber of its faculty and staff. Among those who came and made their mark during this period were Distinguished Teaching Professor Eugene Stelzig (English) and Distinguished Service Professor Daniel Strang (school of business), who arrived in 1972. Distinguished Service Professor Karen Duffy (psychology) came the next year, while Chancellor's Excellence in Teaching awardees Phillip Boger (geology), Walter Soffer (philosophy), and Nicholas Schiavetti (communicative disorders and sciences), joined the faculty in 1976, 1977, and 1977 respectively. Also photographer Ronald Pretzer, who came in 1976, and Jerald Wrubel (career services director), who followed the next year, received Chancellor's Awards for Excellence in Professional Service. In 1978 Distinguished Professor Robert Beason (biology), and Distinguished Teaching Professor Robert Owens, Jr. (communicative disorders and sciences) made their appearances. It goes without saying that these individuals are just a few of those upon whom MacVittie and the College were counting to ensure the enrollment turnaround.

Van E. Quaal served as vice president for business affairs from 1966 to 1985. (1983 *Oh Ha Daih*)

Elephants, the "F Word," Attica, "Cos," Main Street Burns, and the "Braves"

An odd array of events also marked the times. Ironically, none reflected the gloom and doom that the budget crunch, energy conservation measures, and enrollment crisis might have engendered. On the other hand, predictably, the students protested a proposed tuition increase, raising undergraduate tuition from $400 to $550 for the 1972–1973 school year and to $700 the following. And they questioned the mandatory student activity fee, a recurring issue.[33]

Few events matched the parade of circus elephants in the newly dedicated Kuhl gym. Imagine health and physical education director Daniel Mullin's distress about possible damage even after special flooring was purchased to protect the gym floor. More to Mullin's liking, Geneseo's new gym got another workout beginning September 20, 1974, when the Buffalo Braves (later San Diego and L.A. Clippers basketball team) began practicing there after MacVittie signed an agreement with the Braves' general manager.[34]

However, a presentation of *Man of La Mancha* didn't come off. It was cancelled when it was discovered that the acting company's sets would not fit onto the Wadsworth Auditorium stage. (More resourceful Geneseo drama students, including David Girolmo, who played Quixote, and director Scott Ray, pulled it off in 1979 with student-designed and constructed sets.)

Abbie Hoffman's anti-war remarks were popular with the many students who opposed U.S. involvement in Vietnam. (Roemer House Collection)

Other performances during the early seventies brought mixed reactions. Vietnam War protester Abbie Hoffman's repetitious use of "the f word" became "boring" to Elaine Kupi Hinz, B.S. in 1971 and M.S. in 1973. She much preferred the popular musical *1776*, directed by Bob Sinclair in October 1972.[35]

Activity fees also paid for mime Marcel Marceau (1971); Pierre Salinger, press secretary to presidents Kennedy and Johnson (also 1971); Dr. Daniel Ellsburg, who released the Pentagon Papers to the *New York Times* to challenge the government's prosecution of the Vietnam War (1972); Bill Cosby, who performed two shows, at 7 and 10 p.m. on December 1, 1977; Watergate break-in mastermind G. Gordon Liddy (1978); and young Steve Martin that same year.[36]

One of the most troubling events early that decade occurred on September 8, 1971, when inmates at New York State's nearby Attica prison rioted and took hostages. Governor Rockefeller's orders to state troopers and National Guardsmen to take over the prison resulted in eight hostages and thirty-seven inmates dead. Seven members of Geneseo's cross country team, including stars Joe Contario and Doug Colton, protested the state's actions in their own way. They ran to Albany in shifts to carry a petition asking for more humane treatment of prisoners. (By the way, Contario and Colton, members of Geneseo's undefeated 1972 cross country team, were named to the State University of New York Athletic Conference Cross Country Hall of Fame the following year.)[37]

Students Stephen T. Lambert and Mark F. Calicchia made their mark in 1971 in a very different way. They engaged in a sit-down protest at the Selective Service office on Main Street to challenge the military draft and were unceremoniously hauled to the doorway of a nearby department store by Police Chief Bill Roodenburg and a deputy.[38]

Students Stephen Lambert and Mark Calicchia protested the draft in 1971. (1972 *Oh Ha Daih*)

A more indirect student protest was aimed at what came to be called "grade inflation." A study of student grades by department found the average grade an "A," with almost 80 percent awarded (not surprisingly) to student teachers, 73.7 percent to speech and hearing students (a graduate program), and 67 percent to special education students. By contrast, only 25.2 percent of those taking geological science courses and 30.3 percent of those taking biology and Spanish courses earned an A. (One explanation for "grade inflation," not given in this study, was that satisfactory grades generally guaranteed draft deferments.)[39]

The early seventies also marked the last outdoor graduation (1972) for a quarter-century, followed by a chaotic indoor (ice arena) graduation the next year at which graduates' names were read in alphabetical order, but didn't match the student crossing the stage because a number of students protesting "the ills of society" refused to march onstage. (Imagine the audience's confusion.) Another political statement of sorts was the 1972 election of graduate student "Brother Bob" Tegart as homecoming "person" (rather than the traditional "homecoming queen"). Still other extracurricular events that marked the time period were the "streaker" who ran from the Bailey science building to a waiting car near the flagpole at the south end of the upper quadrangle and the nude male sunbather on the upper quad. And—reminiscent of the fires at

Graduate student Robert "Brother Bob" Tegart (second from right) defeated several 1972 homecoming queen candidates to become Geneseo's first "homecoming person." Other members of his court were (from left): Cyril Polansky, Diane Czop, and Nancy Discavage. (Vic Cherubini, *The Lamron*, Oct. 20, 1972)

the time of the stormy debates over funding the College more than a century earlier—there was the destructive November 15, 1972 fire that burned the former Scherline (Rabinowitz) building on Main Street. It blocked the street, delayed faculty trying get to their classes on time, and, of course, offered students an excuse to cut classes and watch the fire.[40]

A local businessman emerged from the fire strengthened by the ordeal somehow. Barry Caplan, who had lived and carried on his business above Gay

Prometheus fraternity's used book sale was a heavily used service that helped many students control their textbook expenditures. (1966 *Oh Ha Daih*)

Brewer's hardware store, barely survived, though he lost his entire inventory of used books. Undaunted, he opened Sundance Books, helped by Al Bruno ("Buzzo") and Fred Mingrino, '74, whose association with Caplan began when he was a student. Importantly, without fanfare, Barry and his wife, Angela (Amedore) Caplan, '74, are important contributors to the village and to the College.[41]

Caplan also may have benefited from the earlier demise of Prometheus fraternity's used textbook sales, which some alums still recall appreciatively. Early each semester the brothers collected upwards of five thousand books from sellers who set a price for the books. The fraternity added fifteen percent to the asking price for its "labor-intensive endeavor," which helped pay for social functions through the semester. So the sellers, buyers, and the fraternity all benefited from what brother and Geneseo Foundation member Robert J. Avalone called a campus and community service.[42]

The Sports Scene

Intercollegiate athletics prospered during this era, including the expansion of women's sports in compliance with Title IX in 1972. Within a decade, Geneseo added seven women's varsity sports. Fittingly, on October 13, 1973, "the new [and much-needed] gym," which Mullin tried so hard to protect from the circus elephants, was dedicated to the late Louise Kuhl. From 1941 to 1967, Kuhl

As a result of Title IX, Geneseo added several women's sports, including the first women's soccer team, coached by Fred Bright (back row, right), in 1980–1981. (Bright collection)

not only headed the health and physical education department, she was acting dean of the College three times, directed summer school for seven years, and supervised construction of Schrader Gym. (Fittingly, that same day the service building was dedicated to L. Watson Clark, maintenance supervisor from 1914 to 1949, which may have been a SUNY first: naming a building for a member of the maintenance staff.)[43]

Men's sports were on the upswing. Martin Kentner's men's cross country team, which held its first SUNYAC meet at Geneseo in 1970, claimed a 17-0 dual meet season two years later. Duncan Hinckley's 1974–1975 men's swimming team too went undefeated, beginning its winning tradition. Early on Tom Basher, now a local businessman, and teammates Harry Ward and Mike Chapman spelled success for Tom Pope's basketball teams, which included Ed Robota, Geneseo's first All-American (1975) and 1980

Ed Robota (24), shown with teammate Gary Witter (15) in the new Alumni Field House gym in 1973, was Geneseo's first All-American in basketball. (Bright collection)

inductee in Geneseo's Hall of Fame. In 1974 Coach Paul Rose's lacrosse team (12-1) took the first of two consecutive ECAC Upstate lacrosse titles. And in 1979 the College hosted the NCAA Division III National Swimming and Diving Championships in the Alumni Field House later renamed for Dr. Myrtle Merritt.[44]

Success Stories

Graduates' successes attest to the College's long tradition of attracting students who would prove their worth. Dr. Leo Lambert, '76, president of North Carolina's Elon College, was honored with the SUNY Doctor of Humane Letters in 2002, while Dr. Arlene "Gidget" Myers Hopf, '72, is CEO of Rochester's Association for the Blind and Visually Impaired. (Among her husband John's accomplishments was co-authoring a study of migrants and the courts for the Migrant Center shortly after he graduated in 1970.) Denise Decker, a 1971 magna cum laude French major, traveled widely as a personnel management specialist in various U.S. government agencies, despite being blind from birth. Glenn Gordon Caron, '75, achieved acclaim for his television series *Moonlighting*, starring a young Bruce Willis and Cybill Shepherd, which ran from 1985 to 1989. Dr. Donald Marozas, '76 (elementary/special education), returned in 1983 to teach special education and was honored with the Chancellor's Award for Excellence in Teaching three years later. Curt Smith, '73, took his writing skills, honed as sports editor for *The Lamron*, to the White House as a speechwriter for the first President Bush, authored a number of books on baseball, and hosted a radio program. His sister, Karen Smith-Pilkington, '78, went on to chair Kodak's Greater Asia region, one of the highest positions held by a woman in the venerable company. Though an unsuccessful candidate for state comptroller in 2007, New York State Assemblyman Joseph Morelle, '79, successfully chaired the Monroe County Democratic Party in

The legal drinking age was still eighteen when students celebrated Spring Happening in 1978, and the yearbook noted "a hundred kegs still wasn't enough." (1978 *Oh Ha Daih*)

the 2006 election. Thomas Strining, '71, served the Webster Central School District for over thirty years, retiring as superintendent, matched by David DeLoria, '69, retired superintendent of Livonia Central Schools. Lawyer and Alumni Association president Donald "Dan" O'Brien, '73, received the Geneseo Foundation's Meritorious Service Award in 1991. Classmate Edward Pettinella, CEO of the prospering Home Properties, and Michael Tantillo, '74, Ontario County district attorney, were recognized by the Alumni Association in 1998 with the Professional Achievement and Distinguished Service Awards respectively. Then there is Brigadier General David Reist, '78, possibly the highest ranking soldier among Geneseo's graduates. Of course, this is only a partial, somewhat random, listing.

The MacVittie Presidency Ends

On Friday, January 26, 1979, after sixteen event-filled years at the helm, Robert MacVittie announced his retirement, effective August 27. *Livingston Republican* editor-owner Ray Sherman recalled that MacVittie had seen the College grow from a small regional teachers college to a "full-fledged liberal arts institution" drawing students from throughout the state. MacVittie had fostered the change despite the turbulence of the sixties, including ongoing construction projects and student protests, and the budget, oil, and enrollment crises of the seventies. Other newspapers echoed Sherman's comments, and tributes poured in.[45]

Ronald Satryb served as vice president for student services and staff relations from 1975 to 1994. (1982 *Oh Ha Daih*)

Before departing, MacVittie did not escape the mandatory "roast," courtesy of Dr. Ronald Satryb, assistant vice president for business affairs and director of personnel, and Delores "Dee" Donnelly, associate dean for college activities and College Union director. While many of the jabs were understandable only to insiders, some were rather obvious. Among the "Things we [Satryb and Donnelly] wanted to get you but couldn't obtain or couldn't afford" were: "A two-week cruise with Steve Allinger" (the Central Council president who had led the 1976 administration building sit-in); a papoose sling for Art Hatton to carry MacVittie through future golf tournaments; the framed retirement applications of two education professors who had been thorns in MacVittie's side; a silver shovel from the Eighth Annual Ground Breaking Ceremony for the Upper Division College at Utica-Rome (a reminder of his ill-fated appointment), and two tickets to the dedication of the Robert W. MacVittie Student Union.[46]

The latter would turn out to be obtainable after all. At the time, SUNY policy forbade naming buildings for living persons. However, ten years later, on November 17, 1989 (after prodding by history professor Fausold and a policy change), President Carol Harter welcomed the MacVitties back for the Dr. Robert W. MacVittie College Union dedication. Harter claimed that MacVittie, with the help of Larry Park, Thomas Colahan, and Van Quaal, had "built a distinguished college and helped put Geneseo on the map." His legacy included "far more than new buildings." Recruitment of "outstanding faculty and staff" was coupled with the development of "new academic programs," initiation of faculty governance "which has stood the test of time," and "creation of the Geneseo Foundation." MacVittie, Harter noted, was characterized by his colleagues as "a man of strength and quiet vision," a man of "grace, style, and good old-fashioned hard work."[47]

The other significant honor was an invitation to deliver the College's 131st commencement address on May 24, 1997. Unfortunately, MacVittie succumbed to cancer shortly before the appointed date, but his son Robert delivered his remarks to an appreciative audience. Graduates were reminded that they were leaving "the gem in SUNY's crown," for which the former president could have taken considerable credit, had he been inclined.

****

MacVittie left quite a legacy. During his sixteen years, he oversaw the opening of twenty-four buildings, a total enrollment that more than doubled (from 2,262 to 5,342), and a faculty that almost tripled in number (113 to 311) before experiencing near-devastating budget cuts. He managed to maintain good relations with protesting students and with the community despite property acquisitions that dislocated some longtime residents. He even managed to stall the closing of the campus school, thus prolonging a tradition. Part of MacVittie's success was due to his style; he was a consensus builder. SUNY Provost Harry Porter believed "anybody could work with Dr. MacVittie."[48]

With the aid of able faculty and staff, President MacVittie also oversaw the College's transition to a multipurpose school with many of the trappings of a liberal arts college. The most obvious example was the introduction of the two four-hour humanities courses. Importantly, during his tenure the College attracted faculty whose academic specializations more closely matched the school's changing mission and initiated measures to assure faculty accountability. Above all, MacVittie presided over unprecedented campus expansion and helped set in motion ambitious student recruitment and fundraising programs that not only saved the College, but set it on its way to national recognition.

In January 1974, the
Chamber Singers made a
two-week concert tour of
Switzerland, Austria, and Italy,
performing in such places as
the Mozarteum in Salzburg,
Austria. (Robert Isgro)

Chapter Nine

State University
of NEW YORK *at* GENESEO

•

A Public College with an Ivy Twist (1979–1995)

It seemed that few events in this era had the impact that the fatal explosion of the spacecraft *Challenger* had—not the election of a cinematic U.S. president, not the first woman Supreme Court associate justice nor the first woman astronaut, nor *M*A*S*H*'s historic goodbye to television audiences, nor the March 1991 ice storm that left the College without electricity for more than thirty hours.

Yet—guided by an economist and then by its first female president—the College was embarking on a transformation that would vault it into national recognition despite falling state support. The teachers college image was fast being erased, replaced by an emphasis on liberal arts, greater diversity of students, and a more "cosmopolitan" faculty, who called Rochester or its immediate suburbs home rather than the village of Geneseo, as faculty typically had.

"The Atmosphere at Geneseo to be Alive"

A big step in that transformation was finding a successor to Robert MacVittie. While that process did not go smoothly, on September 1, 1979 Edward Jakubauskas, a forty-nine-year-old Waterbury, Connecticut

Opposite Page: South Hall was built on the site of a former parking lot behind Fraser and Welles and is connected to those two buildings. (Facilities Planning Office)

Edward Jakubauskas served as president from 1979 to 1988. (1983 *Oh Ha Daih*)

native and former University of Wyoming vice president of academic affairs, took the helm. Given the economy's doldrums, it's not surprising that the first thing the search committee sought from its new leader was "evidence of competence in management" (budget development, finance, etc.). Jakubauskas, who held a Ph.D. in economics from the University of Wisconsin, seemed to fit the bill.[1]

In his first address to the College community, Jakubauskas assured his audience that he wanted "the atmosphere at Geneseo to be alive in the resolve to make Geneseo the very best college it can be." He intended to stress academic quality, meet the "enrollment challenge," and foster partnerships with local businesses.[2]

The new president had a head start in some areas. For example, more than 6,300 students, a thirty-eight percent increase over the previous year, had applied for admission in 1980, and the College could admit only 1,300. Also the B.S. in Accounting had been approved by the State Education Department during the previous summer.[3]

The "admissions turnaround," discussed in the last chapter, was already beginning to pay off. Needed changes were being made and funded: the admissions staff had been increased; more cars had been assigned for travel; young, enthusiastic adjunct recruiters were sent out for a week at a time; and high school students and their families were regularly touring the campus. Ahead lay the real "hype" and more applied programs that appealed to students (and parents of students) unsure of the merits of a liberal arts degree.[4]

Jakubauskas also could rely on most, if not all, of the experienced administrators who had served under President MacVittie. They included vice presidents David A. Young, Thomas Colahan, Van Quaal, and two individuals who were spearheading Geneseo's turnaround, William Caren, assistant vice president for student services and staff relations, and Arthur Hatton, assistant to the president for communications and development. Hatton also was to direct the Geneseo Foundation, replacing Dr. Fred Bennett, who had headed the Foundation from its inception until his recent retirement. Additionally, Jakubauskas counted on Dr. Ronald Satryb, assistant to the president for labor relations, and Mrs. Lenora McMaster, who was named the new president's secretary. On the other hand, he lost the services of Theo Greenman, who had admirably served presidents Moench and MacVittie, and shortly he said goodbye to College Council chairman Joseph Quirk and member Frances Dew, in office since 1958 and 1954 respectively.[5]

In the early 1990s, the Geneseo Foundation Board of Directors included (from left): Spencer Roemer, Thomas Young, John Linfoot, Ruth Linfoot, Jon Porter, Betty Minemier, Stephan Schwartz, Myrtle Merritt, Dean Johnston, Bertha Lederer, John Lockhart, Kenneth Book, Anne Bishop, Edward Pettinella, Anthony Barraco, and Alice Strong. (Ron Pretzer, Roemer House collection, identification by Art Hatton)

"From a Tax-Supported to a Tax-Assisted University"

In February 1980, barely five months into his term, Jakubauskas was discomforted by Governor Hugh Carey's executive budget, which threatened more cuts. The College had lost twenty-four faculty and staff at the beginning of the 1979–1980 school year and "must eliminate another twenty-seven filled positions by March 1981." The only "viable answer" to further cuts was retrenchment and elimination of programs. The College had survived so far only by maintaining its full-time equivalent enrollment at 4,900 and dipping into academic program money for twenty thousand dollars to repair dorm damages and for twenty-five thousand dollars to bring the women's locker room in the Alumni Field House in compliance with Title IX. President Jakubauskas was rudely introduced to the yearly game of "mindless budget cutting." But he knew failure to play the game was ruinous. "Get yourself in the red [allow budget overruns], you were out as president."[6]

Now Geneseo was being asked to cut enrollment from its targeted 4,900 to 4,600. Sounding like his predecessors, President Jakubauskas vowed that Geneseo "will not yield to pressure to phase down enrollment." He had some good arguments. In his words, no "comparable institution" had managed to emerge "as a better institution" while experiencing such deep cuts in personnel and facility maintenance. (The reduction in state supported personnel over the previous five years had been dramatic: Geneseo's workforce had declined from 771 full-time equivalent [FTE], including 294 faculty, to 665 FTE, including 276 faculty.) The College faculty and staff were already do-

President and Mrs. Jakubauskas enjoyed a light moment with professor emerita Bertha Lederer. (Hepler collection)

ing "more with less;" in fact, its productivity was unprecedented.[7]

To Governor Carey, the most obvious way for Geneseo to absorb the cuts was to close the Holcomb School, thus eliminating seventeen full-time and two part-time positions. Carey could easily justify the action. Earlier he had recommended closing all unnecessary campus schools. Moreover, beginning in 1974 the village had an elementary school; it didn't need two, and the College Priorities ("hatchet") committee had recommended closing it. Yet, President Jakubauskas understood earlier reluctance to do so. It had served many village students virtually from the College's inception. It also offered a pre-K program and opportunities for more than 40 student teachers and 180 "participants" per year to work with experienced teachers. Nor was Geneseo Central School prepared for an immediate doubling of its elementary population.[8]

Reluctantly, President Jakubauskas decided to shut down the venerable campus school. After the decision was announced at a heavily attended and acrimonious community meeting, a group of Holcomb supporters immediately, but unsuccessfully, sought to overturn the decision. The campus school had to go by August 31, 1981, a decision that severely strained town-gown relations. "Oh boy. Oh, the hate mail. The violent phone calls and all that,"

The softball (and former baseball) field is named for former New York Yankee star pitcher Victor Raschi, who served as Geneseo's baseball and basketball coach. (Bright collection)

Jakubauskas recalled almost two decades later. He argued that the College was multipurpose; teacher education was only a part, not the primary focus anymore. Further, the village's relatively new school could accommodate the additional students if it obtained the money to hire more faculty.[9]

It took a lot of scrambling by—and caused many anxious moments for—representatives of the College and Geneseo Central School to accomplish the changeover, including Geneseo Central's agreement to hire some of the retrenched Holcomb faculty. Yet, amid the turmoil and the tears that flowed, there were some now-laughable moments, including a minor battle over ownership of various items at the Holcomb School, including computers. Had they been purchased by SUNY or Geneseo Central? Paper shuffling, arguments, and meetings occupied hours. Imagine fighting over Radio Shack TRS 80 computers with barely 4K of memory! About as useful as buggy whips today, they were then "state-of-the-art," enabling students to overtake their elders technologically in short order.

Still more draconian cuts were demanded by Governor Carey's 1982 executive budget, which "sliced" forty-six more positions from Geneseo. Out-of-state travel was suspended, in-state travel was sharply curtailed, purchases of paper and printing supplies were reduced, and a freeze was placed on office furniture purchases. The "powers-that-be [in Albany]…looked to privates [not the public colleges and universities] for quality," Jakubauskas asserted. More damning, SUNY Central Office "never sold the public on the idea that SUNY and public education are really important for the state of New York." Jakubauskas complained that the budget cuts had transformed SUNY "from a tax-supported to a tax-assisted University." While the line may not have been original with him, it delivered the message.[10]

Joyce Wechsler (left, rear) coached the 1986 ECAC champion volleyball team. (Bright collection)

"The Central Core"—Academics in Lean Years

Another momentous decision—also reached reluctantly—was to close the Library School. For many it **was** Geneseo and had been for almost eighty years. But its enrollment had declined, leading it to depend on a large number of foreign students who received tuition waivers. The death blow was struck when the legislature cut off the waivers. Other institutions facing similar enrollment declines, including Columbia University, also anticipated closing their library schools. Further, the college priorities committee had recommended its demise for much the same reasons it offered for closing the Holcomb School. Given Geneseo's mission to serve undergraduates, its library school, "the smallest accredited School of Library Science in the country" (with only ninety-six students) simply had to go. (By contract, the College could not simply cut tenured faculty to achieve savings; it had to eliminate programs.)[11]

The timing of the decision was especially ironic. The Library School had just redefined itself by evolving into a School of Library and Information Science, with increased emphasis on technology. (Its former dean, Dr. Ivan Kaldor, was the first person on campus to have a personal computer.) And it had begun a search for Kaldor's successor. Equally ironic, less than four years earlier the executive director of the American Library Association had praised President MacVittie for his support of and "concern for the best in library education."[12]

In his 1981 draft Budget and Planning Statement for 1982–1983 to 1985–1986, Jakubauskas justified both school closures. The "central core" of the

Library science faculty in 1975–1976 included (front row, from left): Janet Neese, Ralph Black, dean Ivan Kaldor, Josephine Mills, Eula White; (back): Charles Kritzler, John Winkelman, Paul Studer, Leslie Poste. (1976 *Oh Ha Daih*)

College was liberal arts courses "balance[d] by selected professional offerings that are built upon a liberal arts foundation." Geneseo's duty was to offer "a selected and limited number of high quality…programs in areas that have a critical mass of resources of faculty, equipment, and support systems." With the exception of the computer science program, funded through the positions saved by closing the library school, no new programs were "planned or desired."[13]

Jakubauskas was not only carrying out the earlier Priorities Committee recommendations but was following through on the recruitment plans instituted during the 1977 enrollment crisis. That plan, which is credited in large part with Geneseo's amazing turnabout in applications from 1978 to 1981, called for strengthening existing programs as well as implementing professional programs for which there was demand, such as the newly instituted accounting and computer science programs. Such planning was critical, given the expected decline in college-age students.[14]

Reflecting on his first four years, Jakubauskas found some bright spots. Importantly, enrollment exceeded budgeted figures. Despite an "admissions challenge" in 1981, Assistant Vice President Caren reported Geneseo was running almost sixteen percent above the previous year's applications, marking the third straight year that Geneseo topped all other SUNY units in students applying only to a single school.[15]

Further, the much-anticipated, revised common core was in place; the

College had received a laudatory Middle States reaccreditation; the School of Business was in full swing; the "computer revolution" had begun; two new education departments (Elementary and Secondary Education and Reading, and Special Education) had been created out of the former Division of Educational Studies; and facilities were upgraded. The president also could have cited Geneseo's having the highest percentage of women faculty members in SUNY (thirty percent) and offering beginning salaries among the highest in SUNY, partly because of Colahan's "conservative promotion policy."[16]

The Equal Opportunity Program (now Access Opportunity Program) was another success story. With only three full-time staff, including director Isom Fearn, the program had grown to ninety students by 1980. (Enrollment reached an early high of 179 in 1988, exceeding the previous year's high of 145, helped by Candice Bunham, president of the Minority Student Union and Dr. Ramon Rocha, assistant to the vice president for minority affairs.) Aggressive recruiting was matched by the students' academic success, with the program's graduation rate higher than at other SUNY units.[17]

Despite painful economizing, Jakubauskas seemed upbeat in his 1985 annual report. The August 1984 Painted Post planning retreat, with its "informal interaction," had been productive. The central message from the retreat was to emphasize the opportunities Geneseo offered; that the College should tell the "Geneseo story," or in the words of future Distinguished Teaching Professor James Willey, "promote ourselves." After all, the previous year Geneseo had admitted only forty-nine percent of applicants (3,198 of 6,247), making it as selective as some well-known private liberal arts colleges. And the state education department correctly reported that Geneseo's students certifying to teach were attaining a pass rate of between ninety-seven and ninety-nine percent on the National Teacher Exam. Even so, to foster high graduation rates the president formed a retention committee consisting of Barbara Rhodes, Kathy Trainor, Joan Schumaker, and James McNally.[18]

Jakubauskas's Fall 1985 convocation address presented a mixed message. The College had met its targeted enrollment of 4,900 FTE, Andrew Fox from nearby Wyoming County was Geneseo's first Fulbright Scholar, and the annual fund drive had just raised one hundred thousand dollars for scholarships (compared with only sixteen thousand dollars in 1978–1979, its first

Geneseo has had several student organizations representing racial or ethnic groups, including the Minority Student Council (front, from left): D. Clark, M. Farquarson, C. Griffin; (back): A. Constant, V. Powell, M. Broomfield. (1993 *Oh Ha Daih*)

Distinguished Teaching Professor James Willey, a talented keyboardist and composer, taught music theory for more than thirty years. (Fall 1991 *Geneseo Scene*)

year). But newly inaugurated Governor Mario Cuomo's initial budget resembled outgoing Governor Carey's. Geneseo's 1986–1987 operating budget would be almost a million less than requested. If the proposed cuts were not restored, students would be tripled in dormitory rooms and more faculty and staff lines would have be to be left vacant.[19]

The new buzz word was reallocation—shifting faculty lines from low- to high-demand departments, yet keeping options open, a practice with which VPAA Colahan was all too familiar. Math, physics, computer science, and language skills gained full faculty "lines;" music a half. Drama, dance, art, health and physical education, chemistry, and special education (four positions, the most) took hits.[20]

"A SUNY Success Story"

Despite devastating budget cuts, the College garnered unexpected, but highly satisfying, attention. "Geneseo is everything one might expect in a private college," a 1985 Associated Press article reported. It lay "high above the Genesee Valley cornfields...the picture of a comfortable private school." But AP reporter Peter Coy advised the reader that it was not a private college; it was public. Geneseo's "success story" derived from the fact that it was among the most selective in the SUNY system, admitting only forty-nine percent versus eighty-eight percent in 1978. Geneseo not only competed with the privates, it had done so despite "a retrenchment period for SUNY in which Geneseo lost 104 faculty and staff jobs." Coy's only criticism was that Geneseo was "a bit bland to people who have spent time at colleges with more intellectual and cultural ferment," which its faculty readily acknowledged.[21]

The article was music to the ears of Geneseo's administration, faculty, staff, students, and alumni. Faced with the disastrous 1977 enrollment shortfall and caught up in the "transformative environment" that led many public colleges to become "universities," Geneseo bucked the trend. It had opted to retain its small size and undergraduate status and to adapt the private colleges' techniques to "become the public alternative to the small selective private college." And it regularly told the "Geneseo story" to college counselors in high schools throughout the state, touting each entering class as the "brightest" yet and citing SAT scores, high school averages, and career aspirations.[22]

On the other hand, the editors of the March 1983 *Geneseo Compass* viewed the students differently. Reflecting the entering class's imbalance between

Among the many students celebrating their ethnic heritage were 1992–1993 members of Hispanos Unidos en Geneseo (HUG) (front, from left): J. Diaz, S. Masquera; (center): L. Baquero, C. Griffin, C. Sulit, J. Pletz, M. Vasconez, R. Luna, advisor I. Bosch; (back): T. Woolcock, L. Pineda, G. Arce, E. Robinson, M. Fritz. (1993 *Oh Ha Daih*)

men and women (seventy-one percent of the entering class was female), the editors claimed Geneseo's fresh(woman) wore a Levi's jacket, designer baggy jeans, a Rolling Stones concert jersey, and Nike sneakers, and lugged a backpack. She might well be the first generation in her family to attend college, made Geneseo her first choice because Geneseo "has a good academic reputation," came from the top forty percent of her high school class, expected to major in business (accounting, marketing, or management), likely would pursue a master's degree, wanted to be an authority in her field after graduation and make money—and was a feminist.

The Geneseo freshmen (women) not only resembled their private school counterparts in dress, they enjoyed similar program options, such as the B.A. in computer science, the B.S. in Management Information Systems, and the B. S. in biochemistry, and faced more rigorous requirements than most of their predecessors. At the outset over half of the class of 1984 perceived that the College was "demanding," with almost seventy percent opting for Geneseo because of its curriculum.[23]

With faculty backing, Dr. Colahan's ambition to have a core curriculum to rival private liberal arts colleges was beginning to take shape, with two four-hour courses "in the humanistic tradition" (Humanities I and II) and

Students entering and exiting Sturges Hall wore the typical student outfit described in the March 1983 *Geneseo Compass*: jeans, sneakers, and backpacks. (1987 *Oh Ha Daih*)

two three-hour courses "emphasizing rational methods and problem solving" ("Critical Reasoning") plus two courses each in the fine arts, social sciences, and the natural sciences. Clearly, the cornerstone was the two humanities courses, which offered a healthy dose of diverse literature. Little overlapping of courses to fulfill these requirements was allowed: only two core courses could be used to meet requirements in a student's major, and only two courses could be taken at the introductory and intermediate levels.[24]

Despite the liberal arts emphasis, predictions based on preferences of students admitted in 1981—and later borne out—were that almost two-thirds would choose professional programs (business/management science, education, and speech pathology and audiology). Nearly twelve percent of the class of 1984 intended to major in business/management science, second only to special education, confirming that offering popular majors would attract more students. By 1987 nearly twenty percent of the students were enrolled in business programs.[25]

Academic promise (Geneseo enrolled three hundred National Merit Scholars between 1979 and 1987) led to the creation of an honors program, launched in 1988 with the key leadership of professors Bill and Stacey Edgar. Based on high school averages and SAT scores, twenty entering students (or freshmen with a 3.50 GPA), "the best academic students," were invited to enroll in the twenty-one-hour program that continues today. Examples of Geneseo's progress in attracting quality students and faculty were physics students' research projects in 1988. Led by physics professor Dr. Stephen Padalino (2000 Carnegie/CASE Professor of the Year for New York), six students investigated

Swan Lake was performed in April 1990 by (from left): Shelly DeVito, Lenore DePaoli, Lori Flack, and Jeanne Murray. (1990 *Oh Ha Daih*, identification by Jonette Lancos)

the "polarized ion source telemetry link" and "projectile fragmentation in an oxygen-aluminum reaction," and Geneseo native, Marty Putnam, was one of only two undergraduate physics majors to present papers at a major conference in New Mexico that year.[26]

Despite their academic prowess, the students challenged a proposed administrative change in the Pass/Fail option (a "Pass" or "Fail" rather than a letter grade) for selected courses that had been in effect since the early 1970s. Arguing that the purpose of the option was to encourage students to "explore areas outside of their major," *The Lamron* editorialized that forcing students to declare by the drop/add deadline rather than waiting until the final third of the course was unfair. A compromise was reached, allowing students to declare their intent by the end of the first three weeks.[27]

Geneseo Becomes "Wired"

Meanwhile Geneseo became "wired." Every academic building (thirty-three terminals) was connected to the Burroughs B6800 computer in the Erwin building. Although it took five years to deliver personal computers to all faculty, Geneseo was in the vanguard of SUNY units and far ahead of SUNY's promise to spend upwards of one hundred thousand dollars for computers.[28]

Longtime director of admissions Spencer Roemer was one of the College's most generous donors and funded scholarships for many students. (Art Hatton)

The heroes were associate vice president Bruce Ristow and Bill Davis, associate director, Computing and Information Technology (CIT). Rather than waiting for bureaucratic approval to obtain financing and to hire consultants and contractors, Ristow and Davis pulled it off, with the help of technician

Gary Stratton and students hired during the summer to climb down into manholes to snake fiber wires to one building at a time. The first to get desktop computers were science faculty, who sought them to perform laborious statistical research. This was even before the College had its Banner record management system in place, which Mary Nitsche, then manager of administrative systems and programming for the Computer Center, is credited with getting up and running.[29]

By 1987, computers were so much a part of the academic life that students expected—some said "had to have"—total access all hours of the day and night. A December 9, 1988 editorial in *The Lamron* summed it up: "pretty soon scalpers [charging for use of a printer] will be making a buck." Computer

Orchesis members posed at the barre in the Brodie dance studio in 1980.
(1980 *Oh Ha Daih*)

demand had exceeded supply. Still, there were jokes about students being left behind. In February 1991, *The Lamron* asked students whether they needed an imaginary course, "Computers 099." They did if they could not answer the following questions: "The term 'hard drive' refers to: a) 350 horsepower and a sunroof, b) Long Island to Geneseo, c) The last hole on a golf course" or the second question, "To program a computer in BASIC requires: a) a working knowledge of Greek, b) a small miracle, c) a large miracle." Nonetheless, by 1997 even the dorms were "ethernetted," so students could connect their desktops, then laptops, electronically with almost anyone, though increasingly they have opted for cell phones, Blackberries, or iPods. (Does anyone remember painfully slow 9K modems?)[30]

The bootstrap effort had succeeded beyond the originators' wildest dreams. By 1998 Geneseo ranked eightieth on *Yahoo Internet Life's* list of "America's Most Wired Colleges," ahead of Syracuse University, Johns Hopkins, Haverford, Carleton, and other prestigious schools. The following year, it leapfrogged over a number of well-known colleges and universities to forty-ninth. In 2000 and 2001, little Geneseo was lumped with "universities and research schools," again surpassing all other SUNY schools, except Binghamton, which was two places ahead. It was analogous to a school jumping from Division III to Division I in athletics. And in 2004, Geneseo ranked twenty-fifth among Intel's top one hundred "unwired" colleges, i.e., "where students have the freedom to wirelessly access the Internet on notebook PCs without the traditional wired connection." A year later, Davis's CIT successor, alumna Sue Chichester, '79, was the first to be named Information Technology Woman of the Year by the upstate chapter of the Association of Women's Computing. The efforts of Ristow, Davis, Stratton, Chichester, and others have paid off handsomely.[31]

"SUNY Campus in Cornfields Acquires an Ivy Reputation"

AP reporter Coy's article about SUNY and Geneseo seemed to usher in head-turning accolades. The November 25, 1985 *U.S. News & World Report* ranked Geneseo seventh-best of four-year liberal arts and professional schools in the East. Four years later, Geneseo beat out nearby Rochester Institute of Technology, Ithaca College, and fellow SUNY unit, SUNY Buffalo, to place third among the top regional colleges and universities in the North. Factors weighed in the ranking were selectivity, faculty quality, academic excellence, retention, and—of all things—financial resources. Meanwhile, in May 1986

Money magazine called Geneseo one of the "Ten Public Colleges with an Ivy Twist." The College's science departments were "noteworthy academically," while education, music, and philosophy were "humanities standouts." Four years later the magazine ranked Geneseo second among the nation's public colleges. Then in 1991, *Money's Guide to the Best College Buys in America*, which combined private and public schools, ranked Geneseo twenty-eighth of one hundred. Three years later Geneseo was fifteenth and the only four-year SUNY school

Jim Kimball (center) led the popular Geneseo String Band's 1978 Homecoming parade performance. (1979 *Oh Ha Daih*)

ranked in the top one hundred. The higher ranking was attributed to graduation and retention rates and the percent of budget spent on academic quality.[32]

Better yet, on November 12, 1990, the *New York Times* profiled Geneseo. With its "ivy-covered buildings...[which] soar startlingly out of the surrounding cornfields," Geneseo was "becoming one of the nation's most selective, highly regarded public colleges." In fact, a SUNY administrator called Geneseo's achievement a "marvel." The low tuition played a part, a State of Washington educator claimed, but more importantly the attraction was the "increasing [institutional] quality." And the students themselves were different—more affluent, but unwilling to spend money on Ivies like Cornell and Brown. On the other hand, the article acknowledged that the pattern of budget cuts threatened to undermine the College's efforts to advance further.

Closer to home, in 1988 the Rochester chapter of the American Marketing

In the early 1990s, chemistry faculty included (front, from left): Bhairav Joshi, David Johnson, David Geiger; (back): Richard F. Smith, Richard A. Smith, John Deutsch, Glenn Wilkes, James Boiani. (1993 *Oh Ha Daih*)

Association honored the College with its annual Marketer of the Year Award, proclaiming that "Geneseo has become the most sought-after college in the State University system in New York." Recognizing that some might call this the self-promotion award, the association's secretary countered that "it's more difficult to win the award with the kind of activity at (Geneseo) [*sic*] than with a concrete, tangible product. But we want to recognize good marketing wherever we find it." Geneseo's Assistant Vice President Caren was quick to add that "it would have been impossible [for Geneseo to achieve its success] without a substantial, real program to market" and able students. Caren could have cited biologist Dr. Herman Forest's praise of the class of 1990 in the January 30, 1987 issue of *The Lamron* (not the administration's *Compass*, because, Forest asserted, "students do not read it"). Forest and colleague Dr. Robert Simon had developed a course for non-majors and were amply rewarded by the 112 takers. "The performance I would expect out of 5–10% was delivered by about 80%." Intelligence alone did not explain the achievement in a course demanding "comprehension, not rote memory."[33]

By Geneseo's own measures it was succeeding. In 1986, for the sixth consecutive year, Geneseo was the first SUNY unit to close freshman applications with 6,800 applicants, the most of any of the SUNY arts and science colleges. The students' mean 89 high school average and composite 1100 SAT average were the highest yet of any entering Geneseo class. Six years later, the mean high school average of Geneseo's freshmen was 91.3—the first time high school averages exceeded 90—with a mean SAT score of 1121.[34]

Another satisfying statistic was the overall placement record. Geneseo's graduates went from the 1976 all-time low of forty percent employed full- or part-time or attending graduate school a year later to ninety-three percent for the class of 1989. The percentages were almost identical for business, education, and liberal arts graduates. Business and industry were the primary employers (fifty-four percent of Geneseo's graduates), followed by public schools which employed twenty-five percent, and private agencies choosing 15.4 percent.[35]

Importantly, the Rochester *Democrat and Chronicle* wrote that unlike "major institutions" in the area (Rochester Institute of Technology and the University of Rochester), which had "launched expensive public relations campaigns," Geneseo had "quietly" succeeded—and, it could be added, relatively inexpensively. A Pittsford-Mendon High School counselor acknowledged that Geneseo's faculty and staff had "worked very hard to improve their

image and up their standards." Greece Arcadia guidance counselor Ron Zimarino (who was not identified by the reporter as a 1971 Geneseo graduate) was equally impressed that the school's admission standards rivaled "more prestigious schools." Only Cornell, ranked "most competitive" among upstate colleges and universities, had a lower acceptance rate according to *Barron's Profile of American Colleges*.[36]

Philosophy faculty in the mid-1990s included (front, from left): Dennis Bradford, Walter Soffer, Larry Blackman, Jeeloo Liu; (back): Gary Cox, Carlo Filice, Stacey Edgar, William Edgar. (1994 *Oh Ha Daih*)

However, an October 13, 1989 editorial in *The Lamron* expressed some misgivings. Reacting to a special issue of *U. S. News & World Report* identifying "America's Best Colleges," the writer argued that Geneseo "is not Utopia." Rather, it was an "annoyingly homogeneous" campus. Faculty with doctorates (one measure of "America's Best Colleges") did not necessarily mean better teaching, and student involvement was "feeble at best." While "Geneseo certainly is a fantastic school," it must stop reading its press clippings; "there's still work to be done." The editors could have cited the somewhat troubling statistic that only eighteen percent of Geneseo's students were going to graduate school. The percentage had remained the same over a decade, despite higher admissions criteria.[37]

Dr. Jakubauskas Leaves

On February 26, 1988, *The Lamron* announced what had been rumored for some time. After nine years at the helm, President Jakubauskas was leaving to become president of much-larger Central Michigan University. Reflecting on his term at Geneseo, Jakubauskas recalled that "we went from a period when we were searching for survival into a period where we're riding the quest of fame." While "image means a great deal," he added, Geneseo was "damn good academically." Importantly, Geneseo had been successful despite a serious recession and the loss of close to one hundred posi-

Former United Nations ambassador James Jeremiah Wadsworth received the College's first honorary degree in 1982 and is remembered by the Wadsworth Memorial Lecture series. (Winter 1996 *Geneseo Scene*)

tions over the previous twenty years. He said Geneseo's strategy had been to build up programs students wanted, mainly in the field of business, despite some opposition on campus. The biggest challenge ahead was avoiding complacency.

Steven Stubblefield created this set for the November 1984 production of *Joseph and the Amazing Technicolor Dreamcoat*, which was directed by Scott Ray. (Stubblefield)

Jakubauskas had stressed academic quality, met enrollment challenges, and fostered partnerships with local businesses, as he had promised to do when he took office. But he had paid a price for some of his decisions, especially closing the campus school. Reflecting years later, he felt he had to face the issue head-on. "Politically I might have been better off never to have gone near that Campus School....I didn't like the decision." Otherwise, "I would have cut academic programs." While Geneseo "should continue to turn out good teachers," Jakubauskas felt it had to get away from "the teachers college mission" to be truly multipurpose.[38]

It may go without saying that problems remained, including the need to eliminate tripling in student housing, to lower the student-to-faculty ratio (from 22:1 to a more ideal 16:1, like sister school Brockport), and to enjoy more flexible campus budgeting.

Additionally, President Jakubauskas had only papered over a problem with the special education department, which had been "embroiled in dissent and controversy." The festering began in 1984 when he refused to approve an application for federal funding, leading former chairman Dr. Lyle Lehman to resign in protest. Shortly thereafter, seven department members filed grievances against the new department chairman who was reported to be "rather unresponsive." And the decision to eliminate four positions, alluded to earlier, led the administration to discontinue the Visually Impaired and Early Childhood Education certification programs. The underlying problems of the department's enrollment, its certification options, and leadership remained unresolved.[39]

Undoubtedly, the outgoing president's most visible and lasting accomplishment was South Hall, the first new academic building in over three decades, which opened in 1995, six years after he left. Jakubauskas, who disliked driving to and attending meetings in Albany ("talk, talk, talk for hours" without solving budget problems), had hit the road to argue that Geneseo deserved a new building. Geneseo had achieved its lofty status despite severe

The South Hall construction project was progressing well in July 1994. (Facilities Planning Office)

budget cuts: some faculty offices and classrooms remained in converted dorms (Blakes B–E), which should have been torn down years earlier; the computer center was in the Erwin basement storage area; and the computer science department was spread throughout Fraser without adequate computer labs.[40]

Fortuitously, the timing was right. Some SUNY Construction Fund bonds had matured, and a new classroom building meant Geneseo could avoid paying the Dormitory Authority charge for the Blake buildings. Given SUNY's encouragement, Jakubauskas talked with others on campus who advised putting the computer center, computer science and math departments, and the schools of business and education in the building to justify the desired size, which apparently worked. On the other hand, his request for student townhouses was rejected, though in time, that aspiration too was realized. Importantly, he was leaving his successor with one advantage he had enjoyed only briefly, more flexible campus budgeting, which offered greater freedom to transfer funds among programs without Albany approval. Possibly Jakubauskas also left knowing that he was, in the words of one administrator, "a great shot in the arm" for the College.[41]

Around the Quad

Despite obvious successes, Jakubauskas had faced some minor, but vexing, problems shortly after he took office. The discontent included a protest of course titles, accusations of censorship, challenges to mandated measles inoculations, complaints of sexual immorality, and disapproval of smokers.[42]

During the 1980–1981 school year, some students sought gender-neutral course titles. Bio 103-4, "Biology of Man," was the most offensive to the protesters. But the complaint went beyond just the course titles. "Several times this semester my ears and intellect have been assaulted," one student wrote the president, "by the use of masculine pronouns in reference to all people and the use of 'man' for humanity….These archaic terms dominate the lectures of many professors, *Lamron* articles…and students' papers and conversations…."[43]

History faculty in the mid-1990s included (front, from left): Charles Randy Bailey, William Gohlman, William Derby: (back): James Somerville, Meg Stolee, Helena Waddy, Valentin Rabe, David Tamarin, James Williams. (1996 *Oh Ha Daih*)

The issue of censorship was raised by *The Lamron* editors, who charged the administration with trashing copies of *The Lamron*. While President Jakubauskas confessed that "'I don't think it [*The Lamron*] is a very good paper," he denied ordering custodians to dump the papers. Not surprisingly, *The Lamron* editors and their advisor, Doug Lippincott, the College's director of communications, took offense at the president's criticism.[44]

Claims of censorship took other forms as well. *The Lamron's* Todd Church claimed to have unsuccessfully "fought 'tooth and nail'" to persuade faculty to invite creationist Luther Sunderland to deal "a fatal blow to the scientific community…by revealing several inaccuracies and discrepancies in the theory of evolution." It took special funding to bring Sunderland to the campus, Church asserted. Another claim of censorship arose out of Central Council's "defunding" of Geneseo Students for Peace and Justice and the Gay and Lesbian Support Group. *The Lamron* editors blamed the College Republicans. "Whether you agree with them [the two groups whose funding was eliminated] or not is irrelevant if they are functional to a sizeable population of the college community."[45]

Health-related issues also led to protests. A statewide outbreak of measles in 1989 led the state health department to direct inoculation of students, faculty, and staff. Only students safely inoculated were permitted in the classrooms or dining halls, which drew a protest from a state consumer group claiming the students should have a choice. Shortly thereafter, condoms were put in residence hall vending machines, which brought varied reactions. "Making it [sex] safe is not going to solve the problem," Jerry Reynolds, president of the Inter-Varsity Christian Fellowship, protested. Vice President

Satryb countered that it was not a question of morality, "it's strictly a health [AIDS] issue." And it was a health issue that prompted the smoking ban in campus buildings, leading one of *The Lamron's* editors to laugh at "a stodgy professor" suffering a "nic fit" or sneaking a smoke behind "snowy shrubs." The answer, according to the editor, was to "kick the habit."[46]

On the bright side, *The Lamron's* features editor praised the carillon bells atop Sturges for cutting the winter gloom. Bruce Godsave had overcome bureaucratic obstacles to restore the carillon in 1983, and now, however corny, "'The Rainbow Connection' [*The Muppet Movie*], 'Theme from Mahogany' or a fine Christmas carol," lifted spirits. The writer knew that the music was prerecorded—that there weren't real bells up in the tower—but it didn't diminish her pleasure. Students also enjoyed live music on campus, including by the Chamber Singers, directed by Dr. Robert Isgro, before their 1987 concerts in Italy, and a seasonal "Festive Concert" by the Carol Choristers and the Chamber Symphony, conducted by Dr. James Walker.[47]

While the carillon and the concerts were free, the mandatory activities fee, which had to be voted on every four years, again became an issue in the 1980s when William F. Buckley charged $12,000 for a fifty-three-minute talk, or "$226 per minute," according to a critical commentary in *The Lamron*. However, after an October 20, 1984 performance by Red Skelton, "a combination of Peter Pan and Santa Claus," the students approved the fee again 960 to 40 in 1985. So later, Larry Linville (*M*A*S*H's* Major Frank Burns) in "blue pants, penny loafers, and a Geneseo sweatshirt" could entertain an appreciative audience, as did Mary Wilson and the Supremes, whose performance was labeled "supreme." They were followed in short order by James Taylor, actor-dancer Ben Vereen, Abbie Hoffman ("Yippie") versus former war protester and ally, Jerry Rubin ("Yuppie"), whose combined fee was less than half Buckley's, and comic Jay Leno, who performed at Homecoming 1987 for $25,000, more than double Buckley's fee. On the other hand, the talk by then-U.S. Attorney for the Southern District of New York Rudolph Giuliani on tax evasion and government corruption was underwritten by the John Wiley Jones School of Business.[48]

Fees also helped pay for "local" talent who performed *Chicago: A Musical Vaudeville*, featuring Bettina G. Pollard as Velma Kelly, killer of an adulterous husband. (As Bettina DeBell, '87 and '92, she is Geneseo Central School's

Red Skelton posed with coordinator of college activities Tom Matthews after his popular October 20, 1984 performance. (Tom Matthews)

Pippin, a musical about Charlemagne's young son, was well received in November 1986. (1987 *Oh Ha Daih*)

Former President Gerald Ford delivered the first James Jeremiah Wadsworth Lecture in 1989. (Roemer House collection)

much-admired and appreciated play director.) The activities fees also supported *As You Like It*, directed by Dr. John Barrett, which *The Lamron* arts editor asserted "was liked." *Godspell*, performed by the Newman parish in April 1986, also played to an appreciative audience.[49]

It didn't cost anything from 1985 to 1989 to turn on the tube Tuesday nights at 9:00 p.m. to watch alumnus Glenn Gordon Caron's *Moonlighting*. Created and produced by Caron, for a time the program enjoyed the highest TV rating for that evening, surpassing *Who's the Boss, The A-Team, Growing Pains,* and *Spenser: For Hire*.[50]

Also free of charge, Geneseo String Band began its "Pre-St. Patrick's Day Concerts" in March 1979. Led by the incomparable James Kimball, the ever-changing band has performed for almost thirty years to the delight of audiences of various ages.

Not surprisingly, the presidential election campaign was a hot topic in Fall 1988. A straw vote favoring eventual winner George H. W. Bush and the charge that Michael Dukakis was an "inexperienced liberal who represents a grievous threat to social and economic stability" were too much for Rory Lancman, "outspoken" features editor for *The Lamron* and a "budding Democrat." Mid-year he relocated to New York City, "the place [for a Democrat] to be." Others, unhappy with the election results, formed a Democrat Socialists Party, though they recognized that socialist is a dirty word in the United States.[51]

Republicans on campus and in the village prided themselves that one of their own was recognized in May 1982. James Jeremiah Wadsworth, former U.S. Ambassador to the United Nations, grandson, son, and brother of three of Geneseo's Board of Visitors' chairmen, was awarded the College's first SUNY-authorized honorary Doctor of Laws. Six years later, Art Hatton persuaded "Jerry's" daughter and son-in-law, Alice and Trowbridge Strong, to contribute fifty thousand dollars to an endowment to sponsor the James Jeremiah Wadsworth Lecture Series, which has featured ex-U.S. presidents Gerald Ford and George H. W. Bush.[52]

"Dr. Mac is Back"

The search for an interim president was amazingly brief. The obvious choice was former president MacVittie. Speaking for the community, *Livingston Republican* editor Ray Sherman said, "It's like seeing an old friend again." Faculty and staff agreed. Because MacVittie had just served as a consultant to various Pennsylvania colleges and as interim president of Fredonia, he felt he could get back into harness rather effortlessly. Also, his return was helped by Jakubauskas, who thoughtfully appointed MacVittie as adjunct faculty member and consultant from May 15 to June 30. While he was drawn back to see how well Geneseo was meeting its promise, MacVittie made it clear that he was back for only a year. The College needed a dynamic, younger president to accomplish the myriad tasks that remained. Tasks included building repairs, attracting more distinguished scholars as visiting faculty, serving teacher education better than it was being served, developing more public service programs, attracting and accommodating more minority students, enlarging Milne Library (to which basically nothing had been done since its 1966 opening) and countering "over-enrollment," which was badly stretching faculty and staff.[53]

However, Dr. MacVittie was not encouraged by incoming Chancellor D. Bruce Johnstone's warning that Geneseo and the other SUNY schools faced *"permanent reductions"* in base budgets [italics in original]. As if on cue, Governor Cuomo's 1989–1990 "retrenchment budget" threatened the loss of twenty more positions at Geneseo and the delay or cancellation of building maintenance projects. Compounding SUNY's budget woes, Cuomo vetoed a bill increasing tuition by two hundred dollars, arguing that he wanted schooling to be affordable and would not raise tuition unless it was an "absolute necessity."[54]

MacVittie experienced a potentially greater threat when a bomb—a real one—was delivered to dean of students Katie Hayes-Sugarman. At about 10:00 a.m. February 2, 1989, Hayes-Sugarman called Public Safety to report she had received a suspicious package, forcing evacuation of the Erwin building. The Monroe County Sheriff Department's bomb squad x-rayed the package, confirmed that it contained an actual bomb and successfully disarmed it.[55]

Interim president MacVittie celebrated the women's soccer team's 1988 ECAC championship with co-captains Eileen Reagan and Diane Stanitski. (Fred Bright)

Fortunately, no one was hurt, and MacVittie once more departed after a generally trouble-free "homecoming" year.

"Doctor or President is Fine"—Carol Harter

By early March 1989 the presidential search committee had narrowed the candidates to two men and a woman. Successful candidate Carol C.

Harter clearly appealed to a reporter for *The Lamron*. Asked "whether she was a feminist, Dr. Harter replied that she was." Then asked whether she "preferred Ms. or Mrs., Harter quickly replied, 'Doctor or President is fine.'" The reporter learned as other students, faculty, and staff would, that Geneseo's president-to-be was decisive, clear about who she was and forthright about what she intended to do once in office.[56]

Harter, a Queens, New York native with a SUNY Binghamton doctorate and bachelor's degree from Harpur College, had served as Ohio University vice president and brought a memorable style. While she viewed the College's selectivity as an asset, it could be a liability if it resulted in a "'lily-white, yuppie, college community.'" She sought diversity, "a sense of cosmopolitanism," a school known for "quality of academic and intellectual life," and a "dynamic involvement" by students and faculty. Additionally she intended to revitalize faculty and programs through seminars and workshops. Did she anticipate any problems because she was a "woman administrator?" No, she assured the college community, because "'confidence wins friends—even chauvinists.'" Befitting the arrival of a path-breaking president, a full-scale inaugural was held October 14, 1989, attended by individuals representing more than thirty colleges and universities. [57]

Carol Harter served as president from 1989 to 1995. (1990 *Oh Ha Daih*)

Aware that the budget would determine the direction of Geneseo's future, she sought to overcome SUNY's lack of flexibility that resulted in "a game of answering to politicians...unlike Ohio," where, she asserted, universities determined their own budgets. Support for the faculty and staff, upon whom she was counting to achieve the College's mission, was a "top priority." To strengthen college advancement—and under vice president Hatton's guidance—she appointed Dick Rosati, '71, associate vice president for college relations and development, and Debra Grose Hill, '75, formerly director of corporate and special gifts, as director of alumni and parent relations. Both have proved their worth. Harter also emphasized the importance of the Geneseo Foundation's commitment to supporting faculty research, including travel. She was helped early by retired director of admissions Dr. Spencer Roemer, Geneseo's most generous benefactor, followed shortly by a sizeable gift from Gertrude Chanler.[58]

As Harter acclimated to the campus, changes rapidly followed. One of many was purging the campus of its teachers college image by dropping references to "State," as in "Geneseo State," including in the College bookstore

and the wall of the Wilson Ice Arena. However, quite possibly the most significant change was the resignation of Vice President Colahan, who briefly returned to teaching in the history department before retiring. His resignation was followed by Associate Vice President Virginia Kemp's retirement and Dean Joan Schumaker's return to the math department before retiring.[59]

Harter's new chief academic officer was Dr. Donald S. Spencer, who succeeded interim Vice President Bruce Ristow on July 1, 1990 and was given the title of provost rather than vice president for academic affairs. Spencer, a Midwesterner and army veteran who held degrees from Illinois College and the University of Virginia, had earned his spurs as a member of the history faculty at Ohio University and Westminster College before serving as the University of Montana's assistant provost.[60]

Spencer Roemer's generous donations made the Roemer Arboretum a reality in 1990. (Fred Bright)

The new president also counted on many who already were in place, including Kenneth H. Levison, Harvard Ph.D., who continued as vice president for administration and finance; Arthur Hatton, vice president for college relations and development; Ronald Satryb, heading student services and staff relations; and William Caren, Satryb's associate vice president. According to Jakubauskas, the "very bright" Levison, a former state division of the budget administrator, understood how the state budget bureau worked. He needed to, for he was replacing likeable Dr. Van Quaal, "a nuts and bolts person" who knew the campus better than anyone else, though it took a toll on his health, likely leading to his retirement in 1985. Hatton's public relations skills and positive feeling for Geneseo were unmatched. Satryb could play the "heavy," especially in relations with unions,

Jack Johnston was appointed director of the School of Performing Arts and later the School of the Arts. His office, like many faculty offices, was better organized than the cluttered appearance suggests. (Paul Hepler)

with which Jakubauskas was uncomfortable. The imaginative Caren had already proven his worth by promoting Geneseo as a worthy competitor of prestigious private schools.[61]

President Harter found a strong and improving faculty. Two arrivals in 1979 were math professor Dr. Stephen West, who was named Distinguished Teaching Professor in 2000, and anthropology professor Dr. Ellen Kintz, whose research of early Central America civilizations has been widely recognized. Dr. Olympia Nicodemi, recipient of the Deborah and Franklin T. Haimo (mathematics) Award for Distinguished College Teaching in 2003 (four years after her husband Dr. Gary Towsley had received it), came two years later, along with Dr. Kenneth Kallio, who later chaired the psychology department, and Dr. Darrell Norris, National Council for Geographic Education's Distinguished College Teacher (1987). Fulbright scholar Dr. Robert Goeckel (political science), Dr. Celia Easton (English), recipient of the Chancellor's Award for Excellence in Teaching (1989), and Dr. David Geiger (chemistry), who received the Chancellor's Research Recognition Award (2005), arrived in 1982, 1984, and 1985 respectively. In 2004, Dr. Robert O'Donnell (biology), who debuted in 1987, was designated a Distinguished Teaching Professor. Dr. Robert Anemone, an anthropologist who joined the faculty in 1988, brought some warranted attention three years later by discovering (with Drs. William Brennan, James Scatterday and Richard Young) "the most complete [85–90 percent] mastodon skeleton found in New York State." Dr. Rong Lin, who came in 1989, was recognized by the Chancellor's Award for Excellence in Scholarship and Creative Activities and as a First Time Patent Awardee (both in 2002). Sadly, he died just three years after being recognized.[62]

President Harter's hires included Drs. Leonard Sancilio (dean of students), Isidro Bosch (biology and Roemer Professor, 1999–2002), Kurt Fletcher (physics chair) and Irina "Ren" Vasiliev (geography), who came in 1991, 1992, and 1993 respectively. Fletcher and Vasiliev were 1997 winners of the Chancellor's Award for Excellence in Teaching.[63]

The Chancellor's awards were important to Harter, who ordered expensive medallions for award winners—strongly urging recipients to wear them at various College functions—and hung photos of "distinguished" faculty in the Erwin building. However, she could be as firm as she was congratulatory. She did not hesitate to dismiss Dr. Vahakn Dadrian, "an internationally recognized expert on genocide," after an arbitrator found Dadrian guilty of "improper physical contact" with a female freshman.[64]

The new president also could be dismissive of student complaints. After angry protests over the 1994 merger of music, theater, and dance into the School of Performing Arts and a critical editorial in *The Lamron*, Harter bluntly asserted that it was "'an administrative organizational issue. I don't think it's something students should be concerned with.'"[65]

Fulfilling the Mission of the College

After only a year in office, Harter was fighting budget wars, just as her predecessors had done. In a December 10, 1990 news release, Harter growled that SUNY could not survive without more money. For Geneseo to receive a million less than requested was devastating. That same day at SUNY Binghamton, Harter took her wrath out on the state legislature, railing about the "absurdly low tuition—based on the cockamamie idea that higher education is so important it shall be free." Then, beginning just before Christmas, the College had to close for eleven days to save just thirty-five thousand dollars (repairing frozen pipes in some buildings cut that saving) and state workers had to take accrued vacation days. Further, the College was banned from hiring, traveling, and purchasing equipment to save another fifty thousand dollars, and was forced to cancel twenty class sections for Spring 1991.[66]

The 1991 ice storm was beautiful but destructive, leading to fallen trees and widespread power outages. The College fared better than much of the village, with power restored after only thirty hours. (Roemer House collection)

Provost Spencer supported Harter's claims of austerity in a memo in which he pointed out that "our faculty teach more than is usual around the country," yet surveys showed that Geneseo was "doing a good job." SUNY administration did not help by suggesting faculty and staff could work harder.[67]

Possibly President Harter figured a glossy annual report might help the cause. At any rate, the 1990–1991 report was a public relations gem. In it she reiterated her goals: to ensure that students obtained "a broad, superior liberal arts and science education" and to provide necessary administrative support to "fulfill the mission of the college." That is, if the College was not closed. In a December 1991 memo to SUNY presidents, Chancellor D. Bruce Johnstone threatened major budget cuts, including closing three campuses.[68]

Scott Fitch (with ball) and Scott Tudman led the Blue Knights to victory in the 1993 Chase Tournament. Fitch was the leading scorer and tournament MVP. (Tom Murphy, Bright collection)

Undaunted, Harter had created a new planning council to replace the College Priorities Committee. In addition to recommending "a mission statement," which would set priorities rather than simply recommend cuts, she wanted the committee to focus on ways to enhance the students' learning and experiences. She also wanted academic departments to set goals. Toward this end she allocated forty thousand dollars in 1991 and one hundred thousand the next year to fund faculty/staff proposals reflecting the College's mission. And she intended to "restore" the School of Education (promised by MacVittie in 1971) under the leadership of Dr. Mary Jensen.[69]

Health and physical education did not fare as well. Rather, despite Fred Bright's impassioned plea in April 1991 to save the already-reduced program (cut from four to two credits in 1987), the College Senate voted to eliminate the physical education requirement and drop graduation requirements from 124 to 120 hours. The only concession was to grant intercollegiate athletes one credit for participation per sport—over their four years.[70]

The good news was that the quality of students continued to rise. In 1990, Geneseo had admitted only 3,611 of 9,845 applicants, including sixteen percent minorities, with average SAT scores of 1140. Rebecca Surman had received a Goldwater Scholarship, a Geneseo first (Lisa Lucenti was Geneseo's first Mellon Fellowship winner two years later), the seven winter sports teams had compiled an amazing 93-14-3 record, and an eye-pleasing "Valley, Village, College" display in Newton, initiated by Martin L. Fausold, was dedicated in June 1991. Finally, President Harter mentioned that construction on the new academic building ("South Hall"), the first in eighteen years, would begin in March 1993.[71]

On the other hand, transforming the upper quad into a showplace gave students, faculty, and staff plenty to deplore and/or ridicule. Nothing seemed to go right. The original contractor blamed the architect, vice president Levison blamed the contractor for failed planning, and critics blamed the state's policy of accepting the lowest bids. The initial phase, dubbed "carnage" by many, was whacking down trees, most noticeably a large one in front of the Milne Library entrance, shortly after graduation in 1994. This was followed by bulldozing virtually everything fronting the Erwin, Bailey, and Greene buildings, including asphalt walkways, before starting construction on the centerpiece,

The mid-1990s upper quad reconstruction project seemed endless. (Bruce Ristow)

a brick and lattice archway, a sunken area, and a perimeter knee-high brick wall. After an embarrassingly long time and at a cost of approximately seven hundred thousand dollars, a new contractor eventually completed the show-place in 1997.[72]

"From State-Supported to State-Aided to State-Located"

However energetic and positive, barely four years into her term President Harter was less sanguine about sustaining the College's progress. In fact, she was irate over the state's lack of support and adapted her predecessor's complaint: SUNY had gone "from state-supported to state-aided to state-located." By her reckoning, since 1981 the College had maintained a stable enrollment of approximately five thousand FTE students while it lost more than one hundred positions, or 15.5 percent "of its total work force." During that time, the state tax support for SUNY had dropped from sixty to thirty-nine percent. Now Geneseo's operating budget was being reduced another twelve percent, causing the College to lose more faculty.[73]

Given its successful retention rate, Geneseo would have to limit admissions further; the catch was that revenues were based on enrollment. Fewer students meant less money. But one budget protest differed greatly from the past. Instead of negotiating with students to leave the administration building, Harter not only invited them to conduct a sit-in from 10 a.m. to 4 p.m., Thursday February 20, 1992, she even gave the first protest speech. Yet, she and Central Council representatives were fully aware of the dilemma: if the state upped support for students, likely, it would cut more faculty and staff. Nor was raising student tuition the answer, for that meant fewer students could afford to attend Geneseo. Nonetheless, tuition was raised soon thereafter from $500 to $1,325 a semester. But, intersession courses, which were first offered in January 1990 to bring in extra revenue, had not really paid off and would be dropped later.[74]

Geneseo's 1993–1994 All-Americans were (from left): Betsy Balling (soccer), Katie Smith (basketball), Scott Fitch (basketball), Mark Monaghan (swimming), Kim Stone (indoor track), and Keena Bush (indoor track). (Fred Bright)

The 1990–1993 school years were once more good news-bad news for the College. The good news was that a retirement incentive proved successful. A total of thirty-three, mostly senior and higher-salaried, faculty retired between 1991 and 1993. The bad news was that many of the retirees were veteran faculty and staff on whom the College had counted for leadership. The first round in 1991 included administrators Thomas Colahan and Virginia Kemp, chemistry chairman Kevork Nahabedian, former history chairman Valentin Rabe, communications department head Charles Goetzinger, geology chairman James Scatterday, Donald DeMott, Robert Haseltine, Arch Reid, Michel Richard, Paul Schaefer, Dietmar Schenitski, and Carey Vasey plus alums Tom and Brenda Conlon, and Ernie Fox, the incomparable technician. The next year Martin L. Fausold and Herman Forest, representing fifty-one years of service, enjoyed retirement incentives. Among the 1993 retirees were two distinguished teaching professors (Rose Alent and Richard F. Smith) and five former department chairs (William Derby, Helen Foster, Paul Hepler, who really didn't stay retired, Robert Isgro, and John Youngers.) The School of Education lost the most faculty, six: Robert Comley, Muttaniyil Idiculla, Robert Meyer, and Charles Scruggs, plus Foster and Youngers.[75]

Also between 1988 and 1994, eight people who had been important to Geneseo died. Gloria Mattera and Donald Innis were still active faculty, former HPE director Daniel Mullin and former communications department chairman Charles Goetzinger had only recently retired, while former presidents Espy and Moench and professors Ira Wilson and Paul Neureiter were in their nineties.[76]

There were administrative changes as well. In September 1991, Dr. Thomas A. Greenfield, with a doctorate in English from the University of Minnesota and formerly dean at Kentucky's Bellarmine College, became the first at Geneseo to hold the title of dean of the College rather than dean of undergraduate studies. His marked sense of humor was best demonstrated by his songs, accompanied by his guitar playing. Then, less than three years later, in January 1994, Provost Spencer returned to his native Illinois as Western Illinois University's president, replaced by Fred Fidura (psychology) until August 15, 1994, when Dr. Christopher Dahl assumed the post.[77]

"I Have Such Fond Memories…"

Although the College struggled with budget cuts, the loss of faculty, and energy conservation measures, campus life was not entirely grim. Reflecting on his years at Geneseo, Paul Kreher, '93, remembered watching the sunset from the gazebo, listening to the carillon bells, taking calculus with Dr. Gary Towsley, biology with Dr. Harold Hoops, "Christian Thought" with Dr. Bill Cook, and geography with the Lougeays (Ray and Cheryl), reading *Wuthering Heights* and *Gulliver's Travels* in the Humanities courses, watching girls in short skirts, running for Dorm Council on the slogan, "I can't run my own life, so let me run yours," dancing to the Hogs at the Idle Hour, and dating a classmate who would become a spouse. Senior Karen Kraus enjoyed an "all-expense-paid trip" to Washington, D.C., which she had won for submitting the name "Rex" for President Reagan's new dog. Ms. Kraus proudly wore her College Union snack bar hat to the ceremony.[78]

Others remembered either protesting or reluctantly supporting Desert Storm in 1991. A special ten-page issue of *The Lamron* in January 1991 clearly reflected the divide. Yet, a discussion initiated by sociologist Dr. Nancy Kleniewski drew only ten listeners, twice the number of speakers. The issue took on special meaning for Marine Reserves Corporal Mark Maisel, a management science major, who on November 26, 1990, just two-and-a-half weeks before his graduation, was called up for the "Persian Gulf Crisis."[79]

Still others vividly recalled athletic successes. For example, 1972 graduate Linda Piccirillo Hinckley's women's swimming team enjoyed a 15-0 dual meet record in 1980, compiling new records in sixteen of twenty-four events during the 1979–1980 season. Star swimmer Joan Alley, daughter of physics faculty mem-

Students partied in front of a Bank Street fraternity house, now Roemer House. The In Between is in the background. (1980 *Oh Ha Daih*)

ber Dr. Phillip Alley, was Geneseo's first female All-American (1980). That same 1980 season the Ice Knights posted a 16-11-1 season, only to lose out in their playoff bid. It would up its record to 22-8-1 in 1985, winning the conference championship, earning an ECAC playoff berth and helping coach Paul Duffy become ECAC coach of the year. And the men's soccer team, coached by Carl Witzel and relying on Geneseo's first two soccer All-Americans, Ray Maxwell, '81, and Rick Butterworth, '82, made it to the ECAC championship in 1981. In

1979, Marilyn Moore, a Brockport graduate, became Geneseo's trainer, and twenty years later she was named athletics director to succeed Dr. John Spring, who for a dozen years had overseen major growth in the programs.[80]

Though men's baseball, wrestling, golf, and tennis and women's tennis and synchronized swimming were dropped in the 1980–1981 school year for budgetary reasons,

The 1987–1988 basketball team included (kneeling, from left): Mike Guariglia, Kyle Hargrave, co-captain Jim Clar (who holds several basketball and soccer records), co-captain Joe D'Ambrosia, Paul Benz, Tony Whitlow; (standing): coach Tom Pope, Chip Trapper, Joe Boronczyk, Sean Gray, Scott Forrest, Tom Rieflin, Mark Muller, Jamie Palmer, manager Scott Cripps, assistant coach Tom Curle. (Bright collection)

the remaining teams prospered. Cross country runner Mary Ryan took twenty-fifth of 111 runners at the national meet in Atlanta on November 23, 1985, to earn All-American honors. Husky Winton Buddington might not have won any honors as a Geneseo cheerleader in 1986, but he did so later in the hammer throw. The men's cross country team took the SUNYAC championship and a sixth place in the state meet that same year, while the women runners had their best season up to then, earning a second place in the SUNYAC championship. Led by Jim Clar, who became an admissions counselor at his alma mater after graduating, Geneseo's basketball team defeated Brockport, RIT, and Hobart to win the 1989 Chase-Lincoln Trust Bank tournament in Rochester. After

Chris Smith, seen with President Harter, was a hockey All-American who led Geneseo in assists and total points scored and set records that still stood in 2006. (Bright collection)

his women's cross country team won its second straight New York State title, 1969 alumnus Mike Woods was honored as the NYS Women's Collegiate Athletic Association Coach of the Year in 1993, the first of many honors. The Lady Knights soccer team, coached by Fred Bright, enjoyed an impressive fourteen-year record of 177 wins, 62 losses, and 17 ties, and made the Division III final four in 1994. Mathematics education student Scott Fitch, two-time All-American, was named SUNYAC basketball player of the year, All East, All-ECAC and Division III player of the year in 1994.[81]

Students' memories, whether about classroom experiences or participation in the arts or sports, often resulted in contributions to the Geneseo Foundation, which raised almost two million dollars from nearly nine thousand individual donors between 1982 and 1992. By 1994 the cumulative total (from 1979) was almost five million dollars. One tack for raising money was creating the Society of Old Main in 1987. It annually honors successful alumni by awarding them medals featuring Old Main, the school's original building. (By 2005, some thirty individuals had been honored.) Graduates were profiting from their ingenuity and College experience, so it made sense to ask them to "give something back" to help current students. For example, in September 1984, alumnus Donald Zabkar, '77, a speech communications major, related his entrepreneurial experiences to an appreciative audience in the MacVittie College Union. Ten years after graduating, his Zab's Backyard Hots was the official supplier of hot dogs to the Rochester Red Wings baseball team and to the Hartford Whalers hockey team. One way Karen Dewitt, '82, contributes to her alma mater is by achieving prominence as public affairs reporter for public broadcasting in Albany.[82]

One of the most stirring success stories is of the five Huynhs, Vietnam refugees who, by dint of almost unimaginable hard work, graduated from Geneseo. Older brother Bobi Huynh, '90, paved the way, followed by four sisters. Next to graduate was MyHang Huynh, '91, who majored in mathematics and chemistry and later earned a Ph.D. in chemistry from SUNY Buffalo. She was followed by sisters PhuongHang Huynh, '92, DiemHang Kennison Huynh Younes, '93, and MinhHang Kennison Huynh, '93. Their remarkable story and that of the family **they** "adopted," Lynn, '81, and

Sisters (from left) MinhHang, DiemHang, PhuongHang, and MyHang Huynh followed their older brother Bobi to the College. (Marie Zito, Summer 1991 *Geneseo Scene*)

Weston Kennison, '79, is not only unique to Geneseo, it is inspirational. As if out of a fairy tale, in September 2007 Dr. MyHang Huynh was awarded the five-hundred-thousand-dollar MacArthur Foundation's so-called "genius grant," for designing less toxic explosives, which use copper and iron instead of mercury and lead. The timing was perfect. Huynh, who had abandoned lab work early in the year because of "stress-related health issues," was able to take time to consider what to do next with her life.[83]

Harter Leaves Geneseo for UNLV

At the end of June 1995, Carol Harter left to become president of the University of Nevada at Las Vegas. She confessed she was induced to take the UNLV presidency at a salary of $150,000, plus some nice perks, because of the election of Governor George Pataki, whom she had not supported, and the prospect of more SUNY budget cuts. However, in just six short years, the flamboyant Harter had made an impact.[84]

Under her leadership Geneseo enjoyed positive press, increased applications from academically talented students, a more research-oriented faculty, larger annual fund donations, and ongoing growth plans. Harter not only touted Geneseo's academic programs, especially the humanities courses, she found ways to recognize faculty, such as showing faculty art in the president's house and initiating the Lockhart and Alumni professorships to recognize and reward outstanding faculty. She also used savings from energy conservation measures and retirements to fund faculty/staff proposals reflecting Geneseo's academic mission, initiate program reviews, and pursue some of the planning council's recommendations.

The Jakubauskas and Harter Years

Paradoxically, under presidents Jakubauskas and Harter, Geneseo blossomed while SUNY's reputation suffered. *Newsday's* six-part series in 1992 severely criticized SUNY for losing faculty, letting buildings deteriorate, enlarging class sizes, and increasing tuition. Particularly troubling, *Newsday* reported that a third of SUNY faculty believed the quality of education had declined during the previous five years. The paper's editors concluded that "the State University of New York has faltered in its drive to become a first-rank institution of learning," and laid blame on the "state's budget crisis" which "drained dollars out of the system." However, Geneseo, on the brink of disaster with a drastic drop in applications in 1977, had turned itself around by "aggressive marketing, selling itself as a selective liberal arts school equal to an Ivy League school, at less cost." Its "improved quality of students…has invigorated the faculty and helped develop an atmosphere of high academic energy." "That academic alchemy worked so well that Geneseo now hears complaints that it is far too selective for a SUNY campus."[85]

These were "critical years" for the College. While MacVittie was the driving force behind Geneseo's turnaround, both of his successors bought into and added to his vision of what the College might become. And both Jakubauskas and Harter benefited from many of VPAA Colahan's occasionally unpopular plans to transform Geneseo. But the transformation demanded some "daring decisions" by Jakubauskas, most notably closing the Holcomb and library schools. He saw the advantage of offering the business and computer science programs, which were attractive to students, though they did not fit the liberal arts model.[86]

Unlike her immediate predecessor, President Harter was a "lightning rod." She virtually ran academic affairs, including supporting program reviews, initiated by Provost Spencer, to assure the academic quality she sought. She also adopted the total quality management concept, and with Vice President Levison's help, reallocated money where she felt it was needed while obtaining more private donations. Above all, along with Vice President Hatton, she set in motion a capital campaign, possibly the first for a SUNY unit, to coincide with the College's 125th anniversary celebration. Some three hundred supporters attended the campaign Kickoff Dinner held at Rochester's Hyatt Regency Hotel, which featured a new fundraising video produced by Emmy award-winner Gertrude Houston, a Geneseo native and resident. Importantly, Harter "created a momentum" that has re-engaged successful alumni and significantly increased annual contributions and major gifts from alumni and friends of the College.[87]

Basically, Geneseo was always a good institution; it just needed a boost and a little horn-tooting by Jakubauskas and Harter.

Weather was not a problem when commencement was held in the Wilson Ice Arena from 1973 through 1998. (1990 *Oh Ha Daih*)

Chapter Ten

SUNY GENESEO

•

Some Achieve Greatness (1995–2007)

While a millennium catastrophe loomed—and quickly faded—Geneseo was not untouched by outside events. Four Geneseo alumni lost their lives when Muslim terrorists flew hijacked commercial airplanes into the World Trade Center on September 11, 2001, a Muslim Geneseo undergraduate's sister was attacked in a misguided act of revenge, and alumni would serve in Afghanistan and Iraq. However, the College had its own agenda: appointing a new leader; sustaining, if not advancing, its reputation for excellence; and attracting, retaining, and housing students while adjusting to the demands of more activist SUNY trustees.

"A Tradition of Excellence"

The outgoing president was a tough act to follow. A charismatic, highly visible detail person, Carol Harter left when Geneseo's ascent might well have peaked. The question was what kind of leadership the College needed.

The presidential search began in May 1995 after Provost Christopher C. Dahl was appointed interim president. Though the forty-nine-year-old Vermont native with a Harvard B.A. and Yale Ph.D. (English) had served in that post for less than a year, he had impressed both town and gown. His

Opposite Page: In recent years, the village has hung a banner on Main Street in late August to welcome students back to campus. (*Geneseo Scene*, January 2000)

Christopher Dahl was appointed president in 1996 after serving briefly as provost and interim president. (Roemer House Collection)

amiability, scholarship, and experiences as chair of humanities at the University of Michigan-Dearborn and dean of the School of Humanities and Social Sciences at Millersville University of Pennsylvania boded well.[1]

By early October the search committee, which represented virtually every interested group, had narrowed the list of candidates from eighty to six. Two months later, given Chancellor Thomas Bartlett's directive to submit *two* names (breaking with precedent), the committee recommended Dr. Dahl and Dr. Susanne Woods, academic vice president at Franklin and Marshall College. The College Council, by a vote of six to two, opted for Woods. The advisory committee, favoring Dahl, immediately challenged the council, to which it had sent its recommendation, citing trustee policy which required consensus or near consensus. A joint meeting on January 8, 1996, supporting Dahl—and Woods's subsequent withdrawal—paved the way for Dr. Dahl's permanent appointment by the SUNY trustees at the end of February 1996. Following John Milne's precedent, he was only the second head of the school to be appointed from within.[2]

Candidate and then appointee Dahl stressed that the College was "looking for excellence," but he cautioned that attainment was threatened by budgetary constraints and attacks on higher education generally. Nonetheless, a year-long celebration of the College's 125 years was a positive omen. Founders Day, Friday September 27, 1996, was a gala affair, highlighted by President Dahl's installation. In his half-hour address he recalled the College's "metamorphoses" (from Normal School to teachers college to public liberal arts college) and its "tradition of boldness, imagination, and excellence."[3]

President Dahl, his wife Ruth Rowse, and their son George greeted 1995 Homecoming parade spectators. (Ron Pretzer)

While the 125th celebration did not have all the hoopla of the fif-tieth, nor a published history, as the hundredth did, it had its share of events. For example, alumni hosted a coffee hour on September 13, 1996, and students buried a time capsule. Later, faculty, including Dr. Rose Bachem Alent, shared recollections. Alumni Dr. Thomas Sergiovanni, '58, Tom Cook, '75, and "Dutch" Van Ry, '64, offered historical perspectives. The academic departments reviewed their contributions, and various groups prepared exhibits and a videotape to commemorate the occasion. It was a memorable year.

Taking the reins, the new president called for "still higher levels of quality" and counted on a new provost. That search was begun in September 1996, and four months later, Dr. Barbara Dixon, with a doctorate in musical arts from the University of Colorado, emerged from the candidate pool. The former K-12 music teacher most recently had served for two years as Central Michigan University's Dean of the College of Arts and Science.[4]

Students buried a time capsule on September 13, 1996 as part of the College's 125th anniversary celebration. (Winter 1996 *Geneseo Scene*)

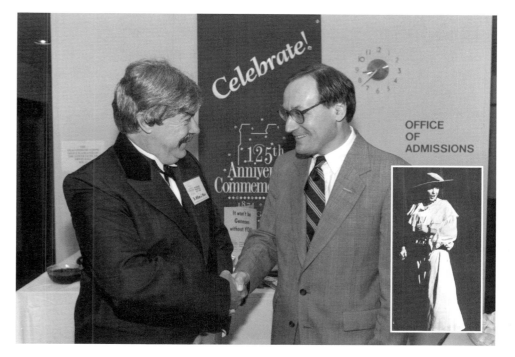

Bruce Godsave showed his flair for the dramatic by playing the part of William Milne during the College's 125th anniversary celebration and by performing as Sophie Tucker during a Delta Kappa Tau revue during his student years. (Winter 1996 *Geneseo Scene*; inset 1964 *Oh Ha Daih*)

"Time for Some Applause"

Outwardly at least it seemed to be a propitious time for the new administrative team. *The Lamron* editors, particularly critical in the recent past, lauded their College. They complimented the University Police for its rape defense pro-gram, the administration for examining the issue of alcohol abuse, the Student

Geneseo's University Police, the last unarmed SUNY police officers, sponsored billboards in 2006 as part of their effort to be allowed to carry guns. They were armed after the spring 2007 Virginia Tech shootings. (Wayne Mahood)

Association for discussing multicultural issues, and Vice President Levison for explaining budgeting in lay terms. The editors' commendation merited framing, given how seldom school administrations receive praise from anyone, let alone students. Recall University of California Chancellor Kerr's facetious dictum that the school administrator's job was to provide parking for faculty, sex for the students, and a winning team for alumni.[5]

Applause was in order. "What a great place to start the rest of your life," former *New York Times* education editor Edward B. Fiske wrote about Geneseo in his 1996 guide to colleges. Fiske's praise was reinforced by *Money Magazine's* 1996 annual ranking, which placed Geneseo sixteenth among the one hundred best college buys. *U.S. News & World Report* and *Time* magazine issued similar, if not better, rankings. *Time* included Geneseo with such universities as the University of California at Berkeley, the University of Virginia, and SUNY Binghamton. This was heady stuff.[6]

However, some old-timers likely remember that this was not the first time Geneseo had received positive press in the esteemed *New York Times*. Rather, on Sunday March 24, 1968, the *Times* ran a big spread on an exhibit of about one hundred Hudson River School paintings in Geneseo's new Fine Arts building, calling it a "very good show." Importantly, the exhibit was highlighted because it brought back paintings expressing "confidence [in] the American vision of a spiritual empire" that had not yet been "debauched." Now, almost thirty years later, Geneseo again was garnering national attention.

"Rethinking SUNY"

The accolades were especially important, given public pressure from recently elected GOP governor, George Pataki, and his SUNY Trustee appointees. They wanted SUNY schools to become "more self-sufficient, more entrepreneurial, more focused, and more creative." The SUNY Faculty Senate was told to gather, summarize, and forward responses from the various campuses, which the Trustees would examine before deciding SUNY's future. This was no idle threat. The Trustees wanted to cut SUNY expenses by ninety-eight million dollars, which would translate into Geneseo losing almost seven hundred thousand dollars, threatening to eliminate as many as nine programs and reducing student aid.[7]

On a positive note, President Dahl pointed out that the Trustees' plan contained a "carrot" that offered greater campus autonomy: carrying forward operational surpluses and possibly charging different tuition levels. The "stick" was that the campuses had to assure higher standards through a new core curriculum, a revamped presidential selection process with annual reviews, and—shades of the 1970s—a performance-based system of reimbursements (measure up or lose money).[8]

The new "hastily passed" core curriculum drafted by four SUNY Trustees and two administrators mandated courses in "mathematics, natural science, social science, American history, Western civilization, other world civilizations, humanities

Barry Caplan's Sundance Textbook Outlet competed for several years against vendors operating the on-campus bookstore and eventually won the contract as the official college bookstore. (1998 *Oh Ha Daih*)

and the arts, foreign languages and basic communication, reasoning and information management." (By contrast, Hamilton College, a private school with which Geneseo has at times compared itself, has eliminated distribution requirements.) This was only the beginning for outspoken SUNY Trustee Dr. Candace de Russy, who spoke at Geneseo in October 1996. While Pataki appointee de Russy did not speak for the Trustees officially, she clearly reflected the majority's thinking, and her message was chilling. She wanted SUNY to raise the student-faculty ratio, increase tuition, eliminate "weak course offerings," and close or merge SUNY schools. Geneseo faculty picket signs failed to dissuade her from pursuing her agenda here.[9]

Ironically, Geneseo had been upgrading regularly. For example, during the 1994–1995 school year the Curriculum Task Force had expanded the College's mission statement, emphasizing student-faculty development, integration of curricular and co-curricular experiences, and more "rigorous" courses. The College had

Access Opportunity Program counselor Betty Fearn (right) and members of the Black Student Union greeted Rochester Mayor William A. Johnson (second from right), who spoke at the group's first leadership conference. (1996 *Oh Ha Daih*)

also implemented new honors criteria and had required all faculty to prepare a prescribed course syllabus format. But system-wide changes were demanded. So, given its internal review (requiring INT 105, an intensive writing course for freshmen, and substituting a symbolic reasoning course for Critical Reasoning) and the Trustees' mandate, Geneseo added U.S. history and foreign language proficiency, effective with the class of 2004. The result was a forty- to forty-seven-hour required "General Education Curriculum" (versus thirty-four to thirty-six hours with the previous "Core Curriculum"). Further, despite the fact that Geneseo's teacher certification students scored well above the national average on national certification exams, the School of Education instituted new admission standards. It was hard to imagine what else was needed to satisfy the Trustees or the public generally.[10]

"The Most Drastic One-Time Reduction in State Support"

Belt-tightening—that's what was needed. Vice president Levison called Governor Pataki's 1995–1996 budget proposal "absolutely devastating." It represented the biggest cut in twenty years. Again Geneseo had to do more with less. The six-year funding history, issued in 1996, clearly demonstrated a pattern of declining support for the SUNY campuses. From 1990 to 1996 Geneseo's budget had risen just over one million dollars, or 4.75 percent. By contrast, the inflation rate had risen an average of three percent *a year*. More telling, state aid for the College's operating budget had fallen from 71.7 percent to 33.5 percent. Geneseo was more than twice as dependent on tuition and fees as it had been six years earlier. So, everything was in jeopardy. Consider faculty hiring and retention—of the SUNY four-year schools, only Cortland paid a lower average salary for assistant professors than Geneseo's $36,100. The students and faculty revived old practices, including rallying, lobbying, and letter-writing—albeit with limited success.[11]

The 1994 women's soccer team, Geneseo's first team to make the NCAA Division III final four, celebrated at the tournament in San Diego. (Fred Bright)

Two years later, in 1998, President Dahl was more hopeful. The SUNY Trustees had revamped campus funding with a plan called "Resource Allocation Methodology" (RAM), which, among other things, allowed campuses to keep the tuition and fees they collected. So, Geneseo received a seven-percent operating budget increase, enabling it to restore the Access Opportunity Program to the 1994–1995 level, to increase the Tuition Assistance Program awards (albeit capped at ninety percent of full tuition) and to hire a limited number of faculty. Additionally, capital improvement money for an integrated science building seemed likely. The president and Dr. Levison were even more upbeat in 2000 at the announcement that the state intended to increase the SUNY budget, but it was a mixed bag. Other factors had to be reckoned with. For example, the cost of fuel for 2001 was double the annual average for the previous five years.[12]

The following years also were roller coaster rides. Beginning in 2000, the new SUNY funding formula recognized campus performance (student and faculty achievement), a real benefit for Geneseo. But Governor Pataki's 2003 executive budget cut support for SUNY by $184 million. To make up some of the loss he called for a $1,200 increase in tuition (one-third more than previously) and got approval for a $950 increase (from $3,400 to $4,350). Nonetheless, SUNY Chancellor Robert King, a Pataki ally, said SUNY could "function well." Students and faculty disagreed, siding with critics who claimed SUNY was in decline. Critics cited the decreasing proportion of students graduating within six years, fewer faculty and course offerings, and larger class sizes. Small consolation, Geneseo's percentage loss of faculty over the past ten years was smaller than SUNY overall. Geneseo took another hit in the 2002–2003 budget. State aid was reduced one percent, forcing cuts in utilities, admission and recruitment, and temporary service (student jobs).[13]

After a November 2003 groundbreaking, the new science building project had reached this point by September 2004. (Don Dannecker photo, Facilities Planning Office)

For all but a select few, state funding formulas are as arcane as Old English. The key element in any of them is allocation. However, there was one difference from the past: instead of New York's Department of the Budget allocating authorized funds to individual campuses, henceforth it was SUNY's responsibility. Yet, regardless of the particular formula, Geneseo remained disadvantaged, compared with the specialized programs in other SUNY schools, e.g., engineering, nursing, technology. As an undergraduate institution with a small enrollment (thus receiving fewer tuition dollars than larger schools) and with a focus on teaching, even basic research, advisement, etc., have to come out of faculty's and staff's hides.[14]

Fortunately, despite some setbacks, campus construction continued apace. The redesigned upper quad—long a source of embarrassment—was finally finished in 1997. But the age-old problem of student housing plagued the administration. A new $4.5-million residence hall was planned to connect to Allegany and Wyoming halls; ground was broken in the summer of 2003 for what would be called Putnam Hall (after the county). Emphasizing "relational learning" to provide a sense of community, it would have all the amenities: "superior" single rooms renting for $2,575, and "standard" rooms for $1,850. But Genesee and Jones halls were closed for renovation, threatening tripling, so Blakes D and E temporarily were put back in service as residence halls.

The Saratoga Terrace Townhouses created a village atmosphere west of the former "tundra" walkway to the southside residence halls. (Ron Pretzer, November 2001 *Geneseo Scene*)

Special student housing arrangements based on a variety of factors, including academic or cultural interests, also were tried—with limited success.[15]

Groundbreaking for townhouses on a blustery September 28, 2000, was one of the more ambitious projects undertaken. These "attractive living spaces would help to retain students" and "connect" with the south campus across the bypass. The ten-million-dollar, three-story, air-conditioned buildings with kitchens, living-dining areas, laundry and seminar rooms to house two hundred students in forty-four units, were to simulate off-campus housing. Though generally pleased when it was completed, the first residents of Saratoga Terrace filed a four-page petition listing complaints about conditions. Items cited ranged from problems with electricity, plumbing, and fire safety, to mold from basement flooding, mice, and half-eaten food left in rooms by construction workers. However, the anticipated protest about the lack of parking spaces—there were only 136 spaces for 200 students—never materialized.[16]

"The Geneseo Zone"

More in character, *The Lamron* editors poked fun at the College, warning newcomers about "the Geneseo Zone." For example, walking uptown was hazardous. No driving rules seemed to apply except for "no parking signs," which were strictly enforced. Students who bundled up to deliver assignments on campus on icy cold mornings often confronted sixty-degree temperatures by noon. Students who went to the health center either received no treatment for a sore throat and cold or were "given every possible cold medicine you can buy."[17]

However, the March 4 "Blizzard of '99" (nearly twenty inches of snow)—the second heavy snowfall in just over a year—was no laughing matter. It forced the cancellation of classes and required ten snow removal crews to work 250 overtime hours. Perhaps a sign of the times, students railed that walks were not sufficiently cleared and that their cars were buried under the plowed snow. It is unlikely that alumni who recall their long trek across "the tundra" to "East Cuylerville" were particularly sympathetic.[18]

After all, those living in the "Geneseo Zone" and townhouses were a different breed. These students and their cohorts have been dubbed the "Millennial generation," "the most watched-over [protected] generation in our history." They were distinguished by seven traits: "special, sheltered, confident, team oriented, achieving, pressured, and conventional." More affluent, better educated, and more ethnically diverse than their predecessors, they liked structure, which was attributed to their "helicopter parents" hovering overhead (a cell phone call away). Necessarily, these students helped the College in its quest for excellence, but they also demanded more from the school, including greater computer access, more accessible and competent faculty, and increased scholarships and attractive housing.[19]

United Students of the Continent of Asia is one of several student organizations that celebrate the increasing diversity of Geneseo's student body (front row, from left): P. Tam, J. Bagasan, R. Rayo, A. Labeste; (second row): R. Mathew, G. Huey, L. Won, T. Jimbo, C. Labeste; (third row): K. Chan, J. Chung, E. Weisent, J. Luk, P. Wirojratana, M. Young; (fourth row): S. Pak, J. Liao, H. Kim, D. Blake, J. Capili, S. Shiledar Baxi, R. Novarrete. (1996 Oh Ha Daih)

While the College was going all out to provide the housing, it was scrambling to keep up with the rapid development of information technology. The bootstrap operation of Associate Provost Bruce Ristow and CIT director Bill Davis that wired the campus was generally successful, and Geneseo had been recognized as one of the nation's more "wired" campuses. However, budget cuts made it difficult to keep up. To fund services, beginning in September 1995, all students were assessed a fifty-dollar-per-semester technology fee, which generated five hundred thousand dollars a year—half the estimated cost for services, which included computer kiosks for student access to College information. Imagine the irritation when the VAX network crashed for twenty-

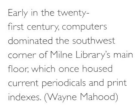

Early in the twenty-first century, computers dominated the southwest corner of Milne Library's main floor, which once housed current periodicals and print indexes. (Wayne Mahood)

Online registration put an end to the old system, with its long lines and confusion in the gym. (1966 *Oh Ha Daih*)

two hours barely three weeks into that fall semester (it would crash again two years later)! The problem had been the "exponential growth" of student use, according to Davis's CIT successor, Sue Chichester. (Ironically, few thought to praise alumna Chichester on January 1, 2000, when there was no "millennial" computer disaster.)[20]

The tech-savvy students wanted online course registration, so a trial run was offered in the spring 1999 semester. Two years later, in November 2001, some 4,900 students registered online. Unfortunately, what should have taken a half-hour, took up to four. Frustrated students regarded this as no better than the old system, except they didn't have to stand in line. Then, beginning spring 2002 students' grades were posted online on the "Knightweb," though that did not go smoothly either. Still, despite demand for computer access, the students and faculty voted down mandatory purchases of laptop computers, the brainchild of Associate Provost Stephen Padalino, which would have taken advantage of Geneseo's wireless technology. Four years later Padalino's goal came to fruition, when the Advisory Committee on Technology called for all students to have laptops, beginning with freshmen in 2007.[21]

Demands for greater computer access and competent faculty intersected in spring 1995. The students wanted to complete the SOFIs (Student Opinion of Faculty Instruction) online, arguing that it would mean less paper, more reflective responses, and faster, more readily accessible results. After the perennial debate over the wording of the SOFIs, an agreement was reached to conduct a trial run, beginning on April 27, 2006, with students in psychology classes asked to complete the SOFIs online. The trial proved so successful that in Fall 2006 all students completed the SOFIs online.[22]

Fortunately, a million-dollar grant from the non-profit Campus EAI and eight hundred thousand dollars from the National Science Foundation would enable Geneseo and three other institutions to create a computational and data grid to pool power for greater student and faculty research. But wants always exceed resources.[23]

Bob Guy's 1994–1995 women's basketball team compiled a 27-2 record, won the SUNYAC championship and advanced to NCAA Division III's final eight. (Bright collection)

The "Most Ambitious Fund-Raising Effort in the College's History"

Given persisting needs, newly appointed President Dahl found himself with hat in hand, emulating his predecessors. Recall that before departing, President Harter, using the College's upcoming 125th anniversary as a prod, had launched a campaign to raise five million dollars. Consultants offered a feasibility study to build the endowment, increase merit and honors scholarships, offer more faculty grants and fellowships, and fund programs for exceptional students. After a visit by Vice President Art Hatton, community philanthropist Dr. James Lockhart made a lead gift of a quarter-million dollars to endow the James and Julia Lockhart supported professorships and Lockhart scholarships. The Lockharts would be recognized again when the Geneseo Foundation purchased an historic house at 26 Main Street, extensively renovated it from 2000 to 2002 out of a special campaign fund and named it the McClellan House with the Lockhart Gallery, honoring the Lockharts and prominent Geneseoans Robert and Jeannette McClellan.[24]

Dick Rosati, '71, and alumna Ella Cline Shear celebrated the announcement of her generous donation supporting the Ella Cline Shear School of Education. (November 2001 *Geneseo Scene*)

In short order, no small thanks to 1971 alumnus Dick Rosati, senior staff associate, Geneseo received the largest alumni gifts in its history. In 1995 Ella Cline Shear, '35 (bachelor's in 1950 and master's in 1959), an unassuming former elementary teacher and wife of a dairy farmer, gave a surprisingly large gift. The Ella Cline Shear School of Education was named for her in 1998.[25]

Affection for Geneseo apparently spurred other gifts, including $250,000 from the estate of Eleanor Trask Baldwin, '32 (library degree in 1954), $570,000 from Elizabeth R. Raynor Neuffer, '36, and an historic $863,052.58 bequest from Mark Scheiber, a seventy-five-year-old Queens librarian who had received his master's in library science in 1970. Two other donors had buildings or parts thereof named for them: the Myrtle Merritt Athletic Center and the Irma Hamer Collins Alumni Center in the McClellan House.[26]

The 125th anniversary goal of raising five million dollars was exceeded by two million. More aggressive efforts to attract major gifts by reaching out and reconnecting with successful alumni paid off. Nearly twenty-three million dollars was contributed by alumni and friends between 1990 and 2005. In 2004 alone, 520 students received almost a half-million dollars in scholarships, another 115 students shared forty-four thousand dollars in research grants, and 260 faculty used approximately two hundred thousand for travel and research. While no substitute for the loss of state aid, the generosity of alumni, friends, faculty, and staff has certainly helped sustain the College. As former Vice President Hatton has observed: "There are no great colleges without philanthropy."[27]

"Claiming Our Place"

On August 23, 2002, President Dahl convened the faculty and staff, and, instead of dwelling on the $1,461,700 budgetary shortfall which required "careful planning and prudent management," offered some welcome news. The previous March the Middle States Commission on Higher Education had renewed Geneseo's accreditation for another ten years, and a month later the Jones School of Business was granted initial accreditation by the Association to Advance Collegiate Schools of Business. Dean Mary Ellen Zuckerman and her faculty prided themselves on being one of just thirty-six undergraduate-only programs in North America so accredited.[28]

Perhaps conveniently, in his convocation addresses President Dahl ignored some events reminiscent of earlier times. For example, he never mentioned the bomb threat called in to the Steuben RA at 2:45 a.m. on August 26, 1997, which required evacuation and a thirty- to forty-minute search. Nor did he mention cancellation of the *Oh Ha Daih* in 2001. (Two months before graduation in 2000, only eighty-five of one thousand seniors had bought the fifty-dollar yearbooks.) The student complaint that "Parking Sucks" too was ignored, though the perennial problem was aggravated in 2000 by the student parking fee spike from seven to ninety-five dollars. Nor was the College spared the anti-war protests that began within weeks of the attack on the World Trade Towers in 2001 and irregularly persisted into 2006.[29]

At the 2003 Convocation, President Dahl again lauded Geneseo's accomplishments despite continued budget constraints, and listed efforts toward "Claiming Our Place." For example, thirty-six percent of the class of 2002 went on to graduate school, expenditures for sponsored faculty and student research exceeded one million dollars and a construction firm had contracted to build a thirty-three-million-dollar integrated science building to foster more research.[30]

But the most satisfying news was that Geneseo would "shelter" "the most prestigious honor society in the country." Just two weeks earlier the charter for a Phi Beta Kappa chapter had been granted to Geneseo—one of only seven out of forty-one applications. (On January 16, 2004, the Alpha Delta chapter recognized founding faculty and installed Drs. Douglas Baldwin,

Geneseo's cheerleaders have long played an important part in raising team spirit at athletic events. (Bright collection)

Among the first sixty-three members of the class of 2004 inducted into Geneseo's inaugural Phi Beta Kappa chapter were (from left): Kara Noto, R. Matthew Gee, Fiona Lee, Amy Norton, Paul Weismann, Chaunise Dorell Johnson, Luke Sworts, Jennifer Gewandter, Daniel Schultz. (2004 *Report of the President*)

Distinguished Teaching Professors Ronald Herzman (left) and William Cook (right) have earned many grants and teaching awards. (May 2000 *Geneseo Scene*)

Distinguished Teaching Professor Margaret Matlin has earned national recognition for her teaching and widely used textbooks. (Linda Monteverdi Kuehn, Summer 2002 *Geneseo Scene*)

Celia Easton, James Williams, Kenneth Levison, and Anne-Marie Reynolds as president, vice president, secretary, treasurer, and historian respectively.)

In short, Geneseo was looking good.

Distinguished Teaching Professors Cook and Herzman had received the first national award for excellence in teaching medieval studies. Distinguished Teaching Professor Margaret Matlin (1987) had been honored nationally three times: the American Psychological Association Teaching of Psychology Award (1985), the American Psychological Foundation Distinguished Teaching in Psychology Award (1995), and the Society for the Psychology of Women's Heritage Award in 2001.[31]

Geneseo was the only undergraduate school to be categorized Tier I by SUNY, signifying that sixty percent of incoming freshmen had a high school average of ninety-five and/or SAT scores of at least 1300. However, the newcomers had big shoes to fill. For example, two biochemistry majors, Summer Raines, '03, and Mathew Fleming, '04, were awarded Goldwater Scholarships in the sciences, making ten Geneseo students in thirteen years to receive that coveted award. Geneseo's athletes had "achieved an historic first," winning the SUNYAC Commissioner's Cup for compiling the "best overall record" in the conference.[32]

One of Geneseo's athletes who also excelled in the classroom was 2001 graduate Melissa White, seven-time athletic All-American and New York State's winner of NCAA Woman of the Year—the first from Geneseo to win at the state level. Topping these achievements, she received a five-thousand-dollar NCAA Postgraduate Scholarship, Geneseo's second athlete to do so. (Christine Sisting, '96, a seven-time All-American in track and cross country was the first, and All-American Tony Gallo, '02, who followed White, used his scholarship to attend medical school.)[33]

Not to be outdone, the School of Performing Arts assigned itself a back-breaking Spring 2004 schedule, beginning January 22 with Vocal Miscellany's *Bat Boy* ("bloody entertaining") and ending April 26 with the Geneseo Percussion Ensemble. In between events, to name a few, were VegSoup's *The Mineola Twins*, the Geneseo Dance Ensemble, whose "performances soar," and GENseng's *Falling Flowers*.[34]

Notwithstanding the College's successes, in his 2003 address Dahl readily acknowledged the need to "maintain forward momentum." That includ-

The School of the Performing Arts, formed in 1994, brought together music, drama, and dance faculty and students: (front, from left): James Willey, Terry Browne, Melanie Blood, James Kimball, William Edwards, '98; (back): Joseph Dechario, Robert Isgro, James Walker, Barbara Mason, James Kirkwood, Jack Johnston, Steve Stubblefield, William Leyerle, Johnnie Ferrell, Elisa Delarm, '98, Ruth Peck, Jeannine Baumgart, '98. (1996 *Oh Ha Daih*)

ed addressing personnel changes, including the July 1, 2003 departure of Provost Dixon to become president of Missouri's Truman State University. Associate Provost David Gordon agreed to serve as interim during the search for Dixon's successor, Stephen Padalino remained as associate provost, Dr. David Geiger (chemistry) was talked into assuming a similar position, and Dr. Susan Bailey traded her interim status for a permanent appointment as dean of the College.[35]

Replacing personnel director Donald Lackey and James McNally, Geneseo's numbers cruncher, who retired in 2003 and 2002 respectively and who together represented close to seventy years of service, proved more difficult. Fortunately, both willingly returned to their posts on an interim basis when needed.

Turnover of faculty and staff was not only ongoing, the pace was picking up. Deaths took active faculty members Daniel Fink in 1995, Ramon Rocha, Lee Bryant, and part-timer Joseph O'Brien in 1996, and Charles R. "Randy" Bailey in 2000. Among the retirees who died during this period were Fred Bennett and Walter Harding (1996), Rose Bachem Alent, Spencer Roemer, Virginia Kemp, Norman Lyon, Robert W. MacVittie, Gifford Orwen, Archibald Reid, William Small (1997), Cecil Coleman, Worth Harder, Gladys Rhodes (1998), Alice Austin (1999), John Herlihy and Donald Watt (2002), and John Barrett (2004).

Incentive pay induced two dozen faculty and staff to retire in 2003 alone, including Distinguished Professor Srinivasa Leelamma (mathemat-

Daniel Fink combined expertise in photography and art history to produce his popular book, *Barns of the Genesee Country, 1790–1915.* (Laura Fink, courtesy Mary Ann Fink)

ics), Excellence in Teaching awardee Phil Boger (geology), former department chairmen Ray Lougeay (geography) and Paul Olczak (psychology), and Excellence in Librarianship awardees Judith Bushnell and Paula Henry (Milne Library).[36]

On the other hand, the College had attracted some able replacements, among whom were Excellence in Teaching awardees Joseph Cope, Emilye Crosby, Carol Faulkner, and Michael Oberg (history), Rachel Hall and Beth McCoy (English), Karla Cunningham (political science), Anne Eisenberg (sociology), Rosemary McEwen (foreign languages), Edward Pogozelski (physics), and Monica Schneider (psychology).

U.S. Senator Hillary Clinton visited the campus in September 2004 to commemorate the new Finger Lakes Trading Cooperative. Shown with Clinton are (from left): Arthur Hatton and Dean Johnston. (Ron Pretzer)

Heady Initiatives Ahead

Dahl also proposed initiatives to build a diverse community of teachers and learners; to foster civic engagement; and to examine faculty roles, rewards, and evaluation. On July 21, 2004, Dr. Katherine Conway-Turner was appointed the College's first African-American provost. "Provost Kate," with a bachelor's in microbiology and a master's and a doctorate in psychology from the University of Kansas, had spent most of her career as a University of Delaware professor and administrator, with a year out as an American Council on Education

In 2006, top administrators included (front, from left): President Christopher Dahl, Katherine Conway-Turner; (back): Becky Glass, Kenneth Levison, Debra Hill, William Caren, Robert Bonfiglio. (Jenn Gaylord)

fellow at the College of New Jersey, before becoming dean of the College of Humanities and Social Sciences at Georgia Southern University. At Geneseo she has shared vice president for student life Dr. Robert Bonfiglio's goal "to make [the] Geneseo campus a community," a priority since he came from Pennsylvania's Cabrini College in 1999.[37]

While fostering civic engagement demanded an equally long-term effort, Geneseo had already made some progress, as mentioned in the president's 2002 convocation address. The College was collaborating with other Council on Public Liberal Arts Colleges (COPLAC) members in the American Democracy Project, co-sponsored by the *New York Times* and the American Association of State Colleges and Universities, with the object of finding and implementing ways to encourage students to take a larger part in government.

Another initiative was examining faculty roles, rewards, and evaluation to meet the needs of the type of students Geneseo was attracting and to avoid the missteps that led to a 1998 gender discrimination finding against the College. Randy Kaplan, former assistant professor of theater and dance, had sued the College after she was not renewed six years earlier. A federal district court judge ruled that "the evaluation process was biased" and that Kaplan was to be reinstated with back pay. Since returning she has successfully directed GENSeng, the Asian American Performance Ensemble.[38]

Regularly revising and administering the SOFIs was one obvious step to improve the evaluation process. Another was expanding the College Personnel Committee (formerly Faculty Personnel Committee) from five to seven members and making associate professors and associate librarians eligible for membership. Incentives to improve faculty performance were chancellor's awards and endowed chairs.[39]

Alumni Affairs staff members were tolerant enough to share McClellan House space with the College History Committee for more than three years. Clockwise from front are *Geneseo Scene* editor Jo Kirk, Suzy Boor, Michelle Walton Worden, '92, Allison Barley, '00, and Patty Hamilton-Rodgers, '85. (Jenn Gaylord, '08)

Good friends socialized at the 1995 President's Recognition Dinner (seated from left): Spencer Roemer, Bertha Lederer, Joan Bright; (standing): James McNally, Shirley McNally, Maurice Alent, Rose Alent, Fred Bright. (J. McNally)

"Some Achieve Greatness"

President Dahl opened the 2004 school year by quoting from Shakespeare's *Twelfth Night*, Act II, Scene 5: "Some are born great, some achieve greatness, and some have greatness thrust upon 'em." Dahl's vision of "greatness" for Geneseo was to be recognized officially as "the premier public liberal arts college in the country." The College had a good start, given the spring 2004 Phi Beta Kappa chapter installation;

Celebrating their thirteenth
year of service, the
Volunteer Emergency
Squad obtained a new van
in 1987. (1987 *Oh Ha Daih*)

the College's eleventh Goldwater scholar, sophomore Daniel Welchons; the Class of 2008 with the highest average SAT scores to date; and recent fund-raising. The latter took on added significance. With the new academic year underway there was still no SUNY budget, appropriations for capital projects had been vetoed by the governor, and the division of the budget was holding back two-thirds of the fifty million dollars the legislature had added to the SUNY operating budget.[40]

Pressure to do more with less continued. Given the need to raise money to compensate for loss of state tax dollars, SUNY chancellor Robert King announced ambitious plans for its sixty-four campuses. The first was to seek three billion dollars in philanthropic gifts to individual SUNY campuses over a seven-year period. (Geneseo's "target" was twenty-one million dollars.) Second, the SUNY schools were asked to prove themselves worthy of these grants and gifts. That is, over the next five years (2005 to 2010) the SUNY Trustees wanted a portion of the funding tied to graduation rates. Chancellor King unsuccessfully protested that it was both premature and too difficult to compare campuses to draw system-wide conclusions about quality. So, while Geneseo proudly proclaimed that its sixty-eight percent four-year graduation rate tied it with Binghamton for the highest in SUNY, it would have to jump through hoops with the others.[41]

As SUNY came under increasing scrutiny, the activist Trustees forced out Chancellor King, who was replaced by Vice Admiral [ret.] John Ryan, who, in turn, left SUNY in 2007, leaving the system unsettled. Further complicating matters for Geneseo and its sister schools, New York's private colleges and universities sought more money from the state. The latter were pacified some-what by the Higher Education Capital Facilities Matching Grant Program, which offered the privates $150 million over four years. If Geneseo wanted more money, it would have to work even harder to build its donor base and, like private schools, develop a culture of philanthropy, according to Geneseo's

Vice President Hatton. While annual gifts had exceeded two million dollars, unrestricted giving was down.[42]

"Advancing Geneseo's Mission": 2005 Convocation Address

To obtain more money, Geneseo had to redouble its efforts, according to President Dahl in his 2005 Convocation Address. Yes, the College had successfully recruited another excellent freshman class. Yes, during the 2004–2005 school year its athletic teams had won eight SUNYAC and three ECAC championships, and Mike Mooney's men's soccer team had reached the NCAA Division III final

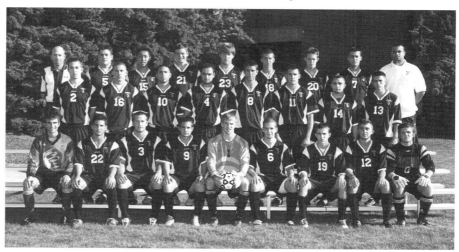

Mike Mooney's 2004 men's soccer team made it to NCAA Division III's final four. (Bright collection)

four. Yes, history professor Cook was one of three finalists for the Robert Foster Cherry Award for distinguished teaching and, yes, Dahl was negotiating with three foreign universities to establish dual-degree programs. (Agreements with Turkey's Hacettepe University, Mexico's Universidad de las Americas and Moscow State University were signed January 17, 2006, April 13, 2006, and late October, 2006, marking firsts for SUNY. An even more historic agreement was reached on November 17, 2006, with South Korea's Yangchung High School, alma mater of assistant professor of the School of Business Seong B. Lim, by which five to ten "distinguished" graduates will attend Geneseo annually.)[43]

However, for President Dahl, truly advancing Geneseo meant being designated an Honors College. And that would require the College to increase tuition or the general fee, reduce the high student-to-faculty ratios, augment student resources, pursue strategic marketing, participate more fully in the Teaching and Learning Center, then administered by Dr. Becky Glass (sociology) and more recently by Cristina Geiger (chemistry), and meet the Diversity Commission's goals.[44]

"What Will You Miss the Most About Geneseo?"

While President Dahl appropriately stressed academics, four of seven 2005 graduates interviewed by *The Lamron's* "Inquiring Photographer" cited Geneseo's sunsets as their lasting memory.[45]

Therein lies an anomaly. Sunsets are the gravy; educational experiences

Physics faculty members Kurt Fletcher (left) and Stephen Padalino (right) celebrated when their former student, Brian DeMarco, '96 (center), received the Outstanding Young Alumnus Award in 2006. (May 19, 2006 *Geneseo EnCompass Weekly*)

are the meat. How are meaningful educational experiences created, let alone measured? On the one hand, it is relatively easy to document academic successes. For example, Michelle Morse, a dual biology-music major, was named to *USA Today's* 1997 All-USA College Academic First Team, representing the twenty best and most remarkable college seniors (out of 12,500 nominees). Morse, headed to medical school at Johns Hopkins, not only carried a 3.91 GPA, she was an accomplished jazz singer, an EMT, and a member of the Geneseo Village Fire and Rescue squad. Or consider Geneseo's third Goldwater Scholar, physics major Brian DeMarco, '95. Four years later, as a University of Colorado doctoral candidate, DeMarco made national news for his research dealing with a new state of matter. (Not surprisingly, in 2006, Dr. DeMarco, assistant professor of physics at the University of Illinois, received Geneseo's Outstanding Young Alumnus Award.) There is no telling what biochemistry major Jessica L. Gucwa, Geneseo's fourteenth Goldwater student since 1992, will achieve.[46]

On the other hand, ignoring the hype for a moment, what genuinely affects Geneseo's students? Few will—can—forget the deadly September 11, 2001 ("9/11") destruction that they witnessed repeatedly on television or heard about from family and friends. Yet, Michael Chin, the departing editor of *The Lamron* also remembered that his class of 2005 saw the Hub transformed into the Knight Spot, Mary Jemison Dining Hall, "once a dormant, moss-covered eyesore," evolve into "the most popular dining facility on campus," and Putnam Hall become "one of the most sought-after residence halls." (Chin also would be remembered for his three novels, two of which were

In May 2002, the College dedicated a memorial in Roemer Arboretum to four alumni who were killed in the September 11, 2001 attack on the World Trade Center: Richard Bosco, '89, Yan Zhu Cindy Guan, '99, James Kelly, '83, and Dennis O'Berg, '95. (Roemer House Collection)

written as an undergraduate while working on behalf of Amnesty International and the Writing Learning Center and editing *The Lamron*).[47]

How representative are Chin, Morse, and DeMarco? How do they compare with earlier Geneseo students? While protected, sheltered, and conventional, ironically, the most recent students were more politically liberal than their predecessors. For

example, fifty-seven percent favored incumbent Bill Clinton in 1996, fifty-six percent preferred Democrat Al Gore to the 2000 winner, George W. Bush, and sixty-seven percent wanted John Kerry in 2004. Shattering a record that had stood for thirty-six years, in 2004 an estimated one thousand College students voted in Geneseo rather than by absentee ballot, likely resulting in the traditionally GOP village and town going Democratic by "several hundred votes."[48]

Students also were socially conscious. Two Resident Advisors, David Hoekstra and Donovan Shirkley, competed to raise money for victims of the 2005 Hurricane Katrina. The loser had to shave his head. Though Hoekstra, the winner, raised $687.18, both shaved their heads. During their 2006 spring break, junior Charles Elliot-Bearce and Dr. Thomas Matthews, Geneseo's Director of Leadership Education, Development, and Training, organized a trek to Mississippi, where students and adjunct professor and 1979 alumnus Wes Kennison and emeritus professor Lyle Lehman helped families rebuild homes. In turn, their efforts were recognized in October 2006 when Geneseo— the only New York State school to be recognized— received a Katrina Compassion Award at the President's Higher Education Community Service Honor Roll Ceremony in Chicago. In fact, ninety percent of the Class of 2008 reported they had performed volunteer service even before attending Geneseo.[49]

Geneseo students were also an economic force. For example, as of 2006 they had raised over one hundred thousand dollars for civic causes ranging

Early in the twenty-first century, Mary Jemison Dining Hall, which had been unused for several years, underwent major transformations and reopened. (Ron Pretzer)

Knightline's well-choreographed and energetic routines have enlivened halftime at men's basketball games for several years. (Roemer House collection)

The 2005 women's cross country team raced their way to the NCAA Division III national championship: (front, from left) Shannon Griggs, Francesca Magri, Liz Montgomery, Marta Scott, Christy Finke; (back): assistant coach Jeff Beck, head coach Mike Woods, assistant coach Dave Prevosti, Christiana Martin, Renne Catalano, Karen Merrill. (Bright collection)

from Alzheimer's relief to breast cancer research. And that year they spent almost ten thousand dollars each, or a total of fifty-two million dollars in the village and town, according to a study done by students of 1968 alumnus and adjunct business professor Paul Scipione.[50]

With their ever-present cell phones, the technologically adept students were also globally connected. For example, two business administration students, seniors Tracy Tillapaugh and Michaela Alissandrellow, participated in a panel discussion in the United Arab Emirates in March 2006. But students also relied on time-honored means to communicate. That is, some used chalk on walkways to initiate dialogue or to advertise an event like a rape prevention colloquy, because they felt the College limited free speech. Next to a chalked message on the sidewalk might be a piece of chalk, so others could enter the exchange. (Eschewing spray paint, the Geneseo students demonstrated a characteristic conservatism.)[51]

Geneseo's athletes and coaches, too, made their presence known. Consider seven-time All-American Beth Shope, who won a national championship—Geneseo's first—in the hammer throw in 1999. Or take the crew team, begun by English professor Dr. John Hoey in 1989, which daily drives to Conesus Lake for 5:30 a.m. practices and in April 2001 won the All-SUNY Regatta. Or the women's swimming team, which in 2004 won its fifteenth straight SUNYAC title, while the men won their eighth in twelve years for coach Paul Dotterwich. Or Jason Lammers, '98, All-SUNYAC defenseman, who in 2006 coached the hockey team to a SUNYAC championship before losing out in the NCAA Division III tournament. Keeping pace, the lacrosse team, coached by Jim Lyons, SUNYAC Coach of the Year for the third time in six seasons, made it to the Division III quarterfinals. Not to be outdone, the men's basketball team won two ECAC titles for coach Steve Minton. Then there was Julie Atwell, class of 2002, a special education major who was born with only one kidney and a short leg that necessitated a prosthesis to compete on the women's swimming team. She placed third in the SUNYAC 1,650-yard freestyle as a freshman.[52]

English professor John Hoey (standing, center) founded the crew club and lacrosse, rugby, and squash teams. Shown with Hoey are Alumni Association president and crew club benefactor Patricia Malet Fennell, '65 (front), crew club president Chris Philips, '03, and crew club historian Karen Rollek McDonnell, '92. (Patricia Fennell)

Geneseo's sports information director and 1988 alumnus George Gagnier rarely interjected himself in the stories. However, in December 2005, he

Members of the crew team worked hard during this early morning practice on Conesus Lake. (Adrian "Bud" Prince)

couldn't help noting the connection between his alma mater and his native Hilton. Geneseo women's and men's cross country coach, Mike Woods, 2005 Division III National Coach of the Year, and Mike Szczepanik, Hilton High's coach, were Geneseo graduates, 1969 and 1994 respectively. Both of their teams won national championships in 2005 (a first for each). Among the top runners on each team was a Griggs: Geneseo's Shannon Griggs, a junior who won the 5,000 meters at the New York State College Track Championship meet in May 2006, and her sister, Hilton's Amanda.[53]

Another kind of playing earned the Geneseo Symphony Orchestra an invitation to tour China for ten days in May 2006. Supported by private and public funds, including from the provost's office and the Geneseo Foundation, the thirty-eight-member orchestra, directed by Distinguished Service Professor James Walker, kicked off its tour with a concert on the Great Wall the morning after its arrival in Beijing. The "appreciative audience" danced "to the Rags of Joplin" and selections from Leonard Bernstein's *West Side Story*. This was followed shortly thereafter by an inside concert at the Beijing Central Conservatory, shared with the National Youth Orchestra of China, which featured "When Johnny Comes Marching Home Again" and dance episodes from Aaron Copland's "Rodeo." A particularly memorable event was at the international Cultural Exchange Theater in the

Among the Geneseo athletes with the most All-American certificates were four swimmers (from left): Mike Houlihan, '98 (ten), Josh Muldner, '99 (at fifteen, Geneseo's most honored All-American), Todd Geary, '99 (seven), Matt VanDerMeid, '98 (ten). (Physical Education collection, identification by Duncan Hinckley)

city of Xi'an, where a huge banner unfurled above the stage with the heartening words, "Warmly Welcome State University of New York at Geneseo Symphony Orchestra."[54]

"A Few Small Public Colleges…Stand Out"

Bolstering President Dahl's call for Honors College recognition, once more

Ontario Residence Hall's 1999 Homecoming float was part of a continuing trend away from the large and ornate floats of earlier years. (2000 *Oh Ha Daih*)

Geneseo received high marks in national publications ranking colleges and universities. For example, in August 2006 the *Princeton Review* named Geneseo a "Best Northeastern College." In *U.S. News & World Report's* 2007 edition of "America's Best Colleges," Geneseo was number two among the "Top Universities—Master's" for the north, behind only the College of New Jersey, which may well have borrowed upon Geneseo's model for its transformation from Trenton State College.[55]

These welcome rankings were reinforced when the *New York Times* labeled Geneseo one of the nation's "hidden gems." The *Times* listed Geneseo as one of only three colleges in the northeast "seen as a first choice for high achievers who cannot or won't do the financial aid dance with private colleges." And the February 2006 *Kiplinger's* ranked Geneseo seventh (up from thirty-second) of its "Kiplinger 100," i.e., the "best values in public colleges." Geneseo ranked just below perennial favorites such as the University of North Carolina at Chapel Hill (1) and New College of Florida (4). "With just 5,375 students and a picturesque campus in the Genesee Valley…, Geneseo competes against small, private liberal arts colleges in the Northeast." (And, it could have added, elsewhere. Sophomore Mallory Howe, who was pursuing a double major in biology and studio arts, chose Geneseo over Bucknell and Carleton.) *Kiplinger's* attributed Geneseo's success to its small size, accessible "top-notch" professors and bargain price. The February 2008 issue was even more complimentary, featuring a two-page spread on Geneseo.[56]

Kiplinger's was not exaggerating when it labeled Geneseo's faculty top-notch. In 2005, Drs. David Geiger (chemistry) and 1970 alumnus Dale Metz (communicative disorders and sciences) received the Chancellor's Research

Recognition Award. A year later three Geneseo faculty, Drs. Isidro M. Bosch (biology), Stephen J. Padalino (physics), and Wendy Knapp Pogozelski (chemistry), were honored with the SUNY Research Foundation Research and Scholarship Award. Drs. Kenneth Deutsch (political science) and Jeffrey Over (geology) were among fifty-eight individuals honored as New York's "most important and innovative scholars and scientists." The honorees, including Deutsch and Over, generated nearly seventy million dollars in research funding.[57]

Well on his way to similar awards is Dr. Anthony Macula (mathematics), who hit a grant trifecta in 2006. With a total of more than a million dollars from the U.S. Air Force, the National Science Foundation, and the CFD Research Corporation, he will work with others on computer operational capability, biomathematical research, and the identification of new diseases. His and others' successes in obtaining funding benefited from the help of long-time director of sponsored research, Dr. Douglas Harke.[58]

And we must not forget two of Geneseo's newer faculty, both alumnae, who were honored in 2006. Dr. Melissa Schmitz Sutherland, '92, (mathematics) received the Chancellor's Award for Excellence in Teaching and Dr. Amy Sheldon, '90, (geology) was given the President's Award for Excellence in Academic Advising.[59]

These accomplishments are all the more remarkable, given that among SUNY units Geneseo regularly has been shortchanged. In 2005 the SUNY Trustees doled out $1.9 billion to thirty-one campuses, an average increase of five percent. However, Geneseo received $37,282,400, only a 3.4 percent increase. Sister school Brockport's take was upped 6.5 percent, and Empire State College's budget jumped 9.7 percent. A year later the SUNY Trustees upped the ante to $2.26 billion. Binghamton got an 11.3 percent boost, but Geneseo received only a 6.2 percent increase, edging out only SUNY IT-Utica/Rome (which had lost enrollment).[60]

Minerva Returns

On a cheerier note, alumni returned to campus June 10, 2005 for a standing-room-only celebration in Milne Library and to a videotape titled "What is Minerva?" For the most senior attendees it was déjà vu: a large statue of the Roman goddess of wisdom was the featured attraction. From 1906 until Old Main's demise in 1951 a 6'2" (not including base), 350-pound, plaster Minerva graced the College library. Year-long efforts by the Milne Library

Two students took a few minutes away from studying to enjoy a light moment on the upper quad. (1980 *Oh Ha Daih*)

Above: In 2005, a replica of the original Minerva statue that long dominated Old Main's library was dedicated in Milne Library's lobby. According to notes on two photos in the county historian's collection, the original statue was bulldozed into a ravine when Old Main was razed. (Wayne Mahood; inset 1937 *Normalian*)

Right: As part of the new science building construction project, Blakes D and E were razed. (Don Dannecker photo, Facilities Planning Office)

staff to find the original, including posting "Wanted" signs around the campus, led only to dead ends. (Likely, Minerva was bulldozed when Old Main was razed, so this was a way to reengage Library School graduates by way of the newly created Friends of Milne Library.) Milne officials decided to have a replica made by the Giust Gallery in Woburn, Massachusetts, aided by a hefty donation from the Class of 2005. Thus, on June 10, the new diet-conscious (weighing between 80 and 120 pounds) 8'3" tall statue was dedicated to an appreciative audience and now greets Milne Library visitors.[61]

"Bringing It All Home: The Honors College"

On August 25, 2006, President Dahl convened the faculty and staff for the eleventh time and proclaimed that the previous year had been a watershed year for the College. The most visible evidence was the new Integrated Science Center, which towers over the campus and was formally opened on November 9. To Dahl it symbolized what Geneseo had been, is, and will continue to be ("poised for great things"): a public liberal arts college that values academics and encourages research, important not only in its own right, but vital to upstate New York. The opening of the building neatly coincided with recent funding for research totaling more than $1.3 million.[62]

These events fit into Dahl's vision of a formally designated "Public Honors College." That designation would go a long way toward fulfilling the College's mission: increasing undergraduate research, attracting even more talented and diverse students, mentoring more students for graduate schools, furthering co-curricular life, enhancing international experiences and study abroad, and fostering greater civic engagement. Consequently, there would be even greater emphasis on private fundraising to make the vision possible. It was a big order, but Dahl, proud of what the College had already accomplished, was optimistic.

****

Reflecting on the "Dahl Years"

Historians tend to be shy about analyzing current events, preferring the perspective of time that fosters more objectivity. So, we must conclude this latest era in Geneseo's history, which is still unfolding, with an all-too-brief summary.

The reconstructed upper quadrangle is surrounded by (clockwise, from lower left): Wadsworth Auditorium, Erwin, Blake A–C, Milne Library, the new Integrated Science Center (with Newton not visible to its north), Greene, and Bailey. (Craig Shaw, Stratus Imaging)

National rankings by respected media support Geneseo's claim that it has become a quality public liberal arts college. These media laud the students, the faculty and staff, the curriculum, and the College's affordability. Their rankings take into account the Phi Beta Kappa chapter, Middle States re-accreditation, the business school's accreditation, the School of Education's NCATE accreditation, the College's membership in COPLAC, dedication of two residence halls (Putnam and Saratoga Terrace), the state-of-the-art integrated science center, and the dual-degree programs with Turkey's Hacettepe University, Mexido's Universidad de las Americas, and Moscow State, as well as the agreement with South Korea's Yangchung High School.

Importantly, these achievements came during a time of particular public scrutiny, a decline in state dollars, cuts in low-enrollment majors and "non-essential" programs, and tuition hikes. Just staying the course might have been an accomplishment.[63]

One observer believes President Dahl resembles former President MacVittie, remembered fondly by many from "another generation" for his affability, accessibility, and responsiveness. According to former Vice President Hatton, Dahl has worked to sustain the positive town-gown relationship that MacVittie fostered. An example is preserving Main Street by renovating the Big Tree Inn, Campus House, and McClellan House. Another ob-

server claims the "defining agenda of Dahl's presidency has been the Honors College initiative." Still another asserts that Dahl "patiently has brought everyone on board." That is, he has expanded President Harter's vision for the College by recognizing faculty strengths and accomplishments, increasing students' opportunities, raising funds, including lobbying in Albany, and redefining Geneseo's mission.

The new Integrated Science Center opened in Fall 2006 and was formally dedicated on November 9, 2006. (Craig Shaw, Stratus Imaging)

William Caren, whose long tenure at the College offers a unique perspective, credits Dahl with having "been remarkably in touch and supportive of a lot of initiatives." Further, Dahl has put money into the physical plant (grounds, residence halls, and academic buildings) to make the College more attractive. The latter "may not be sufficient, but it is absolutely necessary," Caren claims. Attention to the physical plant in the future involves plans to build a new residence hall, raze the 1969 Holcomb School and replace it with a synthetic turf sports stadium, reacquire the Doty building (the old Geneseo High School) and make needed renovations across the campus. Unfortunately, there are no plans for the expanded library slated for 1973 and pursued by interim president MacVittie in 1989–1990.[64]

At the heart of Geneseo's required five-year plan, filed with SUNY in 2006 along with the 2007–2008 budget request, was the "Honors College" proposal. So designated, Geneseo would do in a public setting what "great private liberal arts colleges—Oberlin, Swarthmore, Bucknell"—do: tie greater community service to education and research in part through capstone theses or projects. It would require cutting full-time equivalent students from 5,100 to 4,600 and adding eighty-three faculty to improve the student-faculty ratio. But Geneseo would need greater than $1.8 million the first year, increasing to over eight million dollars in the fifth year, necessitating a higher "fee" from students, starting at two hundred dollars the first year and rising to one thousand dollars the fifth year. Admittedly, some questions have been raised about the import and likelihood, but, as noted, an Honors College designation for Geneseo could well be Dahl's legacy.[65]

This photo collage depicts more than five decades of secretaries to the College's presidents (seated, from left): Theodora Greenman, Mary Noto; (standing): Ann Crandall, Lenora McMaster, Gloria Tarantella. The photo on the wall is Frances Brown. (Ben Gajewski, Lenora McMaster, 1970 *Oh Ha Daih*, 1930 *Normalian*, collage by Hepler)

Evaluating himself, Dahl would like to have raised more private funds, argued more forcefully for a four-course rather than five-course student load (to reduce compartmentalizing the curriculum), and more aggressively pushed the Honors College initiative. However, he cautions that if these are considered "failures," they are "failures of execution rather than failures of principle or strategy."[66]

Certainly Dahl fares well with his peers, who appointed him vice chairman of the Association of American Colleges and Universities for the 2006–2007 academic year and chairman the following year.[67]

Relying on an old cliché, only time will tell how President Dahl will be viewed as the College's chief administrator. He certainly has shone as the College's public face and as its chief booster. Importantly, except for the budget, which is subject to the whims of the economy and state government, the College has prospered during his presidency.

The Geneseo Symphony Orchestra, conducted by Distinguished Service Professor James Walker, performed in China in Summer 2006. (James Walker)

Epilogue

A hot air balloon flight during the mid-1980s provided an excellent view of the campus. (Fred Bright)

The Geneseoans who invested in a Normal School back in the late 1860s and their successors have been repaid many times over. It is not simply the jobs the College provides, the money the students spend on housing and necessities, nor the faculty and staff drawn to the area. It's also the intangibles. There is an agreeable prestige attached to a school that attracts such favorable national acclaim.

From the beginning, the College provided an affordable education for the women and men who came to its campus to start their professional and intellectual lives. Certainly, a payoff has been the contributions of alumni. Some of them have stayed—others have returned—to raise families, start businesses, practice law or medicine, hold elective office, or teach.

Though there has been a concerted effort to bury Geneseo's Normal School "roots," even deny its teachers college past, it and other early public training schools still play a "central role in mass education" in the United States. A twentieth-century United States president and five of Geneseo's chief administrators were Normal School graduates.[1]

Importantly, as Brockport historian Dr. Bruce Leslie has observed, "Geneseo is a remarkable story of a public college finding a niche." Though

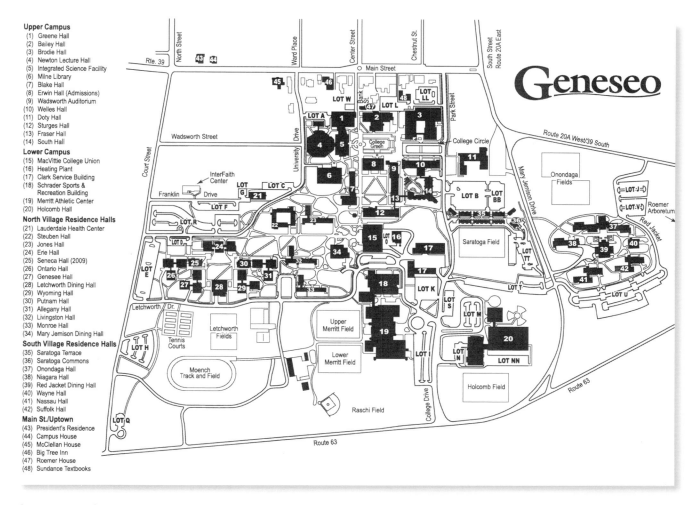

Map: Brian Bennett

three times threatened with extinction due to enrollment declines, it has been acclaimed for its excellence almost from the start. Moreover, though it now possesses many of the trappings of a private school, it has succeeded as a multipurpose public college. [2]

That Geneseo has prospered is a tribute to those who have believed in it from the beginning. Credit for this belongs to the community leaders who found a way to fund the school and constituted its early governing board, including James W. Wadsworth, Sr., Col. John Rorbach, Dr. Walter E. Lauderdale, William A. Brodie, and Lockwood L. Doty.

During their thirty-four years at Geneseo, the Milne brothers, Geneseo's first two principals, set a high standard for those who followed. (And William later garnered national attention for his leadership at Albany and his textbook authorship.) Upon his appointment, which Col. Rorbach subsequently described as "providential," the elder Milne faced the daunting challenge of getting a school up and running, attracting quality faculty, developing a curriculum, constructing buildings, and, of course, attracting students. Above

The Alumni Association celebrated the College's 125th anniversary with a Homecoming float featuring the Sturges clock tower and campus milestones and memories. (Ron Pretzer, winter 1996 Geneseo Scene)

all, he valued scholarship and a sense of community, fostered by the literary societies which evolved into the fraternities and sororities that have long offered a vital social life. In eighteen years under Milne's leadership Geneseo Normal achieved an enviable reputation.

Though his brother John M. Milne was an able successor, precarious health and over-involvement in community affairs may have limited his achievements. Yet, under his leadership the school proved so attractive that its enrollment had to be capped. Moreover, by the time of his departure ninety-five percent of Geneseo's graduates had applied or were applying in their own classrooms what they had learned here, a mark few Normal Schools could match.

At the half-century mark Geneseo claimed a total of more than five thousand graduates, its faculty, led by Principal James V. Sturges, had grown from thirteen to fifty-nine, and the two-year curriculum was replaced by a more rigorous and professional three-year program. Importantly, Geneseo was known for its Kindergarten-Primary Department and Teacher-Librarian program. In fact, at one point a quarter of all New York State school librarians were Geneseo graduates. In time, the newly created special education program, with its connection to Sonyea, enjoyed a similar reputation.

However, by the early 1920s Geneseo suffered from claims of mismanagement, rumors that the school would be moved, inadequate student housing, and the publicized dismissals of two faculty members. But Principal Winfield A. Holcomb, at times heavy-handed, righted the ship by creating a Department of Rural Education to offer more realistic student teaching experiences, by hiring more faculty with professional degrees, by improving student housing, and by opening a new practice school.

The following period, the "Welles era," may best be remembered for Geneseo's having remained open and functional during the depths of the Great Depression and through a taxing world war. Not even the deteriorating buildings, the devastating enrollment decline, rationing, and blackouts proved the College's undoing. In fact, by the time Dr. James B. Welles retired in 1946, Geneseo and its sister schools were degree-granting teachers colleges with a strengthened curriculum and faculty.

However, much was left undone. The facilities were, as his successor Herbert G. Espy wrote shortly after his arrival, "obsolete, unattractive, unsafe, and inefficient." Necessarily, morale was adversely affected. The threat of closing again was all too real. Only the newly created State University of New York in 1948 offered any hope. On the other hand, Espy could claim Middle States accreditation, the awarding of the first master's degrees, and the opening of long overdue residence halls and a college center.

His successor, Francis J. Moench, ushered in the new era, fostered ultimately by ambitious governor Nelson Rockefeller. While construction seemed to take precedence—a library-auditorium, three dorms, a dining hall, and a health and physical education building—it was matched by increased enrollment, faculty recruitment, and the stirrings of a liberal arts curriculum.

Robert W. MacVittie left quite a legacy when he departed in 1979. During his sixteen years, twenty-four buildings opened, enrollment more than doubled, and the faculty nearly tripled. Above all, during MacVittie's tenure the College began a transformation which led to national recognition.

Ironically, while parent SUNY experienced severe budget reductions and a diminished reputation, Geneseo blossomed under presidents Edward B. Jakubauskas and Carol C. Harter. That is, by the mid-1980s the

These graduates probably agreed with Edward Fiske's description of Geneseo as "a great place to start the rest of your life." (1990 *Oh Ha Daih*)

College was selling itself as a selective liberal arts school at a bargain price. In fact, it had to answer complaints that it was too selective for a SUNY school.

While he took a beating, Jakubauskas's willingness to close the venerable Holcomb and library schools and to offer attractive business and computer science programs solidified the transformation begun by MacVittie.

The ambitious Harter picked up where Jakubauskas left off, promoting Geneseo's reputation, adopting the total quality management concept, reallocating money to bolster faculty and student quality, gaining the College's membership in COPLAC (Council on Public Liberal Arts Colleges), dedicating a new academic building, and campaigning for private funding.

Christopher C. Dahl has seen Geneseo recognized by *Kiplinger's*, the *New York Times*, *U.S. News & World Report*, *Princeton Review*, and *Money Magazine*. Accomplishments during Dahl's terms as provost and president include the Phi Beta Kappa chapter, Middle States re-accreditation, the business school's AACSB and the education school's NCATE accreditation, the opening of two residence halls and a state-of-the-art science building, and the creation of international dual-degree programs. Importantly, these achievements have come during a time of particular public scrutiny.

Looking beyond Geneseo's press clippings for the moment, how should we conclude this look at the College's history? Certainly, Geneseo has had its ups and downs, as any institution has. There have been student, faculty, and administrative dismissals, minor scandals, occasional failures of execution, student protests, and near closures.

In the end, former Vice President Arthur Hatton points out, "the true measure of success for any college is the character, success, and loyalty of its alumni." Careers of its alumni, many with modest family backgrounds, testify to Geneseo's success. They range from public school teachers to school superintendents, from television producers to commercial airline pilots and army officers, from college presidents to a presidential speechwriter, from business CEOs to public office holders and from Goldwater Scholars to Division III national athletic champions. With the sunsets overlooking the beautiful Genesee Valley and the opportunities the College has provided its students, it's easy to agree with former *New York Times* education editor Edward Fiske who wrote: "What a great place to start the rest of your life."

Photo opposite page: (1967 *Oh Ha Daih*)

Appendices

Principal/Presidential Succession

Prepared by Fred Bright

1871–1889	Dr. William J. Milne
1889–1905	Dr. John M. Milne
1903–1905	*Dr. Hubert J. Schmitz (Acting)*
1905–1922	Dr. James V. Sturges
1921–1922	*Miss Anne S. Blake (Acting)*
1922–1934	Dr. Winfield A. Holcomb
1934–1946	Dr. James B. Welles
1946–1952	Dr. Herbert G. Espy
1952–1954	*Dr. Kenneth H. Freeman (Acting)*
1954–1963	Dr. Francis J. Moench
1963–1979	Dr. Robert W. MacVittie
1971–1972	*Dr. Thomas S. Colahan (Interim)*
1979–1988	Dr. Edward B. Jakubauskas
1988–1989	*Dr. Robert W. MacVittie (Interim)*
1989–1995	Dr. Carol C. Harter
1995–1996	*Dr. Christopher C. Dahl (Interim)*
1996–	Dr. Christopher C. Dahl

Names Given to the State Educational Facility At Geneseo, New York

1867	Wadsworth Normal and Training School (Chapter 195, Laws of 1867)
1871	Geneseo Normal and Training School (Proposed April 5, Approved August 3)
1875	State Normal School, Geneseo, New York (Letterhead on College Stationery)
1888	State Normal and Training School at Geneseo (First circular and following editions)
1903–1905	Geneseo Normal School (College Bulletin)
1906–1915	Geneseo Normal School, Geneseo, New York (College Catalog)
1915–1917	Geneseo State Normal School (College Catalog)
1918–1936	State Normal School, Geneseo, New York (College Catalog)
1937–1942	State Normal School at Geneseo, New York (College Catalog)
1943–1947	State Teachers College, Geneseo, New York (College Catalog via Feinberg Bill)
1948–1960	State University of New York Teachers College at Geneseo (College Catalog)
	Geneseo State Teachers College (State Education Department Annual Report)
1960–1962	State University of New York College of Education at Geneseo (College Catalog)
	College of Education at Geneseo (Executive Budget)
1962–1969	State University of New York College at Geneseo
	State University College of Arts and Science (Executive Budget)
1969–1979	College of Arts and Science at Geneseo, State University of New York at Geneseo, or State University College of Arts and Science, Geneseo, New York
1986–1992	State University of New York College of Arts and Science, Geneseo, New York (Simply "Geneseo" on letterheads)
1992–2000	State University of New York College at Geneseo (Undergraduate Bulletin)
2002–	State University of New York at Geneseo (Undergraduate Bulletin)

Compiled by William Lane, College Librarian, and adapted.

Enrollment and Graduation History

Prepared by SUNY Geneseo Office of Institutional Research

Year	Students	Diplomas/Degrees	Year	Students	Diplomas/Degrees	Year	Students	Diplomas/Degrees
Sept. 71	71	0	1920-21	314	149	1970-71	5,408	1,001
1871-72	191	10	1921-22	455	277	1971-72	5,905	1,088
1872-73	244	4	1922-23	382	291	1972-73	5,699	1,282
1873-74	307	12	1923-24	281	114	1973-74	6,373	1,355
1874-75	347	24	1924-25	381	84	1974-75	6,567	1,543
1875-76	339	24	1925-26	436	113	1975-76	6,374	1,412
1876-77	308	27	1926-27	501	146	1976-77	5,845	1,338
1877-78	294	24	1927-28	603	151	1977-78	5,153	1,206
1878-79	312	27	1928-29	671	208	1978-79	5,342	1,116
1879-80	394	18	1929-30	686	212	1979-80	5,550	1,234
1880-81	416	12	1930-31	645	227	1980-81	5,571	1,077
1881-82	461	22	1931-32	681	212	1981-82	5,546	1,161
1882-83	458	26	1932-33	683	193	1982-83	5,231	1,178
1883-84	460	30	1933-34	707	232	1983-84	5,319	1,073
1884-85	380	41	1934-35	703	266	1984-85	5,282	1,076
1885-86	425	58	1935-36	723	309	1985-86	5,425	1,091
1886-87	442	57	1936-37	651	293	1986-87	5,333	1,115
1887-88	476	43	1937-38	658	220	1987-88	5,363	1,201
1888-89	486	76	1938-39	584	171	1988-89	5,321	1,194
1889-90	464	73	1939-40	485	244	1989-90	5,373	1,189
1890-91	491	105	1940-41	453	139	1990-91	5,599	1,280
1891-92	535	124	1941-42	440	175	1991-92	5,672	1,450
1892-93	559	75	1942-43	362	126	1992-93	5,651	1,435
1893-94	625	87	1943-44	324	108	1993-94	5,631	1,235
1894-95	730	108	1944-45	349	157	1994-95	5,754	1,383
1895-96	835	160	1945-46	369	106	1995-96	5,719	1,304
1896-97	847	164	1946-47	518	126	1996-97	5,564	1,338
1897-98	810	224	1947-48	570	131	1997-98	5,560	1,367
1898-99	751	195	1948-49	624	140	1998-99	5,497	1,274
1899-00	746	186	1949-50	697	177	1999-00	5,603	1,315
1900-01	673	146	1950-51	774	198	2000-01	5,477	1,251
1901-02	488	149	1951-52	801	187	2001-02	5,649	1,407
1902-03	446	126	1952-53	857	187	2002-03	5,668	1,326
1903-04	413	110	1953-54	783	201	2003-04	5,550	1,314
1904-05	363	91	1954-55	884	190	2004-05	5,573	1,364
1905-06	315	116	1955-56	964	197	2005-06	5,484	1,298
1906-07	281	133	1956-57	1,073	185	2006-07	5,530	1,244
1907-08	212	104	1957-58	1,312	212	2007-08	5,548	
1908-09	203	105	1958-59	1,544	257			
1909-10	239	104	1959-60	1,592	277			
1910-11	254	123	1960-61	1,792	456			
1911-12	270	134	1961-62	2,035	350			
1912-13	273	131	1962-63	2,262	388			
1913-14	327	170	1963-64	2,370	476			
1914-15	325	173	1964-65	2,724	560			
1915-16	461	155	1965-66	3,035	486			
1916-17	416	238	1966-67	3,283	555			
1917-18	326	212	1967-68	3,671	620			
1918-19	248	155	1968-69	4,136	850			
1919-20	303	149	1969-70	4,678	1,017			

SUNY Geneseo Honor Roll of Student Academic Awards

Prepared by SUNY Geneseo Office of Institutional Research

FULBRIGHT AWARD

1998	Tiffany Hopkins	1995	Elizabeth Fraser
1998	David Binns	1985	Andrew Fox

GOLDWATER SCHOLARSHIPS

2006	Jessica Gucwa	1998	Amy Cocina
2005	Scott Meckler	1997	Richele Abel
2005	Amy Zielinski	1996	Kurt Schillinger
2003	Daniel Welchons	1996	Michael Duff-Raffaele
2002	Matthew Fleming	1995	Brian DeMarco
2002	Summer Raines	1992	Elizabeth Hile
2001	Kathryn Weiss	1991	Rebecca Surman

MCNAIR SCHOLARSHIP

1997	Ho-Ling Chack

MELLON FELLOWSHIP

1993	Lisa Lucenti

NATIONAL SECURITY EDUCATION PROGRAM SCHOLARSHIP

1995	Bronwyn Irwin

SUNY CHANCELLOR'S AWARD FOR STUDENT EXCELLENCE

2008	Jared Chester		Marinda Wyant
	Derek Jokic		Joanna Zieno
	Peter Kang	2003	Melissa White
	Colin Kremer		Tracie Klusek
	Pamela May		Summer Raines
2007	Amanda Brownstein		Bethany Lipa
	Christina Finke	2002	Anthony Gallo
	Amanda Gitomer		Jennifer Sahrle
	Jessica Gucwa		Kathryn Weiss
	Sarah Pinchoff	2001	Jeffrey Reingold
2006	Renne Catalano		Danielle Schoen
	Joseph Gianfagna		Jennifer Turkovich
	Salvatore Priore Jr.	2000	Andrew Caffrey
	Taylor Foster Smith		Robert Rubin
	Daniel Welchons		Patrick Winkelman
2005	Nicole Barzee	1998	David Binns
	Felisa Brown		Amy Cocina
	Eric Rathfelder		Tiffany Hopkins
	Erin Walsh	1997	Richele Abel
2004	James Rogers		Michelle Morse
	Paul Weismann		

USA TODAY ALL-USA COLLEGE ACADEMIC FIRST TEAM

1997	Michelle Morse

SUNY Geneseo Honor Roll of Faculty and Professional Staff Award Recipients

Prepared by SUNY Geneseo Office of Institutional Research

National, State, and Regional Awards

AMERICAN PSYCHOLOGICAL ASSOCIATION TEACHING OF PSYCHOLOGY AWARD

Margaret Matlin	1985	Psychology

AMERICAN SPEECH AND HEARING ASSOCIATION FELLOW

Nicholas Schiavetti	1992	Communicative Disorders & Sciences
Dale Metz	1991	Communicative Disorders & Sciences

AMERICAN PSYCHOLOGICAL FOUNDATION DISTINGUISHED TEACHING IN PSYCHOLOGY AWARD

Margaret Matlin	1995	Psychology

CARA AWARD FOR EXCELLENCE IN TEACHING MEDIEVAL STUDIES
(Medieval Academy of America)

William Cook	2004	History
Ronald Herzman	2004	English

CARNEGIE/CASE PROFESSOR OF THE YEAR FOR NEW YORK AWARD

Stephen Padalino	2000	Physics
William Cook	1992	History

CORNARO AWARD (Grand Lodge Order Sons of Italy in America)

Linda House	1992	Communicative Disorders & Sciences

DISTINGUISHED SERVICE TO HIGHER EDUCATION (College Student Personnel Association)

Robert Bonfiglio	2005	Student and Campus Life

FIRST TIME PATENT AWARD

Rong Lin	2002	Computer Science

HAIMO AWARD FOR DISTINGUISHED COLLEGE TEACHING
(Mathematical Association of America)

Olympia Nicodemi	2003	Mathematics
Gary Towsley	2000	Mathematics

INFORMATION TECHNOLOGY WOMAN OF THE YEAR AWARD
(Association for Women in Computing, Upstate New York Chapter)

Susan Chichester	2005	Computing & Information Technology

INSTRUCTIONAL DEVELOPMENT DIVISION OF THE INTERNATIONAL COMMUNICATION ASSOCIATION TEACHING AWARD

Mary Mohan	1987	Communication

MATHEMATICAL ASSOCIATION OF AMERICA'S TEACHING AWARD
(SEAWAY SECTION)

Olympia Nicodemi	2000	Mathematics
Gary Towsley	1999	Mathematics
Stephen West	1993	Mathematics

NATIONAL COUNCIL FOR GEOGRAPHIC EDUCATION,
DISTINGUISHED COLLEGE TEACHER AWARD

Darrell Norris	1987	Geography

NEW YORK STATE SPEECH & HEARING ASSOCIATION
DISTINGUISHED ACHIEVEMENT AWARD

Dale Metz	1994	Communicative Disorders & Sciences
Nicholas Schiavetti	1993	Communicative Disorders & Sciences

SOCIETY FOR THE PSYCHOLOGY OF WOMEN HERITAGE AWARD
FOR CONTRIBUTION TO THE TEACHING OF PSYCHOLOGY AWARD

Margaret Matlin	2001	Psychology

U.S. FULBRIGHT SCHOLAR PROGRAM (FACULTY)

Yanxian Anthony Gu	2005	School of Business
Jeffrey Koch	2002	Political Science
Karen Duffy	2000	Psychology
Robert Goeckel	2000	Political Science
Karen Duffy	1995	Psychology
Robert Goeckel	1995	Political Science

U.S. INTERCOLLEGIATE LACROSSE ASSOCIATION – DIVISION III
COACH OF THE YEAR AWARD

Jim Lyons	2004	Intercollegiate Athletics & Recreation

SUNY Awards

CHANCELLOR'S AWARD FOR EXCELLENCE IN FACULTY SERVICE

Michael Schinski	2008	School of Business
Paul Schacht	2007	English
Mary Ellen Zuckerman	2006	School of Business
Dennis Showers	2005	School of Education

CHANCELLOR'S AWARD FOR EXCELLENCE IN LIBRARIANSHIP

Kimberly Davies Hoffman	2007	Milne Library
Sue Ann Brainard	2004	Milne Library
Paula Henry	1995	Milne Library
Judith Bushnell	1990	Milne Library
David Parish	1979	Milne Library

CHANCELLOR'S AWARD FOR EXCELLENCE IN PROFESSIONAL
SERVICE

Tamara Hurlburt	2006	Judicial Affairs
Roxanne Johnston	2005	College Advancement
Barbara Howard	2004	School of Business
Marilyn Moore	2003	Intercollegiate Athletics
Scott Hooker	2001	Admissions
Susan Bailey	2000	Dean's Office
Donald Lackey	1999	Personnel Office
Isom Fearn	1998	Access Opportunity Program
Ronald Pretzer	1997	College Advancement
Laura Wrubel	1996	Dean's Office
Kathleen Trainor	1995	College Activities
Kathleen Hayes-Sugarman	1994	Dean of Students
Jerald Wrubel	1993	Career Services
William Davis	1992	Computer Center
Edward Reiman	1991	Financial Aid
Janet Graeter	1990	Admissions
Roseann Bellanca	1989	School of Business

Katharyn Crabbe	1988	Graduate Studies
Richard Rosati	1987	Alumni Affairs
Dolores Donnelly	1981	College Activities
William Caren	1980	Student Services & Staff Relations
Joan Schumaker	1979	Undergraduate Studies
Thomas Matthews	1978	College Activities

CHANCELLOR'S AWARD FOR EXCELLENCE IN SCHOLARSHIP AND
CREATIVE ACTIVITIES

Michael Lynch	2008	Psychology
Gerard Floriano	2007	Music
Stephen Padalino	2006	Physics
Steve Derne	2004	Sociology
Yanxian Anthony Gu	2003	School of Business
Rong Lin	2002	Computer Science

CHANCELLOR'S AWARD FOR EXCELLENCE IN TEACHING

Jennifer Katz	2008	Psychology
Michael Rozalski	2008	School of Education
Caroline Woidat	2008	English
Christopher Annala	2007	School of Business
David Geiger	2007	Chemistry
Intekhab Alam	2006	School of Business
Kathryn Rommel-Esham	2006	School of Education
Melissa Sutherland	2006	Mathematics
Joseph Cope	2005	History
Anne Eisenberg	2005	Sociology
Rosemary McEwen	2005	Foreign Languages
Carol Faulkner	2004	History
Edward Pogozelski	2004	Physics
Rachel Hall	2003	English
Michael Oberg	2003	History
Monica Schneider	2003	Psychology
Emilye Crosby	2002	History
Tze-Ki Hon	2002	History
Beth McCoy	2002	English
Patrice Case	2001	Art
Edward Wallace	2001	Mathematics
Isidro Bosch	2000	Biology
Jee Loo Liu	2000	Philosophy
Anne-Marie Reynolds	2000	Music
Harold Hoops	1999	Biology
Thomas MacPherson	1999	Art
Irina Vasiliev	1999	Geography
D. Jeffrey Over	1998	Geological Sciences
Kurtis Fletcher	1997	Physics
Joseph McCartin	1997	History
Paul Schacht	1997	English
Carol Highsaw	1996	English
Jonette Lancos	1996	Dance
Christopher Leary	1996	Mathematics
F. Kurt Cylke, Jr.	1995	Sociology
James Kimball	1995	Music
Wanda Spruill	1995	School of Business
William Leyerle	1994	Music
Olympia Nicodemi	1994	Mathematics
Robert O'Donnell	1994	Biology

Robert Owens	1993	Speech Pathology & Audiology
Laura Doan	1992	English
Stephen Padalino	1992	Physics
Nicholas Schiavetti	1992	Speech Pathology & Audiology
Brian Coffey	1991	Geography
Stephen West	1991	Mathematics
Daniel Fink	1990	Art
David Martin	1990	School of Business
Celia Easton	1989	English
Peter Meiksins	1989	Sociology
Jerry Reber	1989	Physics
Nancy Kleniewski	1987	Sociology
Daniel Strang	1987	School of Business
Stacey Edgar	1986	Computer Science
Donald Marozas	1986	Education
Eugene Stelzig	1985	English
Walter Soffer	1982	Philosophy
Wendell Rhodes	1981	Anthropology
Donald Watt	1981	English
Phillip Boger	1980	Geological Sciences
Gary Towsley	1980	Mathematics
Donald Innis	1979	Geography
Thomas Pray	1979	School of Business
Huston Diehl Hallahan	1978	English
James Willey	1978	Music
Margaret Matlin	1977	Psychology
James Scholes	1977	English
Nona Schurman	1977	Dance
Joseph Dechario	1976	Music
William Edgar	1976	Philosophy
Ronald Herzman	1976	English
Wayne Mahood	1976	Education
Lawrence Casler	1975	Psychology
H. Gordon Miller	1975	Art
Richard Salisbury	1975	History
William Cook	1974	History
William Edgar	1974	Philosophy
John Kucaba, Jr.	1974	Music

CHANCELLOR'S AWARD FOR INTERNATIONALIZATION

Robert Goeckel	2004	Political Science

CHANCELLOR'S RESEARCH RECOGNITION AWARD

David Geiger	2005	Chemistry
Dale Metz	2005	Communicative Disorders & Sciences
Richard Young	2002	Geological Sciences

DISTINGUISHED PROFESSOR

David Meisel	2001	Physics
Robert Beason	1999	Biology
Rita Gollin	1995	English
Srinivasa Leelamma	1995	Mathematics

DISTINGUISHED SERVICE PROFESSOR

Daniel Strang	2006	School of Business
James Walker	1998	Music
Charles Randy Bailey	1997	History
Karen Duffy	1995	Psychology
Wayne Mahood	1994	Education
Robert Isgro	1993	Music
Richard Young	1991	Geological Sciences
Martin Fausold	1985	History
William Small	1985	Mathematics
John Paul	1982	Speech Pathology & Audiology
Richard Stolper	1982	Educational Studies
Bertha V. B. Lederer	1980	Fine Arts
Gifford Orwen	1980	Foreign Languages
Harold Starbuck	1979	Speech Pathology & Audiology
Kathryn Beck	1978	History
Myrtle Merritt	1976	Health, Physical Ed. & Recreation
Hans Gottschalk	1975	English

DISTINGUISHED TEACHING PROFESSOR

Stephen Padalino	2007	Physics
Robert O'Donnell	2003	Biology
Robert Owens	2003	Communicative Disorders & Sciences
Stephen West	2000	Mathematics
Gary Towsley	1998	Mathematics
Eugene Stelzig	1997	English
Jerry Reber	1995	Physics
James Willey	1990	Music
Ronald Herzman	1989	English
Margaret Matlin	1987	Psychology
William Cook	1984	History
William Edgar	1979	Philosophy
Rose Alent	1975	Foreign Languages
Richard F. Smith	1974	Chemistry
Robert Sells	1973	Physics

DISTINGUISHED UNIVERSITY PROFESSOR

Walter Harding	1973	English

SCHOLARSHIP AND RESEARCH IN THE HUMANITIES, ARTS, AND SOCIAL SCIENCES

William Cook	2001	History

Campus Awards

ALUMNI PROFESSOR

Wendy Pogozelski	2004	Chemistry
Kurtis Fletcher	2001	Physics
Robert Beason	1998	Biology
Stephen Padalino	1995	Physics

ART HATTON AWARD FOR EXCELLENCE IN COLLEGE ADVANCEMENT

Amy Sheldon	2007	Geological Sciences

GENESEO ALUMNI SUPPORTED PROFESSORSHIP

Ganie DeHart	2007	Psychology

GENESEO FOUNDATION PROFESSOR

Daniel Strang	2000	School of Business
David Geiger	1997	Chemistry

HARTER MENTORING AWARD

J. Christopher Pruszynski	2007	Communication
Isidro Bosch	2006	Biology
Emilye Crosby	2005	History
Thomas MacPherson	2004	Art
Chi Ming Tang	2003	Mathematics
Mary Mohan	2002	Communication
Stephen Padalino	2001	Physics
Ganie DeHart	2000	Psychology
William Edgar	1999	Philosophy
Stacey Edgar	1998	Philosophy

JAMES AND JULIA LOCKHART SUPPORTED PROFESSORSHIP

Beth McCoy	2007	English
Kenneth Asher	2004	English
Harold Hoops	2001	Biology
D. Jeffrey Over	2000	Geological Sciences
F. Kurt Cylke, Jr.	1998	Sociology
Celia Easton	1997	English
Robert O'Donnell	1995	Biology
Gary Towsley	1994	Mathematics

JOSEPH M. O'BRIEN AWARD FOR EXCELLENCE IN PART-TIME TEACHING

Kimberly McGann	2007	Sociology
Jacalyn Eddy	2006	English
Jeremy Grace	2005	Political Science
Barbara Stewart	2004	Mathematics
Virginia Jurkowski	2002	School of Business
Jonathan Kruger	2001	School of Performing Arts
Pamela Kurau	2000	School of Performing Arts
Luvon Sheppard	1999	Art
Weston Kennison	1998	English
Amelia Braun	1997	School of Education

LOCKHART RESEARCH/CREATIVE ENDEAVORS PROFESSOR

Michael Oberg	2005	History
Eugene Stelzig	2002	English

MACVITTIE PROFESSORSHIP AWARD

Donald Marozas	2002	School of Education
Laura Doan	1999	English

PRESIDENT'S AWARD FOR EXCELLENCE IN ACADEMIC ADVISEMENT

Monica Schneider	2007	Psychology
Amy Sheldon	2006	Geological Sciences
Savitri Iyer	2005	Physics
Susan Salmon	2004	School of Education
Celia Easton	2003	English
Margaret Stolee	2002	History
Gerard Gouvernet	2001	Foreign Languages
Linda House	2000	Communicative Disorders & Sciences

George Briggs	1999	Biology
Jack Johnston	1998	Music
Daniel Strang	1998	School of Business
Melvyn Yessenow	1997	Psychology
Jane Hogan	1996	Education
Donald Trasher	1995	Mathematics
Gary DeBolt	1994	Education
Stacey Edgar	1993	Philosophy
Sharon Bossung	1992	School of Business
Ellen Kintz	1991	Anthropology
Robert Goeckel	1990	Political Science
Jerry Reber	1990	Physics
Archibald Reid	1989	Biology
Lynn Zimmer	1989	Sociology
J. Thomas Conlon	1988	Education

PRESIDENT'S AWARD FOR EXCELLENCE IN RESEARCH AND CREATIVITY

Emilye Crosby	2007	History
Wendy Pogozelski	2006	Chemistry
Mark Mitschow	2005	School of Business
Richard Young	2004	Geological Sciences
Nader Asgary	2003	School of Business
William Cook	2002	History

PRESIDENT'S AWARD FOR OUTSTANDING PROFESSIONAL SERVICE

Andrea Klein	2007	Campus Scheduling & Events
Roy Doane	2006	Facilities & Planning
Debra Hill	2005	College Advancement
Edward Abbott	2004	Campus Auxiliary Services
Isom Fearn	2003	Access Opportunity Program
Leonard Sancilio	2002	Dean of Students
Virginia Geer-Mentry	2001	Campus Auxiliary Services
Kimberly Dalton Ferris	2000	Environmental Health & Safety
Susan Chichester	1999	Computing & Information Technology
William Mathews	1998	College Advancement
Alan Case	1997	School of Performing Arts
Brian Bennett	1996	College Advancement
Gloria Tarantella	1994	President's Office
Ronald Satryb	1993	Student & Campus Life
Frederick Bright	1992	Sports & Recreation
Mary Nitsche	1991	Computing & Information Technology
Michael Dailey	1990	Facilities Services

ROEMER PROFESSORSHIP AWARD

Emilye Crosby	2005	History
Christopher Leary	2002	Mathematics
Isidro Bosch	1999	Biology

Chronology of College Buildings

Dates are based on information provided by the College Facilities Planning office and represent dates of occupancy.

Old Main: 1871—razed 1951–1952

    Normal Hall: 1876

    Training School: 1886

    Gymnasium, science wing, heating plant: 1896

    Library and swimming pool: 1903

Welles Hall (originally Holcomb Campus School): 1932

Sturges Hall: 1938

Blake A–E: 1950–51 (orig. College Center, Bailey, Fraser, Blake, Sturges)—
    D & E razed 2004

Heating plant service building: 1953

Fraser Hall (orig. Milne Library): 1955

Wadsworth Auditorium: 1955

Jones Residence Hall: 1958

Livingston Residence Hall: 1959

Mary Jemison Dining Hall: 1960

Monroe Residence Hall: 1961

Schrader Health & Physical Education Building: 1961

Transformer service building: 1962

Bailey Science Building: 1964

Steuben Residence Hall: 1964

Genesee Residence Hall: 1965

Letchworth Dining Hall: 1965

Ontario Residence Hall: 1965

Wyoming Residence Hall: 1965

Allegany Residence Hall: 1966

Erie Residence Hall: 1966

Lauderdale Health Center: 1966

Milne Library: 1966

Brodie Fine Arts: 1967

Clark Service Building: 1967

Erwin Administration Building: 1967

Nassau Residence Hall: 1967

Newton Hall: 1967

Red Jacket Dining Hall: 1967

Suffolk Residence Hall: 1967

MacVittie College Union: 1969

Holcomb Learning Center: 1969

Greene Science Building: 1970

Niagara Residence Hall: 1970

Wayne Residence Hall: 1970

Onondaga Residence Hall: 1971

Merritt Athletic Center: 1973

South Hall: 1995

Saratoga Terrace residences: 2001

Saratoga Common: 2002

Putnam Residence Hall: 2004

Integrated Science Center and Greenhouse: 2007

Off-Campus Properties

President's Residence and garage, 15 Main Street: purchased 1955, built 1897

Interfaith Center, Franklin Street: 1969

Doty Building: acquired 1974 (built as Geneseo High School 1933), surplused
    1980

Campus House, 17 Main Street: purchased by C.A.S. 1996, built ca. 1816

Roemer House, Bank Street: purchased 1997

Big Tree Inn, 46 Main Street: purchased by C.A.S. 1998, built 1833

McClellan House, 26 Main Street: purchased by Geneseo Foundation 2000,
    built 1825

SUNY Geneseo NCAA Division III All-Americans

Names are followed by class year, sports, and number of All-American certificates. Prepared by SUNY Geneseo Sports Information Director George Gagnier.

Alley, Joan, 1983. Swimming, 1.
Almansberger, Jill, 2002. Softball, 1.
Annabel, Matt, 1998. Cross country/Track, 1.
Anthone, Jennifer, 2011. Swimming, 4.
Balling, Betsy, 1994. Soccer, 1.
Barth, Kate, 2008. Volleyball, 1.
Bazydlo, Owahn, 2007. Lacrosse, 3.
Beck, Jeff, 2005. Cross country/track, 3.
Beck, Jon, 2002. Cross country/track, 1.
Bondi, Rich, 1980. Swimming, 4.
Breeden, Mark, 1999. Ice hockey, 2.
Bush, Keena, 1995. Track, 6.
Butterworth, Rick, 1982. Soccer, 1.
Cascio, Sean, 1990. Ice hockey, 1.
Casey, Jason, 2004. Track & field, 1.
Catalano, Renne, 2004. Track & field, 1.
Cincotta, Beth, 1996. Track & field, 1.
Clark, Sharon, 1995. Swimming, 1.
Cleary, Amy, 1997. Swimming, 1.
Cocco, Jessie, 2009. Swimming, 3.
Cox, Doug, 1980. Swimming, 1.
Culhane, Sig, 2009. Swimming, 2.
Daggett, Richard, 1977. Swimming, 2.
DePrez, Kim, 2006. Track & field, 5.
DeWitt, Jim, 1978. Swimming, 1.
Farry, Tim, 1991. Swimming, 1.
Finke, Christy, 2007. Track & field, 2.
Fish, Pat, 1995. Swimming, 2.
Fisher, Paula, 1995. Soccer, 1.
Fitch, Scott, 1993. Basketball, 2.
Gallo, Anthony, 2002. Cross country/track, 4.
Gardner, Phil, 2007. Lacrosse, 2.
Geary, Todd, 1999. Swimming, 7.
Germain, Lou, 1991. Ice Hockey, 1
Gleason, Tom, 1979. Lacrosse, 1.
Goodspeed, Joe, 2007. Track & field, 2.
Greenan, Bernadette, 1994. Track & field, 1.
Griggs, Shannon, 2006. Cross country/track, 1.
Hake, Charlie, 2008. Swimming, 2.

Haney, Amanda, 2008. Track & field, 5.
Hennigan, Kevin, 2007. Lacrosse, 2.
Hirsch, T. J., 2004. Diving, 1.
Hoercher, Larry, 1975. Diving, 1.
Holzschuh, Scott, 1977. Swimming, 2.
Houlihan, Mike, 1998. Swimming, 10.
Howland, Emily, 2006. Track & field, 2.
Janis, Carey, 1995. Basketball, 1.
Kosloski, Mary, 2006. Track & field, 1.
Kramer, Carly, 2010. Track & field, 1.
Kuhn, Audrey, 2007. Softball, 1.
Lane, Jennifer, 2003. Swimming, 1.
Lewis, Gary, 1975. Lacrosse, 1.
Linehan, Katie, 2010. Swimming, 3.
Litzelman, Don, 1982. Lacrosse, 2.
Mackey, Megan, 1998. Basketball, 3.
Magri, Fran, 2006. Track & field, 2.
Manetta, Judah, 2009. Soccer, 1.
Maxwell, Ray, 1982. Soccer, 1.
Mazurowski, Glen, 1991. Ice Hockey, 1.
McCann, Bridget, 2001. Track & field, 1.
McClosky, Heather, 1997. Swimming, 1.
McDermott, Tim, 2007. Lacrosse, 2.
Menges, Tim, 1993. Swimming, 3.
Miller, Wayne, 1977. Swimming, 1.
Monaghan, Mark, 1995. Swimming, 2.
Montgomery, Liz, 2009. Cross country/track, 5.
Mooney, Mike, 1982. Swimming, 1.
Muldner, Josh, 1999. Swimming, 15.
Nethaway, Amy, 1996. Track & field, 1.
Nolan, Meghan, 2008. Cross country/track, 6.
O'Brien, Bill, 1982. Swimming, 1.
O'Brien, John, 1981. Swimming, 1.
O'Donnell, Charles, 1975. Swimming, 1.
Perrault, Kristen, 1998. Swimming, 2.
Pesch, Dave, 1978. Swimming, 3.
Petrillose, A. J., 1989. Lacrosse, 1.
Pizzuto, Mike, 2008. Lacrosse, 1.
Rettke, Jen, 2003. Cross country/track, 3.

Riehlman, Pat, 2006. Lacrosse, 3.
Robota, Ed, 1975. Basketball, 1.
Rodriguez, Michelle, 2011. Swimming, 4.
Ryan, Mary, 1986. Cross country, 1.
Ryerson, Jack, 2006. Lacrosse, 1.
Scanlan, Brian, 1995. Soccer, 1.
Schoen, Danielle, 2001. Swimming, 1.
Scott, Marta, 2006. Cross country/track, 6.
Shepard, Randy, 1993. Diving, 2.
Shope, Beth, 1999. Track & field, 7.
Sisting, Christine, 1996. Cross country/track, 7.
Smith, Chris, 1991. Ice hockey, 1.
Smith, Katie, 1995. Basketball, 2.
Smith, Sharon, 1983. Diving, 2.
Snyder, Diana, 2008. Track & field, 1.
Sovie, Joel, 2008. Lacrosse, 1.
Spennacchio, Dave, 2004. Lacrosse, 1.
Stenzil, Joel, 1981. Diving, 1.
Stephens, Mitch, 2007. Ice hockey, 1.
Stock, Chris, 2005. Soccer/Lacrosse, 1.
Stone, Kim, 1995. Track & field, 2.
Storch, Mark, 1980. Swimming, 1.
Sugnet, Clint, 2009. Swimming, 2.
Swensen, Lindsay, 2005. Swimming, 1.
Taub, Sarah, 2003. Softball, 1.
Thorpe, Natalie, 2010. Swimming, 2.
Tudman, Ian, 1995. Basketball, 1.
Turner, Ted, 2005. Cross country/Track, 6.
VanDerMeid, Matt, 1998. Swimming, 10.
Verdino, Annie, 2008. Basketball, 1.
Walker, Brett, 2005. Ice hockey, 1.
Wayne, Colleen, 2006. Swimming, 1.
White, Melissa, 2003. Cross country/Track, 7.
Wrighter, Brandy, 2004. Swimming, 1.
Zera, Joe, 2005. Basketball, 1.
Zieno, Joanna, 2004. Cross country/track, 1.
Zolna, John, 2008. Swimming, 2.

Members of SUNY Geneseo's Sports Hall of Fame

Names of alumni are followed by class year and sports played. Compiled by SUNY Geneseo Sports Information Director George Gagnier.

Akers, Frank, Coach/Administrator.

Allan, Jim, 1961, Soccer/Basketball/Baseball.

Andrews, Jim, 1971, Lacrosse.

Balling, Betsy, 1994, Soccer.

Bondi, Rich, 1980, Swimming.

Breeden, Mark, 1999, Ice hockey.

Bright, Fred, Coach.

Brown, Fred, 1955, Soccer/Basketball/Baseball.

Bunker, Lisa, 1982, Swimming.

Burruto, Colleen, 1988, Soccer.

Bush, Keena, 1995, Track.

Butterworth, Rick, 1982, Soccer.

Camera, Christine, 1991, Soccer.

Canale, Aimee, 1998, Soccer, Coach.

Cascio, Sean, 1990, Ice hockey.

Checho, Don, 1960, Soccer/Basketball/Golf.

Clar, Jim, 1989, Basketball/Soccer.

Conboy, Gary, 1968, Basketball/Baseball.

Connor, Lori, 1984, Volleyball/Track.

Contario, Joe, 1975, Cross country.

Dellavecchia, Christine, 1987, Volleyball/Softball.

Derwick, Charlie, 1963, Basketball/Baseball.

Dewar, Robert, Contributor.

DeWitt, Jim, 1978, Swimming.

Dietsche, William, 1933, Baseball.

Dowling, Kathleen, 1977, Synchronized swimming.

Duffy, Paul, Coach.

Ellert, Marjorie, 1975, Synchronized swimming.

Farry, Tim, 1991, Swimming.

Fiala, John, 1954, Soccer/Basketball/Baseball

Fish, Pat, 1995, Swimming.

Fitch, Scott, 1993, Basketball.

Geary, Todd, 1999, Swimming.

Giordano, David, 1975, Soccer.

Gleason, Tom, 1979, Lacrosse.

Gross, David, 1967, Basketball.

Halleran, Carin, 1994, Soccer.

Hamilton, Lynn, 1991, Basketball.

Herrmann, Peter, 1970, Baseball.

Hewson, William, 1969, Soccer.

Hinckley, Duncan, Coach.

Hinckley, Linda, 1972, Swimming.

Hogan, Jen, 1997, Soccer.

Houlihan, Mike, 1998, Swimming.

Janis, Carey, 1995, Basketball.

Keady, John, 1988, Ice hockey.

Keane, Dan, 1995, Basketball.

Kentner, Martin, Coach.

Lewis, Gary, 1975, Lacrosse.

Lind, Sue, 1987, Basketball.

Linfoot, John, Contributor.

Litzelman, Don, 1982, Lacrosse.

Loveland, Bill, 1989, Ice hockey.

Mackey, Megan, 1998, Basketball.

MacVittie, Robert, College President.

Malone, Erin, 1994, Basketball.

Mason, Bill, 1992, Basketball.

Maxwell, Ray, 1982, Soccer.

Mazurowski, Glen, 1991, Ice hockey.

Menges, Tim, 1993, Swimming.

Merritt, Myrtle, Administrator.

Metzger, Tom, 1980, Ice hockey.

Monaghan, Mark, 1995, Swimming.

Muldner, Josh, 1999, Swimming.

Muller, Mark, 1991, Basketball.

Mullin, Dan, Coach/Administrator.

Nelson, Mike, 1969, Basketball.

O'Brien, John, 1981, Swimming.

Pope, Tom, Coach.

Raines, Kristin, 1994, Basketball.

Reilly, Terry, 1988, Ice hockey.

Reist, Chip, 1977, Soccer.

Rich, Paul, 1981, Basketball.

Riedel, Robert, Coach/Administrator.

Rivers, Julie, 1988, Soccer.

Robota, Ed, 1975, Basketball.

Rose, Paul, Coach.

Scanlan, Brian, 1995, Soccer.

Shaw, Craig, 1970, Soccer.

Shope, Beth, 1999, Track & field.

Sisson, Tom, 1971, Basketball.

Sisting, Christine, 1996, Cross country/Track.

Smith, Chris, 1991, Ice hockey.

Smith, Curt, 1973, Sportswriter.

Smith, Katie, 1995, Basketball.

Solomon, Al, 1974, Wrestling.

Spring, John, Administrator.

Toler, Shirley, Coach.

Tudman, Ian, 1995, Basketball.

Usinger, Ed, 1973, Soccer.

VanDerMeid, Matt, 1998, Swimming.

Ward, Harry, 1974, Basketball.

Weber, Ken, 1978, Ice hockey.

Wechsler, Joyce, Coach.

Welch, James, Coach.

White, Mary, 1979, Basketball/Volleyball/Softball.

Williams, Diane, 1986, Basketball.

Wilson, Ira, Coach/Administrator.

Witzel, Carl, Coach.

Notes

Chapter One

1. Rosalind Fisher, ...the stone strength of the past... (Geneseo: by the College, 1971).

2. Martin Fausold, A Draft History of the State University of New York, unpublished paper, 1988, 1, 3, 4.

3. Ibid., 4; Jesse Stuart, The Thread That Runs So True (New York: Charles Scribner's Sons, 1958). After a teaching and administrative career, Stuart gained fame as a prize-winning poet and novelist, with over fifty books to his credit, the best known of which was Taps for Private Tussie, which was the inspiration for the movie, "No Time for Sergeants." He spoke at the College on February 10, 1941.

4. Christine Ogren, The American State Normal School (New York: Palgrave, 2005), 9, 10, 13; Mitchell L. Robinson, "'A Freer Opportunity to Go to College': The New York State Normal Schools & the Development of Public Higher Education, 1890-1914," unpublished paper, 1985, 3, 4. Robinson, who received his doctorate in history from Cornell, has dual degrees from Geneseo, a B.A. in History and an M.S. in Library Science.

5. Robinson, "'A Freer Opportunity to Go to College,'" 5, 6.

6. Fisher, ...the stone strength of the past..., 12; Letter from James Wadsworth to James Samuel Wadsworth, November 29, 1843, Wadsworth Family Papers, Milne Library, State University of New York at Geneseo (SUNY Geneseo). Consistent with that belief, James is credited with obtaining legislation to create district (public) school libraries in New York State, New York State Legislature, Section 4, Chapter 237, Laws of New York, 1838; Thurlow Weed (Harriet A. Weed, ed.), The Autobiography of Thurlow Weed, 2 vols. (Boston: Houghton Mifflin, 1884), 2:344-346. Temple Hill Academy was incorporated March 19, 1827 as the "Livingston County High School Association," by Chapter 64, New York State Laws of 1827 as amended April 9, 1833 by Chapter 122, Laws of 1833; F. B. Hough, Historical and Statistical Record of the University of the State of New York (Albany: Weed, Parsons & Co., 1885), 629-630. The intent was to create a "Collegiate Institution," and it was the next thing to it in many respects, though an unknown number of students attended Canandaigua Academy after leaving Temple Hill.

7. Robinson, "'A Freer Opportunity to Go to College,'" 4, 6; Frank E. Welles, "Review of the First Twenty Years of the Geneseo State Normal School," Milne Library, SUNY Geneseo, College Archives, hereafter College Archives; www.nd.edu/~rbarger/www7/normal.html.

8. New York State Legislature, 90th Session, Chapter 195, Laws of 1867a; J. H. Smith, History of Livingston County, New York (Syracuse, New York: D. Mason & Co., 1881), 398; John Rorbach, "History of the Geneseo State Normal School: Address Delivered By Col. John Rorbach At The Occasion of the Twenty-Fifth Anniversary of Its Establishment," Proceedings of the Twenty-First Annual Meeting of the Livingston County Historical Society, Held at Geneseo, N.Y., January 19, 1897 (Nunda, New York: C. K. Sanders, Book and Job Printer, 1897), 38. While Rorbach summarizes Temple Hill Academy's history well, other sources include: Souvenir of the Reunion, After Fifty Years, of the Excursion Party From Temple Hill High School to Niagara Falls (Cambridge, Massachusetts: John Wilson & Son, 1882); "View of the Livingston County High School" (J. Percival, 1828); Rev. Ferdinand DeW. Ward, "Geneseo Academy," Livingston Republican, October 26, 1865, and Lockwood L. Doty's county history.

9. Rorbach, "History of the Geneseo State Normal School," 35, 41.

10. Minutes of the Local Board of Visitors from December 5, 1896 through June 19, 1906, College Archives, hereafter Local Board Minutes; Records of Students, Book E, 16, College Archives.

11. Interview of Arthur Hatton, vice president for college advancement, 1989; Letter from Arthur Hatton, May 10, 1988.

12. Letter from Arthur Hatton, May 10, 1988, and an update by Roxanne Johnston, formerly associate vice president, college advancement, SUNY Geneseo, 2005.

13. Rorbach, "History of the Geneseo State Normal School," 43-55; Fisher, ...the stone strength of the past..., 9, 10, 32, 33; John J. McCusker, "How Much Is That in Real Money? A Historical Price Index for Use as a Deflator of Money Values in the Economy of the United States," Proceedings of the American Antiquarian Society, 101 (1992), 297-373.

14. Fisher, ...the stone strength of the past..., 33, 254, 10; Smith, History of Livingston County, New York, 398.

15. New York State Legislature, Education Law, 90th Session, Chapter 195, Laws of 1867, College Archives; Frank E. Welles, "Historical Address. Review of the First Twenty Years of the Geneseo State Normal School," delivered before the Alumni Association, June 15, 1891, College Archives; Fisher, ...the stone strength of the past..., 34; Grantor Deeds, Book 85, page 17, Book 86, page 7, Livingston County Court House. William Brodie's description of the site in the Rochester Daily Express is worth quoting: "The point selected is on the brow of the hill between Main street [sic] in our village and the Avon, Geneseo and Mt. Morris Railroad track and about five hundred feet west of Main street," Brodie Scrapbook, College Archives.

16. Rorbach, "History of the Geneseo State Normal School," 57. Sadly, Col. Wadsworth died at age thirty, less than four months after the school officially opened. He was duly cited for securing the Normal School while erecting a "splendid church" (Episcopal) in the village "almost at his individual expense" and while "enthusiastically engaged in the erection of the new 'Wadsworth Library,'" Ibid., 50.

17. Fisher, ...the stone strength of the past..., 38, 62; "Building Specifications of the Wadsworth Normal and Training School," College Archives.

18. Local Board Minutes, January 7, 1872.

Chapter Two

1. Eighteenth Annual Report of the Superintendent of Public Instruction, Documents of the Senate of the State of New York, 95th Session, 1872, 3, Nos. 34 to 53 (Albany, The Argus Company, 1872), 154; William Lane, "Names Given to the Educational Facility at Geneseo, New York," unpublished, undated chronology; Rorbach, "History of the Geneseo State Normal School," 61; Local Board Minutes, January 7, 1872; Clayton C. Mau, Brief History of the State University Teachers College, Geneseo, New York, unpublished manuscript, State University Teachers College, 1956; Jean Trescott, "A History of Education in the Town of Geneseo," unpublished manuscript, 1988. The board itself was alternately referred to as Local Board of Visitors or Local Board of Managers, though Local Board of Visitors was the legal term.

2. Robert W. MacVittie Miscellaneous Papers, courtesy of Mrs. Robert W. MacVittie, hereafter MMP.

3. Letter to Chancellor D. Bruce Johnstone, May 2, 1990, copy to author.

4. William A. Brodie, Brodie Scrapbook, College Archives; Rorbach, "History of the Geneseo State Normal School," 58; Fisher, ...the stone strength of the past..., 47-50; Local Board Minutes. Fuller biographies are in Fisher, ...the stone strength of the past..., 253-259.

5. William A. Brodie, Brodie Scrapbook, College Archives; Local Board Minutes, August 9, 1871, College Archives; Fisher, ...the stone strength of the past..., 51-52; Rorbach, "History of the Geneseo State Normal School," 59. Shortly thereafter Lord moved to Utica to join the law firm of Conkling, Lord and Cox, Livingston Republican, April 4, 1872.

6. Local Board Minutes, August 9, 10, 16, 21, 1871, College Archives.

7. Fisher, ...the stone strength of the past..., 56; Local Board Minutes, College Archives.

8. Fisher, ...the stone strength of the past..., 54, 55, 56; Local Board Minutes, August 21, 1871, June 2, 1875, March 15, 1886, College Archives.

9. Local Board Minutes, November 14 and December 18, 1871, March 18 and April 8, 1872, January 30 and February 3, 1873, College Archives.

10. Rorbach, "History of the Geneseo State Normal School," 63; Local Board Minutes, June 6, 1900; Fisher, ...the stone strength of the past..., 172; Local Board Minutes, September 4, 1903, June 27, 1890, September 4, 1903, College Archives. For his last nine years Morey had an assistant. William Bradley was his first, Local Board Minutes, June 18, 1894, College Archives.

11. Welles, "Historical Address;" Fisher, ...the stone strength of the past..., 106; Pliny B. Seymour, "Geneseo As I Knew It," The Lamron, April 6,

1938. Ms. Fisher claims John Milne began teaching at Geneseo July 16, 1872, while Welles recalled that Milne started in January 1872; Local Board Minutes, August 22, 25, September 2, 1871.

12. There seems to be an inconsistency in that Gloria F. Bennett also is listed as a graduate of the first class, *Livingston Republican*, July 4, 1872; Local Board Minutes; August 22 through September 12, 1871, College Archives; Robinson, "'A Freer Opportunity to Go to College...,'" 8; Local Board Minutes, July 10, 1875, College Archives.

13. Local Board Minutes, September 7, 1871, College Archives; Fisher, *...the stone strength of the past...*, 60, quoting the superintendent's annual report; Robinson, "'A Freer Opportunity to Go to College...,'" 7; *State Normal School, Geneseo, N.Y.*, 1898 catalogue, 8, College Archives.

14. Fisher, *...the stone strength of the past...*, 68; Local Board Minutes, September 9, 7, 1871, College Archives; "50th Anniversary," *The Lamron*, Geneseo State Normal School (Geneseo, New York, 1921), 99; Leonard W. Richardson, *The Normal School Idea* (Washington: Department of Education for the United States Commission to the Paris Exposition, 1900), 41, College Archives, referring specifically to Geneseo's Normal and Training School.

15. Fisher, *...the stone strength of the past...*, 62.

16. Local Board Minutes, September 7, 1871, College Archives; Ferdinand DeWilton Ward, *Livingston Republican*, October 26, 1865; Clayton Mau, *Brief History of the State University Teachers College, Geneseo, New York*, 3; Christine A. Ogren, *The American State Normal School* (New York: Palgrave, 2005), 17, cites a later date.

17. Fisher, *...the stone strength of the past...*, 57-59; "50th Anniversary," *The Lamron*, Geneseo State Normal School (Geneseo, New York, 1921), 60. Admission to the Academic Department was limited to "bona fide" residents "of the territory, whose people have heretofore given Normal School property to the state...," *State Normal School, Geneseo, N.Y.*, 1898 catalogue, 8, College Archives.

18. Robinson, "'A Freer Opportunity to Go to College...'", 20, 23; Fisher, *...the stone strength of the past...*, 121; Robinson, "'A Freer Opportunity to Go to College...'", 48.

19. Fisher, *...the stone strength of the past...*, 67.

20. Ibid.

21. Ibid., 61; Local Board Minutes, February 27, 1874, February 25, 1896, College Archives; *The Lamron*, February 10, 1956.

22. Fisher, *...the stone strength of the past...*, 77.

23. The Wayfarer, "Revels Among Old Time Pictures," *Livingston Republican*, July 7, 1921.

24. *State Normal School, Geneseo, N.Y.*, 1898 catalogue, 7, College Archives.

25. Fisher, *...the stone strength of the past...*, 66, which cites the *Livingston Republican*, April 2, 1872; Letters from Geneseo Town and Village Historian, David W. Parish, September 16, 21, 2006.

26. State University College, Geneseo, Registrar's Books, College Archives; Fisher, *...the stone strength of the past...*, 67; Seymour, "Geneseo As I Knew It," *The Lamron*, April 6, 1938.

27. *Livingston Republican*, July 4, 1872; unidentified newspaper, July 1872, College Archives.

28. State University College, Geneseo Registrar's Books, College Archives. Prior to Oneonta this Milne had been principal of Cortland's academic department and Latin and Greek instructor. After leaving Oneonta he served as a lawyer, writing the Cortland city charter before his premature death in 1905, Ralston, *Cortland College...*, 11; David W. Brenner, *State University of New York College at Oneonta* (Charleston, S.C.: Arcadia, 2002), 11; *Manual for the Use of the Legislature of the State of New York, 1893* (Albany: Frank Rice, Secretary of State, 1893). Miss Fisher, *...the stone strength of the past...*, 70, bluntly asserts that James Milne was unrelated to William and John Milne, but there seem to be too many commonalities between the three to dismiss a possible relationship so curtly.

29. *Livingston Republican*, July 4, 1872; unidentified newspaper, chronologically-arranged ephemera boxes, College Archives. Inexplicably, Gloria Bennett was the only graduate not listed in the "Programme."

30. Fisher, *...the stone strength of the past...*, 66. Salaries for graduates in the 1930s—with three years of schooling versus two—were scarcely higher, if any.

31. *Livingston Republican*, July 11, 1872; *The Lamron*, April 6, 20, 2006; *Livingston County News*, June 29, 2006.

32. Rorbach, "History of the Geneseo State Normal School," 62, 63; Local Board Minutes, June 29, 1875.

33. Rorbach, "History of the Geneseo State Normal School," 64, 65.

34. Ibid., 68; Local Board Minutes, December 5, 1894, October 10, 1898, January 17, 1891, College Archives; *State Normal School Handbook of Geneseo Information for Entering Students, 1927-1928*, 16, College Archives.

35. *Livingston Republican*, July 3, 1913.

36. *Normalian*, June 20, 1903, 3.

37. Ibid., 1926; Fisher, *...the stone strength of the past...*, 69, 169; *Normalian*, June 20, 1903, 3. Fisher, *...the stone strength of the past...*, 169, lists Gamma Sigma and Philalethean, but Mau, *Brief History of State University Teachers College, Geneseo, New York*, 18, does not. When fraternities and sororities were forced to sever ties with nationals in 1954, Delta Kappa became Delta Kappa Tau, *The Lamron*, February 24, 1967. Sigma Tau Psi was formed on November 22, 1963.

38. *Normalian*, June 20, 1903.

39. Local Board Minutes, January 27, 1883, September 28, 1894, October 5, 1894, College Archives.

40. Local Board Minutes, July 16, 1872, November 1, 1889, October 8, 11, 1889, March 5, 1898, January 7, 1905, College Archives.

41. Local Board Minutes, April 4, 1891, October 6, 1899, College Archives; Robinson, "'A Freer Opportunity to Go to College...,'" 26.

42. Fausold, *A Draft History of the State University of New York*, p. 14; Local Board Minutes, April 4, 1891, June 18 and July, 1894, College Archives; Fisher, *...the stone strength of the past...*, 142.

43. Fisher, *...the stone strength of the past...*, 142.

44. Local Board Minutes, March 6, and December 22, 1898, and March 9, 1901, College Archives.

45. Robinson, "'A Freer Opportunity to Go to College...,'" 8, 9.

46. Ibid., 9, 10.

47. Ibid., 10-11.

48. Ogren, *The American State Normal School*, 136. Geneseo fares well in Ogren's very readable examination of Normal Schools.

49. Fisher, *...the stone strength of the past...*, 135, 144; James McNally, *Fact Book 2000* (Geneseo: SUNY Geneseo, 2001), 65; *State Normal School, Geneseo, N.Y. 1898* catalogue, 15.

50. *State Normal School, Geneseo, N.Y. 1898* catalogue, 12.

51. Fisher, *...the stone strength of the past...*, 145, 147.

52. *Normalian*, June 20, 1900, 4, 29, 31. The football teams' fortunes failed to improve, leading to the demise of football in 1916. A second attempt to field a competitive team in the 1920s was no more successful.

53. Ibid., June 10, 1901, 22.

54. *The Lamron*, October 18, 1940.

55. "Normal Life of Past Revealed," *The Lamron*, November 7, 1939; Fisher, *...the stone strength of the past...*, 149.

56. "50th Anniversary," *The Lamron*, Geneseo State Normal School (Geneseo, New York, 1921), 99.

57. Local Board Minutes, July 16 and November 5, 1904, February 10, 1906, College Archives; Fisher, *...the stone strength of the past...*, 172; Local Board Minutes, August 20, 1904, College Archives; "50th Anniversary" *The Lamron*, Geneseo State Normal School (Geneseo, New York, 1921), 60.

Chapter Three

1. Walter Lord, *The Good Years* (New York: Harper & Brothers, 1960), ix.

2. Lane, "Names Given to the Educational Facility at Geneseo;" Robinson, "'A Freer Opportunity to Go to College,'" 12.

3. Douglas R. Skopp, *Bright With Promise, From Normal and Training School to SUNY Plattsburgh, 1889–1989* (Norfolk/Virginia Beach, Virginia: The Donning Company, 1989), 43, 60.

4. Robinson, "'A Freer Opportunity to Go to College...,'" 15, 16.

5. Ibid., 30; Fisher, *...the stone strength of the past...*, 149–152. Nine years later the Board of Regents was named the governing body of the State Education Department, Fausold, *A Draft History of the State University of New York*, 15.

6. Local Board Minutes, July 16 and November 5, 1904, April 8, 15, 29, 1905, College Archives; Fisher, *…the stone strength of the past…*, 172, 181.

7. Fisher, *…the stone strength of the past…*, 167; "50th Anniversary," *The Lamron*, 25, states Sturges earned his doctorate in 1906.

8. Fisher, *…the stone strength of the past…*, 168; Local Board Minutes, February 13, 1909, April 26, 1913, College Archives. Examples of Bailey's ingenuity were "an electric bell mechanism" and a "push-button" apparatus for up to seven cameras he mounted at various bird feeding locations to photograph the birds. The "apex" of his ingenuity was a trailer, a "'small house on wheels'" that he towed behind his car. It served not only as a "photo blind," but also had a small library, oil-stove, writing desk and collapsible bed, Bob Marcotte, *Birds of the Genesee* (Franklin, Virginia: Q Publishing, 2005), 24. Actually, Bailey had two buildings named after him. The Blake dorms B–E originally bore the names of Bailey, Fraser, Blake, and Sturges, Fisher, *…the stone strength of the past…*, 204.

9. Local Board Minutes, July 8, 1905, College Archives; Fisher, *…the stone strength of the past…*, 170.

10. Fisher, *…the stone strength of the past…*, 170.

11. Ibid., 170, 168; Local Board Minutes, July 8, 1905, College Archives.

12. On May 11, 1907, the board had resolved to add a kindergarten program, Local Board Minutes; Fisher, *…the stone strength of the past…*, 176.

13. Local Board Minutes, July 7, 1908, College Archives.

14. Fisher, *…the stone strength of the past…*, 154, 155; Local Board Minutes, July 7, 1908, College Archives; *Livingston Republican*, January 19, 1905.

15. Ivan Kaldor, "New York. State University College of Arts and Science, School of Library and Information Science, Geneseo," *Encyclopedia of Library and Information Science*, vol. 19 (New York: Marcel Dekker, 1976), 390. The "50th Anniversary," *The Lamron*, 43, claims the date was 1906. See also Betty Minemier's "A Retrospective Look at the Library School and Its Dedicated Faculty," delivered at the SUNY Geneseo Alumni reunion, July 12, 1997, which is both entertaining and thoughtful.

16. Local Board Minutes, September 30, 1913, January 3, 1914, January 16, 1914, April 14, 1914, College Archives. The house, given by James W. Wadsworth, was formerly for the baseball team's use.

17. Local Board Minutes, November 2, 1912, May 16, 1918, College Archives; "50th Anniversary," *The Lamron*, 27.

18. Local Board Minutes, May 11, 1907, December 16, 1915, College Archives; Fisher, *…the stone strength of the past…*, 177, 178.

19. "50th Anniversary," *The Lamron*, 31, 37.

20. Local Board Minutes, August 24, 1908, College Archives.

21. Ibid., May 4, 1909; July 21, 1914, September 18, 1914.

22. *JEN-O-SEE* (Geneseo, New York: Yearbook of Geneseo Central School, 1933), 6; Fausold, *A Draft History of the State University of New York*, 21. The agreement between the two boards was modified in 1918 so that the Normal School board paid the Cobblestone School trustees the salaries for the five Cobblestone School teachers, with the money coming from the Town of Geneseo, Local Board Minutes, November 14, 1918, College Archives.

23. *Livingston Republican*, September 12, 1918.

24. Ibid., June 18, 1914.

25. Local Board Minutes, January 19, 1910, October 12, 1918, College Archives.

26. Ibid., August 2, 1910.

27. *Livingston Republican*, January 19, 1905. The Normal's typical opponents were Lima Seminary, Alfred University, R.B.I. and the University of Rochester, as well as Avon, Batavia, Dansville, and Warsaw high schools.

28. Geneseo State Normal School, Geneseo, N.Y. Secretary's Report, Class of 1914, pp. 11, 13, College Archives. The electric trolley ran to and from Rochester for many years.

29. *Livingston Republican*, March 24, 1916. In the 1970s and approaching ninety, Nearing was still espousing his views just as forcefully and clearly.

30. David W. Parish, "A Glance Backward," *Livingston County News*, November 2, 1995. Pliny Seymour, 1878, also recalls the Lawton (later Knox) and Cox (later Newton) houses, Seymour, "Geneseo As I Knew It," *The Lamron*, April 6, 1938.

31. David W. Parish, "A Glance Backward," *Livingston County News*, November 2, 1995; *The Lamron*, November 10, 1959; Tanya Marshall, "Where We Lived," College Archives, a project financed by an undergraduate research grant in 1995, when Ms. Marshall was a student at Geneseo.

32. Seymour, "Geneseo As I Knew It," *The Lamron*, April 6, 1938.

33. Minutes of the Meetings of the Faculty of the Geneseo State Normal School, 1907–1913 and 1924–1926, College Archives.

34. Skopp, *Bright With Promise…*, 64; Fisher, *… the stone strength of the past…*, 181. The "50th Anniversary," *The Lamron*, 71, reported 139 graduates and former students, including, apparently, some from the village who attended the Academic Department (secondary school), with seven cited for bravery. Fine Arts Chairman Bertha Lederer saved Greene's treasured puppets after his retirement.

35. Fisher, *…the stone strength of the past…*, 182.

36. "50th Anniversary," *The Lamron*, 10.

37. Ibid.

38. Local Board Minutes, September 13, 1921, College Archives.

39. *Livingston Republican*, June 27, 1922.

40. Local Board Minutes, January 12, 1922, December 22, 1921, July 28, 1922, College Archives.

41. Ibid. *The New York Times*, July 30, 1922, cited "friction" among faculty committee members and the need for restoring "authoritative rights to one person" as the reason for terminating Sturges's contract. The board did offer Sturges a "subordinate position as instructor," given Graves's aproval, Local Board Minutes, July 28, 1922.

42. Local Board Minutes, July 29, 1922, College Archives; *Livingston Republican*, January 21, 1932.

43. *Livingston Republican*, August 22, 1922; Fisher, *…the stone strength of the past…*, 173.

44. *Livingston Republican*, August 3, 1922; McNally, *Fact Book 2000*, 65. Subsequently, Sturges purchased a controlling interest in the Magee Garage, the Ford dealership on Bank Street, before opening a teachers' agency November 1, 1923. Bucke, who was ordained a Methodist minister shortly after being terminated, was twice honored, once by village friends and another time by the Geneseo Grange. Shortly thereafter he became superintendent of the Collingswood, New Jersey schools "at a substantial increase in salary," but that proved unsuccessful, according to Miss Fisher, though she gave no explanation, *The Lamron*, October 1923, December 1922; *Livingston Republican*, September 7, October 26 and November 30, 1922; Fisher, *…the stone strength of the past…*, 182.

45. Obituary in *The Lamron*, September 30, 1941. In fact, Bucke's credentials were superior to those of his colleagues. He received his bachelor's degree from Dickinson College in 1895 and his first doctorate from Ohio's Wooster College, which was a university until 1915. His subsequent doctorate was under the guidance of eminent psychologist G. Stanley Hall at Clark University in Massachusetts. However, that his subsequent employment after leaving Geneseo was terminated after only a year suggests something was awry. Interestingly, his son, thirty-nine-year-old Private W. Fowler Bucke, Jr., who died December 1, 1944 in New Guinea, was remembered at a memorial service at Central Presbyterian Church on December 21, and is listed on the memorial to fallen soldiers in the Geneseo village park, courtesy Geneseo Town and Village Historian David W. Parish.

46. Minutes of the Meetings of the Faculty of the Geneseo State Normal School, January 18, 1932, College Archives; *The Lamron*, October 20 and November 3, 1931.

47. "50th Anniversary," *The Lamron*, 15, 92.

48. Former student and faculty member Frank E. Welles includes John Milne among the first faculty, making fourteen, but the Local Board Minutes indicate John Milne was not hired until July 16, 1872.

49. The 1916 yearbook, *The Periscope*, quoted in "50th Anniversary," *The Lamron*, 92, 43.

Chapter Four

1. Local Board Minutes, August 22, 1922, College Archives; *Livingston Republican*, September 7, 1922, quoting the *Dansville Express*.

2. Ibid., September 14, 1922. Binghamton was involved in another book censorship issue later over the adoption of Progressive Harold Rugg's social studies textbooks.

3. *Livingston Republican*, November 23, 1922; Local Board Minutes, November 20, 1922, College Archives; *The Lamron*, October 1922; Fisher, *…the stone strength of the past…*, 184.

4. *Livingston Republican*, October 5, 1922.

5. Ibid.; Local Board Minutes, June 23 and 12, 1925, College Archives offer additional reasons, including Holcomb's statement to the board that the faculty had recommended Harper's dismissal.

6. Ibid., October 3, 1922; *The Lamron*, October 1922.

7. *The Lamron*, October 1925, 7; Fisher, *…the stone strength of the past…*, 185.

8. Rochester *Democrat & Chronicle*, July 21, 1925; Rochester *Journal & Post Express*, July 22, 1925; *The Rochester Herald*, July 22, 1925; *New York World*, July 21, 1925; unidentified Rochester paper, July 22, 1925; *The Rochester Herald*, July 23, 1925; *New York Times*, July 21, 1925, 2; Rochester *Times-Union*, July 22, 1925, Winfield Holcomb Papers, College Archives. An unidentified national paper, November 11, 1925, viewed the dismissals as a serious breach of academic freedom, an example of "intolerance" for different opinions.

9. Rochester *Journal and Post Express*, July 22, 1925, College Archives; Henry B. Smith letter to Commissioner F. P. Graves, April 17, 1925, Winfield Holcomb Papers, College Archives.

10. *The Lamron*, October 28, and November 10, 1936, and October 18, 1940.

11. Rochester *Times-Union*, July 22 and 26, 1925. McNally, *Fact Book 2000*, 65, shows 381 students.

12. Winfield Holcomb letter to Dr. George M. Wiley, June 22, 1925, and a very telling unidentified poem, Winfield Holcomb Papers, College Archives.

13. *Livingston Republican*, July 23 and 30, 1925.

14. *New York Times*, July 22, 1925, 19.

15. Fisher, *...the stone strength of the past...*, 196; Clayton C. Mau, *Brief History of the State University Teachers College, Geneseo, New York*, 1954 (updated by Mau in 1956 and reissued by James McNally, June 2001).

16. *The Lamron*, October 25, 1925.

17. *State Normal School, Geneseo, New York Catalog, 1925–1926* (Albany: J. B. Lyon Company, 1925), 17.

18. *State Normal School, Geneseo, New York Catalog, 1926–1927*, 17.

19. *The Lamron*, May 1922. The Colony, established in 1892 and named for Oscar Craig, a Rochesterian and president of the State Board of Charities, was the only institution in the United States responsible for the care of epileptics and lasted until the late 1900s. The school itself was created by the state legislature at the urging of Mrs. Charlotte Glenny of Buffalo, interview of Dr. Gladys Rhodes by Martin Fausold and Wayne Mahood, April 7, 1988. The name Sonyea is of Native American origin, derived either from "Captain Snow, Sonyeawa, or a word meaning 'burning spring' or 'hot valley,'" Ren Vasiliev, *From Abbotts to Zurich, New York State Placenames* (Syracuse: Syracuse University Press, 2004), 211.

20. Interview of Dr. Gladys Rhodes by Martin L. Fausold and Wayne Mahood, April 7, 1988; *State Normal School, Geneseo, New York Circular of General Information and Courses of Study, 1922-1923*, 7; interview of Dr. Gladys Rhodes by Martin Fausold and Wayne Mahood.

21. Interview of Dr. Gladys Rhodes by Martin L. Fausold and Wayne Mahood, April 7, 1988.

22. Ibid.

23. Interviews of Dr. Winfield Holcomb and Dean Anne Blake, *The Lamron*, March 27, 1934; Minutes of the Meetings of the Faculty of the Geneseo State Normal School, 1924–1926, June 5, 1924, and 1931–1935, November 16, 1932, College Archives.

24. Minutes of the Faculty of the Geneseo State Normal School, 1924–1926, June 5, 1924.

25. Ibid., April 7, 1925; *The Lamron*, May 15, 1928. *The Lamron* became a bi-weekly November 10, 1925.

26. *The Lamron*, October 11, 1927.

27. Interviews of Dr. Winfield Holcomb and Dean Anne Blake, *The Lamron*, March 27, 1934. Brockport was the first Normal School to offer rural education courses in 1911–1912, Robinson, "'A Freer Opportunity to Go to College...,'" 42.

28. Skopp, *Bright With Promise...*, 62.

29. *The Lamron*, October 11, 1927, November 10, 24, 1925; Judith Bushnell's "Preliminary Chronology...."

30. Local Board Minutes, June 4, May 18, 1926 and March 4, 1923, College Archives.

31. *The Lamron*, May, October and November 1923, May 1922. Ralston, *Cortland College*, 271, claims "Play Days," originated at the University of Washington, had existed at Cortland since 1929 to encourage "the fair sex of the Normal Schools to participate in a greater number of athletic activities" untainted by the "evils of varsity athletics."

32. *The Lamron*, November 24, 1925.

33. Local Board Minutes, October 13, 1923, April 6, 1925, College Archives.

34. Ibid., October 13, 1926; March 7, 1927; November 11, 1934.

35. *The Lamron*, November 1923.

36. *Minutes of the Board of Education, Geneseo School District #5*, May 11, 1929, Livingston County Historian; Jean Trescott, "A History of Education in the Town of Geneseo," unpublished paper for a graduate class at SUNY Geneseo. This well-researched paper has proved quite helpful. It should be added that Fred Quirk's father, Charles, had been a laborer on the original buildings and sent all five of his sons to the Normal School, Fisher, *...the stone strength of the past...*, 38.

37. Fisher, *...the stone strength of the past...*, 180; Local Board Minutes, December 29, 1933, College Archives.

38. Local Board Minutes, December 29, 1933, College Archives; "Statement of Developments at the State Normal School at Geneseo School Year 1934–35," Local Board Minutes, College Archives. Shortly after the newer Holcomb School was opened in 1969 the older building was renamed for Principal Welles.

39. Comments from former students at the Association for the Preservation of Geneseo meeting, October 19, 2005.

40. Fisher, *...the stone strength of the past...*, 177. An example of the seeming anomaly is the 2005 New York Court of Appeals case brought under New York State's Freedom of Information Law asking Cornell administrators to reveal information about genetically modified crop research. The school maintained that it is "a private college not subject to the law." The issue revolved around Cornell's "hybrid status," specifically its operation of the Experiment Station at Geneva, one of the state's statutory colleges, where crop research is conducted. Reportedly, Cornell received "more than $100 million annually from the state Legislature" as of 2005, Rochester *Democrat & Chronicle*, January 15, 2005.

41. *New York Times*, July 22, 1925, p. 12; *The Lamron*, October 20, 1931.

42. "The Senator" was recommended by the board on December 27, 1926, appointed by the commissioner on January 17, 1927 and elected board president January 31, 1927, Local Board Minutes, December 27, 1926, January 31, 1927, College Archives. Failing re-election to the U.S. Senate in 1926, Wadsworth retired from public life for a time, then was elected Congressman, as his father, "the Boss," had been, Martin L. Fausold, *James W. Wadsworth, Jr.: The Gentleman From New York* (Syracuse, New York: Syracuse University Press, 1975), 199, 231.

43. Fisher, *...the stone strength of the past...*, 177.

44. *The Lamron*, March 27, 1934.

45. Ibid. Worse, possibly, Blakes D and E are no more, having fallen to the wrecking ball in 2004 during construction of the new Integrated Science building.

46. Local Board Minutes, April 10, 17, 22, and May 27, 1934, College Archives.

Chapter Five

1. Ralston, *Cortland College...*, 92; *Draft State Normal School, Geneseo, New York Catalog, 1939-1940* and official copy 1940-1941; McNally, *Fact Book 2000*, 65.

2. Phone call to Harrison Phillips, March 24, 2005. Phillips's record at Geneseo was an enviable one. One of the "Prominent Seniors" in the 1942 *Normalian*, he seems to have been into everything as an undergraduate. His yearbook listings included Cothurnus four years, Interfraternity Council president, Men's Glee Club and Mixed Choir, co-president of Alpha Sigma Epsilon fraternity, and baseball and basketball letterman. Sixty-two freshmen (twenty-eight percent of the class) earned part of their schooling by working. Those earning both board and room worked thirty hours a week, while those paying for their board alone worked twenty hours a week.

3. *The Lamron*, May 29, 1934.

4. Information about Dr. Welles, including his resume, was obtained from papers in the College Archives, from *The Lamron*, May 29, 1934 and February 21, 1946, from "Faculty 1871-1957," and from a letter to Geneseo Archivist William Lane, May 5, 1975 from the Columbia Teachers College Reference Librarian, College Archives.

5. Interviews of faculty who served under Welles. Undated letter from Harrison Phillips, likely written April 1, 2005.

6. The *Livingston Republican*, October 1, 1936. The listing "Faculty 1871–1957" in the College Archives, which Miss Brown prepared, cites her as having begun in 1912, while Miss Fisher, ...*stone strength of the past...*, 184, claims she began in 1922, and the first *Normalian* to list her as secretary is 1921; *The Lamron*, May 15, 1934. Brown belatedly received the College's Distinguished Service Award in 1969.

7. "New Positions, 1937–1938," President James B. Welles Papers, College Archives. The nearest ratio was Oswego's at 269:1. The number of students on which the ratio was based, 666, does not jibe with the "Statement of Developments at the State Normal School at Geneseo School Year 1934–1935," which claims an enrollment of 703, College Archives.

8. "New Positions, 1937–1938," President James B. Welles Papers, College Archives. Refer back to Chapter Four's discussion of the need for new boilers.

9. *Livingston Republican*, August 15, 1935; Rochester *Democrat & Chronicle*, August 19, 1935; "1877–In the Tower–1931," *The Lamron*, February 20, 1935.

10. *The Lamron*, February 8, 1939.

11. Ibid., February 6, 1935, December 10, 1943.

12. Skopp, *Bright With Promise...*, 85, 86.

13. Ibid., 86, 88. Given an enrollment of 666 and excluding Geneseo's campus school, the ratio of students to faculty was roughly 24:1. Assuming the 703 enrollment figure, also cited, the ratio would have been 25:1.

14. Interview of Dr. Robert Redden by Martin L. Fausold, no date.

15. *The Lamron*, September 16, 1936, September 29, 1937.

16. Ibid.; April 28, 1937.

17. Interviews of Drs. Paul Neureiter and Gladys Rhodes by Martin L. Fausold and Wayne Mahood, March 2 and April 7, 1988; Minutes of the Local Board of Visitors, June 16, 1936, College Archives.

18. *The Lamron*, October 10, 1939.

19. Interviews of Drs. Paul Neureiter and Gladys Rhodes by Martin L. Fausold and Wayne Mahood, March 2 and April 7, 1988.

20. "New Applicants to Geneseo State Normal School," College Archives, but *The Lamron*, September 25, 1934 claims only 238 of 420 applicants were accepted. The issue is confounded by the fact that eighty of the applicants had advanced credit and fourteen were college graduates; *The Lamron*, September 16, 1936; Scrapbook of Helen (Williams) Rogers, College Archives.

21. It would be interesting to determine the students' socioeconomic statuses. This might throw light on some of the customs, as well as educational practices of Geneseo as a Normal School. A study might also offer more information about why students attended this and other Normal Schools, given the presumption that many wanted a relatively cheap (tuition-free) education, not a teaching career.

22. *The Lamron*, December 3, 1940, September 17, 1941; Placement Bureau Record, Frederick B. Holcomb, August 1937, January, June and August 1938.

23. Recall of Hyde on January 12, 2005, by Cindy Schmidt, whose father, Joseph Schmidt, too had a Dansville school building named for him.

24. *The Lamron*, April 28 and 14, 1937, February 27, 1940.

25. Ibid., September 25, 1934, September 30, 1936, April 4, 1939, September 25, 1935, September 17, 1941. Centers were established in Canandaigua, Perry, LeRoy, Mt. Morris, Oakfield, Wellsville, Rochester, Dansville, Penn Yan and Avon, Ibid., April 31, 1935.

26. Ibid., January 16, 1941; Skopp, *Bright With Promise...*, 130; *State Normal School, Geneseo, NY Catalog, 1940-1941*. Ohio State would prove to be a magnet for Geneseo faculty seeking doctorates, possibly because Dr. Herman Behrens, Geneseo's Director of Training, was an Ohio State graduate.

27. *The Lamron*, September 25, 1934, September 15, 1937; November 10, 1936, May 20, 1941; Fisher, ...*the stone strength of the past...*, 201, 194.

28. Letter from Harrison Phillips, no date, but likely April 1, 2005.

29. *The Lamron*, March 6, 1935.

30. Ibid., February 8, 1939; Robinson, "'A Freer Opportunity to Go to College...,'" 51.

31. *The Lamron*, December 18, 1934; Fisher, ...*the stone strength of the past...*, 191, 192.

32. *The Lamron*, October 20, 1939; Harrison Phillips's scrapbook, College Archives.

33. Local Board Minutes, February 6, 1939 and January 1940, College Archives; Skopp, *Bright With Promise...*, 88; "Comparative Statement, Personal Service," President James B. Welles Papers, College Archives.

The rank of associate first appears in President Herbert G. Espy's 1950 Annual Report, but not in college catalogs until 1955–1956. So, instructor was equivalent to today's assistant.

34. Skopp, *Bright With Promise...*, 101, 102.

35. Fisher, ...*the stone strength of the past...*, 194; Local Board Minutes January 27, 1942. The first extant letterhead bearing the new title was June 1943.

36. *The Lamron*, April 9, 1940. Of course, *The Lamron* did not change its title, implicitly recognizing Geneseo's Normal School past.

37. Ibid., March 26, 1943.

38. McNally, *Fact Book, 2000*, 84; *The Lamron*, February 22, 1930. Alumni associations had long existed, especially the large New York City contingent, but they were informal groups formed by like-minded graduates living near one another.

39. *The Lamron*, September 25, 1934, December 14, 1938.

40. *The Lamron*, September 25, 1934 and September 16, 1936; Scrapbook of Helen (Williams) Rogers, College Archives; *Livingston Republican*, December 9, 1937; *The Lamron*, November 23, 1937.

41. Scrapbook of Helen (Williams) Rogers, College Archives; *The Lamron*, October 12, 1938.

42. *The Lamron*, April 4, 1939. Miss Mitchell's sister, Betty Mitchell Minemier, '61, also made her mark at Geneseo, including serving many years on the College Council and Alumni Association.

43. President James B. Welles Papers, College Archives.

44. *The Lamron*, February 25, 1938; October 28, 1936. Later Welch was voted into the College's sports Hall of Fame and Geneseo Central School's Hall of Fame.

45. Ibid., February 14, 1941 and February 12, 1943.

46. Ibid., November 11, 1941.

47. *Student Handbook, State Normal School, Geneseo, N.Y. 1931–1932, 1939–1942*.

48. *The Lamron*, April 4, 1939, October 20, 1939.

49. Richard B. Morris and Jeffrey B. Morris, *Encyclopedia of American History* (New York: Harper & Row Publishers, 1976), 432, 436; *The Lamron*, October 1, 1940.

50. *The Lamron*, October 19, 1942. The 1945 *Oh Ha Daih*, 89, identified 266 Geneseo students and graduates on its "World War II Honor Roll," while the 1946 *Oh Ha Daih*, 25, names 285. WAACs was the acronym for Woman's Army Auxiliary Corps, while WAVES (Women Appointed for Voluntary Emergency Service) was the Navy equivalent.

51. *The Lamron*, September 17, 1941, January 16, 1942, September 24, 1943.

52. *Livingston Republican*, August 3, 1944; *The Lamron*, September 15, 1944; 1939 *Normalian*; Francis A. O'Brien, *Battling for Saipan* (New York: Presidio, 2003), 319. Other accounts of Geneseo alumni who served in the military are drawn from various issues of *The Lamron* and *Livingston Republican*.

53. Phone call with Harrison Phillips, March 24, 2005.

54. McNally, *Fact Book 2000*, 65. The Local Board of Visitors claims 714 students in the 1944–1945 school year, but that includes 255 students in the Holcomb School and 109 at the Craig Colony School, Local Board Minutes, September 9, 1945. Geneseo's enrollment would not exceed the pre-war peak enrollment until the 1950–1951 school year (774), McNally, *Fact Book 2000*, 65. The naval and Army Air Corps programs are mentioned in *The Lamron*, March 31, 1942 and October 30, 1942, and Fisher, ...*the stone strength of the past...*, 195.

55. Fisher, ...*the stone strength of the past...*, 195; *The Lamron*, November 20, 1942.

56. *The Lamron*, December 11, 1942.

57. Ibid., November 20, 1942, November 9,1938, March 26, 1943. The yearbook has borne different titles and formats over the years, with *Oh Ha Daih*, the longest lasting (from 1943–2000, when it was discontinued). The first, *The Normalian*, basically a commencement issue, appeared in 1899 and 1900. The next was *Echoes From the Geneseo Normal*, June 1905 and 1906. The *Arista* was the June 1908 yearbook. The *Pivot*, which actually looked like a yearbook, was published in 1915, followed by *The Periscope* in 1916 and 1917. The *Normalian* ran from 1917 through 1942, when *Oh Ha Daih* replaced it, Fred Bright, "Listing of Geneseo Yearbooks," unpublished; Milne Library online catalog.

58. *Livingston County Leader*, May 30, 1945; *Livingston Republican*, May 31, 1945; George Mazuzan and Nancy Walker, "Restricted Areas: German Prisoner-of-War Camps in Western New York, 1944–1946," *New York*

History, 59, no. 1 (1978): 67-71; Interview of Dr. Paul Neureiter, March 2, 1988; *The Lamron*, November 9, 1984; Ted Bondi's recall.

59. "Japs Invade Hunts Corners,"*Livingston Republican*, February 26, 1942; Fisher, *...the stone strength of the past...*, 195.

60. Local Board Minutes, June 15, 1943, College Archives; Interview of Dr. Gladys Rhodes by Martin L. Fausold and Wayne Mahood, April 7, 1988.

61. Skopp, *Bright With Promise...*, 106; Fausold, *A Draft History of the State University of New York*, 29.

62. Various issues of *The Lamron*.

63. *The Lamron*, May 25, 1943, September 15, 1944, May 1, 1944; Skopp, *Bright With Promise...*, 108.

64. Local Board Minutes, April 29, 1944, College Archives; Register of Graduates, College Archives; *Livingston Republican*, July 2, 1925; Local Board Minutes, September 30, 1944, College Archives.

65. Local Board Minutes, September 30, 1944, College Archives. Reasons for first denying Geneseo's request were not revealed, but other denials were based on community objections to dorm construction. Ibid., June 9, 1945, October 6, 1945.

66. "Report of the President on Recruitment," Local Board Minutes, June 9, 1945, College Archives.

67. Letter to Geneseo's Local Board of Visitors, February 8, 1946.

Chapter Six

1. Handwritten informal report on Executive Committee meeting of the Local Board of Visitors, June 9, 1945, President James B. Welles Papers, College Archives.

2. *New York State Education*, October 1946, 70, College Archives; Jacques Cattell & E. E. Ross, *Leaders in Education*, 3rd ed. (Lancaster, Pennsylvania: The Science Press, 1948).

3. "President's Report, State University of New York State Teachers College, Geneseo, New York, 1949," College Archives.

4. Interview of Dr. Charles Foster, retired SUNY Vice Chancellor for Business, by Dr. Martin L. Fausold; *The Lamron*, October 18, 1946; Fisher, *...the stone strength of the past...*, 207; Keller, "What We Were Like and How We Have Changed," *Geneseo Compass*, October 5, 1973.

5. *The Lamron*, October 1, 1948; Interview of Barbara Myers Scoville, October 30, 2004; phone call to Dr. Wilbur Wright, October 2004. Wright's memories of the time are extraordinary.

6. Interview of Barbara Myers Scoville, October 30, 2004; Letter from Mrs. Elizabeth Horek Anderson, October 28, 2004.

7. Fisher, *...the stone strength of the past...*, 204; *The Lamron*, October 18, 1946. Mrs. Anderson purchased the commemorative brick and replied to our letter asking about Valley Hall, which led to contact with Barbara Myers Scoville, one of the occupants of Room 3 in 1948. During the school year 1948–1949 Mrs. Anderson was an advisor to Doris Collins Griffith, Joanna Guest Bowker, Asunta Manti, Barbara Myers Scoville, Marcia Schwartz Waxler, Joyce Sweet Leonard, and Kate Webster Scolley. At least through 2004 Mrs. Anderson and five of the dwellers met regularly and stayed in touch by e-mail, according to Barbara Myers Scoville in an interview, October 30, 2004.

8. Conversation with Tom and Brenda Conlon, '52; Scrapbook of Lois Ann Klehamer, College Archives.

9. Interview of Dr. Walter Harding by "Ms. Baker," Fausold SUNY Oral History Project, November 17, 1989. Over forty percent of the students came from Livingston, Monroe, and Steuben counties, which might support Harding's assessment of the students' provincialism, but their mid-80s high school averages are hardly shabby, "Annual Report, State University Teachers College, Geneseo, New York, 1953–54," 9, 7, 5.

10. Letter to President Espy from Dr. Cooper, December 24, 1946, Espy Papers, College Archives.

11. Letter to Dr. Cooper from President Espy, January 2, 1947, Espy Papers, College Archives.

12. *New York Times*, January 10, 1946; Richard Norton Smith, *Thomas Dewey and His Times* (New York: Touchstone, 1982), 472–473; Jeffrey Stonecash, "Politics and the Development of SUNY," in Martin L. Fausold, *Research Materials, Oral SUNY History Project* (unpublished), 4. Also it may well be that Dewey was being pressured to open schools to Jewish applicants who claimed discrimination by private colleges and universities, including Columbia.

13. Fausold, *A Draft History of the State University of New York*, 29; "The Master Plan (Two-Year Colleges and Four-Year Colleges)," (Albany: State University of New York, June 1950), 9.

14. *Report of the New York State Temporary Commission on the Need for a State University* (Albany: Williams Press, 1948); Interview of Dr. Charles Foster by Dr. Martin L. Fausold.

15. Fausold, *A Draft History of the State University of New York*, 34–37; Robert W. Spencer, "Origins and Development State University of New York," n.d., 17; Interview of Dr. Charles Foster by Dr. Martin L. Fausold. Taking over and supporting two expensive, privately run medical schools (at Syracuse, which became Upstate, and Long Island's College of Medicine, later Downstate) apparently was a precondition for approving SUNY. The "Professional Colleges" included the eleven teachers colleges, two medical schools, the agriculture, home economics, industrial and labor relations and veterinary schools at Cornell, the ceramics college at Alfred, the forestry college at Syracuse, and the Maritime College at Fort Schuyler outside New York City.

16. Spencer, "Origins and Development State University of New York," 17.

17. "Memorandum in Relation to Improvement of Conditions in the State Teachers Colleges," no date, but likely April 1947 from Hermann Cooper, Presidents' Papers, College Archives. Another recommendation was that no one over forty-five could be hired as a faculty member nor serve past sixty-five. Students were required to live in college residence halls (the administration building or Valley Hall) or approved off-campus housing, *Teachers College at Geneseo, New York General Catalogue, 1952–1953*, 15.

18. Local Board Minutes, September 24, 1954, College Archives. Less than half the students (200) lived in campus residence halls, "Annual Report, State University Teachers College, 1953–54," 18; *The Lamron*, September 12, 1947.

19. "Annual Report, State University Teachers College, 1950–1951, Geneseo, New York," President Espy's Papers, College Archives; *The Lamron*, September 15, 1944. Median incomes of college faculty and administrators in the United States in 1950 were the lowest of those with advanced degrees or training, including doctors, lawyers and judges, dentists, architects and civil engineers, Sanford Labovitz, "The Assignment of Numbers to Rank Order Categories," *The American Sociological Review*, 35 (1970), 151–524. They even ranked below locomotive engineers. Data were derived from *United States Census of Population, 1950, Occupational Characteristics*.

20. "Annual Report, State University Teachers College, 1950–1951, Geneseo, New York," President Espy's Papers, College Archives; "Fall Enrollment Trends 1943–1953," prepared by Dr. Wilbur Wright, Presidents' Papers, College Archives. Reports on enrollment tend to differ depending on the reporter and purpose.

21. *The Lamron*, February 18, 1949, February 2, 1952, April 28, 1950, May 12, 1950, May 11, 1951, May 21, 1951.

22. Ibid., October 16, 1950, June 1, 1951.

23. Minutes of the Local Board, June 2, 1951, College Archives; Wilbur Harold Wright, "Homecoming: Memories of Geneseo 1949–1977," prepared April 28, 1998, College Archives; *The Lamron*, January 23, 1948. Declining veteran enrollments played havoc with colleges and universities across the nation, *New York Times*, November 27, 1950, College Archives. Enrollment of veterans had declined from one in two students in 1948–1949 to one in four in 1950–1951. However, Buffalo State, Oswego and Cortland saw increases.

24. Erwin's influence is cited by James S. Fleming, *Window on Congress: A Congressional Biography of Barber B. Conable, Jr.* (Rochester, New York: University of Rochester Press, 2004), 44. The story about Erwin's insistence on money for Geneseo's gymnasium is attributed to SUNY Trustee James Warren in an interview of Warren by Dr. Martin L. Fausold, November 22, 1988.

25. *The Lamron*, October 28, 1957, *Livingston Republican*, October 31, 1957. The bond issue was promoted by the College Council, Alumni Council, and College Steering Committee. Almost fifty years later Hepler vividly remembers frantic efforts to prepare and post the "big signs,"

communication to the Geneseo History Committee, 2005.

26. *The Lamron*, November 8, 1957; *Livingston Republican*, November 14, 1957.

27. *The Lamron*, October 6, 1951; Minutes of the Local Board, 1952, College Archives; Martin L. Fausold, *The Gentleman From New York* (Syracuse, New York: Syracuse University Press, 1975), 410. Indicating the esteem with which James Wadsworth, Jr. was held, the principal speaker at the dinner was General George Marshall, Chief of Staff, U.S. Army, Secretary of State and Secretary of Defense.

28. Letter to Dr. Hermann Cooper from Dr. Herbert Espy, January 11, 1947, Espy Papers, College Archives.

29. Skopp, *Bright With Promise*..., 128. The law was subsequently upheld by the U.S. Supreme Court in *Adler v. Board of Education* 342 U.S. 485 (1952), but fifteen years later was struck down in *Keyishian v. Board of Regents of the University of New York* 385 U.S. 589 (1967). Times and the Court had changed.

30. *The Lamron*, October 6, 1950; Interview of Dr. Walter Harding, November 17, 1989. Fisher's field jacket is displayed in the Livingston County Historical Society Museum in Geneseo.

31. *The Lamron*, October 20, 1950, November 12, 1954. Cothurnus later fell victim to student protests over faculty control, which led to the creation of "Vegetable Soup."

32. Judith Bushnell's "Preliminary Chronology of SUNY Geneseo History." Dr. Greene's retirement was understandably celebrated. After all, he had taught a wide variety of courses, including oral English and industrial arts—clearly out of his biology specialty—for thirty-eight years.

33. Fisher, *...the stone strength of the past...*, 204; B. J. Keller, "What We Were Like and How We Have Changed," *The Geneseo Compass*, October 5, 1973; *The Lamron*, October 1, 1948.

34. The College Facilities office. "Basic BCI, 12/27/2004," lists Blakes A, B, and C as "occupied" July 1951, which may indicate official approval. Initially the residence halls were simply labeled B–E. September 1951 they were rechristened Blake, Bailey, Fraser, and Sturges. Still later, as faculty offices, they reverted to "Blakes B–E," *The Lamron*, September 14, 1951. An alternate version is that the residence halls were renamed in 1965 when the new library was dedicated to Principals William and John Milne. The library, built in 1955, was renamed the Bertha Paine Fraser Library, and the former administration building was named for Principal James Sturges. Bailey became a men's dorm in 1958, *The Lamron*, March 11, 1958.

35. *The Lamron*, April 28, 1950.

36. Special edition of *The Lamron*, sometime after March 2, 1951; *Livingston County Leader*, May 24, 1951; Dr. Wilbur H. Wright, "Homecoming: Memories of Geneseo—1949–1977," College Archives.

37. Keller, "What We Were Like...," *Geneseo Compass*, October 5, 1973.

38. Scrapbook of Barbara Bishop, College Archives; Interviews of Dr. Walter Harding by "Ms. Baker," Fausold SUNY Oral History Project, November 17, 1989, and of Dr. Paul Neureiter by Dr. Martin L. Fausold and Wayne Mahood, March 2, 1988. Fisher, *...the stone strength of the past...*, 206, claims Espy left at the end of the 1951–1952 school year. *The Lamron*, December 5, 1952, announced Espy's departure date as December 12, 1952, relying on Chancellor William Carlson's November 21, 1952 announcement. "Annual Report, State University Teachers College, Geneseo, New York, 1953–54," 1, states that Dr. Espy resigned as president in January 1953. Further confusing the issue, Maine's website alternately lists Espy's term as commissioner of education as 1952–1955 and 1953–1956, www.state.me.us/education/150yrs.... Correspondence in the Presidents' Papers supports the claim of a December 1952 departure.

39. *The Lamron*, September 14, 1951; *New York Times*, July 19, 1951. Freeman returned to Christian College as president in January 1957, *The Lamron*, December 7, 1956. Kuhl was remembered by an $80,485 bequest to the Geneseo Foundation from her sister's estate, *Geneseo Scene* (Winter 1998), 4.

40. *The Lamron*, October 30, 1953; Minutes of the Local Board, May 23, 1952; Senate Bill 1670, passed April 6, 1953, Presidents' Papers, College Archives; *New York Times*, July 23, 1958. Old-timers could not help but remark on Quirk's appointment by Democratic Governor Averell Harriman in this strongly Republican conclave. Quirk was reappointed in February 1967, effective July 1, for nine more years, *Livingston Republican*, February 2, 1967.

41. *The Lamron*, September 17, 1954; *New York Times*, July 16, 1991; *Faculty Bulletin*, State University College at Geneseo, December 3,

1962. Recognized early, Moench spoke to the New York City Alumni Association after his graduation from Cortland Normal School in 1916 as "a representative of the student body," Ralston, *Cortland College...*, 89, 90. In 1968, he received Cortland College Alumni Association's Distinguished Achievement Award, www.ccclub.net/memberDetail.asp?hofid=86.

42. Moench was recognized by Geneseo in 1989 when the College's outdoor track was named for him.

43. Fisher, *...the stone strength of the past...*, 207; Interview of Ms. Cottone, initiated by Curriculum Librarian Barbara Clarke, August 9, 2005; *Livingston Republican*, May 28, 1970; President MacVittie's commencement talk in 1997, delivered by his son, Robert Jr. '69; *Geneseo Compass*, February 8, 1999.

44. Interview of Theodora Greenman by James McNally and Wayne Mahood, January 25, 2005. Miss Greenman, who had worked for Dr. Moench at Cortland and would serve him and Dr. MacVittie for over two dozen years, knew Moench both as a boss and family friend.

45. Beginning in June 1955, his second year, Dr. Moench and his wife moved into what now is commonly referred to as "the president's house" at 15 Main Street, which was purchased from Steve and Ruth Shepard, a Geneseo graduate and a Holcomb teacher respectively, *The Lamron*, May 20, 1955; Deeds, Livingston County.

46. *The Lamron*, October 30, 1953, "Annual Report, State Teachers College, Geneseo, New York, 1953–54" by acting president Freeman, announcing the "dissolution of relations with Craig Colony." The listing of buildings was obtained by committee member Hepler from the Facilities Office. Enrollment data are from James McNally, *Fact Book 2000*, 65. Wadsworth Auditorium was completed pretty much on time, but Milne Library (later named Fraser), was delayed by a carpenter's strike, Judith Bushnell's "Preliminary Chronology of SUNY Geneseo History."

47. *The Lamron*, October 12, 1954, May 4 and February 10, 1956.

48. Ibid., April 12, 1957 and November 19, 1956. Whether the opportunity to opt for Social Security, which first became available to New York State college and public school faculty beginning in 1957, was an inducement is unknown, ibid., October 11, 1957. Employees paid 2.25 percent of the first $4,200 of salary, which the State matched.

49. Ibid., September 14, 1956, *Geneseo Scene*, June 2005. The Walter Harding Lecture recognizes Harding, who died in 1996. His unparalleled 15,000-item Thoreau collection and diaries were donated to the Thoreau Institute Library, www.walden.org/institute/Collections/Harding/Harding.htm. Thanks to Judith Bushnell for this information and website.

50. *The Lamron*, February 10, 1956, December 12, 1947.

51. Ibid., May 4, 1956 and September 22, 1959. After graduating from Geneseo Normal School in 1921, and bowing to parental wishes, Dr. Delehanty taught two years before beginning medical school, Fisher, *...the stone strength of the past...*, 215.

52. Interview of Dr. Harry Porter by Wayne Mahood, March 27, 1989; Fisher, *...the stone strength of the past...*, 215–216; *The Lamron*, September 16, 1955, February 24, 1959, September 22, 1959.

53. *The Lamron*, January 13, 1959; Betty Mitchell Minemier, "A Retrospective Look at the Library School and Its Dedicated Faculty," Remarks delivered as part of the SUNY Geneseo alumni reunion, July 12, 1997.

54. *The Lamron*, September 16, 1955; Interview of Dr. Stanley Rutherford, June 11, 2005; *The Lamron*, October 16, 1953 and February 24, 1959; John Paul, "A Brief Personalized Anecdotal History of the Department of Speech Pathology and Audiology, State University of New York College of Arts & Science at Geneseo, May 1982," 3, 4, 6, 10, College Archives.

55. Interview of Charles Foster by Martin L. Fausold.

56. *The Lamron*, December 10, 1954, November 2, 1956, May 5, 1959; March 4, 1961; Marquis *Who's Who on the Web*; Research eLert Issue no. 3, June 2005.

57. www.escondidosunriserotary.org/newsletters/Octpober [sic] %2016-2003.pdf.

58. *The Lamron*, September 14, 1956.

59. Ibid., September 28, 1956.

60. Ibid., November 18, 1955, January 13, 1959.

61. Ibid., April 29, October 4, 1958, September 14, October 19, 1956, May 10, 1957, November 25, May 13, September 23, 1958, February 4, 1959.

62. Letter from Gordon Schiller, '63, recalling his time at Geneseo.

63. Memorandum from James G. Eberhardt to the "Library Staff and Patrons," Presidents' Papers, College Archives; "This week in Geneseo history," *The Lamron*, March 9, 2006; "Memories at SUNY Geneseo, Paul H. Hepler 1956-2001," unpublished ms.

64. *The Lamron*, December 7, 1956, March 20, 1959, November 11, 1960. While 465 students claimed to be Republicans, 247 were Democrats, and 1 preferred Alfred E. Neuman, the hero of *Mad* magazine.

65. Recall of Charles "Dutch" Van Ry, '64, one of the three first students to obtain the master's degree in physics under Dr. Robert Sells.

66. Email message from George Wilkerson to Dr. Bruce Godsave, October 27, 2005, courtesy of Wilkerson and VanRy.

67. Phone call from James Brunner, November 1, 2005.

68. Interview of Paul Neureiter by Drs. Martin L. Fausold and Wayne Mahood, March 2, 1988.

Chapter Seven

1. Dr. John Black to President Robert W. MacVittie, March 14, 1979, MacVittie Miscellaneous Papers, courtesy of Mrs. Robert W. MacVittie, hereafter MMP.

2. Martin L. Fausold, Dedication of the "Valley, Village, College" Exhibit, June 6, 1991.

3. Excerpted from "Remember" by the Class of 1967, MMP. We learn much about Dr. MacVittie and his sense of humor from his retaining this among his miscellaneous papers.

4. "Rockwell Jeered on Race Policy," Rochester *Democrat and Chronicle*, February 5, 1965; "Geneseo Integrates," *Livingston County Leader*, December 12, 1963; WGSU–FM schedule for an unidentified day in 1963, Presidents' Papers, College Archives.

5. Dr. Lawrence Park, then vice president for academic affairs, was the other candidate who came out of a teachers college background.

6. President Robert W. MacVittie, "The Lamp of Knowledge Needs Wiring," Inaugural Address as President of the State University at Geneseo, April 23, 1964, MMP. MacVittie quoted from John Henry Cardinal Spellman, Woodrow Wilson, Alfred North Whitehead, and C. P. Snow. President MacVittie shared another commonality with President Kennedy, Catholicism. In fact, at his interview with the College Council one of the members who supported another candidate asked MacVittie what his religion was, and though MacVittie thought the question improper, unhesitatingly told the member he was Catholic and that it should make no difference, interview of President MacVittie by Martin L. Fausold and Wayne Mahood, June 26, 1989.

7. Letter from Dr. Robert W. MacVittie to Theodora Greenman, July 15, 1963, MMP.

8. This anecdote among MacVittie's papers reveals a lot about him as a person, MMP.

9. Interview of Dr. William Cotton by Laura Freedell, December 10, 1989 for Martin Fausold's SUNY Oral History Project; Fausold, *Draft History of the State University of New York*, 59. Ironically, Gould, then Antioch College president, was Geneseo's commencement speaker May 1957, when he looked ahead to "The Teacher in the World Tomorrow."

10. Fausold, *Draft History of the State University of New York*, 58, 59, 62. Former Vice President for Academic Affairs at Geneseo Larry Park found Gould "the most influential figure" in SUNY's struggle for greatness, undated letter to Martin Fausold.

11. Skopp, *Bright With Promise…*, 138; MacVittie, "Perceptions of SUNY," SUNY History Conference, Brockport, New York, April 19, 1991. That is, a student who failed student teaching had to make it up or leave without a degree, for the only option until then was the B.S. in Education.

12. MacVittie, "Perceptions of SUNY," SUNY History Conference, Brockport, New York, April 19, 1991.

13. The first to receive the M.A. in English was Mrs. Lakshmi Mani from Bombay, India, who had abandoned her pursuit of a Ph.D. in economics at the University of Wisconsin, Livingston News Service, undated; Rochester *Democrat and Chronicle*, April 26, 1967.

14. MacVittie, "Perceptions of SUNY," SUNY History Conference, Brockport, New York, April 19, 1991. TIAA-CREF, the acronym for Teachers Insurance and Annuity Association-College Retirement Equities Fund, is a private company established by the Carnegie Plan and resulted in more faculty mobility.

15. Interview of President MacVittie by Martin L. Fausold and Wayne Mahood, June 26, 1989.

16. *Buffalo Evening News*, May 19, 1967; *Livingston Republican*, June 8, 1967; phone call to Mrs. Robert L. Sells, August 5, 2005. Competitive salaries continued into the early 1970s, when state budgets reflected the national doldrums. However, Sells's fifteen-thousand-dollar salary exceeded all but the director of and four department heads in the Division of Education five years later, per handwritten notes on a list of departmental faculty in the Division of Education, miscellaneous papers given by Dr. William Cotton to the Geneseo History Project.

17. Meredith Drake, "Recalling a Life with Raptors, Reptiles and Rodents," *The Geneseo Emeritus*, vol. 11, (2005) no 1: 2–3.

18. Interview of Dr. William Cotton by Laura Freedell, December 10, 1989; Public Employees' Fair Employment Act, Civil Service, Article 14, New York State Laws.

19. "Center is Established For Migrant Studies," *Geneseo Alumni News*, May 1968.

20. Interview of President MacVittie by Martin L. Fausold and Wayne Mahood, February 1, 1989; "College Seal for Geneseo," *Geneseo Alumni News* 3, (1964), no. 3: 22; "College Unveils Its New Emblem," Rochester *Democrat and Chronicle*, July 16, 1968; "A Look at the College Seal," *The Lamron*, September 11, 1971, 3.

21. Dr. David Martin was never persuaded that Geneseo was a true liberal arts college, at least during his three decades at the College. Rather, to him it was a distinguished multipurpose college, "Beyond the Myth of Geneseo as a Liberal Arts College," *Faculty Forum: A Collection of Essays Originally Published in The Geneseo Compass*, ed. Judith Bushnell (Geneseo: SUNY Geneseo, 1992), 17–18.

22. McNally, *Fact Book 2000*, 65; cf. News release, February 6, 1964, MMP.

23. Maps obtained by Paul Hepler from the College Facilities Office. The number of lots to be acquired changed between 1961 and 1967, but the general boundaries remained much the same.

24. "Home Owners Get Notice from the College," undated clipping in the College Archives; "We Don't Feel The Village Is Ours…," Rochester *Times-Union*, July 24, 1967. Contractor Joseph Vitale sued the state.

25. Newspaper clippings retained by Dr. MacVittie, MMP.

26. College Facilities Office; Rochester *Democrat and Chronicle*, January 23 and April 23, 1965, May 14, 1967; *Livingston Republican*, February 6, 1964. The costs of the respective buildings were: Fine Arts, renamed Brodie ($2,405,160), Lauderdale Infirmary ($526,051), Milne Library ($1,813,560), Newton Hall ($1,487,105), and the campus school ($2,594,880).

27. This borrows heavily on a note from former associate vice president Bruce Ristow, who nominated Tafel for an honorary Doctor of Arts degree, which was awarded by the College in 1989. Tafel was a senior apprentice of Wright, News Release, SUNY Geneseo, September 16, 1999.

28. Letter from Professor Willard Peterson to Dr. MacVittie, March 29, 1965, MMP; MacVittie's response, March 31, 1965, Presidents' Papers, College Archives.

29. Memo from Dr. James McNally to Dr. James Somerville, March 20, 1998. Between 1962 and 1970 the students came from the same geographic areas, roughly a third from nine counties that represented the "Rochester Region," between seven and nine percent from the Elmira area, approximately fourteen percent from the "Niagara Region," though there was a jump from about eleven to seventeen percent from the New York Metro area. Twenty-two percent of families were in the ten-thousand to fourteen-thousand-dollar range in 1962, while sixty percent were in 1970. Males claiming probable careers in teaching dropped from forty percent in 1967 to twenty-four percent, barely three years later. The drop among women was less, from sixty-six to fifty-three percent, James McNally, *Geneseo Freshmen, 1967 and 1970: A Comparison Profile, February 1971* (Geneseo: Office of Institutional Research, 1971).

30. "Editor to Transfer: Upset over Students," Rochester *Times-Union*, May 2, 1967; *The Lamron*, February 15, 1963; Rochester *Democrat & Chronicle*, February 5, 1965. The paper recalled the students jeering Rockwell, but Betty Kent (Walrath), '65, remembered that at the conclusion of his talk students silently walked out of Wadsworth Auditorium, Reunion of the 1964, 1965 Classes, June 11, 2005. "The Dissonant Sound—Loud, Discordant But Clear," *Geneseo Alumni News*, 4, (1967), no. 6: 12. This

article and the bulk of the others dealing with the campus protests of the 1960s are from MMP. The fact that over the years Dr. MacVittie retained so many articles about campus protests of the 1960s, pro and con, attests not only to the effect the events had on him, but the balanced approach that he seems to have taken.

31. Freedom Fighter, "Geneseo Women Demand Freedom-Equal Station," *Livingston County Leader*, January 25, 1967.

32. "Revision Seen For College's Curfew Rules," Rochester *Democrat & Chronicle*, January 24, 1967; "Position Paper and Proposal to the Faculty Undergraduate Student Affairs Committee concerning Women's Hours at Geneseo State" [*sic*], MMP. Roark was particularly troubled by a quote from Paul Goodman, whom Roark claimed was "very 'far left,'" note attached to the "Position Paper…" by Roark.

33. "Protestors Assail College at Geneseo," Rochester *Democrat & Chronicle*, Februrary 7, 1967.

34. "Pointless Protest Technique," Rochester *Democrat and Chronicle*, January 24, 1967; "Geneseo Prexy Talks to SFF on Coed Case," Rochester *Times-Union*, February 10, 1967; "Dormitory Hours Set At College," Rochester *Democrat and Chronicle*, April 29, 1967; "MacVittie Liberalizes Dorm Hours," Rochester *Times-Union*, February 22, 1967.

35. "'Unrest Is Healthy, Not Disruptive,'" Rochester *Times-Union*, February 28, 1967; "Teachers Frame Reply to Park," Rochester *Times-Union*, March 5, 1967; "Geneseo Staff Mulls College Atmosphere," Rochester *Times-Union*, March 3, 1967. Ironically, Rockas and Nadelhaft had received grants-in-aid for research from the SUNY Research Foundation.

36. "College Colloquy Raises Eyebrows," Rochester *Times-Union*, March 16, 1967.

37. "College Paper Shows Fervor at Geneseo," Rochester *Times-Union*, February 27, 1967 (which refers to *The Lamron*, February 24, 1967); "Student Vote Backs Fees at Geneseo," Rochester *Times-Union*, April 27, 1967; "College Fee Decision Likely in September," Rochester *Times-Union*, May 25, 1967.

38. "Faculty Backs March to Protest Dismissal," Rochester *Times-Union*, May 25, 1967.

39. "5 of 7 Protest Professors Leave Geneseo," Rochester *Democrat & Chronicle*, June 9, 1967; "An Open Letter," copy in MMP; "Dissenters Ask Geneseo Probe," Rochester *Times-Union*, July 31, 1967. John Collinson, Professor of Independent Study, left the College in 1967. Lonero remained a year, but Forest would remain and retire in 1992 after a very long and distinguished career. Additionally, Paul Worthman, history instructor on leave to work on his doctoral dissertation at Yale, also resigned, arguing that "the intellectual climate at Geneseo remains incompatible with serious scholarship," "Fourth Prof Leaves College, Hits 'Climate,'" undated article in MMP; Worthman's resignation was received on February 15, 1967, President's Papers (Mail Log); "Faculty Governance Subcommittee Report on Visit to State University College At Geneseo," MMP. Subcommittee members who visited the campus came from Fredonia, Oswego, and the Maritime College.

40. "State Report Hails System at Geneseo," Rochester *Times-Union*, February 22, 1967; "He Accepts Dissent, But Has 'Faith in the Majority,'" Rochester *Times-Union*, February 20, 1967; "A New Look at Geneseo," Rochester *Democrat and Chronicle*, April 11, 1967.

41. Letter to the Editor by Elwood B. Ehrle, carbon copy to MacVittie, March 22, 1967, MMP. The headline, which particularly irritated Ehrle, read, "Professor's Resignation Rocks Geneseo State," Rochester *Times-Union*, March 22, 1967. Arthur Brooks, the College spokesman, protested Bickel's columns directly with the editors of the Rochester papers.

42. The Board also noted that MacVittie had "displayed admirable composure" and had "steadfastly maintained his commitment to democratic principles…." "A Pat on the Back," Rochester *Democrat and Chronicle*, June 3, 1967.

43. Seymour L. Halleck, "Alienation in Students," *Think*, March–April 1967, MMP.

44. *The Lamron*, May 14, 1965. We are indebted to Dr. James Somerville, upon whose meticulous research we relied heavily.

45. Dr. Somerville's unpublished data; *Geneseo Scene*, 14 (Spring 1989) no. 1: 1.

46. Interview of President MacVittie by Martin L. Fausold and Wayne Mahood, June 26, 1989; statement by Rosati at the Geneseo Emeritus breakfast, September 23, 2005.

47. Interview of President MacVittie by Martin L. Fausold and Wayne

Mahood, June 26, 1989. The first issue of the *Geneseo Compass* was May 8, 1970. It appears *The Lamron* editors were battling with themselves over treatment of the Vietnam War in the paper, leading the editor-in-chief to "quit," though he remained as an "Executive Editor," *The Lamron*, October 17, 1969; *Livingston Republican*, May 7, 1970.

48. SUNY Geneseo Faculty Senate Minutes, May 5, 7, 1970, 414, 416. Four students were killed and nine wounded at Kent State, while two students were killed and twelve wounded at Jackson State. Geneseo students were obligated to notify faculty if they were not taking the final, and the students' instructors had the option of giving a letter grade for student performance to date, or recording an Incomplete, "Satisfactory" or "Unsatisfactory." Also a committee was created to hear appeals of instructors' grading, ibid., May 7, 1970, 419-420.

49. *Livingston Republican*, May 14, 21, 1970.

50. *Livingston Republican*, June 4, 1970.

51. Martin L. Fausold's recollection, October 4, 2005.

52. *The Lamron*, October 9, 1964, Rochester *Democrat & Chronicle*, May 1, 1967; Rochester *Times-Union*, May 15, 1967; *Livingston Republican*, May 24, 1967; *Hornell Tribune*, August 5, 1968; *The Lamron*, November 8, 1968, September 25, 1970.

53. B. J. Keller, "What We Were Like and How We Have Changed," *The Geneseo Compass*, October 5, 1973; emails from Rand and Janine McCoy, '72, Bill Brewer, '69, Barbara Finkle, '68, August 2005, and Doug Brode, '65, September 2005.

54. Thanks to Suzanne Boor, Administrative Associate, Alumni and Parent Relations, for the information about Coughtry. Scipione's story is told in *The Geneseo Scene* 14 (Spring 1989), no. 1 and Sciarrino's in *The Lamron*, September 22, 2005. Jordan was featured at a special night in November 2005 when Geneseo alumni and friends were invited to enjoy his play, *Shear Madness* at Rochester's GEVA. Mrs. Vosburgh-Canedo's honor was featured in an undated article, MMP.

55. Interview of Harding by "Ms.Baker," January 17, 1989, Fausold SUNY Oral History Project. One has to be a bit careful with numbers, for faculty include part-time instructors and some non-teaching personnel. For example, in 1965 the "teaching" faculty was reported to be only 189. Also graduate students and part-time students are included in enrollment totals.

Chapter Eight

1. *The Lamron*, October 22, 1971. The September 28, 1971 *Utica Observer-Dispatch* had already announced MacVittie's appointment, MMP.

2. *The Lamron*, October 22, 1971.

3. "MacVittie Returning to Geneseo," Rochester *Democrat and Chronicle*, January 29, 1972. Governor Rockefeller subsequently came up with close to a million dollars to try to jumpstart the Utica-Rome technical college after protests by community leaders in those cities.

4. Assessment of Colahan by Dr. James McNally; undated letter from Dr. Lawrence Park to Martin L. Fausold; McTarnaghan became Associate Director of Virginia's State Council of Higher Education.

5. Interview of Bruce Ristow, assistant VPAA by Martin L. Fausold, July 8, 1997; discussion with Dr. Leslie, summer 2003.

6. "Comprehensive Site Plan Report, 1969–1974," College Archives; interview of Dr. Thomas S. Colahan, VPAA, by Martin L. Fausold, April 15, 1997.

7. Interview of Dr. Thomas S. Colahan by Martin L. Fausold, April 15, 1997; *The Lamron*, December 11, 1970, January 15, 1971; *Livingston County Leader*, August 23, 1972; interview of Dr. Thomas S. Colahan by Martin L. Fausold, April 15, 1997; *Geneseo Compass*, August 30, 1974.

8. *Livingston County Leader*, August 23, 1972; interview of Dr. Thomas S. Colahan by Martin L. Fausold, April 15, 1997.

9. "The Hundredth Year," *Geneseo Compass*, August 31, 1973.

10. Curriculum proposals and changes had to be approved by the Faculty Senate, which relied on committees and subcommittees to examine proposals and, after their approval, to bring them to the full Senate.

11. "College Has Option Now on For. Langs.,"*The Lamron*, February 5, 1971.

12. *The Lamron*, November 12, October 6, 1970; January 22, October 29, November 5, 1971; "College Upheld in Suspensions For Sleep-In," Rochester *Times-Union*, November 20, 1973.

13. *The Geneseo Compass*, February 5, 1971.

14. *The Lamron*, January 23, 1970.

15. *The Lamron*, April 6 and 13, 1973.

16. "Geneseo State students 'occupy' building," Rochester *Democrat and*

Chronicle, May 1, 1976; "Students Rally," *Livingston County Leader*, May 5, 1976; interview of President MacVittie by Martin L. Fausold and Wayne Mahood, June 26, 1989; James Allan, "Campus Life Enriches The Collegiate Experience," *Geneseo Compass*, December 16, 1996.

17. "Rally Ends With Erwin Takeover," *The Lamron*, May 7, 1976; interview of President MacVittie by Martin L. Fausold and Wayne Mahood, June 26, 1989; Colahan memo to President MacVittie, November 3, 1976; "SUNY tuition hike needed—MacVittie," Rochester *Times-Union*, March 11, 1979.

18. Interview of Dr. Harding by "Ms. Baker," November 17, 1989, Fausold SUNY Oral History Project.

19. "MacVittie Raps Cuts By State for Geneseo," Rochester *Times-Union*, February 23, 1973; "College Tightens Belt," *Livingston County Leader*, August 23, 1972; "Cuts Put College in Dormitory Bind," Rochester *Times-Union*, January 21, 1972; "From the President," *Geneseo Compass*, February 12, 1971; Letter to Charles Fake, SUNY Assistant Director of Facilities Planning, from Donald Pebbles, Geneseo Facilities Program Coordinator, January 15, 1970, Presidents' Papers 1969–1970.

20. Edmund J. McMahon, "Déjà Vu All Over Again: The Right Way to Cure New York's Looming Budget Gap," *Civic Report*, No. 9 (October 2002).

21. "Holcomb Center granted full funding for this year," *Geneseo Compass*, April 11, 1975; "MacVittie comments on proposed campus school budget cutbacks," *Geneseo Compass*, January 30, 1976; "Geneseo State wins delay on school closing," Rochester *Democrat and Chronicle*, February 27, 1976.

22. *Geneseo Compass*, January 13, 1975; Interview of Dr. Bruce Ristow by Martin L. Fausold, July 8, 1997.

23. Interview of Dr. Thomas S. Colahan by Martin L. Fausold, April 15, 1997; Paul Hepler, "Geneseo Art Department History, 1871–2000," unpublished. The art department claims to have lost seven full-time faculty from 1971 to 1976, Paul Hepler, "Historic Record of the Art Department Staff, SUNY Geneseo, 1873–July 1, 2005," unpublished.

24. News Release (1976 Convocation address), August 30, 1976; *The Lamron*, January 22, 1971; James McNally, "SUNY Geneseo Student Reactions to Faculty Instruction, 1969–1998;" *The Lamron*, November 5, 1976.

25. *Geneseo Compass*, January 18, 1974; "From the Vice President for Academic Affairs," ibid., October 27, 1972; *Faculty Senate Bulletin*, 1972/73, 28–29, 68, 158, 214, 220, 253, 284, 289; *Faculty Senate Bulletin*, 1973/74, 296. Other members of that first committee were Drs. Walter Harding (English), Hans Gottschalk (English), Edward Janosik (political science) and Bruce Klee (drama). Librarians became eligible to serve during the 1986–1987 school year, and beginning in the 1998–1999 school year the committee, renamed College Personnel Committee, was enlarged to seven and modified to include associate professors and associate librarians, *Faculty Senate Bulletin*, 1985/86, 117, 35; *College Senate Bulletin*, 1998/1999, 2.

26. McNally, *Fact Book 2000*, 123–125; James McNally, "Faculty/Staff Awards (2005);" *Faculty Senate Bulletin*, 1972/73, 65, 162, 167, 293, 326; *Faculty Senate Bulletin*, 1973/74, 105, 165, 179, 241, 264.

27. *Geneseo Compass*, November 21, 1973; *The Lamron*, September 16, October 28, 1977.

28. This section and the following rely heavily upon an interview of Dr. William Caren, Associate Vice President for Enrollment Services, by James McNally and Wayne Mahood, January 3, 2005.

29. "MacVittie appoints task force on student recruitment," *Geneseo Compass*, April 22, 1977; "Student recruitment and retention discussed," ibid., September 16, 1977; "Tuesday's Faculty Meeting Discusses Enrollment Crisis," ibid., September 16, 1977; "Student Enrollment Declines, College Admissions Revised," ibid., September 9, 1977; Frank Kemerer, "Enrollment Policy and Planning," July 5, 1977, Presidents' Papers, College Archives; *News Release*, July 8, 1977, Presidents' Papers, College Archives.

30. Comments by Arthur Hatton to the committee, October 10, 2006; Caren interview; memo from President MacVittie to Dr. Van Quaal, July 14, 1977, Presidents' Papers, College Archives; memo from Dr. Frank Kemerer to President MacVittie, November 1,1977; Christopher C. Morphew, J. Douglas Toma, Cora Z. Hedstrom, "The Public Liberal Arts College: Case Studies of Institutions That Have Bucked the Trend Toward 'Upward Drift'...and the Implications for Mission and Market," paper presented at

the Association for the Study of Higher Education, Richmond, Virginia, November 2001, 26.

31. "College priorities committee draft report," *Geneseo Compass*, May 5, 1978. Education actually was taking a larger hit, for it also lost the assistant dean. Morphew, Toma and Hedstrom, "The Public Liberal Arts College...," 4.

32. Hatton's report to the president's "Cabinet," October 15, 1980, Presidents' Papers, College Archives; http://foundation.geneseo.edu/privsupp.shtml. At the first Dinner honorees were Geneseo Mayor Ann Duff and Emeritus Professor Ira Wilson. The second group included presidents Moench and MacVittie, longtime College Council chairman Joseph Quirk and Livingston County Judge J. Robert Houston, a Holcomb and Geneseo Central School graduate. Subsequent ones recognized Theodora Greenman and Wilbur Wright (1991), President and Mrs. Jakubauskas and Dr. Myrtle Merritt (1992), President Harter (1995), Fred Bright (1996), and Dr. Phillip Alley (1997), to name just a few.

33. *The Lamron*, January 29, February 26, April 23, 1971.

34. College Union Activities Director Dr. Thomas Matthews's conversation with the Geneseo History Committee, October 24, 2005; "Buffalo Braves to Train at Geneseo State," *Livingston Republican*, July 25, 1974.

35. College Union Activities Director Dr. Thomas Matthews's conversation with the Geneseo History Committee, October 24, 2005; *Geneseo Compass*, October 5, 1979; "Thoughts on Geneseo," Elaine Kupi Hinz; *The Lamron*, October 27, 1972.

36. *The Lamron*, January 26 and 29, 1971; October 27, 1972; December 1, 1977; January 27, 1978, April 29, 1977.

37. Ibid., September 17 and 24, 1971, October 3, 1972.

38. Ibid., October 8, 1971.

39. *The Lamron*, January 29, February 26, March 5, September 17, 24, October 8, 1971.

40. These are among Judith Bushnell's and James McNally's recollections of the period.

41. Recall and records of Barry Caplan, November 2, 2005. See also an interview by News Editor, Jay Kleinman, in which Barry is just as self effacing and enigmatic as ever, *The Lamron*, November 6, 1987, and "Bookish Overdrive," Rochester *Democrat & Chronicle*, June 10, 2007.

42. Email from Robert J. Avalone to Dr. Paul Hepler, July 18, 2006. Of course, the sellers were paid or their books returned.

43. *Geneseo Compass*, October 5, 1973; Fisher, *...the stone strength of the past...*, 173. Women's sports were basketball and tennis in 1974, softball in 1976, cross country and track in 1978 and soccer and indoor track in 1980. Unfortunately, women's synchronized swimming and tennis and men's baseball, wrestling, golf, and tennis were dropped in 1979, though women's tennis was reinstituted in 1994. Women's lacrosse and field hockey teams were added in 1995 and 1997 respectively.

44. *The Lamron*, October 16, 1970, October 3, 1972; *Geneseo Compass*, February 5, 1971, May 24, 1974; McNally, *Fact Book 2000*, 107, courtesy of sports chronicler Fred Bright.

45. "Dr. MacVittie Plans to Retire August 27, 1979," *Livingston Republican*, February 1, 1979; "MacVittie to Retire From Geneseo Post," *Buffalo Evening News*, January 26, 1979, MMP.

46. Copy of remarks by Satryb and Donnelly, MMP.

47. Copy of remarks made by President Carol Harter, November 7, 1989, MMP.

48. "Remarks of Robert W. MacVittie on the occasion of the Dedication of the Robert W. MacVittie College Union, November 17, 1989, SUNY College of Arts and Science, Geneseo, New York," MMP; Interview of Dr. Harry Porter by Wayne Mahood, March 27, 1989. The enrollment for 1978–1979 includes 634 graduate students. The total faculty for 1962–1963, but not for 1978–1979, includes the Holcomb School faculty.

Chapter Nine

1. "Search" note book, Presidents' Papers, College Archives; *Geneseo Compass*, September 7, 1979.

2. *Geneseo Compass*, September 7, 1979; Rochester *Times-Union*, March 11, 1979.

3. The President's Annual Report to the College Council, September 19, 1980,

Presidents' Papers, College Archives.

4. Interview of Dr. William Caren by James McNally and Wayne Mahood, January 3, 2005.

5. *Geneseo Compass*, September 7, 1979; February 8, 1980.

6. President's Annual Report to the College Council, September 19, 1980, Presidents' Papers, College Archives; *Geneseo Compass*, January 29, 1982; interview of President Jakubauskas by Martin L. Fausold, August 18,1988. Splitting the field house locker room to equalize space came about through an agreement after a threatened suit under Title IX by women who objected to having to use the older Schrader locker room.

7. *Geneseo Compass*, September 11, 1981.

8. Ibid., March 6, 1981. Plattsburgh also was told to close its campus school.

9. Interview of President Jakubauskas by Martin L. Fausold, August 18, 1998.

10. *Geneseo Compass*, January 29, 1982, March 1983; interview of President Jakubauskas by Martin L. Fausold, August 18, 1998; *Geneseo Compass*, January 29, 1982. In 1983 new governor Mario Cuomo and the legislature tried to ameliorate the situation by announcing a plan to offer retirement incentives for personnel over age fifty-five.

11. *Geneseo Compass*, February 6, 1981; interview of Dr. Bruce Ristow by Martin L. Fausold, July 8, 1997; *Geneseo Compass*, November 6, 1981.

12. Letter from Robert Wedgeworth, Executive Director, American Library Association, July 26, 1979, MMP.

13. Presidents' Papers, College Archives.

14. Ibid.

15. 1981 Report on Admissions, Presidents' Papers, College Archives.

16. "Four-Year Progress Report—Submitted to the College Council—May 13, 1983," Presidents' Papers, College Archives; *Geneseo Compass*, September 5, October 17, 1980; interview of Dr. Bruce Ristow by Martin L. Fausold, July 8, 1997.

17. *Geneseo Compass*, February 22, 1980; *The Lamron*, October 30, 1987, February 6, 1987, February 12, 1988, November 6, 1981; Annual Report, 1993-1994, Presidents' Papers, College Archives.

18. Annual Report 1984–85, Presidents' Papers, College Archives; *The Lamron*, October 19, 1984.

19. 1985 Convocation Address, Presidents' Papers, College Archives.

20. *The Lamron*, February 22, 1985.

21. "Geneseo in the News," undated article from the Associated Press New York State wire, Presidents' Papers, College Archives.

22. Christopher Morphew, et al., "The Public Liberal Arts College…", 4; interview of Dr. William Caren, January 3, 2005; "Class of '84 Termed 'Brightest in Years,'" *Geneseo Compass*, September 5, 1980, for example. Two other colleges bucked the trend: Truman State (once Northeast Missouri State College at Kirksville) and the College of New Jersey (formerly Trenton State). The latter owes its transformation in part to Dr. Gordon Goewey, formerly music department head and graduate dean at Geneseo.

23. "Incoming Freshmen Have a Clearer Geneseo Picture," *Geneseo Compass*, January 23, 1981.

24. *State University College of Arts and Science, Geneseo, New York Undergraduate Bulletin 1980–82*, 51–56.

25. "Incoming Freshmen…"; Annual Report of the President, 1987, Presidents' Papers, College Archives.

26. Annual Report 1986–1987, Presidents' Papers, College Archives; *The Lamron*, February 6, 1987, October 21, 1988.

27. *The Lamron*, February 26 and March 11, 1988.

28. Interview of Dr. Bruce Ristow by Martin L. Fausold, July 8, 1997.

29. Ibid.; *The Lamron*, February 7, 1991.

30. *The Lamron*, February 21, 1991. It truly was a revolution. Recall that personal computers had been in existence less than a decade. For example, the first Apple I was sold in May 1977, while Radio Shack's TRS 80—like one the College and Geneseo Central fought over when Holcomb closed— was first sold three months later.

31. *Yahoo Internet Life*, May 1998, May 1999, May 2000, May 2001; News Release, "SUNY Geneseo Ranks Among Top 'Unwired' Colleges in the U.S.," April 22, 2004.

32. *Geneseo Compass*, October 13, 1989; *Geneseo Scene*, Winter 1986, Summer 1991; *The Lamron*, September 8, 1994.

33. "Marketers give award to college," Rochester *Democrat & Chronicle*, April 30, 1988; Annual Report, 1993–1994, Presidents' Papers, College Archives; *The Lamron*, January 30, 1987.

34. *Geneseo Scene*, Winter 1986; *The Lamron*, February 20, 1987; Annual

35. *Geneseo Compass*, January 18, 1980; placement data from Dr. James Allan, Presidents' Papers, College Archives.

36. Rochester *Democrat and Chronicle*, March 29, 1987; Annual Report, 1986-87, Presidents' Papers, College Archives; Rochester *Democrat and Chronicle*, March 29, 1987.

37. "Don't Let Publicity Get in the Way of Progress," *The Lamron*, October 13, 1989; Placement data by Dr. James Allan, Presidents' Papers, College Archives.

38. Interview of President Jakubauskas by Martin L. Fausold, August 18, 1998.

39. *The Lamron*, October 24, 1986, April 17, 1987. Two of the "cuts" were Dr. Donald Marozas, who moved over to the department of Elementary and Secondary Education and Reading, and Dr. Ramon Rocha, who was appointed assistant to the vice president for minority affairs.

40. Interview of President Jakubauskas by Martin L. Fausold, August 18, 1998.

41. Ibid.; interview of Dr. Bruce Ristow by Dr. Martin L. Fausold, July 8, 1997; Annual Reports, 1986–1987, 1984–1985, Presidents' Papers, College Archives; Dr. Douglas Harke, quoted by *Newsday* reporter Robert Keeler in a letter to Dr. Martin L. Fausold, May 11,1992.

42. Letters from students, Presidents' Papers, College Archives; *The Lamron*, September 19, 1986, September 26, 1989, November 3, 1989, October 23, 1987, May 5, 1989, February 12, 1988.

43. Letters from a student, Presidents' Papers, College Archives.

44. *The Lamron*, September 19, 1986, September 26, 1986.

45. Ibid., March 7, 1986, October 25, 1990.

46. Ibid., May 5, 1989, October 31, 1987, February 12, 1988.

47. Ibid., October 28, 1988; John Brasser, "The Bells of Sturges," 1988, College Archives; *The Lamron*, December 9, 1989. In 1997 the broken system was replaced by applying seven thousand dollars from the Student and Alumni associations, *The Lamron*, February 13, 1997.

48. *The Lamron*, March 1, 1984, April 19, September 20, 27, October 11, 25, November 1, 1985, September 25, 1987, May 6, 1988.

49. Ibid., November 15, 1985, February 28, April 11, 1986.

50. *Geneseo Scene*, Winter 1986.

51. *The Lamron*, September 23, 1988, February 3, 17, 1989.

52. McNally, *Fact Book 2000*, 46, 48; *The Lamron*, September 23, 1988.

53. Rochester *Democrat and Chronicle*, May 4, 1988; *The Lamron*, September 16, 1988; Letter to Dr. MacVittie from Dr. Jakubauskas, May 11, 1988, Presidents' Papers, College Archives; "Remarks at Convocation," September 6, 1988, MMP. Jakubauskas also set up a meeting of his wife and Mrs. MacVittie "to discuss transitional items related to the President's Residence and social functions."

54. "Remarks at Convocation," September 6, 1988, MMP; *Geneseo Compass*, January 27,1989; *The Lamron*, February 10, 1989, May 5, 1989.

55. *The Lamron*, February 10, 1989; *Geneseo Compass*, February 10, 1989.

56. *The Lamron*, March 3, April 28, 1989.

57. Ibid., September 15, April 28, 1989.

58. Ibid., September 15, 1989, *Geneseo Scene*, Summer 1991; *Geneseo Compass*, February 2, April 6, 1990; *Geneseo Compass*, October 13, 1989.

59. *Geneseo Compass*, November 3, 1989, February 7, 1991, April 6, 1990.

60. Ibid., April 6, 1990.

61. Interview of President Jakubauskas by Martin L. Fausold, August 18, 1998.

62. McNally, Fact Book 2000; *The Lamron*, February 7, 1991; *ENCompass*, December 5, 2005.

63. McNally, *Fact Book 2000*.

64. *The Lamron*, April 25, 1991.

65. Student protests were in *The Lamron*, September 8, 1994, while President Harter's response was in ibid., September 22, 1994.

66. Ibid., February 2, 1990; News Release, Presidents' Papers, College Archives, *Geneseo Compass*, December 5, 1990.

67. Memo from Dr. Spencer to President Harter, October 31, 1990, Presidents' Papers, College Archives.

68. Annual Report, 1990–1991, Presidents' Papers, College Archives; "SUNY closings are threatened," Rochester *Democrat & Chronicle*, December 6, 1991.

Report, 1991–1992, Presidents' Papers, College Archives. *The Geneseo Scene*, Summer 1991, reported that the class of 1995 (1991 freshmen) had a high school average of 92.7, with an SAT mean of 1173, which differs from President Harter's 1991–1992 annual report.

329

69. *Geneseo Compass*, September 8, 1989; Annual Report, 1990–1991, Presidents' Papers, College Archives.

70. *The Lamron*, February 28, April 18, 1991. Bright's appeal appears verbatim in *College Senate Bulletin*, 1990/1991, 223–224.

71. *The Lamron*, December 6, 1990; Annual Report, 1990–1991, Presidents' Papers, College Archives.

72. *The Lamron*, September 8, 1994, September 7, 1995.

73. Annual Report, 1992–1993, Presidents' Papers, College Archives.

74. *The Lamron*, February 7, 1991; *Livingston County Leader*, February 19, 1992; Annual Report, 1991–1992, Presidents' Papers, College Archives; *The Lamron*, November 1, 1990.

75. Annual Report, 1992–1993, Presidents' Papers, College Archives; McNally, *Fact Book 2000*, 119, 120.

76. Annual Report 1991–1992, Presidents' Papers, College Archives; *Geneseo Scene*, Summer 1988; *Geneseo Compass*, March 2, 1990; *The Lamron*, September 16, 1988, November 3, 1994.

77. *Geneseo Scene*, Summer 1991.

78. Partial listing of memories by Paul Kreher, '93, who subsequently earned a master's degree in physical therapy; *The Lamron*, December 13, 1985.

79. *The Lamron*, January 31, March 21, 1991, December 6, 1990.

80. *Geneseo Compass*, February 22, 1980; *The Lamron*, Summer 1985; McNally, *Fact Book 2000*.

81. *The Lamron*, December 6, 1985, February 26, 1986; McNally, *Fact Book 2000*.

82. Annual Report 1991–1992, 1993–1994, Presidents' Papers, College Archives; *The Lamron*, September 14, 1984.

83. *Geneseo Scene*, Fall 1991; data from Suzanne Boor, Administrative Assistant, Alumni and Parent Relations; phone call to Lynn and Wes Kennison, January 18, 2006; Rochester *Democrat & Chronicle*, September 26, 2007.

84. *The Lamron*, February 16, 23, 1995.

85. "SUNY has stumbled badly in its quest to excel," reprinted in *The Buffalo News*, June 7–13, 1992.

86. We owe thanks to vice president Kenneth Levison and associate vice president William Caren for offering insightful comments about the College during this period.

87. Remarks of Arthur Hatton to Geneseo History Committee, January 8, 2007.

Chapter Ten

1. *The Lamron*, May 4, 1995; www.geneseo.edu/CMS/display.php?dpt=president; Curriculum Vitae.

2. *The Lamron*, May 4 and December 14, 1995 and February 1, 29, 1996.

3. Ibid., November 2, 1995, October 3, 1996.

4. Ibid., October 3, 1996, September 12, 1996, February 6, 1997, February 12, 1998.

5. Ibid., November 6, 1997; Clark Kerr, *The Gold and the Blue: A Personal Memoir of the University of California, 1949–1967*, 2 vols. (Berkeley: University of California Press, 2001) I:126.

6. *The Lamron*, September 7, 14, 1995, September 19, 1996, September 11, 1997, March 20, 1997.

7. Ali Shehzad Zaidi, "Dismantling SUNY:The Faculty Revolt," www.unm.edu/ncjm/governance/SUNY.txt; *The Lamron*, October 5, 19, 1995, February 8, 1996.

8. *The Lamron*, December 7, 1995; Rochester *Democrat & Chronicle*, April 25, 1999; Zaidi, "Dismantling SUNY…."

9. Zaidi, "Dismantling SUNY…;"*The Lamron*, September 23, 1999, September 28, 1996, October 24, 1996.

10. *The Lamron*, September 4, 11, 1997; "A Quest for Excellence: Geneseo's Plan for a Decade, 1990-2000," Presidents' Papers, College Archives; Memo from President Dahl, January 3, 2000, Presidents' Papers, College Archives; *The Lamron*, September 23, 1999, April 6, 2000, April 19, 2001.

11. *The Lamron*, February 9,1995; College Planning Council, 1995–1996, Presidents' Papers, College Archives; *The Lamron*, February 9, 1995; December 10, 1998; Rochester *Democrat & Chronicle*, December 12, November 30, 1998. Private Nazareth College paid about three thousand dollars and public Brockport four thousand dollars more for assistant professors than Geneseo. Geneseo's School of Education, heavily hit by attrition, blamed the problem on low salaries. Institutional Research Director McNally attributed Geneseo's low salaries to the number of replacements of higher-salaried retirees.

12. *Geneseo Compass*, September 11, 1998; *The Lamron*, March 19, 1998; *The Facilitator*, February 2001, Presidents' Papers, College Archives.

13. *Geneseo Compass*, September 11, 1998; *The New York Times*, February 12, 2003; Rochester *Democrat & Chronicle*, September 8, 2003.

14. *The Lamron*, October 24, 2002.

15. *The Lamron*, March 18, 1999, *Geneseo ENCompass*, October 6, 2003; *Livingston County News*, September 2, 2004; *The Lamron*, February 13, 1997, November 4, 1999, February 24, November 16, 2000.

16. *The Lamron*, October 5, 2000, September 18, 2003, October 21, 1999, March 7, 2002.

17. Ibid., April 6, 1995.

18. Ibid., March 11 and 18, 1999.

19. Sarah Keeling, "Advising the Millennial Generation," *NACADA Journal*, 23:31, 35. We credit Betty Fearn with recommending we read this article.

20. *The Lamron*, September 21, 1995, October 5, 1995, October 2, 1997, October 9, 1997.

21. Ibid., November 29, 2001, February 7, 2002, February 22, 2001, April 26, 2001, May 3, 2001, September 20, 2006.

22. Ibid., April 20, 27, 1995; March 30, 2006. By College Senate policy the SOFIs must be reviewed every three years, James McNally, "SUNY Geneseo Student Reactions to Faculty Instruction, 1969–1998." Phone call to Jacqueline Connor, Office of Institutional Research, SUNY Geneseo, September 20, 2006; *The Lamron*, November 30, 2006; *ENCompass Weekly*, October 30, 2006.

23. *The Lamron*, April 1, 2004; Rochester *Democrat & Chronicle*, November 26, 2006.

24. *The Lamron*, September 22, 1994; Presidents' Papers, College Archives; undated note from Arthur Hatton.

25. Rochester *Democrat & Chronicle*, July 17, 2001. She was also remembered by Rosati, who drove ninety miles to the Wellsville hospital to visit her the night before she died seven years later, email message from Rosati, November 21, 2005.

26. *The Lamron*, November 17, 2005; *Geneseo ENCompass Weekly*, May 19, 2006; News Release, SUNY Geneseo, July 21, 2005, Presidents' Papers, College Archives; "Some Achieve Greatness," Fall Convocation Address, August 27, 2004; Rochester *Democrat & Chronicle*, August 9, 2005.

27. Former vice president Hatton's recall; *Livingston County News*, December 23, 2004.

28. "Looking Inward and Outward: The Year Ahead," Fall Convocation Address by President Dahl, August 23, 2002.

29. *The Lamron*, September 4, 1997, March 9, 2000, September 21, 2000, September 27, 2001, February 13, 2003, March 23, 2006.

30. "Claiming Our Place," Fall Convocation Address by President Dahl, August 21, 2003.

31. Ibid.; *The Lamron*, November 19, 1992.

32. "Claiming Our Place," Fall Convocation Address by President Dahl, August 21, 2003; Rochester *Democrat & Chronicle*, October 3, 2003.

33. *Geneseo ENCompass*, October 6, 2003; Fred Bright, "Chronology of Sports at Geneseo," McNally, *Fact Book 2000*, 104.

34. *The Lamron*, January 22, 29, February 26, April 8, 2004.

35. "Claiming Our Place," Fall Convocation Address by President Dahl, August 21, 2003.

36. McNally, "Faculty/Staff Awards," n.d.; *Geneseo ENCompass*, March 21, 2003.

37. News Release, March 19, 2004, Presidents' Papers, College Archives: Rochester *Democrat & Chronicle*, March 23, 2004; *The Lamron*, April 15, 2004; September 16, 1999. As of 1999, eighty-nine percent of Geneseo's students were white, compared with seventy-three percent at public four-year colleges and universities generally, *The Lamron*, October 21, 1999.

38. Rochester *Democrat & Chronicle*, September 25, 1998; *The Lamron*, October 1, 1998.

39. *College Senate Bulletin*, 1998/1999, 2, 1999/2000, 12.

40. "Some Achieve Greatness," Fall Convocation Address by President Dahl, August 27, 2004.

41. Rochester *Democrat & Chronicle*, September 17, November 25, 2004, January 26, 2005.

42. Ibid., January 1, 13, 14, March 2, April 6, 12, December 20, April 28, 27, 2005; Arthur Hatton communication to the Geneseo History committee, January 8, 2007.

43. "Advancing Geneseo's Mission," Fall Convocation Address, August 26, 2005; *The Lamron*, April 13, 2006; email from Mary E. McCrank, Media Relations Officer, SUNY Geneseo, November 8, 2006; *ENCompass Weekly*, December 11, 2006.

44. "Advancing Geneseo's Mission," Fall Convocation Address, August 26, 2005.

45. *The Lamron*, April 28, 2005.

46. President Dahl's report to the College Council, February 5, 1997, Presidents' Papers, College Archives; *The Lamron*, April 27, 1995, *Geneseo ENCompass*, September 15, 1999, March 27, 2006. Almost forty percent of Geneseo's 2005 graduates attended graduate school and fewer than five percent were unemployed. These figures hold fairly steady, despite the "dot.com" collapse and post 9/11 upheavals, "Geneseo Class of 2005 Follow-up Study," Career Services Office, "Class of 2001 Follow-Up Study," Presidents' Papers, College Archives. At seventy-seven percent business graduates enjoyed the highest employment rate in 2005, while teacher certification graduates' full-time employment in 2005 declined to forty-three percent from an aberrant 2001 high of seventy-one percent. Liberal arts graduates' employment declined from forty-eight percent in 2001 to thirty-eight percent in 2005.

47. *The Lamron*, April 28, 2005, March 13, 2003, January 26, 2006.

48. *The Lamron*, October 31, 1996, November 2, 2000, October 28, 2004; November 4, 2004.

49. *Geneseo ENCompass Weekly*, March 6, 2006; *New York Teacher*, March 16, 2006; *Geneseo Scene*, Winter 2006, p. 17; *The Lamron*, April 6, 20, 2006.

50. *The Lamron*, October 26, 2006; April 6, 20, 2006, *Livingston County News*, June 29, 2006. Not surprisingly, the bulk of that fifty-two million dollars was spent by students on housing.

51. Rochester *Democrat & Chronicle*, March 12, 2006; *The Lamron*, October 6, 2005.

52. *The Lamron*, March 19, 1998, February 21, 1998, October 9, 1997, April 26, 2001; Fred Bright, comp., "Chronology of Sports at Geneseo," McNally, *Fact Book 2000*, 105; *Geneseo ENCompass Weekly*, May 2, 2006; Rochester *Democrat & Chronicle*, February 16, 2002.

53. Rochester *Democrat & Chronicle*, December 14, 2005; *Geneseo ENCompass Weekly*, May 2, 2006; *Geneseo Scene*, Winter 2006, 5.

54. Dr. James Walker shared his tour description with the Geneseo History Committee, September 20, 2006.

55. News Release, SUNY Geneseo, August 22, 18, 2006.

56. Randal C. Archibold, "Off the Beaten Path: Twenty Colleges Worth a Trip or at Least a Detour," *New York Times*, July 30, 2006, sec. 4/A, 22–25; *Kiplinger's*, February 2006, 90.

57. *Geneseo ENCompass*, Summer 2005; *Livingston County News*, April 27, 2006; *ENCompass News*, December 16, 2003.

58. *The Lamron*, November 30, 2006.

59. *ENCompass News*, December 16, 2006; "Expanding the Experience: 2006 Report of the President & Honor Roll of Donors" (Geneseo, 2006). A Geneseo History Committee member cannot help but recall what an outstanding undergraduate Dr. Sutherland was.

60. Rochester *Democrat & Chronicle*, May 6, 2005, May 26, 2006.

61. *Livingston County News*, June 16, May 12, 2005; personal observations.

62. *Livingston County News*, October 26, June 26, 2006; *The Lamron*, September 21, 2006. The funding included a $522,800 grant from the NYS Office of Science, Technology and Academic Research for research into commercial applications for a lightweight shield against explosives and an $800,000 National Science Foundation grant to study bird flu.

63. Zaidi, "Dismantling SUNY…"

64. Interview of Dr. Wiliam Caren, January 3, 2005; *The Lamron*, September 14, 28, 2006.

65. Rochester *Democrat & Chronicle*, December 25, 2006.

66. Interview of President Dahl by Drs. James McNally and Wayne Mahood, July 19, 2005.

67. Rochester *Democrat & Chronicle*, May 25, 2006.

Epilogue

1. Ogren, *The American State Normal School*, 2.
2. Email correspondence from Dr. Bruce Leslie, September 3, 2006.

Index

Page numbers in bold indicate illustrations. The appendices are not indexed.

A

A & P store, 187
Abbott, Adoniram, J., 32, 50, 51, 60
Abbott, John B., 80, 102, 103, 110
Academic Department, 26, 30, 37-40, 42, 44, 56, 63, 67
Academic divisions created, 192
Access Opportunity Program see also *Equal Opportunity Program*, 222, 280
Accounting program, 242, 246
Accreditation, 121, 157, 176, 247, 286, 301, 307, 308
Adam, Miss, **167**
Administrative reorganization, 192, 230
Admissions office, 230
Advanced English curriculum, 40
Advisory Committee on Technology, 284
Adwell, Paula, **222**
African-American students, 71; "sleep-in" 222
Agonian Sorority, 47, 48, **49**
Akers, Frank, 151, **151, 164,** 166, **230**
Alent, Maurice, **291**
Alent, Rose Bachem, **145,** 165, 228, 268, 277, 289, **291**
Alissandrellow, Michaela, 296
All-Americans, **235, 268,** 269, 270, **270,** 288, 296, **297**
Allan, H., **168**
Allan, James, **168,** 169, 224
Allegany Residence Hall, 199, 282
Allen, Hezekiah, 32
Allen, Jerome, 34, **36,** 56
Allen, Mary P., 42, 44
Allewelt, Miss, **167**
Alley, Joan, 269
Alley, Phillip, 194, **219,** 269
Allinger, Steve, 224, 237
Alpha Delta Sorority, 47
Alpha Sigma Epsilon fraternity, **129,** 130

Altmeyer, Miss, **143**
Alumni and Parent Relations, 23, **291**
Alumni Association 76, 159; founded, 122
Alumni Field House see *Merritt Athletic Center*
Alumni Professorships, 272
Amedore, Angela see *Caplan, Angela Amedore*
American Association of Colleges for Teacher Education (AACTE), 135
American Association of State Colleges, 291
American Association of Teachers Colleges, 121
American Democracy Project see *Council on Public Liberal Arts Colleges*
American Marketing Association, 253-254
Amey, Katherine, **95**
Anderson, Elizabeth, 143
Anemone, Robert, 264
Angel, Benjamin Franklin, 23, 25, **25**
Anniversaries, 25th, 53
Anniversaries, 50th, 76, **98**
Anniversaries, 100th, 215, **216**
Anniversaries, 125th, 276-277, **277, 306**
April, Frank, 74
Aprile (basketball player), **72**
Aprile, Anthony, 65, 67
Arce, G., **249**
Archery, **126**
Arethusa Sorority, 47, 48, 77, **112,** 130
Art department, 227
Art education, **39**
Artist Series, 171
Associated Press, 13, 248, 253
Association to Advance Collegiate Schools of Business, accredits School of Business, 286
Attica Prison riot, 216, 232-233
Atwell, Julie, 296
Austin, Alice, **153,** 157, **170,** 219, 289
Austin, Alice Theater, **184**

Avalone, Robert J., 235
Averill, Clarence, **54**
Avery, Marian, **77**
Avon, Five Arch bridge, **72**
Ayrault, Allen and Bethiah, **30**

B

Babb, Harold, 208
Bachem, Rose see *Alent, Rose*
Bagasan, J., **283**
Bailey (women's basketball player), **96**
Bailey, Charles Randy, 210, **258,** 289
Bailey, Guy A., 62, 74, **88, 102, 115,** 117, 123, 199
Bailey, Susan, 289
Bailey science building, 62, **181, 182,** 198, 199, **301**; groundbreaking, **181**
Baker, Emily, **62**
Baker, Frances, **119**
Balding, Corneil, 132
Balding, Della, **56**
Baldwin, Douglas, 287
Baldwin, Eleanor Trask, 286
Balling, Betsy, **268**
Bancroft, Mrs., **143**
Band, **201**
Bannan, Mary Frances, **94**
Banner system, 252
Baquero, L., **249**
Barber (basketball player), **72**
Barber, Leonard, **68**
Barkin, Leonard, **154**
Barley, Allison, **291**
Barnum, Gertrude, **56**
Barnwell, Ysaye, **205**
Barraco, Anthony, **243**
Barraco, Fred, 169
Barrett, John, 219, 260, 289
Barron's Profile of American Colleges, 255
Barry, S. **167, 193**
Bartlett, Thomas, 276
Bartoo, Leland, **55**
Baseball, 54, **71, 96,** 98, 124, **244,** 270
Basher, Thomas, 235
Basketball, 54, 71, **72, 91,**

93, **97,** 124, **124, 150, 212,** 235, **235, 266,** 270, **270,** 296
Basketball, Intramural, **222**
Basketball, women's, **69, 96, 285**
Battersby, Harold, 219
Baumgart, Jeannine, **289**
Baxi, S. Shiledar, **283**
Beale, Richard, 196, **196**
Beason, Robert, 231
Beck, Jeff, **296**
Beck, Kathryn, **156,** 157
Beebe, Penny, **205**
Behrens, Herman, **115,** 116, **121,** 122, **129,** 155, **155,** 160
Benjamin, Alice, **133**
Bennett, Fred, **191,** 242, 289
Bennett, Gloria, 35
Benz, Paul, **270**
Bergman, R., **168**
Bergstrom, Ann, **209**
Berkness, Hazelle, **155**
Besser, J., **167, 193**
Bickel, Robert, 207
Big Tree Inn, **30,** 302
Bigelow, Daniel, 32
Bikel, Theodore, 211
Biondollilo, Anna Marie see *Loncao, Anna Marie*
Birdseye-Snyder canning factory, 131
Bishop, Anne, **243**
Black box theater, **201**
Black Student Union, **279**
Black studies program, 222
Black, John, 165, 166, **166,** 187
Black, Lillian, **199**
Black, Ralph, **246**
Blackman, Larry, **255**
Blake, Anne S., 66, **67,** 78, 95, 97, 98, 102, 103, 117
Blake, D., **283**
Blake buildings, 15, 80, 103, 133, 134, 158, **179,** 200, 225, 257, 282, **300, 301**
Blakely, Mark, 217
Blakmer, Anna, **62**
Blizzard (1966), 189, **190**
Blizzard (1999), 283
Blood, Melanie, **289**

Bloomer, Richard, **157**
Board of Visitors see also *College Council*, 22, 32-34, 38, 40-41, 44-45, 48-51, 55, 64, 67, 71, 77-78, 85-87, 90, 98-100, 102, 103, 108, 133, 140, 153-154
Boger, Phillip, 231, 290
Boiani, James, **254**
Boles, Mary, **117**
Bolt House, 74, **82**
Bomb threats, 223, 261, 286-287
Bond, Julian, 211
Bondi, Theodore, 131
Bonfiglio, Robert, **290**, 291
Book, Kenneth, **243**
Bookman, Susan, **207**
Boor, Suzy, **291**
Boronczyk, Joe, **270**
Bosch, Isidro, **249**, 264, 299
Bovill, Joseph, **149**
Bovill, Thomas, 105, **149**
Boyd, Helen, **155**, **157**
Boyer, Ernest, 215
Bradford, Dennis, **255**
Braem, Helen, **117**
Breid, Mary, **164**
Brennan, William, 264
Brewer, Bill, 211
Brewer, Gay, 234
Bright, Fred, 6, 212, **230**, **235**, 266, 270, **291**
Bright, Joan, **291**
Brode, D., **173**
Brode, Douglas, 211
Brodie, William A., 21, 23, **24**, 30, 32, 60, 305
Brodie building, 153, **184**, **186**, 198
Bronfeld, Mr., **167**
Bronson, Barnard, **62**
Brooks, Arthur, 30
Brooks, Monty, **222**
Broomfield, M., **247**
Broudy, Harry, 216
Brown, B., **173**
Brown, Cal, 211
Brown, Frances, **107**, 108, **303**
Brown, Fred, 150-151
Brown-Steiner, Terrence, 223
Browne, Terry, **289**
Brunner, James, 175
Bruno, Al, 234
Bryant, George, **91**
Bryant, Lee, 289
Bucke, W. Fowler, 78, 79-80, **79**, 87, 89, 94

Buckley, Julian, 78
Buckley, William F., 259
Buddington, Winton, 270
Budget, 216, 225, 226, 243, 245, 248, 256-257, 261, 262, 265, 267, 272, 279-281, 283, 286, 292, 299
Budget, Planning Statement (1981) for 1982-83 to 1985-86, 246
Budget, SUNY Trustees, 147
Buell, Lucy, 69
Buffalo Braves (basketball team), 232
Bunham, Candace, 247
Burdick, Myra, **51**
Burke, John, **95**
Burns, Mary, **51**
Bush, George H.W., 260
Bush, Keena, **268**
Bushnell, Judith, 6, 290
Butler, Nicholas, 53
Butterworth, Richard, 269
Buzzo see *Bruno, Al*

C

Calicchia, Mark, 233, **233**
Camp Union (Geneseo, N.Y.), 23
Campbell (basketball player), **72**
Campbell (football player), **68**
Campbell, Archibald, **54**
Campus aerial views, **104**, **179**, **180**, **181**, **182**, **304**
Campus Auxiliary Services (CAS), 158
Campus House, 302
Campus maps, **178**, **305**
Campus planning, 197
Campus School, 14, 29, 35, 38, 45, 52, 63, 65, 67-68, 79, 99-102, **101**, 107, 111, 116, **120**, 135, 153, 166, **183**, 198, 200, 211, 219, 225-226, 244, 256, 272, 302, 307
Capili, J., **283**
Caplan, Angela Amedore, 234
Caplan, Barry, 234
Caragher, Mary, 81
Carbaugh, Gaile, 117, **121**, **155**, **157**, **172**
Caren, William, 230, **230**, 242, 246, 254, 263, 264, **290**, 302
Carey, Hugh, 225, 243-245, 248
Carillon bells, 259
Carls, B., **148**
Carlson, William, 163, **163**

Carmer, Carl, 123
Carnival of Gymnastics, 54, 81, 163
Carol Choristers, **95**, 111, 259
Caron, Glenn Gordon, 236, 260
Carrington, David, **164**
Carroll, Betty, 90
Carter, David, 208
Case, Leslie, 62
Casler, Lawrence, 228
Catalano, Renne, **296**
Censorship accusation, 258
Centennial see *Anniversaries, 100th*
Center Street School see *Geneseo Union Free School District No. 5*
Central Council, 224, 258, 267
Chamber Singers, 194, **205**, **239**, 259, **263**
Chamber Symphony, 259
Chamberlain, Ella, 44
Chan, K., **283**
Chancellor's Award for Excellence in Librarianship, 290
Chancellor's Award for Excellence in Professional Service, 231
Chancellor's Award for Excellence in Scholarship and Creative Activities, 264
Chancellor's Award for Excellence in Teaching, 228-229, 231, 236, 264, 290, 299
Chancellor's Research Recognition Award, 264, 298-299
Chanler, Gertrude, 262
Chapman, Mike, 235
Cheerleaders, **287**
Chen, James, **219**
Chichester, Maria, **51**
Chichester, Susan, 252-253, 284
Chin, Michael, 294-295
Christmas caroling, **159**
Christmas dinner (1951), 157
Christmas pageant, **158**
Chung, J., **283**
Church, Todd, 258
Cicoria, Ronald, 213
Clancy, John, **54**
Clar, Jim, 270, **270**
Clark, D., **247**
Clark, L. Watson, 64, 79, **80**, 105, **129**, 235

Clark, L. Watson service building, 79, **182**, 198, 235
Class of '67, recall of the times, 189
Class of 1893, 46, **47**
Classical curriculum, 40
Climensen, Helen, **95**
Clinton, Hillary, **290**
Clionian Sorority, 47, **48**, **87**, 158, 197
Cobblestone School see *Geneseo Union Free School District No. 5*
Coe, Jennie, **51**
Coffin, Ruth see *Underhill, Ruth Coffin*
Colahan, Thomas S., 209, **209**, **217**, 217-220, 223, 224, 226-228, 238, 242, 247-249, 263, 268, 272
Coleman, Cecil, 289
Collective bargaining, 195
College Center (Blake A), 134, 157, **172**, 175, **179**, 208, 211
College Council see also *Board of Visitors*, 21, 30, 31, 161, 167, 190, **199**, 203, 204, 217, 242, 276
College Personnel Committee see also *Faculty Personnel Committee*, 228, 291
College planning, 230, 247, post World War II, 132-133
College Planning Council, 266
College Priorities Committee, 230, 244-246, 266
College Republicans, 258
College seal, 196-197, **196**
College Senate see also *Faculty Senate*, 266
College Union (MacVittie College Union), 142, 157, 198, 210, 238
Collins, Irma Hamer, 286
Collins Alumni Center, 286
Colton, Douglas, 233
Columbia University, 139
Comley, Robert, 268
Computer Science program, 246
Computerization, 251, 283-285
Computing and Information Technology (CIT), 251
Comstock, Laura, **62**
Condoms, 258
Conlon, Brenda, 268

Conlon, James Thomas, 150, **193**, 268
Constant, A., **247**
Construction, 111-112, 163, 176, 197, 225, 282, 302, 307
Contario, Joseph, 233
Conway-Turner, Katherine, 290, **290**
Cook, J. **168**
Cook, Thomas, 277
Cook, William, 219, 228, 269, **288**, 293
Cooper, Hermann, **89**, 93,103, 111-113, 116, 121, 132, **133**, 134, 140, 144, 148, 152, 154, 167, 176, 215, **216**
Cooper, Mrs., **216**
Cope, Joseph, 290
Copeland, E. Stanley, **199**
Core curriculum see also *Curriculum*, 249-250, 279-280
Cornell University, 101, 139
Cosby, Bill, 232
Costello, Lee, **95**
Cothurnus, **114**, 157, 171
Cotton, William, **157**, 165
Cottone, Joan, 162
Coughtry, Jay, 202, 213
Council on Public Liberal Arts Colleges (COPLAC), 291, 301, 307
Countryman, Martha Jane, 124
Countryman, R. Leroy, **88**, **94**, **115**, 124
County Days, 216
Course-Teacher Evaluation see also *Student Opinion of Faculty Instruction*, 227-228
Cox, Gary, **255**
Coy, Peter, 13, 248, 253
Craig Colony, Sonyea, 79, **92**, 94-95, 106, 163
Crandall, Ann, **303**
Crew, 296, **296**, **297**
Cripps, Scott, **270**
Crosby, Emilye, 290
Cross country, 54, 233, 235, 270, 297
Cross country, women's, 270, **296**
Crossett, Floyd, 60
Crowell, Fern, **77**
Culver, C., **173**

Culver, Lucille, 117
Cunningham, Karla, 290
Cuomo, Mario, 248, 261
Curfews, 74, 125
Curle, Tom, **270**
Curriculum, 40, 49-50, 55, 63, 65, 69, 93, 113, 115, 118-120, 149, 166-168, 192, 206, 217-221, 238, 242, 246, 249-250, 279-280, 306
Curriculum Task Force, 279
Curtiss, Emeline McMaster, **51**, **62**
Czop, Diane, **234**

D

D'Ambrosia, Joe, **270**
Dadrian, Vahakn, 265
Dahl, Christopher C., **7**, 31, 268, **276**, **277**, 277-278, 280-281, 285-288, 290, **290**, 291, 293, 298, 300, 302, 303, 307; appointed interim president and president, 275-276; installed, 276
Dahl, George, **276**
Daley, Helen, **62**
Dalton, R., **148**
Dance ensemble, **200**, **250**, **252**, 288
Dances, **81**, **122**
Daniels, Charles, 209
Dates, Sylvia, **95**
Davey, Alice, **56**
Davis (basketball player), **72**
Davis (football player), **68**
Davis, Gilbert, 208
Davis, John, **171**
Davis, William, 251-253, 283
Deal, Marjorie see *Lewis, Marjorie*
DeBell, Bettina G. Pollard, 259
DeCarne, Miss, **167**
Dechario, Joseph, 228, **229**, **289**
Decker, Denise, 236
DeFord, Ruth, **229**
Delarm, Elisa, **289**
Delehanty, Julia, 166, **168**
DeLoria, David, 237
Delphic Fraternity, 29, 43, **43**, 44, 47, 130
Delta Kappa Fraternity, 47

Delta Kappa Tau fraternity, **213**
DeMarco, Brian, 294, **294**
DeMarco, Roland, **91**
DeMocker, Carroll, **149**
Democrat Socialists Party, 260
Demonstration and Practice School see *Campus School*
DeMott, Donald, 218, 268
DePaoli, Lenore, **250**
Department of Rural Education, 97, 103, 306
Derby, William, **156**, 165, 210, **258**, 268
de Russy, Candace, 279
Desert Storm, 269
DeSeyn, Donna, 168
Deutsch, John, **254**
Deutsch, Kenneth, 299
DeVito, Shelly, **250**
DeVoto, Bernard, 123
Dew, Frances, **199**, 242
Dewey, Thomas E., 146, 161,163, **163**
Dewitt, Karen, 271
Diaz, J., **249**
Dietsche, James, **97**, 115, 159
Dietsche, William, **97**
Dievendorf, Mark, **205**
Diploma, 1872, **42**
Discavage, Nancy, **234**
Disparti sisters, 198
Distinguished Professors, 289-290
Distinguished Service Award, 157, 237
Distinguished Service Professors, 231, 297
Distinguished Teaching Professors, 194, 219, 228, 231, 247, 264, 268, 288
Diversity Commission, 293
Diving, **97**, **211**
Division of Educational Studies, 221
Dixon, Barbara, 277, 289
Domm, Jim, **205**
Donnelly, Delores, 237-238
Dotterwich, Paul, 296
Doty, Lockwood L., 20, 23, **24**, 305
Doty, Lockwood R., 60, 78, 103, 110
Doty building see also *Geneseo Central Junior-Senior High School*, 73, **150**, 225, 302

Dowdle, Harold, **91**
Downing, Augustus S., 63, 78
Drake, John, **42**, 43
Dramatic arts program, approved, 149
Dramatic productions, 47-48, **77**, **91**, **95**,**152**, **173**, **175**, **209**, **256**, **260**
Draper, Andrew Sloan, 61-62
Dudley (football player), **68**
Duff, Ann, **225**
Duffy, Karen, 231
Duffy, Paul, 269
Duggan, Marie, 124
Duncan, Vernon, **222**
Dunn, "Herb", **54**
Durkin, Robert, **164**, **168**

E

Easton, Celia, 7, 264, 288
Eaton, Robert, 218-219
Eberhardt, James G., **143**, 171
Ebrite, Ethel, **118**
Eccles, John, 216
Edgar, Stacey, 229, 250, **255**
Edgar, William, 219, 228, 250, **255**
Educational Opportunity Program see also *Access Opportunity Program*, 222
Edwards, William, **289**
Egan, Mrs., **143**
Ehrle, Elwood B., 207
Eisenberg, Anne, 290
Elementary and Secondary Education and Reading department, created, 247
Elementary English curriculum, 40, 49
Elliot-Bearce, Charles, 295
Ellsburg, Daniel, 232
Emerson Hall, 73, **82**
Energy costs, 229
Enrollment see *Student enrollment*
Equal Opportunity Program, 247
Erie Residence Hall, **183**, 199
Erwin, Austin W., Jr., **100**
Erwin, Austin W., Sr., 80, 134, 152, 161, 163, **163**, 199
Erwin, Howard, **147**
Erwin building, 133, 152, **182**, **183**, 198, 199, 251, **301**

Espy, Herbert G., **140**, 141,142,144, 148-149, 151, 154,155, 157, 160, 162, 176, 193, 197, 307; appointed president, 140; dies, 268
Eurich, Alvin, C. 146
Evans, Maurice, 171

F

Faculty, 1871, **36**
Faculty, 1891, **51**
Faculty, 1904-1905, **62**
Faculty, 1914-1915, **79**
Faculty accountability, 227
Faculty Council, **115**, **121**
Faculty—evaluation by students, 227-228
Faculty Personnel Committee see also *College Personnel Committee*, 228
Faculty recruitment, 193
Faculty salaries, 35, 105, 199
Faculty Senate see also *College Senate*, 203, 204, 210, 221, 228
Faculty Senate, Student Affairs Committee, 203
Faculty/staff cuts, 226, 229-231, 243, 245, 256, 261, 267
Faculty Student Association (FSA), 157
Faculty tenure, 227
Fadiman, Clifton, 123
Fallbrook, **84**
Farquarson, M., **247**
Farrell, Cathy, **205**
Faulkner, Carol, 290
Fausold, Martin L., 18, 49, **156**, 165, 193, 210, 238, 266, 268
Fawcett, S., **173**
Fearn, Betty, **279**
Fearn, Isom E., Jr., 222, **222**, 223, 247
Fedder, Miss, **143**
Fees, student activity, 205, 259
Fees, technology, 283
Feinberg, Benjamin, 119-120, 154
Felton, Cornelius, 19
Fennell, Patty Malet, **296**
Fenton, Reuben E., 20
Fernan, Mary, **117**
Ferrell, Johnnie, **289**
Ferriss, Bill, 124
Ferriss, Lester, 125
Fess, Simeon, 76

Fidura, Fred, 193, 268
Fielder, Charles, 60
Filice, Carlo, **255**
Final examinations, 210
Fine arts building see *Brodie building*
Fink, Daniel, 218, 289, **289**
Finke, Christy, **296**
Finkle, Barbara, 211
Fisher, Rosalind, 17, 23, 42, 86, 143, **145**, 156, **164**, 207, 215
Fiske, Edward, 278, 308
Fitch, Scott, **266**, **268**, 270
Fitzgerald, Jim, **230**
Flack, Lori, **250**
Flansburg (football player), **68**
Fleming, Mathew, 288
Fletcher, Kurt, 264, **294**
Fletcher, Sara or Sarah, 35, **36**
Flynn, Thomas, 128
Flynn, William, **55**
Foland, Elbert and Ina, 73
Football, 53, **54**, **68**, 71, 98
Ford, Gerald, 260, **260**
Foreign language department, 165, 221
Forest, Herman, 203, **221**, 254, 268
Forrest, Scott, **270**
Forrester, J., **167**, **193**
Foster, Charles, 141, 147
Foster, Helen Vance, **157**, 165, 166, 268
Fox, Andrew, 247
Fox, Ernie, 268
Fraley, Mrs. J., **62**
Fraser, Bertha Paine, 85
Fraser, John, **71**
Fraternities and Sororities see also names of specific groups, **40**, 46-48, 171; Houses, **83**; National affiliates banned, 161
Freeman, John, **71**
Freeman, Kenneth, 161, **161**, 164,**164**, 215, **216**
Freeman, Mrs., **216**
Freiburger, Robert, 169, **171**
Freshman Beanies, **148**, 170
Freshmen, 170
Frey, Barbara, 155
Friar (football player), **68**
Friends of Milne Library, 300
Fritz, M., **249**
Frost, Robert, 123
Fulbright Scholars, 247
Fuller, Betty Jo, **164**
Fuller, Blanche, 88
Fuller, R. Buckminster, **209**

Fundraising, 45, 231, 247, 270, 273, 285, 286, 292
Funnell, R., **193**

G

G. I. Bill of Rights (Servicemen's Readjustment Act), 132-133, 139
Gagnier, George, 296
Gallo, Anthony, 288
Gamma Sigma Fraternity, 47, 48, 71
Garver, Francis M., 85-86
Gault, Benjamin J., 126
Gay and Lesbian Support Group, 258
Gazebo, **199**
Geary, Todd, **297**
Gee, R. Matthew, **287**
Geiger, Cristina, 293
Geiger, David, **254**, 264, 289, 298
Gender-neutral language, 258
Genesee College (Lima, N.Y.), 20
Genesee Residence Hall, 199, 282
Genesee Valley National Bank, 187
Genesee Valley Park Association, 46
Geneseo Academy see *Temple Hill Academy*
Geneseo Afro-American Student Society, 209
Geneseo Central Junior-Senior High School, 14, 25, **99**, 101, 225, 302
Geneseo Central School, 244, 245
Geneseo Central School District, 197
Geneseo Community Players, 157
Geneseo Compass, 209
Geneseo Foundation, Inc. 22, 122, 235, 238, 242, **243**, 262, 270, 285, 286, 297, created 231
Geneseo, N.Y., **16**, 19, **28**, **32**, **58**, **76**, **138**, **140**, **188**, **198**, **216**, **274**, 304; Bridges, **22**; Fires, 17, 22, **23**, **214**, 234; Indebtedness, 23
Geneseo Normal and Training School see *SUNY Geneseo* and more specific headings

Geneseo Normal High School, 67, 69
Geneseo Sports Hall of Fame, 235
Geneseo String Band, **253**, 260
Geneseo Students for Peace and Justice, 258
Geneseo Symphony Orchestra, performs in China, 297-298, **303**
Geneseo Union Free District No. 4, 197
Geneseo Union Free School District No. 5, 67, **68**, 98-100, 108; trustees, 100
GENseng, 288, 291
George's, **187**
Gewandter, Jennifer, **287**
Giles, M., **193**
Gillam, Tim, **212**
Gillen, James "Fred", 218
Girolmo, David, 232
Giuliani, Rudolph, 259
Glantz, B., **175**
Glasgow, Miss, **143**
Glass, Becky, **290**, 293
Glynn, Helen, **155**
Godsave, Bruce, 213, 259, **277**
Godspell, 260
Goeckel, Robert, 264
Goetzinger, Charles S., 218, 268
Goewey, Gordon, **173**
Goheen, Sara, **51**, **62**
Gohlman, William, **258**
Goldwater Scholarship, 266, 288, 292, 294
Golf, 270
Gollin, Rita, 193
Goodale, Jack, 128
Gooding House, 73
Gordon, D., **193**
Gordon, David, 289
Gorham, J.B., 35, **36**
Gottschalk, Hans, **145**
Gould, Samuel, 191,192, 206, 218
Graber, Edward, **62**
Grading, 251
Graduate programs, 149, 206, 307; Chemistry, 219; English, 192; Library science, 157, 167, 192, 245-246, 272; Mathematics, 192, 219; Physics, 219; Speech and Hearing, 168
Graduates, salaries, 114-115

Graduation requirements, 115
Graduations, **80**,160, **197**, 233, **273**, **307**, **309**; 1872, 29, 42, 43; 1955, 162; 1970, 162; 1973, 162; 1994, 238
Grammar or Junior High School, 65
Grand Ole Opry, 211
Grants, Campus EAI, National Science Foundation, 285
Graves, Francis P., 76, 78, 86, 89, 91
Gray, Sean, **270**
Great Depression, 105-106, 108, 110-111, 135, 306
Greek tree, 211, **211**
Green, Sam, 222
Greene, Robert A., 74, **94**, **102**, **116**, 117, **121**, 123, 157, 199
Greene building, 74, **185**, 199, **301**
Greenfield, Thomas, 268
Greenman, Theodora, 162, 191, **191**, **199**, 242, **303**
Greenwood, Miss W., 48
Gregoire, J. Peter, 173-174
Grey (football player), **68**
Griffin, C., **247**
Griffin, C., **249**
Griggs, Amanda, 297
Griggs, Shannon, **296**, 297
Grose, Debra see *Hill, Debra Grose*
Gross, Mae, **77**
Grove, Mary, 166, **167**, **193**
Grow, Alice, **207**
Guariglia, Mike, **270**
Gucwa, Jessica, 294
Gunther, Emma, **62**
Guy, Bob, **285**
Gymnasium, Old Main see *Old Main Gymnasium*
Gymnasium, planned, 112

H

Hacettepe (Turkey) University, 293, 301
Hadley, Jim, **212**
Hagen, Jack, 131
Hakes, Elizabeth, **167**
Hall, Phebe, **37**, **51**, **62**
Hall, Rachel, 290

Hall, Robert, 157
Hall, Truman, **157**
Halleck, Seymour L., 207
Hamilton, Thomas, **133**
Hamilton, William, **116**, 129
Hamilton-Rodgers, Patty, **291**
Hanley, Joseph, 112, 118
Hanson, Daryl, 165, 171, **173**
Harder, Worth, 289
Harding, Ruth, **77**
Harding, Walter, 143-144, **145**, 156, 160,165, 205, 208, 213, 224, **228**, 289
Hargrave, Kyle, **270**
Harke, Douglas, 194, 299
Harmon, Lucy, **94**, **115**, 116, **118**, **121**, 125, **145**, 156
Harper, Manley H., 87-91, 93
Harriman, Averell, 163
Hart, M., **168**
Harter, Carol, 31, 238, 262, **262**, 264-267, **270**, 272, 273, 275, 285, 302, 307; appointed president, 261-262; inauguration, **263**; leaves, 271
Hartzell, Karl, **121**
Haseltine, Robert, 268
Haspiel, George, **170**
Hatheway, Richard, 218, **219**
Hatton, Arthur, 13, 230-231, **231**, 237, 242, 260, 263, 273, 285, 286, **290**, 293, 302
Hayes-Sugarman, Katie, 261
Health and physical education classes, **145**
Health and physical education requirement eliminated, 266
Heating plant, 133, **141**, 163
Hellmich, Lillian, **117**
Henry, Paula, 290
Hepler, Paul, 6, 14, 153, **153**, 165, **167**, 172, **196**, 268, 289
Herrala, Miss, **167**
Herzman, Ronald, 219, 228, 288, **288**
Hickey, James A., 48
Hicks, Hazel, 117
Hide and Seek, Whoop!, **38**
Higgins, Marion, 122
Higgins, Smith, 128
Hill, Debra Grose, 262, **290**
Hillel Club, **154**
Hilton, N.Y. High School, 297

Hinckley, Duncan, 212, **212**, 235, 269
Hinckley, Linda Piccirillo, 269
Hinz, Elaine Kupi, 232
Hispanos Unidos en Geneseo, **249**
History department, 220
Hockey, 269, **270**, 296
Hoekstra, David, 295
Hoey, John, 296, **296**
Hoffman, Abbie, 232, **232**, 259
Hoke (women's basketball player), **96**
Holcomb, Frederick, 101, **115**, **121**
Holcomb, Winfield A., 86-88, **86**, **88**, 90-91, 93, 95-99, 102, 103, 140, 306; appointed principal, 86; retires, 103
Holcomb School see *Campus School*
Holland, Carol, **95**
Holland, Henry, 208
Homecoming, **14**, 163, **164**, **174**, **200**, **213**, **227**, 233, **234**, **253**, **276**, **298**, **306**
Honors college, 293, 298, 301, 302, 303
Honors program, 250
Hooker, Ava, **56**
Hooker, Naomi, **56**
Hoops, Harold, 269
Hoover, Coach, **97**
Hopf, Arlene Myers, 236
Hopf, John, 236
Horek, Elizabeth see *Anderson, Elizabeth*
Horseback riding, **130**
Hotchkiss, Mary, **77**
Hotel Geneseo, **203**
Houce, Belle, **56**
Houlihan, Mike, **297**
Houston, Gertrude, 273
Houston, Robert, **218**
Houston House, 73
Howe, Harmon, 33
Howe, Mallory, 298
Howe, Richard, 156, **156**
Howerton, Glen, 206
Hub, The, 294
Hubbard, Solomon, 32, 33, 60
Huey, G., **283**
Huff, G. Bradley, **219**
Hughes, R., **193**

Humanities core courses, 220, 249-250
Humphrey, Hubert, 173
Hurlburt, "Jap", **54**
Hurricane relief efforts, 295
Huynh, Bobi, 271
Huynh, DiemHang Kennison see *Younes, DiemHang Kennison Huynh*
Huynh, MinhHang Kennison, 271, **271**
Huynh, My Hang, 271, **271**
Huynh, PhuongHang, 271, **271**
Hyde, Ellis, 115

I

Ice storm (1991), **265**
Idiculla, Muttaniyil, 268
Idle Hour, **224**
In Between, **269**
Influenza, 70
Innis, Donald Q., 195, 208, 210, 268
Integrated Science Center, 280, **281**, 287, 300, **300**, 301, **301**, **302**, 308
Interfaith Center, 211
Intermediate Department, 26, 37, 38, 65
Intermediate program, 93
International programs, 206, 293, 301, 308
Intersession courses, 267
Inter-Varsity Christian Fellowship, 258
Intramurals, 222, **222**
Isaf, R., **193**
Isgro, M., **193**
Isgro, Robert, 194, **205**, **229**, 259, **263**, 268, **289**
Ives, Nancy, **222**

J

Jacuzzo, Tony, **149**
Jakubauskas, Edward, 141, **153**, 242-247, **242**, **244**, 256-258, 261, 264, 272, 273, 307; appointed president, 241; leaves Geneseo, 255-256
Jakubauskas, Ruth, **244**
Jam Kitchen, 74, **75**
Janosik, Edward, 218
Jaquay, Bob, **205**

Jensen, Mary, 266
Jimbo, T., **283**
Johnson, Bess, **155**
Johnson, Chaunise Dorell, **287**
Johnson, David, **254**
Johnson, Mary Jo Armstrong, **158**
Johnson, Philip, **156**
Johnson, William A., **279**
Johnston, Dean, **243**, **290**
Johnston, Jack, **264**, **289**
Johnstone, D. Bruce, 31, 261, **263**, 265
Jones (women's basketball player), **96**
Jones, Lydia, **62**, **165**
Jones Residence Hall, 163, 200, 282
Jordan, Bruce, 213
Joshi, Bhairav, 219, **254**
Junior high program, 93

K

Kadashaw, Miss, 21
Kaldor, Ivan, 246, **246**
Kallio, Kenneth, 264
Kaplan, Randy, 291
Karnath, Steve, **212**
Katrina Compassion Award, 295
Kaufman, Bel, 211
Kaul, Patricia Brown, 168
Keane, Vincent, 219
Keller, B. J., 156, 157
Kellogg, G., **173**
Kelly, John, **199**
Kelly, William, 208
Kelsey, Madame, 41
Kelsey, Otto, 46, **47**, 60, 64
Kelsey field, 46, 65, 76, **96**, 124
Kemerer, Frank, 229-230
Kemp, Virginia, 219, 220, 263, 268, 289
Kennison, Lynn Melizzi, 271
Kennison, Weston, 271, 295
Kentner, Martin, 212, **230**, 235
Killip, Lizzie, 35, **36**
Kim, H., **283**
Kimball (basketball player), **72**
Kimball, James, **253**, 260, **289**
Kindergarten-Primary program, 63, 65, 66, **66**, **67**, 81, 93
King, Robert, 281, 292
Kinsey, Kenneth, 194, **219**
Kintz, Ellen, 264
Kiplinger's, 298

Kirk, Jo, **291**
Kirkwood, James, **289**
Klapper, Miss, **167**
Klehamer, Lois Ann, 143
Kleniewski, Nancy, 269
Knight, Miss, **167**
Knight Spot, 294
Knightline, **295**
Knightweb, 284
Kraus, Karen, 269
Kreher, Paul, 269
Krisher, Elwood ("Fritz"), 127-128
Kritzler, Charles, **246**
Krumrine, Dave, **211**
Krupsak, Mary Ann, **195**
Kucaba, John, **173**, 228, **229**
Kuhl, Louise, 117, **121**, 151,161,**164**, 176, 235
Kuhl gymnasium, 117; dedicated 235
Kupi, Elaine see *Hinz, Elaine Kupi*
Kyle, John, **149**

L

Labeste, A., **283**
Labeste, C., **283**
Lackey, Donald, 289
Lacrosse, 235, 296
Ladies Athletic Association, 47
Ladies Literary Club, 47
Lafferty, Beulah, **157**
LaGattuta, Nicholas, 221
Lagootie, Pete, story, 173
Lambert, Leo, 236
Lambert, Stephen, 233, **233**
Lamron, 50th Anniversary, **78**
Lancman, Rory, 260
Land acquisition 25, 197
Lane, William, 30, 31, **218**
Lanphear, Carol, **200**
Latorella, Henry, 219
Lauderdale, Walter E., Jr., 60
Lauderdale, Walter E., Sr., 32, 33, 60, 305
Lauderdale Infirmary, **182**, 198
Laurini, V., **168**
LaVerdi, Mrs., **143**
Lavery, Edward, **95**
Least, Joe, **149**
Lederer, Bertha, 153, **153**, **167**, **193**, **243**, **244**, **291**
Lederer Gallery, 153, **153**, **207**
Ledoux, Miss, **167**
Lee, Fiona, **287**
Leelamma, Srinivasa G., 193-

194, 289
Lehman, Clarence, 94, 103, **115**, 115-116
Lehman, Herbert, 118, 120
Lehman, Lyle, 256, 295
Leith, K., **175**
Leno, Jay, 259
Lent, Edna, **119**
Lent, R., **175**
Leslie, Bruce, 218, 304
Letchworth Dining Hall, 199
Lettermen's Club, **168**
Leventer, Herbert, 219, 227
Levison, Kenneth H., 263, 266, 273, 278, 280, 288, **290**
Lewis, C., **168**
Lewis, Marjorie, 219
Lexington (Massachusetts) State Normal School, 20
Leyerle, William, **229**, **289**
Liao, J., **283**
Liberal arts programs, 166-167, 192, 217-218
Library Club, **119**
Library education, 64, 80, 81, 93, 118, 149, 272, 307; M.S. in library science approved, 157; M.S. in library science program starts, 167; School of Library and Information Science closed, 245-246
Library, Fraser, 112, 133, **143**, 162-163, 171, 200
Library, Milne (for the original Milne Library built in 1956, see *Library, Fraser*), **194**, 198, 199, **218**, **226**, 261, **284**, 299-300, **300**, **301**, 302
Library, Old Main, 53, 55, 64, **65**, 81, **87**, **123**, 142
Liddy, G. Gordon, 232
Lim, Seong B., 293
Lin, Rong, 264
Linfoot, Benjamin, 187
Linfoot, John, **243**
Linfoot, Ruth, **243**
Linville, Larry, 259
Lippincott, Douglas, 258
Lipson, Frances Willey, 166
List, Eugene, 171
Liu, Jeeloo, **255**
Livingston County Court House, **18**
Livingston County High School see *Temple Hill Academy*
Livingston County Historical Society, 101
Livingston County Republican

dinner, 210
Livingston Republican, 44, 57, 62, 68-69, 71, 73, 76, 79, 86, 88, 91, 131, 210, 237, 260
Livingston Residence Hall, 163, 200
Lockhart, James, 285
Lockhart, John, **243**
Lockhart Gallery, 23
Lockhart Professorships, 272
Loncao, Anna Marie, 166, **167**, **193**
Lonero, Joseph P., 205
Lord, Scott, 31, 32
Lotz, Catherine, **56**
Lotz, Crystine, **56**
Lougeay, Cheryl, 269
Lougeay, Ray, 269, 290
Lowell, Grace, **77**
Loyalty oaths, 75, 155
Lucenti, Lisa, 266
Luk, J., **283**
Luna, R., **249**
Lupardo, William, **207**
Lynch, H., **193**
Lynch, Mrs., **167**
Lynch, Robert, **196**
Lynds, Dorothy, **170**
Lyon, Norman, **157**, 289
Lyons, Jim, 296

M

M & B (Statesmen), 171
Mack, Edna, **169**
Macula, Anthony, 299
MacVittie, Margaret, **207**, **216**, **225**
MacVittie, Robert W., 31, 37, 164, **190**, 191-200, **191**, **196**, **197**, **199**, **200**, 202-203, 204, 205-209, **207**, **209**, 213, 215-218, **216**, **217**, **218**, 220, 222-228, **225**, 230, 232, 238, 241, 242, 261, **261**, 266, 272, 289, 302, 307; appointed president, 190; acting president, 260-261; retires, 237; dies, 238
MacVitttie, Robert W., Jr., 238
Magri, Francesca, **296**
Mahood, Wayne, 6, 228
Maintenance staff, **149**
Maisel, Mark, 269
Malson, Sally, 224

Man of La Mancha, 232
Mandatory fees see *Fees,
    student activity*
Mangione, Chuck, 216
Manly, David, 215, 216, 226
Mann, Horace, 19
Marceau, Marcel, 232
Marchewska, C., **173**
Marcy, Laura, **205**
Mark, Joan, 157
Marks, Leo, 170
Marozas, Donald, 236
Marshall, D., **193**
Martin, Christiana, **296**
Martin, David A., 195, 204,
    219
Martin, Steve, 232
Mary Jemison Dining Hall, 15,
    163, **180**, 294, **295**
Mason, Barbara, **289**
Masquera, S., **249**
Mastodon, 264
Mathematics department
    created, 168
Mathew, R., **283**
Matlin, Margaret, 288, **288**
Mattera, Gloria, **167**, **195**,
    196, 268
Matthews, Thomas, **259**, 295
Mau, Clayton, **88**, **90**, 93,
    115, **121**, 126, **172**
Maxwell, Raymond, 269
Mazuzan, George, 219, 227
McBride, Elizabeth, **51**, **62**
McCaffery, B., **193**
McCarthy, Jerry, 208
McClellan, Jeanette and
    Robert, 285
McClellan House, 23, 143,
    213, 285, 286, 302
McCluskey House, **82**
McCoy, Beth, 290
McCurdy (women's basketball
    player), **96**
McCurdy, Archie, **149**
McCurdy House, 73
McDonald, William, 128
McDonnell, Karen Rollek, **296**
McEwen, Rosemary, 290
McKibben, Frank, 128, **128**
McMaster, Emma, 35, **36**
McMaster, Lenora, **191**, 242,
    303
McNally, James, 6, 226, 247,
    289, **291**
McNally, Shirley, **291**
McNaughton, Howard, **71**

McNaughton, Maggie, 44
McQuilkin, W., **168**
McTarnaghan, Beverly Boyce
    172
McTarnaghan, Roy, 169, **170**,
    172, 217
Meagher (women's basketball
    player), **96**
Measles, 258
Megathlin, Gerrard, **116**, 117,
    129
Meisel, David, 194, **219**
Meisenheimer, Jill, **205**
Melizzi, Lynn see *Kennison,
    Lynn Melizzi*
Mellon Fellowships, 266
Mendenhall, Ida, 64
Merchant, E. J., **95**
Meritorious Service Award,
    237
Merrill, Karen, **296**
Merritt, Myrtle, **145**, 155,
    164, **230**, 235, **243**,
    286
Merritt Athletic Center, 155,
    185, **225**, 235, 243, 286
Metz, Dale, 298
Meuser, John, 175, **175**
Meyer, Harold, 187
Meyer, Robert, 150, **167**, 268
Middle States Commission on
    Higher Education, 157,
    176, 247, 286, 301, 307
Migrant Center see *New York
    State Center for Migrant
    Studies*
Military Draft, 127, 223, 233,
    233
Miller, H. Gordon, **210**, 228
Miller, Nathan, 74
Miller, Peter, 32
Miller, R. Dudley, **92**, 95,
    117, **157**
Mills, Josephine, 165, 166,
    246
Milne, James M., 43
Milne, John M, 34, **36**, 43, 48-
    50, **50**, **51**, 53, 55, 57,
    276, 306; dies, 56
Milne, William J., 33, **33**, 34,
    36, 40-45, 48-49, **51**, 57,
    61, 230, 305-306
Minckler block, **58**, **140**
Minemier, Betty, **243**
Minerva statue, 123-124, **123**,
    299-300, **300**
Mingrino, Fred, 234

Minority Student Council, 247,
    247
Minton, Steve, 296
Miskell, Charles, 165
Mitchell, June, 124
Moench, Francis J., 102, **133**,
    153, **158**, **161**, 162-164,
    162, **163**, 174-177,
    177, **181**, 192-193,
    193, **196**, 197, 213, 215,
    216, 242, 307; appointed
    president, 161-162; dies,
    268
Moench, Katharine, **158**,
    161, 162, **162**, **216**
Moffat, Mr., 63
Moldram, R., **168**
Monaghan, Mark, **268**
Money magazine, 253, 278
Monroe County Sheriff's
    Department, 261
Monroe Residence Hall, 163,
    200
Montgomery, Liz, **296**
Montgomery, Mildred, **77**
Mooney, Mike, 293, **293**
Moonlighting, 260
Moore, Bruce, **155**
Moore, Marilyn, 270
Moran, J. Louise, **102**
Moratorium (October 1969),
    208-209
Morelle, Joseph, 236-237
Morey, L. Charles, 33, **34**, 64
Morse, Michelle, 294
Moscow State University, 293,
    301
Mothersell, Lawrence, 170
Mower, George, 205-206
Mulcahy, Helen, **133**
Muldner, Josh, **297**
Muller, Mark, **270**
Mullin, Daniel, 212, **225**,
    230, 232, 235, 268
Murphy, Margaret, **77**
Murray, Jeanne, **250**
Murray, Merrill, **157**
Mussman, Emanuel, **145**
Myers, Arlene see *Hopf, Arlene
    Myers*

N

Nadelhaft, Jerome, 205-206
Nader, Ralph, 211
Nagle, Florence, **118**

Nahabedian, Kevork, 218, 268
Nassau Residence Hall, 199
National Council for
    Accreditation of Teacher
    Education, 301
National Teacher Examination,
    247
National Youth Administration
    (NYA), 106
NCAA Woman of the Year, 288
Nearing, Scott, 73
Neese, Janet, **246**
Neighborhood School see
    Pestalozzi-Froebel School
Netzer, Royal, 116, **121**, **129**,
    149, 155, 161
Neuffer, Elizabeth R. Raynor,
    286
Neureiter, Paul 114, 116,
    116, 129, 131, **142**, 157,
    160, **172**, 176, 210, 268
New York State Board of
    Regents, 18, 61, 86, 113,
    118, 120
New York State Center for
    Migrant Studies, 195-196,
    195, **196**
New York State Dormitory
    Authority, 134, 148, 257
New York State Education
    Department, 18
New York State Legislature,
    20, 21
New York State Temporary
    Commission on the Need
    for a State University, 146
New York Temporary Emergency
    Relief Administration
    (TERA), 106
New York Times, 253, 278, 298
Newman Club, 98, 260
Newton, Charles, D. 76
Newton, Dallas, **71**
Newton, George, **133**, 134,
    199, **199**
Newton building, 165, **183**,
    198, 199
Niagara Residence Hall, 199
Nicholson, Evelyn, 172
Nickerson (women's basketball
    player), **96**
Nicodemi, Olympia, 264
Niles, Clay, **49**
Nitsche, Mary, 252
Nodar, R., **168**
Normal Department, 26, 29,
    35, 37, 39, 52

Normal Grill, **125**
Normal Hall, 44-45, **45**
Normal schools, origin, 19; professionalism, 55
Normalian see *Yearbook*
Norris, Darrell, 264
North, Ellen, 74, **75**
North, H.P., 42
Northrup, Cora, **51**
Norton, Amy, **287**
Norton, Vera, 72
Noto, Kara, **287**
Noto, Mary, **303**
Novarrete, R., **283**
Nowak, Arthur, **195**

O

Oberg, Michael, 290
O'Brien, Donald, 237
O'Brien, Joseph, 289
O'Donnell, Robert, 264
Office of Research and Extension, 116
Oh Ha Daih see *Yearbook*
O'Hara, Stephanie, **164**
Olczak, Paul, 290
Old Main, 26, **27**, 33, **34**, **35**, **37**, **38**, **39**, **40**, 45, **45**, 56, **60**, 65, **65**, **66**, **87**, **89**, **100**, **108**, **109**, **142**, 176, 299-300; clock tower razed, 109; condition, 98-99, 108, 111, 141-142; razed, 142, 158-159, **159**
Old Main gymnasium, 45, **46**, 54, **56**, **81**, **122**, **124**
Old Main Library see *Library, Old Main*
Old Main swimming pool, 63-64
Olmsted, Mrs., **95**
O'Neal, Harold, 157
Onondaga Residence Hall, 199
Ontario Residence Hall, 199
Orchesis, **200**, **252**
Orchestra, **50**, **61**, **88**, **303**
Orlando, Carmen, 169
Orlando, Nicholas, 169
Orlando, Samuel, 169
Orton, James S., **24**, 25
Orwen, Gifford, 165, 289
Orwen, William, **145**, 165
Osborne, James, **91**
Over, Jeffrey, 299
Owens, Robert, Jr., 231

P

Padalino, Stephen, 250, 284, 289, **294**, 299
Page, Dr., 71
Pageants, 76
Painted Post retreat, 247
Pak, S., **283**
Palladine, Jackie, **205**
Palmer, Jamie, **270**
Palmer, Josephine, **117**
Parent, Mary, 166, **193**
Parish, David W., 73
Park, Lawrence, **166**, 176, 193-194, **197**, 205, 217, 238; appointed dean, 164
Parking, 172, 217, 218, 282, 287
Parks, Mary, 35, **36**, **51**, **62**
Parry, John, **103**, **115**, 117, **118**, **121**
Parry, Sarah, **51**, **62**
Parsons, Emma S. see *McMaster, Emma*
Pass-fail option modified, 251
Pataki, George, 271, 278-281
Patall, Mr., **143**
Patchin, "Can", **54**
Patten, Henry, **56**
Paul, John, 165, 168, **170**
Peacock, Elsa, 127, **128**, 132
Pearl Harbor, 126
Peck, Ruth, **289**
Pennington, Walter, 169
Percussion Ensemble, 288
Pestalozzi-Froebel School, 65, **67**
Peterson, Willard, 200, **210**, **220**
Pettinella, Edward, 237, **243**
Phi Alpha Fraternity, 47, **88**
Phi Beta Kappa, 287-288, **287**, 291, 301, 308
Phi Sigma Epsilon Fraternity, **14**, 47, **174**, **189**, **227**
Philalethean Fraternity, 47, 48, **49**; Track Team, **55**
Philips, Chris, **296**
Phillips, Harrison, 105,106,108, 117, 128, **129**
Piccirillo, Linda see *Hinckley, Linda Piccirillo*
Pierce, T., **148**
Pineda, L., **249**
Planetarium, **202**
Play Days, 98
Pletz, J., **249**
Pogozelski, Edward, 290
Pogozelski, Wendy Knapp, 299

Polansky, Cyril, **234**
Pollard, Bettina G. see *DeBell, Bettina G. Pollard*
Pope, Thomas, 212, 235, **270**
Porter, Harry, 192, 238
Porter, Jon, **243**
Poste, Leslie, **169**, **246**
Postwar Public Works Planning Commission, 148
Powell, Donnie, **222**
Powell, V., **247**
Practice School see *Campus School*
Presidential elections—1932, 1936, 1940, 89; 1960, 173; 1988, 260; 1996, 2000, 2004, 295
President's Donor Recognition dinner, 231, **291**
Presidents, Hiring see also *Principals, Hiring*, 140, 161, 190, 241-242, 261-262, 275-276
President's house, 102, **163**
Pretzer, Ronald, 231
Prevosti, Dave, **296**
Primary department, 26, 37, 38
Princeton Review, 298
Principals, Hiring see also *Presidents, Hiring*, 32-33, 48, 62, 85-86, 103, 140
Prisoner of war camp, 130-131, **131**
Professional Achievement Award, 237
Prometheus fraternity, used book sale, 234-235, **234**
Protests, 202-203, **202**, **204**, 205, **206**, 208-210, **208**, **209**, 222, 223-224, **223**, 233, **233**, 257, 267, 269, 287
Psychology department, 155, 227
Public Safety see *University Police*
Publicity, 248, 307; American Marketing Association, 253-254; Associated Press, 253; *Barron's Profile of American Colleges*, 255; *Kiplinger's*, 298; *Money*, 253, 278; *New York Times*, 253, 278, 298; *Newsday*, 272; *Princeton Review*, 298; *Time* 278; *U.S. News and World Report*, 253, 255, 278, 298; *Yahoo Internet Life*, 252

Purdy, "Jo", **54**
Putnam, Marty, 251
Putnam Residence Hall, 15, 282, 294, 301
Pyper, R., **193**

Q

Quaal, Van, **231**, 238, 242, 263
Quick, Richard, **217**, **218**
Quirk, Fred, 100
Quirk, Joseph, 100, 161, **199**, 242

R

Rabe, Valentin, 218, **258**, 268
Racial tensions, 216, 222
Radio club, **171**
Railroads, 25, **52**, 53
Raines, Summer, 288
Ransbery, Irene, **77**
Raschi, Victor, 166, **168**
Raschi Field, **244**
Rathskeller, 205-206, **206**
Rationing, 129-130, **130**
Raub House, 73
Ray, Scott, 232
Rayo, R., **283**
Razey, Helen, **77**
Reagan, Eileen, **261**
Reber, Jerry, 194
Rebisz, Joe, **212**
Red Jacket Dining Hall, 199
Redden, Robert, 111, 114, **114**, 132, **196**
Reed, J., **168**
Regents see *New York State Board of Regents*
Registration, **284**; online 284
Reid, Archibald, 268, 289
Reidel, Robert, 212
Reist, David, 237
Rensselaerville "retreat", 230
Residence halls see also names of specific residence halls, 199
Resource Allocation Methodology (RAM), 280
Retirement incentives for faculty and staff, 268
Rex Theater, 74
Reynolds, Anne-Marie, 288
Reynolds, Jerry, 258
Reynolds, Richard, **169**
Rhodes, Barbara, 247
Rhodes, Gladys, 94-95, **117**, **155**, **157**, 289

Rhodes, Wendell, 165, **194**
Rich, Bob, **205**
Richard, Michel, 268
Richardson, Mary, 64, **65**, **115**, 117
Richardson, Mrs., **167**
Rider, Alice Damon, **119**, 167, **169**, 176
Riedel, Robert, **225**, **230**
Rieflin, Tom, **270**
Riesch, Kenneth, 157, **157**, 165
Rigney, C. Agnes, 63, **64**,**103**, 117, 168, 176
Rippey House, 73
Ristow, Bruce, 219, 251, 253, 263, 283
Ritter, Edward, 195
Ritter, Tex, 211
Roark, Richard, 203, 208
Roberts, Ken, **205**
Roberts, Lynn, 132
Robinson, E., **249**
Robinson, Sidney, **94**
Robota, Edward, 235, **235**
Roby, Helen, 35, **36**
Rocha, Ramon, 247, 289
Rockas, Leo, 205-206
Rockefeller, Mrs. Nelson, 124
Rockefeller, Nelson, 191-192, **192**, 198, 210, **210**, 225, 233, 307
Rockwell, George Lincoln, 189, 201, 206
Rodamaker, Ruth, 166, **167**
Roecker, Robert, 195
Roemer, Spencer, **243**, **251**, 262, **263**, 289, **291**
Roemer Arboretum, **263**, **294**
Roemer House, **269**
Roffe, George A., 128
Rogers, Clarence, **71**
Rogers, Helen, 123
Rogers, James Gamble, campus plans, **136-7**
Rogers, Lena, **115**, **121**
Roodenburg, Bill, 233
Roodenburg, Eleanor Woelfel, 166, **167**, **193**
Roosevelt, Eleanor, 163, **165**
Roper, Maybell, **56**
Rorbach, Elizabeth, **62**
Rorbach, John, 20, 23, **24**, 25, 30-33, 44-45, 53, 60, 305
Rosati, Richard, 209, 262, 286, **286**
Rose, Paul, 212, **230**, 235

Rowland, Marcia Heath, **51**
Rowles, Elizabeth, **118**
Rowse, Ruth, **276**
Rubin, Jerry, 259
Ruffo, D., **173**
Rutherford, Stanley, 156, **170**
Ryan, A., **193**
Ryan, John, 292
Ryan, Mary, 270

S

Sacco, Pat, **170**
Saddlemire, Gerald, 155-156, **158**, 176
Saddlemire, Mrs., **158**
Saetveit, Joseph, **121**, **129**
Salinger, Pierre, 232
Salisbury, Harrison, 211
Salisbury, Richard, 219, 227, 228
Salter, Miss, **167**
Sancilio, Leonard, 264
Sandburg, Carl, 123
Saratoga Terrace Residence Hall, 15, 282, **282**, 301
Sargent, John, 170
Satryb, Ronald, 237-238, **237**, 242, 259, 263
Saunders, Angie, **217**
Scatterday, James, 264, 268
Scavilla, Norma, 219
Schaefer (football player), **68**
Schaefer, Paul, 268
Scheiber, Mark, 286
Schenitski, Dietmar, 268
Schiavetti, Nicholas, 231
Schilling, Mrs., **167**
Schlageter, Mr., **167**
Schlesinger, Arthur, Jr., 211
Schmitz, Hubert J., **51**, 56-57, **57**, 62, **62**
Schneider, Monica, 290
Scholarships, 21
Scholarships, Regents, 67
Scholes, James, **145**, 165-166, 228
Scholfield, Frank, 195, 206, 208
School of Business, 246, 259, 301
School of Education, 266, 280; accredited, 301; promised, 220
School of Library and Information Science see *Library education*

School of Performing Arts, 265, 288
Schrader, Carl, 54, **62**, **71**, 163
Schrader, Howard, **91**
Schrader gymnasium, 55, 133, 152, 153, 163, **164**, **180**, 212
Schultz, Daniel, **287**
Schumaker, Joan, 219, 247, 263
Schussele, K., **148**
Schutz, Mrs., 14
Schwartz, Stephan, **243**
Sciarrino, Alfred, 213
Sciarrino, Raymond, 169
Scipione, Paul, 208, 213, 296
Scondras, George, **187**
Scopes trial, 89
Scott (basketball player), **72**
Scott (football player), **68**
Scott, Marta, **296**
Scott, Virginia, 127
Scruggs, Charles, 268
Secondary education programs, started, 167-68
Seegler, Dorothea, **92**
Seger, Garretta, **115**
Selective Training and Service Act see *Military draft*
Sells, Robert, 194-195, **219**, 228, **228**
September 11, 2001, 275, 294; Memorial, **294**
Sergiovanni, Thomas, 169, 277
Sexual harassment, 265
Seymour, Pliny, 43, 74
Shady, Jeanette, **205**
Shanahan, Carl, 218, **218**
Shank, Alan, 219
Shear, Ella Cline, 286, **286**
Shearing (George) Quintet, 171
Sheen, Fulton, 211
Sheldon, Amy, 299
Shepard, Elizabeth V. R., 98
Shepard, Steve, 132
Sheppard, Mrs., **167**
Sherman, Ray, 210, 237, 261
Shinny Team, **56**
Shirkley, Donovan, 295
Shope, Beth, 296
Shubert, Joseph, 168-169
Shults, C. Everett, **133**, **199**
Sigma Pi Sigma honorary society, 97
Sigma Tau Psi fraternity, **188**; Sig Tau Regatta, **224**

Simmons House, **82**
Simms, Thomas, 71, **71**
Simon, Robert, 254
Sinclair, Robert, 157, **158**, **170**, **171**, 174, **201**, 232
Singer, S., **173**
Sisting, Christine, 288
Sitler, Ronald, 219
Skelton, Red, 259, **259**
Skinner, Julia, 44
Slavick, William, 203, 205
Small, William, 195, **195**, 289
Smith, Chris, **270**
Smith, Curt, 236
Smith, Gerald, **145**,157, 228
Smith, Harry B., 87-91
Smith, J. Irene, **118**, **145**
Smith, Katie, **268**
Smith, Morgan, **212**
Smith, Nancy, **205**
Smith, Olive, **77**
Smith, Richard A., **254**
Smith, Richard F., 195, 228, **228**, **254**, 268
Smith, Roger, **192**
Smith, Sherry, **205**
Smith-Pilkington, Karen, 236
Smoking, 41, 259
Smokoski, F., **168**
Snow, Barbara, 151, **164**
Snow sculptures, **160**, **189**
Snyder, James, 163
Soccer, **151**, **212**, 269, 293, **293**
Soccer, Women's, **235**, **261**, 270, **280**
Social Studies program, Early Secondary (N-9), 167; 7-12 220-221
Society of Old Main, 159, 270-271
Sociology department, 221, 227
Soffer, Walter, 231, **255**
Softball, **244**
Somerville, James, 208, **258**
South Hall, **240**, 256-257, **257**, 266
Special education see also *Craig Colony, Sonyea*, 69, 79, 81, 93-95, 131-132, 163, 247, 256
Speech and Hearing, Master's degree program started, 168
Speech Pathology and Audiology program, 167-168
Speech program, approved, 149

Spencer, Donald, 263, 265, 268, 272
Spencer, Robert, 106
Spring, John, 270
Spring Happening, **236**
Stadium, proposed, 302
Stanitski, Diane, **261**
Starbuck, Harold, 165, 168, **170**
Stare, Jane, **157**
State University of New York (SUNY), 13, 18, 145-147; headquarters, **146**
Statesmen, 171
Statt, Thomas, 208
Stefansson, Vilhjalmur, 123
Stelzig, Eugene, 231
Stephens, Clarence, **195**
Steuben Residence Hall, 199, 286-287
Stevens (basketball player), **72**
Stevens (football player), **68**
Stevens, Rise, 171
Stickney, John, **71**
Stolee, Meg, **258**
Stolper, Richard, **157**
Stone, Kim, **268**
Stovall, Theodore, **195**
Strang, Daniel, 231
Strang, John, 23, **24**, 60
Stratton, Gary, 252, 253
Stratton, L. M., 41
Stratton, Sue, **205**
Streaker, 233
Streamer, Mary, **56**
Strining, Thomas, 237
Stroetzel, Bernice, **118**, **167**
Strong, Alice, **243**, 260
Strong, Trowbridge, 260
Stuart, Jesse, 18
Stubblefield, Steve, **289**
Stuber, Homer, **91**
Student admissions, 37, 50, 113, 242, 246, 247, 254, 266, 267, 280
Student Association, 277-278
Student Christian Fellowship, 98
Student Co-op Bookstore, **148**
Student Cooperative Government, 95
Student demographics, 200-201, 248-249
Student discipline see Student regulations
Student dress code, 171-172
Student enrollment, 29, 39, 50, 52, 79, 81, 103, 105-106, 128, 132, 133, 148-151, 160, 163, 200, 213, 218, 226, 229, 238, 242, 243, 247, 254, 267

Student evaluation, 55
Student government, **93, 94**
Student grades, 233
Student Handbook, 97
Student health, measles outbreak, 258
Student housing, 26, 41, **41**, 73, **73**, 80, **82-83**, 134, 142, 143, 148-149, 158, 163, 225, 256-257, 282, 302
Student mailboxes, **175**
Student Opinion of Faculty Instruction see also Course-Teacher Evaluation, 227-228, 284-285, 291
Student placement, 39, 44, 114, 254
Student protests see Protests
Student recruitment, 134, 229, 230, 242, 246, 254
Student regulations, 40, 51, 171
Student retention, 247, 267
Student Senate, 227
Student surveys, 96
Student teaching, 116, 118, 306; centers created, 97
Student-Faculty Service, 157
Students—Economic Impact, 44, 295-296
Students For Freedom (SFF), 202-203
Studer, Paul, **246**
Sturges, James V., 62-63, **63**, 65, 67, 69, 74, **79**, 87, 116, 187, 306; terminated, 77-79; dies, 80
Sturges, Ruth L., 78
Sturges building, **12**, 80, 107, **110**, 111, **112**, **141**, 142-143, **183**, 191, 200, 259
Stuttering clinic, 168
Sub-Frosh Day, 121
Suffolk Residence Hall, 199
Sulit, C., **249**
Summer school, begins, 69
Sundance Books, 234, **279**
Sunderland, Luther, 258
Sunter, Mr., **129**
SUNY Albany, 20, 37, 48-49, 51, 61, 99, 113, 118, 139
SUNY Board of Trustees, 280; ask SUNY schools to upgrade, 278; Master Plan 2005-2010, 292; prescribe core curriculum, 279

SUNY Brockport, 20, 33, 43, 54, 134, 151
SUNY College at Buffalo, 118, 132, 139
SUNY Construction Fund, 257
SUNY Cortland, 20, 94, 99, 113, 133
SUNY Fredonia, 20, 26, 54, 94, 99, 134
SUNY Geneseo—for most listings, see more specific headings
SUNY Geneseo—names, 30-31, 59-60, 120
SUNY Geneseo, to be multipurpose college, 167
SUNY Master Plan, 191-192, 218
SUNY New Paltz, 99
SUNY Oneonta, 69, 99
SUNY Oswego, 19, 20
SUNY Plattsburgh, 71, 74, 97, 99, 116
SUNY Potsdam, 20, 94
SUNY Research Foundation Research and Scholarship Award, 299
SUNY Utica-Rome, 237
Supremes, 259
Surman, Rebecca, 266
Sutherland, Melissa, 299
Swimming, **212**, 235, 296, **297**
Swimming, women's, 269, 296
Sworts, Luke, **287**
Synchronized swimming, women's 270
Syracuse University, 20, 139
Szczepanik, Michael, 297

T

Tafel, Edgar, **153**, 198-199
Tallchief, Flora B., 21
Tam, P., **283**
Tamarin, David, **258**
Tantillo, Michael, 237
Tarantella, Gloria, **303**
Taylor, James, 259
Taylor Law, 195
Teacher education see also Normal Schools, 19, 63, 69, 118, 192, 218; debate over focus, 51-52; professionalism, 50-51, 59-61, 113
Teacher-Librarian program see Library Education
Teachers College, Columbia University, 51

Teaching and Learning Center, 293
Tegart, Robert, 233, **234**
Temple Hill Academy, 19-22, **21**, 23, 25, 31, 32, 38
Temple Hill Fund, 21-22
TenEyck, Lucy, **77**
Tennis, 270
Tennis, women's, 270
Teres, Michael, **226**
Terrorism, 294
Thau, Morton, 151
Thoman, Joe, **205**
Thomas, Mary, **103**, 117, **118**, 157
Thomas, Norman, 123
Thompson, Dorothy, 123
Thompson, Meredith, **205**
Thompson, Phyllis, **221**
Thorndike, Edward L., 91
Tiffany, Joyce see Zobel, Joyce Tiffany
Tillapaugh, Tracy, 296
Time, 278
Title IX, 235, 243
Titsworth, Adelene, **92**
Todd, Keith, **222**
Tolan, Marie, **77**
Toler, Shirley, 212, **230**
Tolley, William P., 146
Toole, Charles, **55, 71**
Total quality management, 273
Totten, Fred, 128
Towsley, Gary, 264, 269
Track, 54
Training Department see Campus School
Training School see Campus School
Trainor, Kathleen, 219, 247
Trapp family, 130
Trapper, Chip, **270**
Traying, 211
Tripp, Earl, **71**
Trolley, **72**
Truman, Harry S., 146
Tudman, Scott, **266**
Tuition, 42, 171, 261, 267, 281; first imposed, 192; rumored, 161
Tuition Assistance Program, 280
Turner, Pete, **222**
Tuttle, Howard, **149**
Twiman, Bertrand, 71

U

U.S. News & World Report, 253, 255, 278, 298
Ulmer, Harold, 162
Ulmer's Drug Store, 187
Ulrich, Marjorie, **95**
Underhill, Irvin, **217**
Underhill, Ruth Coffin, 166, **167**, **193**
Unification Act of 1904 see also Teacher education, professionalism, 61, 63
United Students of the Continent of Asia, **283**
Universidad de las Americas (Mexico), 293, 301
University of the State of New York see New York State Education Department
University Police, 261, 277, **278**
Upper Quadrangle construction, 266-267, **267**, 282

V

Valley Hall, 142-143, **144**
Valley, Village, College display, 266
Vance, Helen see Foster, Helen Vance
Vanderbilt, Delia, 35, **36**
VanDerMeid, Matt, **297**
VanDerWall, Clarence, 128
VanDeusen, Neil, 117-118, **119**, **121**, **129**
Vangalio, M., **193**
VanHusen, Nancy, 35, **36**
VanNorman, C. Elta, **119**, **169**
VanRy, Charles, 173-174, 277
Vasconez, M., **249**
Vasey, Carey, 268
Vasiliev, Irina ("Ren"), 264
VAX network, 283
VegSoup, 288
Vereen, Ben, 259
Vickers, Edna, **119**
Vienna Boys Choir, 123
Vietnam War protests, 208-210, 216, 223, 233
Village Taverne, **174**
Villard, Oswald Garrison, 123
Vitale, Joseph, 197

Vocal Miscellany, 288
Volleyball, Women's, **245**
Volunteer Emergency Squad, **292**
Volunteerism, 295
Vosburgh-Canedo, Marion, 213

W

Waddy, Helena, **258**
Wadsworth, Craig W., 23, **24**, 25
Wadsworth, Elizabeth P. 85, **85**, 100, 110, 157
Wadsworth, James, 19, 20
Wadsworth, James Jeremiah, 102, 123, **255**; receives Doctor of Laws from the College, 260
Wadsworth (James Jeremiah) Lecture Series, 260
Wadsworth, James Samuel, 19, 25, 46
Wadsworth, James W., Jr., 76, 101-103, 111, 127, 153-154, 159-160, 165
Wadsworth, James W., Sr., 32, 48, 60, 85, 305
Wadsworth, Mrs. William Austin see Wadsworth, Elizabeth
Wadsworth, Penelope, **218**
Wadsworth, Reverdy, 127, 154, 163, **199**
Wadsworth, William, 19
Wadsworth, William Austin, 60
Wadsworth, William P., **218**
Wadsworth Auditorium, 112, 133, 163, 200, 232, **301**; cornerstone-laying, 162-163, **163**; dedicated, 163
Wadsworth Library, 46, 53, **53**
Wadsworth Memorial Fountain, **147**, **188**
Wadsworth Nursing Home, **70**, 110
Wadsworth Trust, 23
Wahlgren, Hardy, 155, **155**, **157**
Walker, James, 219, **229**, 259, **289**, 297
Walker, S. Jay, 208
Walton, James, 163
War bond stamp sales, **127**
War Council, 129
Ward, Harry, **222**, 235

Ward, James, **230**
Warfield, William, 171
Warford, Edith, **56**
Warner (basketball player), **72**
Washington, Booker T., 123
Waterbury, Reuben A., 34, **36**, **51**
Watson (football player), **68**
Watson, Sarah, 44
Watt, Donald, 193, 289
Wayne Residence Hall, 199
Weaver, Abram B., 31, 38, 39
Wechsler, Joyce, 212, **230**, **245**
Weekley, C., **193**
Weisbrod, Steve, **195**
Weisent, E., **283**
Weismann, Paul, **287**
Welch, James, 124, 187
Welch, Mark, 152
Welch, Robert, 201
Welchons, Daniel, 292
Weller, Gene, **54**
Weller, Paul, **205**
Welles, Frank E., 42-44, **51**, 56, **62**, 106
Welles, James B., 106-108, **106**, 112, **115**, 116, 117, 119, **121**, 122, 124, 132-135, 140, 211, 230, 306; appointed principal, 103; retires, 135
Welles building, 14, 101, **101**, 200, 211
Werner, A., **68**, **72**
Werner, K., **68**
West, Stephen, 264
Westland House, **82**
Westmoreland, Gladys, **107**
WGSU-FM, 189
White, Eula, **246**
White, Melissa, 288
Whitlow, Tony, **270**
Whitmore, William, **55**
Wilbert, Martha, **205**
Wilbur, James, 218
Wilcox, Homer, **149**
Wilcox House, 73
Wiley, George, 91
Wilkerson, George, 173-175
Wilkes, Glenn, **254**
Wilkinson, Ara, 43
Willard, Kenneth, **133**, **199**
Willey, Frances see Lipson, Frances Willey
Willey, James, **229**, 247, **248**, **289**

Williams, Helen see Rogers, Helen
Williams, James, **258**, 288
Wilson (basketball player), **91**
Wilson, Claire, **54**
Wilson, Ira, **91**, 93, 124, 126, 129, 151, **156**, **164**, **172**, **225**, 268
Wilson, Mary, 259
Winans, Anna, **56**
Winkelman, John, **246**
Winnie, Frank, 29, 42, 43
Winter Weekend, **160**, **189**
Wirojratana, P., **283**
Witter, Gary, **235**
Witzel, Carl, 212, **212**, **230**, 269
Woelfel, Eleanor see Roodenburg, Eleanor Woelfel
Women faculty, 247
Women's hours, 202, 204
Won, L., **283**
Wood, James, 32
Woods, Michael, 270, **296**, 297
Woods, Susanne, 276
Woodward, Dick, **212**
Woolcock, T., **249**
Woolston, Loren, 156, **156**
Worden, Michelle Walton, **291**
Works Progress Administration (W.P.A.), 112
World War I, 74-75, **75**; honor roll plaque, **58**; parade, **76**
World War II, 126-131, **127**; plaque, **132**
Wrestling, 270
Wright, Wilbur, 151, **151**, **155**, 176
Wrubel, Jerald, 231
Wyoming Residence Hall, 199, 282

Y

Yahoo Internet Life, 252
Yangchung (South Korea) High School, 293, 301
Yearbook, 48, 130, 200, 205, 287
Yoos, Frederick, 208
York, J., **168**
Younes, DiemHang Kennison Huynh, 271, **271**